Personal Fina...

. . . .

3rd edition

Jonquil Lowe

Child Poverty Action Group

CPAG promotes action for the prevention and relief of poverty among children and families with children. To achieve this, CPAG aims to raise awareness of the causes, extent, nature and impact of poverty, and strategies for its eradication and prevention; bring about positive policy changes for families with children in poverty; and enable those eligible for income maintenance to have access to their full entitlement. If you are not already supporting us, please consider making a donation, or ask for details of our membership schemes, training courses and publications.

Services Against Financial Exclusion (SAFE) is an innovative project of Toynbee Hall that is dedicated to eradicating financial exclusion through providing practical services, such as supporting individuals to access bank accounts and financial education, as well as facilitating Transact, the national forum for financial inclusion.

Published by Child Poverty Action Group
94 White Lion Street, London N1 9PF
Tel: 020 7837 7979
staff@cpag.org.uk
www.cpag.org.uk

A CIP record for this book is available from the British Library

ISBN: 978 1 906076 32 0

Child Poverty Action Group is a charity registered in England and Wales (registration number 294841) and in Scotland (registration number SC039339), and is a company limited by guarantee, registered in England (registration number 1993854). VAT number: 690 808117

Cover design by Devious Designs
Typeset by David Lewis XML Associates Ltd
Printed in the UK by CPI William Clowes Beccles NR34 7TL
Cover photo by Jess Hurd/Reportdigital

The author

Jonquil Lowe trained as an economist and worked for several years in the City as an investment analyst before moving to *Which?* where she was head of the Money Research Group. Jonquil now works as a freelance researcher and journalist and is also Lecturer in Personal Finance at The Open University. She holds the Diploma in Personal Finance (formerly called the Advanced Financial Planning Certificate). Jonquil writes extensively on all areas of personal finance and is author of several other books, including *Be Your Own Financial Adviser*, *The Which? Essential Guide to Giving and Inheriting*, *The Pension Handbook* (published by Which?), *The Which? Essential Guide: finance your retirement*, and, with Sara Williams, *The Financial Times Guide to Personal Tax*.

iii

Acknowledgements

I would like to thank Adam Clark and the staff at Toynbee Hall, and Carolyn George for their valuable comments on the draft, Alison Key for editing the book and managing its production, Kathleen Armstrong for proofreading the text and Paul Levay for producing the index.

I remain indebted to Faith Reynolds, formerly of SAFE, who had the original inspiration for the *Handbook* and to Teresa Fritz, Michelle Gerwitz, Mark Berman, Alice Rogers, Barbara Williamson, Beth Lakhani and Peter Ridpath whose contributions to the first edition continue to shape the *Personal Finance Handbook* today.

Jonquil Lowe

SAFE and CPAG developed the original *Handbook* with the support and expertise of a working group, including the Financial Learning team at NIACE, the Financial Services Authority and the Institute of Financial Services.

Financial Services Authority

This *Handbook* has been written by Toynbee Hall and Child Poverty Action Group, and funded by the Financial Services Authority as part of the National Strategy for Financial Capability

Foreword

....

I welcome the publication by the Child Poverty Action Group and SAFE at Toynbee Hall of this, the third edition of the *Personal Finance Handbook*.

The financial landscape has altered dramatically since the publication of the second edition in 2007. We have witnessed the near collapse of some of Britain's biggest banks, followed by recession, a steep rise in unemployment, mortgage arrears and, potentially, home repossession. At the same time, there is a reluctance among banks to lend to solvent business and individuals. In this context there is a heightened awareness of the need to manage personal finances as prudently as possible.

I have long been a strong advocate of a national network of advice centres to help people with unbiased, disinterested advice which is very belatedly taking stage. There is also an important role for financial education, and schools are beginning to develop accredited courses. I have been impressed too by the initiative of the Scout movement which, alongside rock climbing and kayaking, has introduced programmes on personal finance. I am impressed – and a little surprised – to discover that the Scouts I meet hold genuine enthusiasm for these classes and are asking for lessons on personal finance at school. This is an encouraging model to emulate.

The *Personal Finance Handbook* is a useful addition to these educational initiatives. Whether for planning school lessons or trying to communicate the complexities of a company pension scheme, this book offers a comprehensive resource to anyone seeking to widen financial understanding.

It is thoroughly comprehensive and deals with the full gamut of subjects: tax, benefits, pensions, insurance, mortgages and savings products. It is a mine of essential information for advisers and educators, but will also be of use to those who are themselves facing financial difficulty or who wish to improve their own personal finances.

Vincent Cable MP
MP for Twickenham & Liberal Democrat Deputy Leader
and Shadow Chancellor of the Exchequer

Contents

Abbreviations

AA	attendance allowance	JSA	jobseeker's allowance
ABI	Association of British Insurers	MA	maternity allowance
AER	annual equivalent rate	MVA	market value adjustment
APR	annual percentage rate	MVR	market value reduction
ASU	accident, sickness and unemployment	NI	national insurance
BIBA	British Insurance Brokers' Association	NS&I	National Savings and Investments
CA	carer's allowance	OFT	Office of Fair Trading
CGT	capital gains tax	PAYE	Pay As You Earn
CTB	council tax benefit	PC	pension credit
CTC	child tax credit	PCP	personal contract plan
DLA	disability living allowance	PEP	personal equity plan
DMO	Debt Management Office	PET	potentially exempt transfer
DRO	debt relief order	PIN	personal identification number
DWP	Department for Work and Pensions	PPF	Pension Protection Fund
EEA	European Economic Area	PPI	payment protection insurance
EC	European Community	PTM	Panel on Takeovers and Mergers
EHIC	European Health Insurance Card	RPI	Retail Prices Index
ESA	employment and support allowance	S2P	state second pension
FAS	Financial Assistance Scheme	SAP	statutory adoption pay
FLA	Finance and Leasing Association	SDA	severe disablement allowance
FOS	Financial Ombudsman Service	SERPS	state earnings-related pension scheme
FSA	Financial Services Authority	SHIP	Safe Home Income Plans
FSCS	Financial Services Compensation Scheme	SMP	statutory maternity pay
		SPP	statutory paternity pay
HB	housing benefit	SSP	statutory sick pay
HP	hire purchase	TER	total expense ratio
IB	incapacity benefit	TPAS	The Pensions Advisory Service
IHT	inheritance tax	UAP	upper accruals point
IS	income support	UCAS	Universities and Colleges Admission Service
ISA	individual savings account		
IVA	individual voluntary arrangement	WTC	working tax credit

Chapter 1

Financial planning

This chapter covers:
1. The importance of financial products (below)
2. Financial exclusion (p2)
3. The need for financial planning (p6)
4. How financial planning works (p6)
5. Choosing the right products (p8)
6. Keeping track of your finances (p12)

Basic facts
- Ninety-one per cent of British households have a current account and 7 per cent have a basic bank account.[1]
- Ninety-seven per cent of households have at least one savings or investment product.[2]
- Sixty-eight per cent of Britain's 21.4 million households own their own home. This includes just under eight million who have a mortgage.[3]
- Low-income households pay a 'poverty premium' of £1,000 a year on average because of exclusion from financial services.[4]
- Financial firms produce nearly one-quarter of the UK's output and provide one-fifth of all jobs.[5]

1. The importance of financial products

Increasingly, the Government expects citizens to take responsibility for their own financial wellbeing – eg, by managing financial stress, saving for retirement, protecting themselves from financial emergencies and funding higher education. In addition, as both the public sector and private companies embrace new technologies, barriers and extra costs are driving out old ways of managing money, such as paying by cash and cheque. As a result, it is becoming ever more important to have at least some basic financial tools, and households, whatever their level of income, are having to understand and engage with financial products and services.

The Government is encouraging the take-up of financial products – eg, through the new Saving Gateway accounts, child trust funds, continued tax relief on pension savings and, from 2012, automatic enrolment in a new national pension scheme. However, the choice of products across the whole market is bewildering. For example, even after the mortgage credit freeze that followed the onset of a global financial crisis from 2007, it is estimated that there are still 6,500 different mortgages (though well below the peak of over 27,000 in 2007). It is therefore important for households to choose carefully, matching the products on offer to their own particular needs and circumstances. Selected and used appropriately, financial products can give households not only security now, but also cost savings and the ability to achieve goals (rather than just fight financial fires) in the future, and even, according to some studies, better physical and psychological health.

2. Financial exclusion

What is financial exclusion

Financial exclusion is a phrase first coined by the Office of Fair Trading in the late 1990s.[6] Since then, the concept has been widely debated and developed, but at its simplest can be defined as 'a state where individuals cannot access the key financial products and services they need'.[7] It is the opposite to financial inclusion which has been defined as:

> . . . a state in which all people have access to appropriate desired financial products and services in order to manage their money effectively. It is achieved by financial literacy and financial capability on the part of the consumer and access on the part of financial product, services and advice suppliers.[8]

Financial inclusion is important because, without financial products, consumers are likely to be financially worse off than people who do have them.
- **They are vulnerable to financial loss.** Without a bank account, households are more likely to keep their week's funds or any savings in cash. This makes them vulnerable to theft and accidental loss.
- **They are forced to pay more.** Fuel and phone companies, in particular, often charge less if the consumer agrees to pay by direct debit (though consumers need to guard against being required to pay too much in advance – see Chapter 3). Direct debit payments are impossible if consumers have no bank account. Also, if households cannot pay with plastic or cheques, they cannot shop by internet or phone and so may miss out on the best bargains. A household without savings may have little choice but to borrow to buy large items, and poor credit ratings typically mean paying over the odds for credit. Mainstream retailers are increasingly refusing to accept payment by cheque or charging

extra for this payment mode, forcing consumers to embrace newer alternatives. Overall, it has been estimated that low-income households pay an extra £1,000 a year on average due to lack of basic financial products and services. This has been dubbed the 'poverty premium'.[9]

- **They are vulnerable to financial shocks**. Illness, job loss or even something as simple as a broken washing machine can tip a household into debt.
- **They are denied other products**. Many lenders are unwilling to lend at competitive rates to people who have not got a bank account or do not own their own home. Some services have shifted to new forms of delivery (eg, state benefits by direct payment, and insurance and mortgages by internet) which require consumers to have specific financial products or particular ways of accessing them.
- **They are unable to afford other products**. If a household cannot spread payments by, for example, direct debit, they might not be able to afford to buy an item.
- **They may have difficulty accessing employment**. Having a bank is a prerequisite for most jobs.[10]

An important factor in financial inclusion is **'financial capability'**. The Government has defined this as:

> ... a broad concept encompassing people's knowledge and skills to understand their own financial circumstances, along with the motivation to take action. Financially capable consumers plan ahead, find and use information, know when to seek advice, and can understand and act on this advice, leading to greater participation in the financial services markets.[11]

Without financial capability, there is an increased risk that, even where consumers do buy financial products, they will get poor value for money, end up with products which do not suit their needs and fail to take steps required to improve their financial wellbeing. The UK's main financial regulator, the Financial Services Authority (FSA), has identified five components of financial capability:[12]

- making ends meet;
- keeping track of your finances;
- planning ahead;
- choosing financial products;
- staying informed about financial matters.

Why does financial exclusion happen

Financial exclusion is closely associated with having a low income. The problem, however, is not simply being unable to afford financial products – products do not always meet the needs of low-income households and financially excluded people are more likely than average to live in deprived areas where, for example, the cost of insurance is high and providers do not seek out business. However, as

Transact, a national forum for financial inclusion, points out, financial exclusion does not just affect poorer people; the 2009 recession and tightening of credit have also created problems for more affluent households.[13] Factors that tend to make financial exclusion more likely include:

- **geographical location:**
  - in some poorer areas, banks and other financial firms are thin on the ground because financial firms prefer to target wealthier potential customers;
  - in rural areas there may be few financial firms because customers tend to be thinly spread and so expensive to target. Exclusion is exacerbated if car ownership is low and public transport poor so that customers find it difficult to travel to regional centres where firms are present;
- **other physical access problems.** People with disabilities and families with children may find it hard to access financial products and services, especially if access involves travelling. Phone- and internet-based services may help;
- **procedural barriers to access:**
  - customers may need to pass credit checks before they can have a product, even if they do not want to use any credit facilities. This can be a problem for people with either a poor credit history or no credit history at all because they have not previously used financial products;
  - money laundering regulations mean that financial firms are required to check the identity and address of new customers and sometimes they take an inflexible approach over the forms of proof they will accept. This causes difficulties if someone does not have the more traditional documents, such as passport, driving licence or household bills;
- **language and cultural barriers**. People whose first language is not English may need literature and sales staff that can explain products in their own language. Some products that involve interest on loans, savings or insurance may be unacceptable on cultural or religious grounds;
- **unsuitable products**. Financial products may be poorly designed for low-income consumers – eg, products may require regular payments; have a high minimum payment, balance or level of cover; have charges that eat heavily into small savings; offer poor rates of interest on low balances; or insurance cover might exclude people in temporary or insecure work. Insurers may also refuse cover to offenders, ex-offenders and their families;
- **confusing products**. Some products are overly complex and explained in confusing terms. Not all consumers feel confident enough to ask questions and are put off buying. People with low literacy and numeracy skills or with learning difficulties are particularly vulnerable;
- **pre-conception and past experience**. In surveys, low-income consumers have said they believe financial firms are not interested in people like themselves. Other consumers have been turned down for financial products in the past. Both these factors promote a situation in which people no longer bother to seek financial products;

- **inter-generational transmission**. It is widely accepted that there is a 'generational cycle of poverty' so that children who grow up in poor households are more likely to be poor themselves as adults than children in better-off families.

Tackling financial exclusion

Tackling financial exclusion is high on the agendas of both the Government and the FSA. A number of strategies are being employed.

The FSA has a statutory duty of 'promoting public understanding of the financial system'.[14] This involves increasing consumers' awareness of the benefits and risks of different financial products and ensuring they are provided with appropriate information and advice. The FSA does this through the requirements it places on financial firms themselves, as well as by providing its own factsheets, leaflets and its Moneymadeclear consumer website which includes comparative tables (see Appendix 2). The FSA is also heading a national strategy to increase financial capability. Working with partners, it is promoting financial education through schools and workplaces, and also targeting specific groups, such as young adults and new parents.[15] The FSA has conducted a survey (the 'Baseline Survey')[16] to assess the nation's current level of financial capability and will repeat the survey from time to time to measure progress.

The Government has promoted the introduction of new products which it hopes are better suited to low-income consumers' needs. These include basic bank accounts (see p43), the Saving Gateway (p76), child trust funds (p80) and stakeholder pensions (p195). Several of these products give the consumer a cash subsidy to boost their savings. This is a departure from previous government policies that have attempted to encourage saving through tax reliefs, which are of little or no value to consumers whose income is too low to pay much or any tax. The latest product initiative is to establish a national scheme of pension accounts to promote retirement saving (see p212). Many of these policies are part of a relatively new approach to welfare support first pioneered in the USA, called 'asset-based welfare'. Rather than just tackling immediate lack of income, this approach aims to help low-income consumers build up assets which may provide a more stable, long-term route to financial inclusion.

The Government has established a financial inclusion strategy, mainly focused on increasing access to bank accounts, affordable credit and money advice, working with, for example, the banking industry, credit unions and voluntary bodies.[17] It has also targeted extending the take-up of insurance products by low-income households.

Government initiatives include the Financial Inclusion Champions campaign, which builds and co-ordinates partnerships with organisations that already deal regularly with financially excluded people, such as local authorities, housing associations and Citizens Advice Bureaux, to help increase demand for and access to basic financial services. In 2009 a new money guidance scheme is being piloted by the FSA, which offers free generic financial advice to all. Provided the pilots are successful, the aim is, in time, to roll out the service nationwide. See Chapter 2 for more information.[18]

3. **The need for financial planning**

Research suggests that consumers do not generally have a good understanding of their financial needs. On the whole, consumers are reactive and their focus tends to be limited to building up an emergency fund and saving for a deposit on a house. There is little forward planning for protecting household finances against mishap or for long-term future needs. Consequently, insurance products have a low profile, debts often fail to be paid off in a timely fashion, and saving for retirement – while recognised as important – tends to get buried in more pressing needs.

The problem with this approach is that, if the worst happens, consumers are ill-prepared. An event which might have been merely unpleasant could turn into a financial crisis. Consumers also risk being unable to fulfil financial targets (eg, retirement) in situations where, if saving starts too late, it may be impossible to build up enough money. Failing to plan means consumers may also miss out on other opportunities (eg, the chance to train or start a business) through lack of savings to finance the venture. Finally, without planning, consumers may be losing money through buying the wrong products for their needs, buying products that are overly expensive, or using products in an expensive way – eg, running up an unplanned overdraft or failing to pay off loans in good time.

In the past, employers have often, through life insurance, pensions, and extended sick pay schemes, provided some financial protection for employees. But faced with mounting costs, many employers are cutting back, especially in the case of pension schemes. This makes it all the more pressing that consumers consider how they or their families might cope financially in the event of, for example, illness, death or retirement. This need is even more important for people who do not work for an employer and must rely purely on their own resources.

4. **How financial planning works**

Financial planning follows the following broad stages.
- **Stage 1: identify and prioritise your financial needs.** Although everyone is different, some basic needs are common to everyone and can be roughly prioritised as shown in the table below. Beyond these basic needs, you will have your own personal goals. Many are likely to involve either saving to buy

something later (see Chapter 4) or borrowing to buy now (see Chapter 5). Planning is especially important if your circumstances are unusual or about to change – eg, you are getting divorced, or you about to become a student, a lone parent or retire.

- **Stage 2: check your resources (budgeting).** Consider the resources you have available to meet your needs. For most people, resources will be the income (if any) left after you have paid for essentials, and any savings or other financial products that you already have. If you are not sure how much money you spend, you might find it useful to keep a note of your spending over the course of a few weeks to get an accurate picture.

- **Stage 3: review your goals in the light of your resources.** If your resources are not sufficient to meet all your goals, you will need to think again and decide whether to scale back your plans – eg, pay off debts more slowly, aim for a lower income in retirement or wait longer before buying your own home. You might decide to drop some goals altogether, in which case these should be the goals you previously decided were your lowest priority. Alternatively, you might be able to boost your resources – eg, by working more hours, selling something valuable or taking a lodger.

- **Stage 4: identify suitable financial products.** A suitable product is one which can help you meet a goal and has features which are a good match for your needs and resources – eg, involving no more risk than you are comfortable with and offering the degree of flexibility you need, such as being able to vary the amount you pay. Chapters 3 to 7 of this *Handbook* aim to help you identify suitable products.

A financial adviser can help you with all the above stages. You can also use an adviser to help you with just one aspect of your financial planning – eg, finding a mortgage or investing a lump sum. Make sure you choose the right sort of adviser for the task you have in mind (see Chapter 2).

The new money guidance service being piloted by the FSA in 2009 does not recommend specific products (Stage 4 of the planning process), but covers the first three stages, focusing in particular on the areas of budgeting, saving, borrowing, insurance, retirement planning, tax and benefits, and demystifying the jargon often used by financial services firms.

Basic financial needs

Priority	Need
1 (top priority)	**Get your debts under control**
	See Chapter 5
2	**Build up an emergency fund**
	(Money you can draw on in a crisis – eg, if the washing machine breaks, the roof starts to leak or your car breaks down)
	See Chapter 4

3   **Replace enough income if you stop work because of illness**
(Check what the state provides, what your employer provides and how
to arrange your own cover if needed)
See Chapters 7 and 9

4   **Make sure your family could cope financially if you died**
(Check what the state provides, what your employer provides and how
to arrange your own cover if needed)
See Chapters 7 and 9

5   **Save for retirement**
See Chapters 6 and 9

6   **Buy your own home**
(Not essential if you are able to rent or live with other family members,
but a goal many people have)
See Chapter 5

Comparison websites

At Stage 4 of the financial planning process, you may want to shop around to find suitable
products and providers. Internet comparison sites are a convenient aid to doing this, but
be aware of their limitations.

– Most internet comparison sites do not cover the whole market and different sites include
different providers, so check out two or three sites and see if there are other important
providers you might want to contact direct for information.

– The comparison site may receive commission from providers if you click through from
the site to make a purchase or take out an investment. This means the information you
get may not be completely impartial.

– Often the focus is on finding the best price, but a cheap product will not be a best buy if
its features and conditions are unsuitable for you. Make sure you have enough
information to make a considered choice. This is especially important if your
circumstances are non-standard – eg, you are looking for travel insurance and you have
a health condition, since you may find you have to pay more than the standard price
quoted.

The FSA runs its own comparison websites (at www.fsa.gov.uk/tables) for a limited range
of products. In general, you can rely on these to provide reasonably comprehensive,
impartial information.

5. **Choosing the right products**

Choosing the right financial products to help you meet a goal involves a variety
of factors, which are outlined on pp9–12.

Your attitude towards risk

You cannot be sure how some products will turn out in the future. This is particularly true of products designed to help you save over long periods of time – eg, to build up a pension or eventually pay off a mortgage. Many of these products offer a return linked in some way to the stock market. This means you do not know in advance what return you will get and, in most cases, the value of your money might fall. This is called 'capital risk' – ie, the risk that you might lose some of your original investment and/or some of the growth you have built up so far.

There are other sorts of risk. 'Inflation risk' is the risk that, although your money might grow in cash terms, the buying power falls because prices have risen by more than your money grew. For example, suppose £1 buys a bottle of sauce – you invest the £1 and get back £1.05 at the end of the year but sauce prices have jumped to £1.10 a bottle. Although your money has grown, it is worth less because it is no longer enough to buy the bottle of sauce.

Another type of risk is 'interest risk'. When you put money into a savings account, you earn interest. This might be at a fixed rate (an interest rate which stays the same throughout the whole time your money is invested) or a variable rate (an interest rate which is raised or reduced from time to time). Interest risk relates to the choice you make between a fixed or variable rate. If you choose a variable rate, you risk the income from your savings falling if the interest rate goes down. But if you save at a fixed rate, you could be locked into a poor deal if the variable interest rate on other savings products increases. Similarly, when you borrow money, the interest rate you pay might be fixed or variable. You risk a rise in your monthly payments if you borrow at a variable rate and the rate goes up. But you risk missing out on falling payments if you borrowed at a fixed rate and variable interest rates on other loans have since fallen.

'Shortfall risk' occurs where you have a particular target in mind (eg, building up enough money to pay off a mortgage) and your investment fails to grow by enough.

Sometimes you have to weigh up these risks against each other. In an ideal world, you would like the highest possible return for the lowest possible risk, but capital risk and return go hand in hand. You can minimise capital risk as long as you are prepared to settle for a modest return. If you want a higher return, you have to take on extra capital risk. This relationship is so established that if anyone offers you a great-looking return at low risk, you should be very suspicious. If it looks too good to be true, it probably is.

Examples of how the different sorts of risk interact include the following.

- Opting for savings or investments with low capital risk could increase the shortfall risk – although you have reduced the risk of losing money, you have also increased the likelihood that your investment will grow too modestly to meet your target.

- In times when inflation is high, it may be necessary to accept extra capital risk to reduce the risk of a fall in the buying power of your money.

Timescale

The period of time over which your financial needs must be met will influence your choice of product. For example, if you are taking out life insurance to protect your family, you will usually want a policy that runs until your youngest child stops being financially dependent on you. This might be when s/he reaches age 18 (and starts to work or qualify for a student loan) or older if, say, you plan to help fund her/him through university.

With savings and investments, timescale is also important. If you can save or invest for only a short time (eg, up to five years), you should normally avoid investments that have capital risk (see p9). This is because their value might fall and, although stock markets do tend to bounce back in the long run, you cannot be sure that the value will have recovered by the time you need your money.

Over the long term (eg, 10 years or more), stock market investments usually produce better returns than low capital risk products like bank and building society savings accounts, which are vulnerable to inflation risk (see above). So, unless you would be very worried about taking some capital risk, you should normally consider having at least some stock market investments if you are investing for the long term.

If you are investing for the long term, you might need your money back at a set time – eg, at retirement. Stock market investments may be suitable at first but you could lose some or all of the money you have built up if the stock market were to fall in the last few years before retirement. To guard against this, you could gradually shift your investments during the last 10 years or so before you reach retirement age away from the stock market and into products with a lower capital risk. This strategy lets you lock in the earlier gains that you made. However, you may want to adapt the strategy if you are within 10 years of retiring but the stock market is low and switching would mean locking in losses. You might want the help of a financial adviser with this strategy (see Chapter 2).

Some savings and investments are designed to run for a particular period (eg, five years) and you either cannot get your money back early or stand to lose some of your return or capital if you do. Make sure you understand the terms and conditions before you commit yourself. Otherwise, you could run into financial difficulties if you need your money back early but find you cannot have it or you stand to lose a large chunk in early surrender charges.

How much you can afford

You may have to adjust your goals or the products you choose because of their price. For example, insurance to protect your income if you cannot work because of illness can be very expensive. However, you could reduce the cost by limiting the amount it would pay out or the length of time for which it would pay out. If you are buying a house, there are several ways you could consider to reduce the cost of a mortgage – eg, you could buy a cheaper property. Alternatively, you could consider a mortgage with a longer term – this reduces the amount you have to pay each month but has the drawback of increasing the overall cost of the loan (see Chapter 5). Another option could be a discounted mortgage. This starts with low payments in the first year or two but the payments then increase to a more normal level. It is very important that you plan in advance how you will afford the higher payments once the discount period has come to an end (see Chapter 5).

Some investments involve flat-rate or minimum charges or dealing costs, which make small investments uneconomic but become better value if you can invest a larger sum.

Some products have a minimum investment or premium and would not be available to you if you could not afford that amount.

Tax and benefits

You need to consider how both you and the financial product are treated for tax purposes. For example, some investments (such as shares and most insurance-based investments) pay you a return from which tax has already been deducted and you cannot reclaim the tax. Such products are unsuitable for non-taxpayers and, in some cases, for all but higher rate taxpayers.

Other savings and investments (such as cash individual savings accounts) pay tax-free returns. This is good for all taxpayers, but of greatest benefit the higher your tax rate.

When deciding how much insurance to buy (eg, to replace your income in the event of illness) you will need to consider whether the payout from the policy and any income from other sources are tax-free or taxable.

You also need to consider the impact of any insurance payout or investment income and lump sums on your eligibility for means-tested state benefits.

See Chapter 8 for information about tax and Chapter 9 for information about benefits.

Your health

Your state of health and some factors that affect your health (eg, whether you smoke) are important when buying certain types of insurance and if you invest in an annuity (a type of investment that typically pays out an income for the rest of your life – see p200). If your health is poor, you are likely to have to pay more for life and health insurance and might be refused cover altogether. However, poor health can mean you qualify for a better deal when you are shopping around for an annuity.

Your ethics and beliefs

Your choice of financial products may be affected by your ethical stance or religious beliefs. For example, many people are not comfortable investing in companies involved in gambling, alcohol or defence. You might want to support companies that have a good record of treating employees fairly, sharing profits equitably with developing world traders or tackling climate change. Islamic (*Shariah*) law requires Muslims to share in risk as well as reward when investing and regards investing for interest as exploitation. This rules out ordinary bank and building society accounts, bonds, traditional mortgages and companies involved in these activities, but there is a growing range of *Shariah*-compliant products available.

Ethical Investment Research Services is an independent body which provides information to help organisations and people seeking to invest ethically. See Appendix 2 for contact details.

6. Keeping track of your finances

An important part of managing your money effectively is keeping track of it on a weekly or monthly basis, by getting and checking bank statements, keeping track of spending, and accounting for unexpected expenditure which might hamper your ability to pursue longer term savings and goals.

You also need to keep track in a bigger sense. Financial planning is not a one-off exercise. Having decided your needs, set your targets and chosen your products, you should review your plan from time to time – eg, once a year or maybe once every three years for a long-term goal. You should also carry out a review whenever your circumstances change – eg, if you start to live with someone, get married, have a child, get divorced, and so on. The aim of the review is to check whether your needs have changed and to see whether the products you have bought are still on target to meet them. To carry out a review, you will need the paperwork relating to your original purchase or investment and statements that have been issued since. You might prefer to ask a financial adviser to carry out the review (see Chapter 2).

It is very important that you keep all the paperwork from the time you made your original purchase or investment. It is equally important to make sure that you:

- receive regular statements. With most products, you should be sent a statement at least once a year (and more often with most bank accounts). Make a note of when you expect each statement to arrive and, if it does not turn up, contact the provider;

- check statements on arrival and raise any queries immediately with the provider; *and*
- store the statements in a safe place. You may need to keep them all the while you have the product or investment (which could be many years and even decades) or, if the product earns you taxable income, at least until no longer required under the tax rules (see Chapter 8).

Not only do these papers help you to keep track of your finances, they are also essential if something goes wrong later and you need to make a complaint (see Chapter 10).

Notes

1 Department for Work and Pensions, *Family Resources Survey 2007/08*, DWP, 2009
2 Department for Work and Pensions, *Family Resources Survey 2007/08*, DWP, 2009
3 Department for Communities and Local Government, *Housing Statistics: live tables*, Table 801, www.communities.gov.uk/documents/housing/xls/141491.xls, accessed 27 September 2009
4 Save the Children and Family Welfare Association, *The Poverty Premium*, Save the Children, 2007
5 Office for National Statistics, *United Kingdom National Accounts: The Blue Book*, Palgrave Macmillan, 2009

2. Financial exclusion
6 Office of Fair Trading, *Vulnerable Consumers and Financial Services*, January 1999
7 Resolution Foundation/Transact, *Financial Inclusion and Financial Capability Explained*, 2009
8 Resolution Foundation/Transact, *Financial Inclusion and Financial Capability Explained*, 2009
9 Save the Children and Family Welfare Association, *The Poverty Premium*, Save the Children, 2007

10 Resolution Foundation/Transact, *Financial Inclusion and Financial Capability Explained*, 2009
11 HM Treasury, *Financial Capability: the Government's long-term approach*, 2007
12 Financial Services Authority, *Establishing a Baseline*, 2006
13 Resolution Foundation/Transact, *Financial Inclusion and Financial Capability Explained*, 2009
14 Financial Services and Markets Act 2000
15 Financial Services Authority, *Building Financial Capability in the UK*, available at www.fsa.gov.uk/financial_capability
16 Financial Services Authority, *Levels of Financial Capability in the UK: results of the baseline survey*, 2006
17 HM Treasury, *Financial Inclusion: the way forward*, 2007
18 HM Treasury, *Financial Capability: the government's long-term approach*, 2007

Chapter 2

• •

Getting advice

This chapter covers:
1. When you might need advice (below)
2. Types of financial advice and where to get it (p17)
3. How advice is regulated (p26)
4. What to expect and how to prepare (p29)

• •

Basic facts
- Seven out of ten people do not use an adviser when taking out their most complex financial product.[1]
- Around one in seven say that an adviser or broker was the most important source of information when buying a financial product.[2]
- The Government aims to ensure that all adults in the UK have access to generic financial advice 'to help them engage with their financial affairs and make effective decisions about their money'.[3]

• •

1. **When you might need advice**

The financial planning process

Financial planning involves several stages (see p6) and you might want help with any of these stages.

It is important to distinguish information from advice. There are many sources of information and guidance – eg, articles in newspapers, books, television programmes, personal finance websites, money education in schools and adult learning classes, informal opinions from family and friends, and so on. By advice, we normally mean recommendations personal to you that may lead to buying specific products or to taking particular courses of action. There is also the relatively new concept of 'generic financial advice', which is being piloted through a new money guidance scheme (p25).

Help choosing the right product

Some objectives are pretty straightforward – eg, if you buy a car, you need car insurance. This is a top priority because it is illegal to drive without insurance. You will have to find the money from somewhere, so if you cannot afford insurance, think twice about whether you can afford to run a car at all or consider other areas of spending where you can cut back. You probably do not need any help with these stages.

However, you might want some help deciding what sort of insurance to get – eg, third party, fire and theft or comprehensive, protected no-claims discount or not, and which is the best policy for you.

More complicated situations

Other objectives can be more complex. For example, nearly everyone needs to save for retirement so this should be an objective which is on everyone's list. Deciding how much retirement income you might need, whether this should be a top priority or whether other things, like buying a home, are currently more important, what pension you have already built up, how much you need to save, what sort of pension scheme or plan to choose, and which company to invest with are all difficult decisions. You might want help with all these stages.

If you have several different objectives, such as planning for retirement, building up some savings for your children and sorting out life cover, you might want to ask an adviser to sort out an overall plan for meeting all your objectives.

Who should think about getting advice

At any stage of life you may need the help of an adviser, but particularly in the following situations.

You have debt problems

Common triggers for debts suddenly becoming unmanageable are unemployment and relationship breakdown. Money advisers can help you sort out your debts and make sure you are claiming all the benefits to which you are entitled.

You have a lump sum to invest

This may arise because of, say, redundancy, a life insurance pay out, compensation if you are injured or an inheritance. An independent financial adviser can help you work out your investment goals and choose suitable ways to invest.

Retirement

With many types of pension scheme, you need to turn the pension fund you have built up into a pension. An independent financial adviser can help you find the best way to do this.

Your circumstances change

If you have a change in your circumstance, such as getting married, divorced or having a child, this could bring a change in income, liabilities, priorities or attitude to risk. This may require a review of your financial planning and products to ensure that your dependants are still adequately protected – eg, if you are ill.

Your health deteriorates

This may require specialist advice to accommodate changing levels of income and needs.

Reasons for seeking advice

You might want to get help from a professional financial adviser for all sorts of reasons, including if:

– you do not know much about the financial products you need;
– it is a long time since you last bought the product and you are not up to date with changes;
– some aspect of your planning involves specialist knowledge – eg about tax;
– you are fairly sure what to do but you would like some reassurance;
– you do not have time to do the research yourself into what to do and which product to choose;
– your circumstances are changing in a complicated way – eg, you are getting divorced or you have just won or inherited some money.

Sources of advice

Research for the Financial Services Authority (FSA) shows that consumers rely on many different sources for guidance when thinking about financial products, including:

• family and friends, particularly favoured by younger people;
• personal finance pages of newspapers. This tends to be most popular with people in their mid-40s and older;
• leaflets from banks and building societies. Around one-third of people use these;
• other sources, such as specialist financial newspapers and magazines, the internet and TV and radio programmes.

These can all have drawbacks. For example, although family and friends are most likely to have your best interests at heart, they may lack the relevant knowledge or be basing advice on their own, sometimes out-of-date, experiences. Personal finance articles in newspapers and magazines are often, but not always, useful and objective but will not necessarily be relevant to your own particular circumstances. Literature from banks, building societies and other providers is unlikely to be completely objective, since the company issuing the leaflets presumably wants you to do business with it.

To find literature or web pages which give you impartial information, it is better to stick to independent bodies, such as the FSA (which provides all types of personal financial information on its Moneymadeclear website at www.moneymadeclear.fsa.gov.uk), government departments (eg, the Department for Work and Pensions and HM Revenue and Customs), Citizens Advice and Age Concern-Help the Aged. Trade bodies, such as the Council of Mortgage Lenders (for mortgages), the Association of British Insurers (all types of insurance), the Investment Management Association (unit trusts and similar investments) and the Association of Investment Companies (investments trusts), all publish useful guidance about the products offered by their members. See Appendix 2 for contact details.

For advice that is tailored to your circumstances, well-informed and up to date, you should seek professional advice. The rest of this chapter considers the various sources of professional advice, how you are protected when using an adviser, and what to expect.

---

2. **Types of financial advice and where to get it**

This section outlines the sorts of advisers you can visit for help with different types of financial products. Before contacting an adviser, see p29 for what to expect and how to prepare. If you need help sorting out a debt problem, see p167. The different types of adviser are due to be changed from 2012 as part of the Retail Distribution Review. The changes are outlined on p28.

Types of financial advice

Financial product	*Source of advice*	*Type of advice*
Debt (see Chapter 5)	Independent money advisers	Independent
Bank and savings accounts (see Chapter 3)	Provider	Tied
	There are no specialist independent advisers just for these products, but advice about them might be included if you visit a debt adviser (see p167) or independent financial adviser	Usually independent

Packaged investments – eg, a life insurance policy investing in one or more different investment funds, personal pensions, unit trusts and investment trust savings schemes (see Chapter 4)	Provider Distributor firm Independent financial adviser Appointed representative	Tied or multi-tied Multi-tied Independent Tied, multi-tied or independent – check which
Stock market investments – eg, shares and bonds (see Chapter 4)	Stockbroker	Independent
Mortgages and lifetime mortgages (see Chapter 5)	Provider Distributor firm Independent financial adviser Appointed representative	Tied or multi-tied Multi-tied Independent Tied, multi-tied or independent – check which
Home reversion schemes (see Chapter 5)	Provider Other	Usually tied Tied, multi-tied or independent – check which
Occupational pension schemes (see Chapter 6)	Pensions administrator at work	Tied
Non-investment insurance (see Chapter 7)	Provider Other	Tied Tied, multi-tied or independent – check which
Tax (see Chapter 8)	HM Revenue and Customs Independent tax advice charities Tax adviser, accountant	Government Independent Independent
State benefits (see Chapter 9)	Relevant government department or local authority provider Independent advice agency, charities	Government Independent

Note:

'Tied' means advice about the products of a single provider.

'Multi-tied' means advice based on the products of several different providers.

'Independent' means advice that can be based on all the products on the market.

Advice about debts

If you are having problems managing your debts, it is important to get help as soon as possible. Free, independent advice and help are available from many organisations, including:

- Citizens Advice Bureaux;
- Community Legal Advice (England and Wales only);
- Consumer Credit Counselling Service;
- Money Advice Scotland;
- National Debtline;
- independent advice centres.

See Appendix 2 for contact details.

Many commercial firms also advertise that they can help you with debt, typically by consolidating all your loans into one new debt or by going onto a debt repayment scheme which the firm manages for a large fee. Avoid these firms. They are not independent and recommend only their own products and schemes rather than looking at the full range of options to find the most appropriate solution for you. Moreover, you will be paying unnecessarily, since the organisations listed above not only offer fully independent advice, but it is also free of charge. For further information about dealing with problem debts, see Chapter 5.

Advice about bank accounts and savings

For advice on whether a particular account is suitable for you, talk to the particular bank or building society concerned or National Savings and Investments if this is the provider (see Chapters 3 and 4). Most providers used to be signed up to the Banking Code, which, among other things, required providers to explain clearly to customers the products on offer and to help customers choose products that meet their needs. From 1 November 2009, the Banking Code was replaced by Financial Services Authority (FSA) rules which impose similar requirements.

There are no advisers specialising in giving independent advice about bank and savings accounts. However, a debt adviser or a voluntary organisation (see Appendix 2) might suggest where you can open a basic bank account. Although you would not normally go to an independent financial adviser (see p20) just for advice about bank or savings accounts, any advice given might well include recommending suitable savings products.

Advice about 'packaged investments'

Packaged investments

'Packaged investments' include personal pensions, stakeholder pension schemes, investment-type life insurance including annuities, unit trusts, open-ended investment companies, investment trust savings schemes and individual savings accounts that invest in any of these. See Chapters 4 and 6 for details.

Product providers

If you go directly to a product provider, most will be able to give you advice. Some deal only on a no-advice basis; with others, you can choose whether to buy with or without advice. If you decide not to take advice, you have less protection if something goes wrong later (see p26).

If you take advice, the provider is required to get to know your details and to recommend only products which are suitable for you, given your objectives and personal circumstances. The provider can generally recommend only products from its range and, if the range includes nothing suitable, the provider should admit this and not sell you anything. The provider can adopt the products of other companies into its range in order to offer you a wider choice.

'Distributor' firms

This is a firm which does not have any products of its own, but has built up a range of products adopted from other companies. There could be few or many different companies' products in the range. The firm's salespeople and agents can sell and give advice about any products from the range. Some of these firms deal only on a no-advice basis; with others, you choose whether to buy with or without advice.

The companies that provide the adopted products are responsible for how their products are run, but the distributor firm is responsible for the selling process and any advice you get. Advisers must get to know your objectives and circumstances and recommend only products which are suitable.

Independent financial advisers

Independent financial advisers can help you with any or all of the stages of financial planning. To do this, they must get to know your objectives and circumstances. They must then recommend only products that are suitable, but can select from the full range of products and companies in the market. In practice, they will not necessarily check the whole market for every customer, but are allowed to draw up shortlists from time to time of products suitable for particular types of customer, provided these lists are reviewed and updated regularly.

An adviser wishing to use the description 'independent' must allow you to pay for advice through fees (see p32). S/he may also offer you the option of paying by commission.

To find an independent adviser, contact IFA Promotion, the Institute of Financial Planning or the Personal Finance Society, which can all provide a list of members in your area. Some advisers specialise in helping you shop around for an annuity (ie, an investment typically used to provide a pension at retirement – see Chapter 6). The main ones are listed in Appendix 2.

Appointed representatives

Some firms of investment advisers act as appointed representatives (sometimes called 'tied agents') for another firm. The firm to which an appointed representative is tied is responsible to the FSA for the regulation and conduct of the representative. An appointed representative can be tied to any type of firm. If they are:

- **tied to a single provider**, they can give advice only about that provider's investments and any adopted products the provider has taken into its range. If there are a lot of adopted products, this may be referred to as 'multi-tied advice';
- **tied to a distributor firm**, they can give advice about the range of products offered by the firm. This may be referred to as multi-tied advice;
- **tied to an independent adviser**, they can give independent advice based on all the products in the market; *or*
- **tied to a network**, they give independent advice. A network is an organisation which typically provides its tied agents with various centralised services, such as dealing with regulatory requirements, administration and research.

Advice about stock market investments

The main source of advice about investing directly in shares, corporate bonds, gilts and similar investments (see Chapter 4) is a stockbroker. Most offer a range of different services. With an 'execution only' service, the stockbroker just carries out your instructions to buy or sell and does not give you any advice. If you opt for a 'dealing with advice' service, the broker may recommend which investments to buy and sell or when, and should respond to requests for an opinion on deals that you are considering.

Stockbrokers are obliged to give independent advice and, if you ask them to buy or sell investments for you, to get the best price they can.

For a list of stockbrokers, contact the London Stock Exchange or the Association of Private Client Investment Managers and Stockbrokers (see Appendix 2).

Advice about mortgages

The details given below reflect the FSA rules governing advice about most mortgages. However, they do not apply to advice about buy-to-let mortgages and loans which are a 'second charge' on your home – ie, where you already have another mortgage on your home which would be paid off first if your home had to be sold to repay the loans. Chapter 5 gives details about these products.

Product providers

Mortgage providers may just give you information about the mortgages they offer or might also give you advice. They must make clear at the outset which sort of service they are offering.

A provider must find out about your personal circumstances, including how you feel about risk and what amount of mortgage you can afford. Based on this, the provider must recommend only mortgages that are suitable for you.

The provider can recommend only products from its range. These might be limited to just its own loans or it might have adopted several other companies' products into its range in order to offer you a wider choice.

Distributor firms

This type of firm does not make loans itself, but offers a range of mortgages adopted from other companies. There could be few or many different companies' loans in the range. The firm's salespeople and agents can sell and give advice about any mortgages from the range. The firm must make clear whether it is giving advice or just information.

The companies that provide the adopted products are responsible for how their mortgages are run. But the distributor firm is responsible for the selling process and any advice you get. Advisers must get to know your objectives and circumstances and recommend only products which are suitable.

Independent advisers

Independent mortgage advisers must check your personal circumstances and what you can afford, and then recommend only products which are suitable, although they can select from the full range of loans and companies in the market. In practice, they will not necessarily check the whole market for every customer, but are allowed to draw up shortlists from time to time of products suitable for particular types of customer, provided these lists are reviewed and updated regularly.

A mortgage intermediary can use the description 'independent' only if it allows you to pay for advice through fees (see p32). It may also offer you the option of paying by commission.

To find a mortgage broker in your area, contact IFA Promotion.

Appointed representatives

Some firms of mortgage advisers act as appointed representatives (sometimes called 'tied agents') for another firm. The firm to which an appointed representative is tied is responsible to the FSA for the regulation and conduct of the representative. An appointed representative can be tied to any type of firm. If they are:

- **tied to a single provider**, they can give advice only about that provider's mortgages and any adopted products the provider has taken into its range. If there are a lot of adopted products, this may be referred to as 'multi-tied advice';
- **tied to a distributor firm**, they can give advice about the range of products offered by the firm. This may be referred to as multi-tied advice;
- **tied to an independent adviser**, they can give independent advice based on all the products in the market; *or*
- **tied to a network**, they give independent advice. A network is an organisation which typically provides its tied agents with various centralised services, such as dealing with regulatory requirements, administration and research.

Advice about equity release schemes

Equity release schemes provide a lump sum and/or income funded by taking out a mortgage against your home (lifetime mortgage) or by selling part or all of your home (home reversion scheme). See Chapter 5 for details. If you seek advice about an equity release scheme, under FSA rules, the adviser is required to recommend only a suitable plan taking into account your objectives and personal circumstances, including your attitude towards risk. This includes considering whether a lifetime mortgage or home reversion scheme would best suit your needs and the impact that an equity release scheme might have on your eligibility for state benefits and your tax position.

Many independent advisers who offer advice about packaged investments (see above) also give advice about lifetime mortgages and home reversion schemes. Some advisers specialise in this area and are then usually members of the trade body Safe Home Income Plans, which, in addition to FSA regulation, requires members to abide by its own code of practice (see Appendix 2).

Since these schemes involve taking out a large mortgage on your home or selling part of your home, it is essential that you also get advice from a solicitor (see Appendix 2). The solicitor will advise you on the legal implications of the plan or scheme, but will not advise on whether the scheme is financially suitable for you.

Advice about occupational pension schemes

You can get information, but not usually advice, from the trustees or pensions administrator for your pension scheme at work. Your scheme booklet or staff noticeboard or human resources department should be able to give you contact details.

If you seek advice about pensions from a product provider, its tied agent or an independent financial adviser, it should check whether you are eligible to join an occupational scheme and, if this would be more suitable for you, should not then recommend that you invest in an alternative, such as a personal pension.

If you are thinking about transferring substantial pension rights from an occupational scheme to another pension arrangement, you might want to get advice from a consulting actuary. You can get a list of members from the Association of Consulting Actuaries and Society of Pension Consultants (see Appendix 2). Such advice is expensive, so possibly not worth the cost if you have only a small pension to transfer. For details about pensions, see Chapter 6.

You can get advice about all aspects of pensions, including occupational pensions, from The Pensions Advisory Service (see Appendix 2).

Advice about non-investment insurance

Product providers

Non-investment insurance products (eg, for a car, home, travel, term, most health insurance and so on) are covered in Chapter 7. FSA rules require the salesperson you deal with to make sure as far as possible that the product s/he is selling you is suitable for your needs and to draw your attention to any unusual or particularly onerous terms. Insurers generally sell you just their own policies. If you want a wider choice, you need to visit a tied agent, multi-tied agent or independent intermediary.

Tied agents and multi-tied agents

There are all sorts of tied agents selling insurance. They include travel agents selling holiday insurance, shops selling extended warranties and building societies selling home buildings and contents insurance and mortgage payment protection policies. Often these agents are tied to a single provider and cannot offer you a choice of products.

Other tied agents are 'multi-tied' and can sell you insurance from several providers. You get a bit more choice, but do not confuse these types of agents with independent intermediaries.

Whichever type of agent you use, they must abide by the FSA regulations on selling insurance. **Note:** travel insurance sold through travel agents, which was previously not covered by the FSA regulations, was brought within their scope from January 2009.

Independent intermediary or insurance broker

An independent intermediary can, in theory, give you advice based on all the products and companies in the market. In practice, it usually restricts its advice to a fairly large panel of insurers. To count as independent, intermediaries must base their recommendations on a sufficiently large number of policies to give a 'fair analysis'.

In the past, any intermediary using the name 'broker' had to be independent. Although legal restrictions on using the name 'broker' have now gone, most are members of the British Insurance Brokers' Association (BIBA) which requires its members to give impartial advice. Contact BIBA (see Appendix 2) for a list of its members.

Advice about tax

For general guidance about tax and queries about your own tax affairs, contact HM Revenue and Customs. It can help you understand the system and correctly report and pay tax, but will not give you advice on how to save tax. For this, consult a professional tax adviser (eg, a member of the Chartered Institute of Taxation) or an accountant. See Appendix 2 for contact details.

If you are on a low income (around £17,000 a year or less), you may be able to get free tax advice from TaxAid or TaxHelp for Older People. For more information about tax, see Chapter 8.

Advice about state benefits

The UK benefits system is complicated and it can be extremely hard to work out or check your entitlement or challenge a decision. Although the government or local authority department concerned should be able to help with general information or specific queries regarding your claim, you may want independent help. Organisations, such as Citizens Advice, money advice agencies (which also give debt advice) and Community Legal Advice can help you work out which benefits and tax credits you may be able to claim, assess the impact of working or taking out equity release on your entitlement, challenge an award, and so on. Many charities are also able to give benefit advice relevant to particular situations, such as being a lone parent, having a disability, being a carer or being an older person. See Appendix 2 for a range of useful contacts.

Money guidance (generic financial advice)

Anyone giving the sort of financial advice described in the previous pages that directs you towards buying a specific product from a particular adviser must be authorised by the FSA; they are giving what is called 'regulated advice'. For some years, the FSA and the Government have recognised a widespread need for people to be able to get less formal, less expensive and more general advice that helps them understand their financial affairs and the options available, and to decipher often complex information about financial products. The term 'generic financial advice' has been coined, though to date there is no single view about what this is. At one extreme, some experts suggest generic advice should mean broad financial solutions that could apply to a wide range of people, but is in no way tailored to a particular person. At the other extreme, others believe generic advice should include specific guidance on, say, how much life cover a particular individual should have and perhaps even point to a range of products or providers that might be considered.

By 2012, a new national pension scheme of personal accounts is due to be introduced (see Chapter 6). The Government recognises that people will need advice about personal accounts but, to keep costs down, does not want people to have to rely on regulated advice. Therefore, the introduction of personal accounts is acting as a catalyst for the parallel introduction of a national network delivering generic financial advice to all who want it and covering all areas of personal finance, not just pensions. In early 2007, the Government appointed a review body (the Thoresen Review) to investigate how this advice could be delivered.

As a result of the Thoresen Review recommendations, in 2009, the FSA began piloting a generic financial advice service, which the Thoresen Review called 'money guidance'. Under the pilot, which has been given the FSA's Moneymadeclear brand name, two money guidance services have been established in the north of England in conjunction with a number of other organisations, including Citizens Advice. Anyone can get in touch and receive advice either face to face or by phone (Tel: 0300 500 5000). Alternatively, you may be able to find the information you need on the FSA's Moneymadeclear consumer website (www.moneymadeclear.fsa.gov.uk). The service provides free, impartial guidance covering budgeting, saving and borrowing, retirement planning, tax and benefits, and demystifying the technical language often used by the financial services industry. The service aims to deliver information, guidance and tools that are tailored to the individual so they have the confidence to make informed choices. Where a person's needs are complex, the service will signpost her/him to an appropriate regulated adviser for more in-depth advice. The money guidance service does not recommend specific courses of action, products, types of products or providers.

3. How advice is regulated

Investments, mortgages, equity release and insurance

The need for advisers to be authorised

It is illegal for anyone to give advice about investments, mortgages, equity release or most insurance in the UK without being authorised by the Financial Services Authority (FSA). You should deal only with authorised advisers because, if you deal with an illegal adviser, you are unlikely to be protected if things go wrong.

For this purpose, 'advice' means recommending specific products and companies. So a person or firm does not have to be authorised if they are giving just information or general advice about the types of product you might need (called 'generic advice'). Although 'investment advice' covers advice about most of the things you would consider to be investments, it does not include advice about bank and building society current or savings accounts (this will be covered by separate FSA rules from 1 November 2009 onwards) or National Savings and Investments products. Similarly 'mortgage advice' covers only mortgages secured as a first charge (ie, the first loan that would have to be paid off if the home were repossessed) on UK property, at least 40 per cent of which is for use as a home by the borrower or a close relative (husband, wife, unmarried partner (of same or different sex), parent, brother, sister, child, grandparent or grandchild).

There are some exceptions to the need for authorisation, in particular:

- 'appointed representatives' (also known as tied agents and multi-tied agents). An individual or firm does not have to be authorised itself provided it is an appointed representative of some other firm which *is* authorised (the 'principal'). The principal is responsible for the conduct of its appointed representatives;
- firms based in other European Economic Area (EEA) countries. These are allowed to do business in the UK without being authorised by the FSA provided they are regulated by an equivalent body in their home country or, in the case of an internet firm, the EEA country from which they operate. The EEA comprises the member states of the European Union plus Iceland, Liechtenstein and Norway.

When considering investments, pensions, mortgages, lifetime mortgages or insurance, make sure you deal only with advisers that are authorised by the FSA or tied agents of an authorised firm (or EEA firms regulated by a body equivalent to the FSA). To do this, check the firm's entry on the FSA Register by calling the FSA's Moneymadeclear Helpline on 0300 500 5000 or visiting www.fsa.gov.uk/register/home.do.

The advantages of dealing with an authorised adviser

Firms authorised by the FSA are required to be solvent, run by trustworthy and competent people, and to be operated in an honest and fair way. They must abide by a set of general principles that include treating customers fairly, and often also have to comply with very detailed conduct of business rules that govern advice given to customers. If any advice given breaches the rules (eg, you are sold a product which is unsuitable for you given your attitude towards risk), you can complain and ask for compensation.

Authorised firms are required to have a proper complaints procedure and must have either insurance or adequate resources to pay redress to customers with a valid grievance. They must also belong to an independent complaints body, the Financial Ombudsman Service, which can order a firm to pay redress (see Chapter 10).

If you have lost money through an authorised firm's negligence or fraud, but you cannot get it back because the firm has gone bankrupt you may be eligible for compensation from the Financial Services Compensation Scheme (see Chapter 10).

An authorised firm is required to make sure that its appointed representatives also comply with the FSA's rules and is ultimately responsible for the actions of its representatives.

You lose all these forms of protection if you deal with a firm that is not authorised by the FSA or the representative of an authorised firm. This would be the case if you did business with a firm trading illegally in the UK or with a foreign firm.

If the foreign firm is an EEA firm allowed to do business here, you are covered by the rules of another EEA regulator. The rules will not be quite the same as those of the FSA, but should be broadly equivalent, so, for example, you should still have access to proper complaints procedures if something goes wrong.

If you deal with a foreign firm based outside the EEA, there may be no system for protecting consumers. You could lose your money and have no way to get it back.

Buying without advice ('execution only')

If you use an authorised adviser and the advice turns out to have been unsuitable and causes you to lose money, you have grounds for complaint and may be able to get compensation. If you buy without advice, the decisions are down to you – you cannot blame anyone else for a bad choice or get compensation if you lose money.

Advice about occupational pensions

If advice involves a choice between an occupational pension and other arrangements which count as investments (eg, personal pensions or stakeholder schemes), the rules already described above concerning investment advice apply.

If the advice is purely concerned with an occupational scheme, what protection you have depends on who gave the advice. If advice was given by the trustees or officials of your scheme at work, the scheme is required to have a formal complaints procedure you can use if something goes wrong. If that does not resolve the matter, you can take your case to The Pensions Advisory Service and, ultimately, the Pensions Ombudsman (see p330). If the advice was from a consulting actuary, the rules of the actuary's professional body (such as the Institute of Actuaries) apply and you could seek redress through the courts (see p331) if you think you have lost financially because of bad advice.

Future changes: the Retail Distribution Review

There is a confusing array of different types of advice and a risk that the system of payment by commission could distort the advice you receive. Consumer bodies have been campaigning about these issues since the 1980s when comprehensive financial regulation was first introduced. Over the last few years, the FSA has been reviewing the existing situation and consulting on making changes (the Retail Distribution Review). In June 2009, the FSA announced proposals that aim to:

- improve the clarity of the descriptions of the different advice services;
- remove the potential for advice to be distorted by the method of paying for it; *and*
- increase the professional standards of advisers (who currently must pass only fairly basic exams, although many choose to take additional qualifications).

Under the proposals, which are due to come into effect from 2012, there will be two types of advice: independent and restricted. For advice to be independent, recommendations must be based on a comprehensive and fair analysis of the relevant market and the advice must be unbiased and not restricted in any way. Advice that falls short of this standard – eg, because recommendations can only be made from a limited range of products, will be called restricted advice. Before doing business, an adviser must tell you which type of service s/he offers. You will also continue to be able to buy or invest on a non-advised (execution-only) basis if you want to.

The scope of independent advice will be widened. At present, it applies only when you are buying packaged investment products. Under the new regime, it will apply to a much broader range to be called 'retail investment products' that will include existing packaged products, many other types of investment fund and more complex investment products. Independent advisers should be knowledgeable about, and able to make recommendations from, the full range of these products.

Payment for advice by commission will be abolished. Advisers, whether independent or restricted, will have to set out and agree their own charges with their customers. The charges can be paid in the form of fees or as a deduction from the investment. In general, this should be a one-off charge for one-off advice, but can be spread over time if the investment involves you investing regular sums or you will be receiving ongoing advice. Providers may not be involved in setting charges for advice, but can collect the charges from the investment to pass on to the adviser if that is how the customer would prefer to pay.

4. **What to expect and how to prepare**

Different sorts of advice

There are three main sorts of adviser:

- those advising on and selling the products of a single provider (either working for the provider itself or as tied agents);

- those advising on and selling the products of several providers. They may be employed by, or be agents for, a provider which has adopted the products of other companies into its range – eg, some banks and building societies will go down this route. In the case of non-investment insurance, they may be agents tied simultaneously to several providers; *and*
- those who are independent – ie, making recommendations based on all (or a fair analysis of) the products and companies in the market.

At the start of doing business with you, an adviser should clarify whether the advice is tied or independent and, if tied, tell you whose products can be recommended.

Key facts from the Financial Services Authority

Advisers and providers regulated by the Financial Services Authority (FSA) are required to give you certain documents setting out specified important information. These include initial disclosure documents, guides to the cost of services, key facts documents and key facts illustrations. If you read nothing else, you should read these documents because the information they contain is important and will help you make an informed choice. You can spot these documents by the 'key facts' logo on the front (see p363).

The fact find

Under the FSA rules, advisers are required to 'know the customer' so that they are in a position to give suitable advice. To do this, the adviser will usually take you through some kind of fact-finding process. This will involve asking you a lot of questions and taking down your answers. What questions are asked will depend on the type of advice you are seeking. For example, if you want an adviser to consider your whole situation, s/he will need to know:

- your name, address, age, marital status and state of health;
- details of members of your family and any other dependants;
- about your financial objectives and the timescale over which you hope to achieve them;
- your attitude towards risk;
- your income;
- your tax position;
- whether you have savings and other assets;
- about your existing financial commitments, such as mortgage, other debts and the amounts you are already saving on a regular basis;
- about existing financial products, such as life insurance;
- whether any financial products are available through your work, such as an occupational pension scheme or health insurance;
- whether you expect your financial circumstances to change in the foreseeable future.

Finding out about and comparing products

Packaged investments

If you are considering packaged investments, such as a personal pension, investment-type life insurance or unit trust, when recommending a particular company's product, an adviser should give you, or arrange for the provider to send you, a Key Facts document. This sets out the important features of the product in a format that makes it easy for you to compare this product with other similar ones. The sort of information you will find in the document includes:

- the aim of the product;
- your commitment – eg, how much you must save regularly or invest as a lump sum;
- how your money will be invested;
- how the investment is taxed;
- what charges are deducted.

A Key Facts document will also include a key facts example. This shows the impact that charges may have on your investment and, if you are investing to reach a particular target (eg, investing in a pension to give you a target level of retirement income), the example will include a projection showing how your investment might grow, assuming a particular growth rate specified by the FSA. Bear in mind that this is just an example to give you some idea and a baseline against which to measure subsequent progress of your investment. No one can say what will actually happen in future – your investment might grow by more or less than the amount in the example.

Mortgages and lifetime mortgages

For each mortgage or lifetime mortgage recommended by an adviser, you should be given a key facts illustration. This lists in detail the features of the mortgage or lifetime mortgage in a set format so that you can easily compare one product with another. The illustration is personalised, based on the information you gave the adviser during the fact find.

Non-investment insurance

If you buy face to face, through the post or over the internet, you should normally be given a policy summary and information about what you must pay, any charges, any unusual exclusions or conditions, and the claims procedure before you buy. If you are buying by phone, this might not be possible, in which case you should be sent this information and the full policy document as soon as possible after purchase.

Cancellation periods

After you have invested in, or bought, a financial product, you will be sent various documents. Depending on the type of product, these may include a cancellation notice giving the option to withdraw from the contract.

With packaged products, you usually have 14 days in which to cancel, but only if you received advice, except in the case of pensions and investment-type life insurance when the cancellation period applies even if you did not receive advice. In some cases, if you invest through an individual savings account, the period may be reduced to seven days.

With stock market investments, there is usually no cancellation period. The same is true for mortgages.

For non-investment insurance, the standard cancellation period is 14 days, but 30 days in the case of long-term care insurance, term insurance and critical illness insurance. See Chapter 7 for an explanation of these products.

How advisers are paid

Currently, there are two ways in which a firm of advisers may make its money.

- **Commission** received from the provider of a product you have bought. You pay the adviser indirectly because the commission comes out of charges built into the product. Typically, commission has two elements so your adviser may get an immediate lump-sum payment and then 'renewal commission' (also called 'trail commission') of a given amount for each year you keep the product.
- **Fees.** You pay the adviser directly for the advice given. This might be at a fixed rate or, more often, based on the hours the adviser spends on your case. If the adviser recommends products which pay commission, the commissions received will be set off against the fee, in which case you pay the adviser less in fees but also pay something indirectly through the product charges.

The advantage of the commission system is you do not have to pay a lump sum up front for the advice you get (which may cost hundreds of pounds). Instead, the cost of the advice is spread over several or many years, being deducted bit by bit through the product charges.

There are several disadvantages to the commission system, which are avoided if you pay by fee. First, with commission, the adviser stands to make more money the more products s/he can sell or the more you invest. Also, different products and providers pay different levels of commission, so the adviser will earn different amounts depending on the products you buy. An unscrupulous adviser might be swayed by these factors to sell you products you do not need, to encourage you to invest more in, or buy more of, a product than you really need or to recommend products because they pay the highest commission, not because they suit you best.

Another drawback is that the commission system is obscure. It is hard for you to know how much your adviser is getting for the advice given and, if you do know the amount, hard to tell whether the amount is reasonable. You might be surprised to find that your adviser could still be getting renewal commission many years after you originally sought her/his advice.

Key facts documents (and key features documents) tell you how much commission your adviser stands to make as a result of selling you a particular product. In addition, your adviser should tell you this if you ask. Mortgage advisers and investment advisers wanting to call themselves 'independent' must offer you the option to pay by fees rather than commission.

Getting the best from an adviser

Follow these steps to prepare for seeing an adviser to make sure that you get the best from her/him and to protect yourself from problems.

- **Decide whether you want independent advice** or would be happy with an adviser who can recommend only the products of one or a handful of providers.
- **Check if an adviser is authorised** before you make contact by consulting the FSA Register (see p26). The entry will tell you what sort of products the adviser is allowed to deal with.
- **Visit two or three advisers.** You will be giving the adviser a lot of sensitive information about yourself and relying on her/him to help you make important decisions which may affect you for a long time to come, so it is important to feel comfortable with the person you choose.
- **Do some groundwork**. Think in advance about your objectives and try to find out for yourself something about the ways in which you might set about achieving those objectives. Chapters 3 to 7 will help you do that. You will then be in a good position to have a productive discussion with the adviser and to spot if the advice seems inappropriate.
- **Gather together the information the adviser will need**. For example, have details of your income, spending, tax, existing investments and insurance products, details of your occupational pension scheme, and so on. Think about your attitude towards risk.
- **Be sceptical**. If you do not feel comfortable with the advice given, do not go ahead. If a deal sounds too good to be true, it probably is. Remember that risk and reward always go hand in hand – there is no such thing as a completely safe investment offering amazingly high returns.
- **Make payments directly to the company whose products you are buying or investing in** rather than to the adviser. Few advisers are allowed to handle clients' money. You can see whether this applies to your adviser by checking her/his entry on the FSA Register (see p26).

- **Check the arrangements for keeping your investments safe** if the adviser will be responsible for looking after them.
- **Take notes and keep all documents.** Keep a note of the conversations you have with the adviser. Keep these notes and all the documents you are given in a safe place in case of a dispute later on.

Advice scams

Debt advice. Do not pay for help with debt problems. Get free, independent advice from organisations such as Citizens Advice Bureaux and National Debtline.

Investment advice. If it sounds too good to be true, it probably is. To get a better-than-average return, you must always take on extra risk. So be very sceptical if any adviser suggests a scheme offering amazing returns with little or no risk.

Commission bias. Be on your guard against being recommended an unsuitable or less-than-best product just because it earns extra commission for the adviser. Ask how much the adviser stands to make. Query the recommendation if the amount seems large. Better still, go to an adviser who charges a fee instead of relying on commission.

Mortgage advice. Do not be persuaded to lie about your income or other circumstances in order to get a mortgage, Not only is this fraud, but you increase the risk of being unable to afford your repayments which could mean you lose your home.

Notes

1 Financial Services Authority, *Levels of Financial Capability in the UK: results of a baseline survey*, FSA, 2006
2 Financial Services Authority, *Levels of Financial Capability in the UK: results of a baseline survey*, FSA, 2006
3 HM Treasury, *Financial Capability: the Government's long-term approach*, 2007

Chapter 3

Everyday money

This chapter covers:
1. Managing your everyday money (below)
2. Types of bank account (p42)
3. How bank accounts work (p45)
4. Different ways of banking (p55)
5. What an account costs (p56)
6. Who offers accounts (p58)
7. How to open an account (p58)
8. Regulation and complaints (p61)

Basic facts

- Six per cent of British households have no bank account (current or basic).[1]
- Four per cent of households have no account suitable for receiving direct payments of state benefits. One in 14 has a Post Office card account.[2]
- Paying by direct debit could save you around £230 a year on your electricity, gas and telephone bills.[3]
- Having a bank account is often a gateway to other financial products and services – eg, affordable credit deals.[4]

---

1. **Managing your everyday money**

The cash economy

If your affairs are fairly simple, you might manage your money totally in cash – eg, cashing an order at a post office, paying bills in person at a local bank branch, and buying fuel with a pre-payment meter. The main advantage of cash is that, in theory, it is easy to budget; you can see exactly how much money you have at any time and can keep good track of where it goes. But managing your everyday money in cash has a number of drawbacks.

- **Cash is insecure.** It is easily lost or stolen and virtually impossible to trace.
- **People do not necessarily want to pay you in cash.** Most salaries and benefit payments are paid direct to an account, not in cash. This includes, for example,

tax credits, state pensions, education maintenance allowance and student grants and loans.

- **Cheques cost you money.** Most cheques can be cashed only by paying them into an account. If you do not have a bank account, you may have to use a cheque cashing service, for which there is a fee.

- **Bills paid in cash are often more expensive.** If you arrange to pay regular bills by direct debit, you often get a discount. Pre-payment meters charge you extra for fuel compared with paying against a bill.

- **Some suppliers will not accept cash.** If you are buying life insurance or paying a mortgage, you might have to arrange regular payments directly from an account.

- **You might have no alternative to paying lump sums.** If you are buying something expensive (eg, car insurance), you might prefer to pay by instalments. Sometimes the instalment option is available only if you can pay from an account. You might find it hard to raise the money to pay the full amount in a single cash sum.

- **You have to make sure you pay bills regularly.** With cash, there is a risk of missing payments – eg, if you are ill and cannot get to a branch, you are on holiday, or you forget.

- **You might miss the best deals or be excluded from some products.** You often pay less if you can buy over the internet, by phone or by mail. But you cannot pay by cash if you shop in these ways. In addition, some products or services may only be available in non-cash transactions.

- **Cash in your pocket does not grow.** If you put spare cash into an account until needed, it could be earning you interest (although in 2009, interest on many accounts was close to zero).

All of these drawbacks can be overcome if you use a bank account.

Advantages of having a bank account

A bank account lets you store your money safely until you need to spend it or transfer it somewhere else – eg, to a savings account (see Chapter 4). A bank account also gives you a variety of ways to make payments and to receive money from other people.

People can pay you by transferring money from their own bank account directly to yours. This is both a cheap and secure way of transferring money. Some organisations insist on making certain payments this way – eg, student loans and, since 2005, most state benefits. Increasingly, other forms of state support are being replaced with cash payments that must be paid direct to your bank account – eg, help with your housing costs that were formerly paid direct to your mortgage lender or landlord. These also include social care where, instead of receiving services from your local authority, you are now more likely to receive cash which you can then use to buy in the services you have selected yourself. You might receive cheques, which you pay into your account, usually at no cost to you (but see p57). You can still accept cash, of course, and, if you want to, pay it into your account.

You can pay other people by withdrawing cash from your account. Alternatively, you can pay by debit card or, if your account comes with a cheque book, write a cheque to the person you want to pay. Paying in these ways makes it possible to buy by phone, mail order and online, so you have more scope to shop around for better deals. If you have regular bills (eg, for electricity, telephone, a mortgage or your car insurance) you can arrange for these to be paid directly from your account by direct debit or standing order. Sometimes, by agreeing to pay by direct debit, you get a reduction in your bill (but beware of being asked to pay too much in advance – see p50).

Other things to think about if you have a bank account

At first, you might find it a bit harder to keep track of your money, but the bank will send you regular statements showing the money coming in and going out. You should check that statements are correct by comparing the entries with your receipts from shopping, cash machine slips, cheque book stubs and bill statements. You can readily check how much money is in your account (the 'balance') at any time.

You might be worried that you will spend more money than you have in your account (ie, go overdrawn), but you can choose accounts, called basic bank accounts (see p43) that aim to prevent you doing this.

There are usually no charges for running a basic bank account or a standard current account provided you do not go overdrawn. But there are charges for some special services (see p57). Increasingly, banks offer 'packaged current accounts' with additional features and which do have charges (see p42).

Alternatives to a bank account

Post Office card account

In the past, if you received state benefits or pensions, you could choose to be paid either in cash (by cashing pre-printed orders from a book or presenting a girocheque at a post office) or by direct payment to your bank account. Now, nearly everyone must receive benefits by direct payment.

To receive direct payments, you must either provide the Department for Work and Pensions with details of a bank or savings account (see Chapter 4) into which your benefits will be paid, or you can open a Post Office card account.

A Post Office card account is a special account that can receive only certain state benefits and lets you withdraw them in cash by presenting a plastic card at any post office and keying a personal identification number into a keypad on the post office counter. The cashier then hands over the money. You choose how much cash to draw out each time (up to the maximum in the account), so you can draw out your benefits in several amounts at different times, rather than as one lump sum. It does not have any other banking features – eg, you cannot pay in salary, cheques or cash and you cannot pay bills directly from the account. If you rely on someone else to pick up your benefits for you, you can ask to have a second card for use by another named person. There are no charges and you cannot go overdrawn.

If you cannot manage using a Post Office card account or a bank or savings account, you may be able to get your state benefits paid by weekly girocheque instead. These cheques can either be cashed (in full) at a post office or paid into a bank account. This might be the most suitable option if you rely on a variety of different people to collect your pension or benefits for you.

The Post Office card account is currently used by around 4.3 million people and is offered by post offices through a government contract that runs until 2010. This contract has been renewed for a further five years, so some form of direct payment account will continue to be available through post offices until at least 2015. At the time of writing, it is unclear whether, under the new contract, the card account might be redesigned – eg, to include more features, such as bill payments.[5]

Pre-payment cards and mobile phones

Technology is increasingly offering consumers new ways to pay for goods and services. Pre-payment cards are plastic cards onto which you load your own cash. You can then use the card in cash machines and to pay for goods and services in shops, online, over the phone, and so on. The main advantages of pre-payment cards include the following.

- **No credit checks and no need for a bank account.** As the card is loaded with your money, no one else is at risk. So you can have a pre-payment card even if you have no credit history or a poor one. You can use a pre-payment card even if you cannot get a bank account – eg, you are under 18, although you will usually need to prove your identity and address when you apply.
- **No risk of debt.** The most you can spend is the money you have loaded onto the card.
- **Convenience and cheap deals.** Depending on the card you choose, you may be able to use it in most of the places where you could use a debit or credit card, including being able to buy over the internet and by phone, which often offer lower prices than the high street. You are not limited to spending in the UK, so pre-payment cards can be a good way of taking holiday money abroad.
- **A money transfer facility.** Most cards let you add other cardholders to your account, so they can spend cash that you have pre-loaded. This can be a simple way to transfer money to someone else – eg, a family member in another country.
- **Security.** The card can be locked if it is lost or stolen so that no one else can use it.

You can top up a pre-payment card in various ways – eg, at post offices, Paypoints (found mainly in convenience stores and other shops), by voucher, or using a debit or credit card over the phone or internet. The maximum card balance is usually at least £1,000 and can be as high as £15,000.

The main drawback of these cards is charges. There is usually an upfront charge of around £10 when you get the card and then a monthly fee of around £5 and/or a charge (eg, 3 per cent or £1.25) each time you top up the card. You do not earn any interest on the pre-loaded money.

Some pre-payment cards have a more restricted use – eg, cards to pay for public transport or as gift vouchers. The Oyster card has been available since 2003 as a way to pay for public transport journeys in London. The Oyster function can be included on a credit card that additionally allows 'contactless payment' (passing the card over a scanner) for any small purchases (up to £10) at retailers with the appropriate equipment.

The mobile phone industry is also looking at ways in which you can use your mobile phone to pay for all sorts of items instead of having to produce a plastic card or cash – eg, some car parks allow you to call a number on your mobile and the parking fee is then billed to your phone account. Pilot schemes are underway to enable you to transfer money abroad using your mobile phone without the need for a bank account and more cheaply than through a bank.

Savings accounts

If your banking needs are modest, you might manage without a current or basic bank account and have just a savings account. This will let you pay in cash and cheques and draw out money in cash, but does not usually have any other banking features. There are no charges and you cannot go overdrawn.

While your money is in the account it earns interest. However, the highest rates are often from postal, phone and internet accounts. To operate these, you usually need to have a bank account as well because you pay money in and draw it out by transferring money electronically between your savings account and bank account. See Chapter 4 for more information about savings accounts.

Bank accounts if you are self-employed

If you run your own business as a company, the company needs its own bank account. If you are self-employed, you could put your business income and spending through your personal bank account. The main advantage of doing this is that there are usually no charges for personal accounts and you might earn interest on the money in the account. By contrast, with a business account, you normally either have to pay each time money goes into or comes out of the account, or earn no interest. However, you might be offered a special deal for the first year.

The drawback to running your business through a personal account is that you need to keep accurate and detailed records so that you can separate out the business transactions when you come to draw up your accounts and pay your tax. For information about tax if you are self-employed, see Chapter 8.

Who should think about bank accounts

Most people will use a bank account throughout their lives. Usually, these are straightforward products that require little attention beyond occasional switching to reduce charges or secure better features. At some life stages, however, there are some issues to consider.

Relationships

Getting married, entering a civil partnership or starting to live with someone means you may need to review how you manage your day-to-day budget and share income and expenses with your partner. You might consider a joint account (see p54), on which either of you can draw – eg, to meet the main household bills. It is important to be aware that, when you have a joint bank account with your partner (or anyone else), you are each 'jointly and severally liable' for the whole account. This means that, if your partner runs up an overdraft, this is also your debt. If your partner cannot or will not pay off the debt, you will have to instead. Therefore, if your relationship breaks down, an urgent first action is to talk to your bank. Either freeze the account or change it so that both of you (not just one of you) must sign to make any withdrawals. As soon as possible close the joint account. You will need to agree how any positive balance or overdraft should be split between you. If your partner used to manage all the household finances, on separation, you might find you do not have sufficient credit history to be able to open your own current account. However, you should still be able to open a basic bank account (see p43).

Young people

Children can have their own savings account, usually from age seven, (see p82) and this can be a useful tool for teaching children to save up for things they want and to get them used to the idea of banks and other financial institutions. From age 11, some banks will let children have a restricted bank account with just a cash card which is a good introduction to managing money and using cash machines. Banks are usually keen to attract students who may go on to become lifelong customers. Therefore they offer accounts with a range of special features, including interest-free overdrafts. See p44.

Disability

If your disability makes it hard to write or sign your name, there are a number of features and options that might help:

- banking by phone or internet. You will be required to use passwords rather than your signature (see p55);
- setting up direct debits to pay regular bills (see p50);

- using cash machines with a personal identification number (PIN) rather than drawing money out by signed cheque (see p47);
- using a variety of aids, such as an adapted pen, a weighted cuff to reduce tremor, or a non-slip board to prevent the paper you are writing on from slipping;
- using a rubber stamp that gives a facsimile of your signature. This is recognised in English (but not Scottish) law as being valid in the same way as your original signature. They are fairly cheap (around £20), but make sure you store the stamp securely to prevent misuse.

Using PINs and keypads or passwords and keyboards are not solutions for everyone. You may find it hard to remember a PIN and/or lack the dexterity or co-ordination to manage a keypad. Although keying in a PIN is becoming the norm in the UK when you pay with a plastic card, you can ask instead to have a card where you authorise the transaction with a signature. If you also have difficulty writing, you could consider using this type of card in conjunction with a rubber signature stamp. Discuss the options with your bank or credit card provider.

If you have more widespread problems managing your financial affairs, you might enlist the help of someone else – eg, your partner, carer, family member or close friend. The main point is to choose someone you can trust. You could:

- instruct your bank, using a third-party mandate (see p54) to accept instructions from the other person. To keep some control over this arrangement, consider opening a separate account into which you can transfer a limited sum of money (eg, using phone banking) and limit the third-party mandate to this account;
- consider a opening a joint account with the other person with either of you being able to sign instructions (see p54). Again you might want to limit the amount of your money available through the account;
- grant a power of attorney, giving the other person the right to manage your affairs (see p55).

Coming to the UK from abroad

If you have come to the UK to work, you may want to send some of your earnings back to your family in your home country. Banks have traditionally charged a lot for transferring money across borders, but new options are now available. For example, you could take out a pre-payment card (see p38) that you load with your own money and which can be used in cash machines and at retail outlets worldwide. You could either send your loaded card to someone abroad or arrange for her/him to be a second user of the card.

Most employers in the UK insist on paying your wages or salary direct into a bank account. To open an account you will have to provide proof of your identity and address (see p58). You may not be able to produce the standard documents that banks prefer, such as a passport, driving licence or utility bills. However, banks have the flexibility to accept other documents – including, for example, a document or letter from the Home Office, a letter from a doctor or social worker, or a letter from the Department for Work and Pensions concerning state benefits. Take care to ensure your name is spelled correctly and consistently on all documents issued to you. What is acceptable varies from one bank to another and even one branch to another. Branch staff are sometimes not well trained in head office policy for dealing with non-standard documents. If you have problems, ask to speak to the manager or other person in the bank who is authorised to deal with exceptional cases. You may also experience difficulties because you will have no credit history and so may be turned down for a current account. However, a bank should be willing to offer you a basic bank account (see p43).

2. **Types of bank account**

Current account

A typical current account has all the following features:
- cheque book;
- plastic card that usually acts as a cash card, debit card and cheque guarantee card;
- direct debits;
- standing orders;
- overdraft facility. This might include a small free overdraft, known as a 'buffer-zone';
- monthly interest on the amount in your account (though often only a negligible amount).

See p45 for how these features work. With a standard current account, there are usually no charges for running the account, provided you stay in credit. However, banks are under pressure to reduce the charges they levy when accounts are overdrawn and some banks have suggested that the alternative might be an end to free banking. Some accounts are available only if you agree to pay in a set amount each month – the amount varies from around £250 a month or more.

Packaged current account

Packaged current accounts – which often have names like 'platinum', 'gold' or 'premier' – have all the features of a standard current account but come with higher interest on credit balances and a variety of free or cheap extras, such as travel insurance, commission-free travel money, car breakdown cover, cheap flights and lower than normal overdraft rates.

However, with many of these accounts, you have to pay a monthly or yearly fee and you might have to pay in a large sum each month (eg, £1,000) to qualify. To make these accounts worthwhile, you must make use of the extras. So, before signing up, check they are really things you want and that you cannot get them as cheaply elsewhere.

Basic bank account

With standard current accounts, you can go overdrawn if you spend more than the money you have in the account. This can happen, for example, if you write a cheque for more than is in the account or pay for something by debit card. A basic bank account should not let you go overdrawn because it has only a limited range of features. These are:

- no cheque book and no cheque guarantee card;
- a special sort of cash and debit card – eg, branded Solo or Electron. With this, your account balance is normally checked before each withdrawal or transaction. If there is not enough money in the account, the transaction cannot go ahead. However, some accounts now offer debit cards with the same level of functionality as a current account. See the Financial Services Authority (FSA) booklet *Just the Facts about Basic Bank Accounts* for more information. Some basic bank accounts have just a cash card and no debit card;
- direct debits and standing orders. Your account is checked before each payment from your account and should go ahead only if you have enough money to cover it. If there is not enough money in the account, your bank may charge a fee for the failed payment, may cancel the direct debit or standing order, and might even close your account. Moreover, you will still have to pay any bill that the direct debit or standing order was meant to cover and may incur penalties if that bill was paid late. Therefore, it is important to make sure that you have enough in the account to cover these regular payments.

A few basic bank accounts give you a very small free overdraft (eg, £10), also referred to as a 'buffer zone'. This is because, when you withdraw cash from a cash machine, the smallest amount issued is usually £10. The small overdraft ensures that you are able to withdraw, for instance, the last £8 in your account through a machine.

Although, in general, your account is checked before each transaction, faults and delays can occur, so you should not rely purely on the bank to limit your spending – it is still your responsibility to avoid going overdrawn. If you do accidentally overdraw by more than any free limit, your bank will normally charge you and the charges will be added to your account, taking you even further overdrawn.

About one-third of the basic accounts available pay no interest on the money you have in your account; the rest do, although the rate is usually very low.

A basic bank account could be a suitable choice if you are uncomfortable with the risk of running up any debt and want the extra discipline that a basic bank account imposes. It may be the most appropriate choice and might be the only option if you have a poor credit rating or no credit history at all (see Chapter 5).

A further feature of basic bank accounts is that, with most, you can withdraw cash from your account at post office branches (see p55).

When you have had a basic bank account for a while, or if your income increases, your bank may be willing to upgrade you to a full current account if so desired (see p42).

Credit union bank account

Some credit unions operate a bank accounts offering a debit card, direct debits and standing orders. Some charge a monthly fee for their current account. Credit unions are mutual organisations owned and run by their members. They offer savings accounts and loans and sometimes other financial services too, such as insurance and bill payment services. Members must have a common bond – eg, living in the same area, or working for the same employer or in the same industry. To find out if there is a credit union you are eligible to join, see www.abcul.org or ask your local authority.

Accounts for young people

You cannot usually get full current account with all the features listed on p42 until you reach age 18.

From 16, some banks offer a **'youth account'** with most of the features but excluding an overdraft and, in most cases, without a guarantee card to back your cheques. The bank might overlook one or two occasions if you go overdrawn, but will generally close your account if you persistently spend more than you have got.

Below age 16, you will have to make do with a savings account (see Chapter 4) but a couple of banks do offer children's accounts with debit cards from age 11. These are the special type of debit card (Solo or Electron) where the balance of your account is checked before each transaction to guard against your going overdrawn.

If you go on to further education, you must normally have a bank account if you will be getting a student loan and will usually be eligible for a **'student account'**. These are full current accounts with a large free overdraft (eg, up to £2,750 by the end of a three-year course) and a variety of free gifts, such as CD and book vouchers or offers on railcards and driving lessons. For two or three years after graduation, you can usually have a **'graduate account'** which continues to offer a free overdraft that reduces each year while you gradually pay off the overdraft you built up while studying.

3. **How bank accounts work**

Paying money in

Depending on the features offered by the particular account, you can pay money into a bank account by:

- cash or a cheque at a bank branch, some cash machines and, with some accounts (including some basic bank accounts), at a post office;
- direct transfer (also called 'automated credit') from the account of the person paying you to your account. Wages are often paid this way;
- direct transfer from another account you have – eg, from your savings account to your current account.

The clearing cycle

The 'clearing cycle' refers to the time it takes between paying money in and it being available for you to use. It is based on cheques. When you pay in a cheque, it is sent to the bank of the person who wrote it. That bank will honour ('clear') the cheque, providing it seems genuine, is correctly made out and there seem to be enough funds in the person's account or the cheque is backed by a cheque guarantee card. This process takes time – typically about three working days but sometimes longer.

Even though many transactions are now by automated credit transfer (also known as 'direct payment' or 'direct transfer') between accounts and do not involve physically moving paper cheques, banks still often insist on allowing a few days before money paid in reaches your account. While your money is being processed, the bank may be earning interest on it, although some banks do start to pay you interest on the money before it has cleared.

Since May 2008, a new Faster Payments Service has been introduced which allows transactions by phone, internet and standing order (but not direct debit or cheque) to be made within two hours (and often in just seconds). Participating banks are gradually introducing the service, so contact your bank to find out if it has adopted it. To make a payment using the faster service, the account that will receive the payment must also be in the scheme and you can check this by using the website www.ukpayments.org.uk/sort_code_checker/. Most banks do not charge for the service if you are a personal (rather than business) customer. Be aware that, once a payment has been initiated using the Faster Payments Service, it cannot be cancelled.

The time it takes a payment to clear therefore depends on how you paid it in and the rules of the particular bank and account. The table on p46 shows examples, but you need to check the terms and conditions to find out the clearing times for your own account. Some accounts have much longer clearing times than those shown, especially for paying in cheques.

Examples of clearing times

How you pay the money in	Number of working days to clear	Day you can use the money if it is paid in on a Monday
Faster Payments Service (for phone and internet payments, standing orders if your bank offers this service)	0	Monday
Automated credit transfer (also known as direct payment)	0	Monday
Cash on its own over the counter at a branch of your own bank	0	Monday
Mixture of cash and cheques over the counter at a branch of your own bank	1	Tuesday
Cash over the counter at another bank	3	Thursday
Cash at a cash machine	1	Tuesday
Cheque drawn on branch of your own bank and paid in over the counter at that branch	1	Tuesday
Cheque drawn on another branch or another bank	3	Thursday

Cleared and uncleared balances

Payments received via the Faster Payments Service are available for use as soon as they reach your account – ie, normally within hours. With any other payment, even though it has yet to clear, money you have paid in is usually added immediately to your account balance. This is called your **'uncleared balance'** and generally is what you will see on the printed statements you get by post or from cash machines.

Despite appearing on your statement, uncleared payments are not normally available for you to withdraw or spend. This is because the cheque or other payment could be refused if the person paying you does not have enough money in their account. In that case, the cheque or other payment will 'bounce' and the money will be subtracted from your balance.

If an uncleared payment bounces and is subtracted from your balance, but you had already spent the money, you might find yourself overdrawn, in which case you will usually have to pay interest and charges (see p57). Alternatively, your bank might refuse to honour payments you have made but which are still being processed. In other words, your own cheques and debit card payments might bounce and any direct debits and standing order payments you have set up could go unpaid. You will normally be charged (typically around £30) for each refused payment. The charges are deducted directly from your account and could create or worsen an overdraft.

Some accounts let you use uncleared balances, provided your credit standing is good. If this does not apply and you are relying on a payment in to cover an expense, you should phone your bank to check the **'cleared balance'** (ie, your balance not counting any uncleared amounts) before you go ahead.

Getting money out

Depending on the features offered by the particular account, you can take money out of a bank account:

- in cash at a branch by writing yourself a cheque or using your cash card at the counter. With some accounts, you can also make withdrawals at post office branches (see www.postoffice.co.uk for details);
- in cash at a cash machine or in a supermarket offering a 'cash-back' service, using your cash or debit card at a cash machine or your debit card in a supermarket;
- by automated credit transfer – eg, to your savings account. Usually this is done using a direct debit arrangement;
- to pay regular bills, such as for electricity, telephone or mortgage, by direct debit, standing order or cheque. Standing orders can also be used to make regular payments to people – eg, pocket money to your children;
- by paying for things you buy using either your debit card or a cheque.

Your bank will carry out your instructions provided you have enough money in your account to cover the payment or you have arranged an overdraft (see p52). Otherwise, your bank can either refuse to make the payment as instructed (and will charge you for each refused payment) or will make the payment but will normally charge you for going overdrawn (see p57).

Account features

Cash card

A cash card is a plastic card you can use to withdraw money from cash machines both in the UK and sometimes abroad. Usually you can use the card in the machines of your own and other banks, but some cash cards with basic bank accounts are limited to the issuing bank's machines only. You put your card into the slot in the machine, key in your personal identification number (PIN) and follow the instructions on the screen.

With some cards (eg, Solo and Electron), most machines check your account first and issue the cash only if you have enough money in your account.

There is usually no charge for using cash machines at banks, building societies and many larger supermarkets. Other machines at, for example, garages, nightclubs, convenience stores and motorway service areas, do charge (ranging from £1.50 to £5 per transaction). A message onscreen will warn you if there is a charge and ask if you want to proceed.

Keep a note of cash machine withdrawals or the receipts so that you can check them against your bank statement (see p52).

Keep your PIN safe and be safe at the cash machine or card reader

Your PIN is a four-digit security number which you need in order to use your cash or debit card. To prevent anyone else using your card, it is essential that you keep your PIN secret.

- You will get a slip by post telling you your PIN. Memorise your PIN and destroy the slip immediately. If you forget your PIN, contact the card issuer who will send you a new notification slip by post.
- The banking industry advises that you never write down your PIN. If you really must make a note of it, disguise the number – eg, counting letters from a favourite passage in a book or turn your PIN into a word. Never keep a note of your PIN, however well disguised, in the same bag or place as the card.
- Never write the PIN on your card.
- You can change the PIN originally issued to something your find easier to remember, but avoid numbers that can easily be guessed – eg, your birthdate, house or phone number, 1234, 9999 or similar combinations.
- Never tell anyone your PIN. The police and genuine bank officials do not ask for PINs under any circumstances. If someone does ask, s/he is almost certainly a criminal. Have nothing to do with her/him and report the incident to the police.
- If you want someone else to be able to use your account, do not let her/him use your card and PIN. Instead, ask your bank to issue a second card with its own PIN (see p54).
- Make sure you are not watched when you key your PIN into a cash machine or card reader and shield the keypad with your hand.
- Do not use a machine if you feel uneasy – eg, the machine is in a deserted area or someone is standing uncomfortably close to you.
- Do not use a machine if it seems odd in any way. Criminals sometimes fit machines with devices that steal cards or card information.
- Do not accept offers of help using the machine. The person could be trying to steal your PIN.
- As soon as possible, withdraw your card, money and any receipt and quickly put them away before leaving the cash machine.
- Do not discard receipts carelessly – they contain information about your account that could be used by criminals.
- Cancel your card immediately if it is retained by the machine. It is a good idea to carry the emergency number for this with you at all times.

Cheque book

You have a book of cheques which are instructions to your bank to pay a particular person or organisation a certain sum of money in accordance with the details you write on the cheque. The cheques are pre-printed to show you what to write. Typically, there will be lines for you to put the date, the name of the person or organisation you are paying, the amount you are paying both in words and in figures, and a line for your signature.

Nearly all cheques are crossed (pre-printed with two parallel lines) and carry the words 'account payee' which means the cheque can be paid only into a bank account and, moreover, it must be the account of the person or organisation whose name you have put on the cheque. This is a security feature which makes it less likely that the cheque could be misused if it were stolen. You can add the crossing and words 'account payee' if they are missing from a cheque you write.

You can use cheques to pay for something in person at, for instance, a shop or restaurant or to pay for something by post. However, a number of large retailers have ceased to accept cheques because they are less secure than plastic card payments and, increasingly, most customers prefer to pay by plastic.

When used with a cheque guarantee card (see below), your bank will honour the cheque even if you do not have enough money in your account. If this happens, however, you will go overdrawn and face charges (see p57).

When you write a cheque, make sure you also fill in the stub in the book so you have a record of the transaction to help you check your bank statement (see p52).

Cheque guarantee card

This is a plastic card that you present to the person you are paying when you buy something using a cheque. The card has an amount printed on it – eg, £50 or £100 (the '**cheque guarantee limit**') and a number which the person you are paying writes on the back of the cheque. As long as the cheque is for no more than the guarantee limit, your bank will honour the cheque, even if you do not have enough money in your account to cover the payment. In this way, the person you are paying can be certain of getting the money.

You cannot get round the guarantee limit by writing two or more cheques for a single transaction (eg, two £100 cheques for something costing £200) – the limit applies to a single cheque per transaction. However, you could write a cheque up to the guarantee limit for part of the transaction and pay the rest in another way – eg, in cash.

Note: the cheque guarantee scheme will end in 2011.

- -

Many functions of a plastic card

This chapter describes how several types of plastic card work: prepayment cards, cash cards, cheque guarantee cards, and debit cards. In practice, you will normally get just one card with your bank account which has one or more functions depending on the features offered with your account. For example, a single plastic card may work as both a cash card and a debit card. If you have a cheque book with your account, the same card is also the cheque guarantee card. Any pre-payment card or credit card (see Chapter 5) is usually a separate plastic card.

- -

Debit card

This is a plastic card that you can use to pay for things when you are shopping, either in person or by post, phone or internet. Using the card is an instruction from you to your bank to take the required payment direct from your bank account.

When you use your card in person, it is swiped or inserted in a card reader. You may be asked to sign a payment slip and the sales assistant will check your signature against a specimen you have written on the back of the card. But increasingly, instead of signing, you are asked to key your PIN into the card reader. This is known as 'chip and PIN'.

If you are buying by post, phone or online, you will be asked to give details printed on the card: the name, the card number, its expiry date, a security number from the back of the card and, sometimes, the issue date and issue number. You will never be asked for your PIN.

With some debit cards (eg, Solo and Electron), your account is checked in advance and a transaction goes ahead only if you have enough money in your account.

Keep the receipts when you pay by debit card or, if buying by post or phone, make a record of what you bought, when and how much it cost, so that you can check your bank statement (see p52).

Direct debit

This is an instruction to your bank to let an organisation take regular payments direct from your account and is commonly used to pay utility bills (such as gas, electricity, telephone and water), insurance premiums and subscriptions to magazines, clubs, and so on. You have to set up the arrangement before the first payment is due by filling in a form (called a 'mandate') supplied by the organisation. Usually you send it back to the organisation, which then passes it to your bank.

Most direct debits are set up to pay a fixed amount each month or each year. The organisation can change the amount but must give you 10 days' notice. To cancel a direct debit, contact your bank – although, to avoid confusion, let the organisation know as well.

If anything goes wrong (eg, a payment is mistakenly taken twice) your bank takes responsibility and guarantees to make good any loss.

Direct debits are very convenient and some companies (eg, gas and electricity suppliers) charge you less if you agree to pay by direct debit. There are some pitfalls to watch out for.

- Make sure the timing of direct debit payments fits in with the timing of payments into your account – eg, that your gas bill payment goes out after your pay has gone in. If the timing is wrong, ask the company you are paying to alter the date of the direct debits.

- It is easy to forget what direct debits you have. Once a year or so, ask your bank for a list of your direct debits (and standing orders) and make a point of cancelling those which are for things you no longer need.
- Some contracts (eg, for gym membership or subscription TV) require you to sign up for a minimum period and pay by direct debit. If you cancel early, the direct debit payments still continue until the minimum period is completed. Do not sign up for this type of contract unless you are prepared to pay for the full minimum period.
- If you pay for gas or electricity by direct debit, you will be required to pay a fixed amount each month for a year. At the end of the year, the amount is reviewed and set at a new level for the next year, and so on. Typically, the payment is set too high so that you pay a bit too much each month and can over time build up a substantial overpayment. If this happens, ask for your monthly payments to be reduced to a more realistic level and insist that any surplus on your account is paid back to you.

Standing order

This is an instruction to your bank to pay a set amount at set intervals (eg, monthly) to a person or organisation you name. You set it up by filling in a form supplied by your bank and returning it to your bank. Contact your bank to alter or cancel the order.

Although standing orders seem similar to direct debits, they are in fact very different. With a direct debit, the organisation you are paying initiates the payments and can alter the amount. With a standing order, only you can do this. As a consequence, most organisations no longer accept payment by standing order, preferring direct debits instead.

Automated credit transfer

You can transfer money direct from your account to another and there are different ways of doing this. If your bank offers the Faster Payments Service (see p45) and you are making a payment by phone or online, this is a fast and free way of making an immediate transfer. If the Faster Payments Service is not an option and you want to make a one-off payment quickly to someone, you could ask your bank to make a 'CHAPS transfer' – this is a same-day electronic transfer between the accounts for which your bank will make a charge (eg, £20).

If you want surplus money from your current account to be automatically moved each month to a savings account, your bank might offer a free 'sweeper service' to do this. However, it will only transfer money to a savings account offered by your own bank and often you will be able to get a better interest rate on your savings elsewhere.

If you have a phone-based savings account (see Chapter 4), typically you pay into and draw out of the account using your current account. The savings organisation gets you to complete a direct debit mandate (see p50), but you do not have to use it to make regular payments. Instead, transfers between the savings account and current account happen only when you phone the savings provider to instruct a payment. A similar arrangement is used with internet accounts to enable you to pay bills of varying amounts at varying times.

Interest on credit balances

Most current accounts and some basic bank accounts pay interest on the money you have in your account. However, especially with the big high street banks, the rate is usually very low and, in 2009, has been reduced close to zero. The best interest rates tend to be offered by internet banks (see p55).

Bear in mind that, unless your average balance is high, the total interest you earn is likely to be low. If you do have a high balance, you might do better by regularly transferring any excess to a savings account.

Bank interest is normally paid with tax at the savings rate (20 per cent in 2009/ 10) already deducted. There is only extra tax to pay if you are a higher rate taxpayer. Starting-rate taxpayers can reclaim some of the tax. Non-taxpayers can reclaim all the tax or arrange to have the interest paid without any tax deducted. See Chapter 8 for information about tax.

Some mortgages (called all-in-one mortgages) are combined with a current account and, often also, with a savings accounts. Money in these accounts, in effect, earns tax-free interest at the mortgage rate. See Chapter 5 for details.

Overdraft

An overdraft is a way of borrowing from your bank through your current account, by running the balance down below zero. You might do this by arrangement with your bank (ie, an **'authorised overdraft'**) or without (an **'unauthorised overdraft'**).

With some accounts, you are allowed a free overdraft up to a set limit. The limit is usually fairly low – eg, £20, £50 or £250 – but higher for student and graduate accounts.

If you do not have a free overdraft or you go over the free limit, you will be charged (see p57). The charges for unauthorised overdrafts are particularly high, so it is best to avoid them.

Statements

All accounts include regular statements. These are essential to help you keep track of your money. The example on p53 shows a typical statement and what it tells you. With some accounts, it is standard to get a statement once a quarter, but this is not often enough if you are using the account actively. Ask instead to be sent monthly statements – there should be no charge for this.

If you lose a statement and need a replacement, most banks will charge you – eg, £5 or £10 – so keep your statements in a safe place.

Example of a bank statement

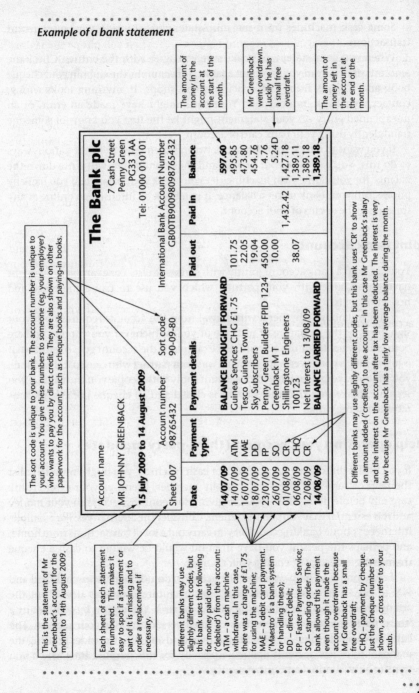

The amount of money in the account at the start of the month.

Mr Greenback went overdrawn. Luckily he has a small free overdraft.

The amount of money left in the account at the end of the month.

The Bank plc

7 Cash Street
Penny Green
PG33 1AA
Tel: 01000 010101

International Bank Account Number
GB00TB9009809809765432

Account name
MR JOHNNY GREENBACK

15 July 2009 to 14 August 2009

Account number
98765432

Sort code
90-09-80

Sheet 007

The sort code is unique to your bank. The account number is unique to your account. You give these numbers to someone (eg, your employer) who wants to pay you by direct credit. They are also shown on other paperwork for the account, such as cheque books and paying-in books.

Date	Payment type	Payment details	Paid out	Paid in	Balance
14/07/09		**BALANCE BROUGHT FORWARD**			**597.60**
14/07/09	ATM	Guinea Services CHG £1.75	101.75		495.85
16/07/09	MAE	Tesco Guinea Town	22.05		473.80
18/07/09	DD	Sky Subscribers	19.04		454.76
23/07/09	FP	Penny Green Builders FPID 1234	450.00		4.76
26/07/09	SO	Greenback M T	10.00		5.24D
01/08/09	CR	Shillingstone Engineers		1,432.42	1,427.18
06/08/09	CHQ	100123	38.07		1,389.11
12/08/09	CR	Net interest to 13/08/09			1,389.18
14/08/09		**BALANCE CARRIED FORWARD**			**1,389.18**

This is the statement of Mr Greenback's account for the month to 14th August 2009.

Each sheet of each statement is numbered. This makes it easy to spot if a statement or part of it is missing and to order a replacement if necessary.

Different banks may use slightly different codes, but this bank uses the following for money paid out ('debited') from the account:
ATM – a cash machine withdrawal. In this case, there was a charge of £1.75 for using the machine;
MAE – a debit card payment. ('Maestro' is a bank system for handling these);
DD – direct debit;
FP – Faster Payments Service;
SO – standing order. The bank allowed this payment even though it made the account overdrawn because Mr Greenback has a small free overdraft;
CHQ – payment by cheque. Just the cheque number is shown, so cross refer to your stub.

Different banks may use slightly different codes, but this bank uses 'CR' to show an amount added ('credited') to the account – in this case Mr Greenback's salary and the interest on the account after tax has been deducted. The interest is very low because Mr Greenback has a fairly low average balance during the month.

Some cash machines print out mini-statements showing your most recent transactions.

When you get a statement, make sure you agree with the entries. Check the amounts drawn from your account against, for example, the stubs in your cheque book and receipts from cash machines and shops. If anything looks wrong, contact your bank immediately. Your bank might have made an error, or an unexplained entry on your statement might be the first you know of someone fraudulently using your bank card or account.

If you want to check your balance between statements, there are various ways to do this. You can visit your branch and the counter staff will write down the balance for you. Some cash machines let you check your balance. If you bank by phone, call your bank to get a balance. If you bank by internet, go online at any time to see the details of your account.

Joint bank accounts

You can hold a bank account jointly with someone else. For example, you might have an account with your partner, which you use to pay a mortgage and household bills.

You can choose whether a withdrawal from the account requires both your signatures or the signature of just one of you. Whichever you choose, you are both equally liable for the account. For example, if the account goes overdrawn it is just as much your overdraft, even if it was your partner who caused it. Therefore, you should take care to have joint accounts only with people you trust and, if you separate, make sure that the account is closed and all cheque books and cards returned to the bank.

Help operating your account (third-party mandate)

If you find it difficult to get to a bank or cash machine, you might want to enlist the help of someone else – eg, a family member, friend or your carer. Think carefully before doing this – you are giving someone else access to your money and it is essential that you can trust them. Consider the alternatives. For example, internet or phone banking could let you carry out a lot of transactions from home, and perhaps the person you have in mind would be willing to cash a cheque themselves instead of operating your account.

If someone is to help you with the account, do not give them your card and PIN to use. It will be easier to sort out any future problems if you put the arrangement onto a formal footing with your bank. You do this by completing a **'third-party mandate'**, which gives a named person access to your account. The bank may issue the person with her/his own card and PIN. Consider limiting the mandate to a new account opened especially for this purpose into which you transfer only a limited amount of money.

To let someone take over completely the running of your account, use a **power of attorney**. This is a legal arrangement giving someone else the power to run your affairs. You must be of sound mind when you set up such an arrangement. A power of attorney can be temporary and this could be useful if, for instance, you will be going abroad for a year. A lasting power of attorney (called a continuing power in Scotland or enduring power in Northern Ireland) puts someone permanently in control of your affairs. You can set up a lasting power of attorney in advance and specify that it comes into effect only if you lose your mental capacity.

4. **Different ways of banking**

Branch

With a branch-based account, you can go to your bank in person to pay money in, draw it out and discuss your needs – eg, for an overdraft, with members of staff. However, if you phone your bank, you will usually talk to a call centre rather than your own branch.

Post office

Many basic bank accounts let you draw out cash and check your balance at post office branches. With a few, you can also pay in money. A few banks have arrangements so that you can draw cash from and, in some cases, pay money into their full current accounts at post offices. You can get details from any post office but will need to contact the bank concerned to open the account.

Phone

Many banks offer phone banking which lets you pay bills, transfer money from one account to another, order cheque books and so on by phone. You operate this type of account using an identification code and password. To keep your account secure, you should never tell anyone your full code or password. The bank will only ask you for selected letters or digits when you phone.

Internet

Many banks also offer internet banking. This lets you view statements, check your balance, pay bills, transfer money and order cheque books online, 24 hours a day, every day of the year. Again, you operate the account using an identification code and password and it is very important that you keep these secret. Most of the big high street banks are starting to issue internet banking customers with card readers for use at home. Before you start an internet banking session and before setting up a new payment arrangement, you must insert your debit card in the reader which generates a one-off code that you enter in addition to your normal security details. You can operate internet banking from a computer or, with a few banks, via interactive digital TV or a WAP phone.

From time to time, criminals send emails to internet bank customers asking them to confirm their security details either in a return email or by logging onto a bogus site. Genuine banks never ask you to do this. Do not act on messages like these and report them to the bank concerned and the banking industry's Bank Safe Online website at www.banksafeonline.org.uk.

Protect yourself when banking online

- While banking online, make sure you are not being overlooked by people or security cameras.
- Beware of crooked emails and bogus websites. If something does not seem quite right, do not go ahead.
- Never email sensitive information.
- Choose 'strong' passwords that are difficult to crack – eg, at least eight characters, a mix of numbers and letters, upper and lower case, and avoid combinations that spell words found in a dictionary.
- Do not key in identification codes, passwords or account information unless you are certain you are on the genuine bank's site.
- Only send codes, passwords, personal information and payment details over a secure link – look for 'https' at the start of the address bar and other security symbols such as a closed padlock.
- If you are using a computer shared with other people, make sure you log off properly before you leave the machine.
- Do not store identification codes and passwords on your computer where they might be vulnerable to hacking.
- Protect your computer with a firewall and up-to-date anti-virus software.

5. **What an account costs**

Ordinary services

With most personal bank accounts, there are currently no charges for ordinary services provided you are in credit. The exception is using some cash machines.

Special services

You are normally charged extra for special services, such as stopping a cheque at your request (eg, £10), duplicate statements (£10 to £15), or cashing a cheque written in another currency (eg, 1.5 per cent of the cheque's value).

If you choose a packaged account (see p42), there is often an annual fee.

Overdrafts

If you arrange in advance to have an authorised overdraft, a few banks levy an arrangement fee (eg, 2 per cent of the amount you borrow). The main charge is interest on the amount by which you are overdrawn. This varies greatly from one bank to another – in mid-2009, from 3 per cent up to 20 per cent a year. A few banks also charge a monthly or quarterly fee.

If you go overdrawn without arrangement (an unauthorised overdraft), you are normally charged a punishing rate of interest (up to 39 per cent in mid-2009). In addition, you may have to pay a monthly or weekly fee and possibly transaction charges for each item paid into and out of your account. Where you have an unauthorised overdraft, your bank is not obliged to make payments as you instruct (except in the case of cheques backed by a guarantee card – see p49). You will normally be charged for each cheque that bounces and for any other payment your bank refuses (eg, £30 per item) and possibly a similar charge for misuse of the guarantee for each cheque your bank is forced to honour. An unauthorised overdraft can therefore work out very expensive, even if you go overdrawn by only a small amount for a short time. In addition, you may face extra problems when cheques bounce and regular payments, such as insurance premiums and mortgage payments, fail to be made.

To guard against an unauthorised overdraft, keep track of your spending, be aware of direct debits and standing orders and the dates on which these payments are made, check your bank statements each month, and request a balance between statements if you're not sure how much you have in your account.

Reclaim excessive overdraft charges

At the time of writing, the Office of Fair Trading (OFT) is investigating the charges banks make for unauthorised overdrafts to assess whether they breach laws which require consumer contracts to be fair. When you have a bank account you enter into a contract with your bank and technically you breach that contract if you run up an unauthorised overdraft. Under contract law, charges for any breach should be in proportion to the costs incurred, but unauthorised overdraft charges (interest, charges for returned payments and so on) are thought to exceed many times over the administration costs a bank actually incurs. Banks disagree, but when challenged have usually refunded the charges involved rather than settling the matter through the courts. Some of the largest banks and the OFT agreed to go to court to test the law.

In spring 2009, the Court of Appeal ruled that the OFT is entitled to assess the fairness of the charges and the OFT expects to report its findings by the end of 2009. In the meantime, if you think you have been overcharged, it is worth writing to your bank to reclaim the excess – you can go back up to six years. For guidance on how to make your claim, see websites such as www.which.co.uk or www.moneysavingexpert.com.

Banks have indicated that, if the outcome of the report is that they are forced to charge less for overdrafts, other customers will have to pay more and, in particular, free banking for customers in credit could be abolished.

6. **Who offers accounts**

Current accounts are offered by banks and some building societies. For simplicity, we refer to them all as 'banks' in this chapter. Larger banks offer basic bank accounts. To compare the main features of accounts, check out surveys published from time to time by *Which?* magazine (available in most public libraries), comparisons on websites such as www.moneyfacts.co.uk and www.moneysupermarket.com, or specialist magazines such as *Moneyfacts* (available in larger reference libraries). Bear in mind the limitations of comparison websites (see p8) and use two or three sites rather than relying on just one.

The main factors to consider when choosing an account are:

- eligibility – if your credit history is poor, you might be restricted to a basic bank account (see p43);
- what features you want (see p47);
- how you want to bank – eg, by branch, phone or internet (see p55);
- availability of branches and/or cash machines near where you live or work;
- the rate of interest offered on credit balances (although this is unlikely to be important if your average balance is low);
- what extras are on offer (if you are looking at a packaged account or a student account), but only let these influence you if the account meets your needs in all other ways.

7. **How to open an account**

To open an account, you must fill in an application form and return it to the bank in person or by post. Alternatively, you can fill in an online version of the form.

You are entering into a contract with the bank, so make sure you have read the terms and conditions and are happy with them. If you are applying online be sure to print a copy.

Under the money laundering regulations, most firms that hold money for customers are required to check that new customers are who they say they are.

Therefore, you will normally have to supply the bank with at least two proofs – one of your identity and another separate one of your address. The regulations allow for reliance on a single document, such as a passport, but in practice most firms insist you provide two. Official documents are preferred since they are more difficult to forge. The table below lists the types of proof that are generally acceptable. However, each bank draws up its own list for guidance and each branch has the discretion as to what identification it will accept. Individual branch staff are held liable if something goes wrong, so the more standard your documents, the easier it will be to open the account. If you are not sure what documents you will need, ask to speak to a member of staff or the manager. They should be able to provide you with a list of documents acceptable to that bank or advise on which of any documents you do have would be acceptable.

Examples of documents usually acceptable as proof when opening an account

Proof of identity	*Proof of address*
Preferred documents:	**Preferred documents:**
Full UK passport	UK photocard driving licence
Identity card if you are from another European Union country	Full older style driving licence
	Recently paid gas or electricity bill
UK photocard driving licence	Recently paid phone bill (but not a mobile phone bill)
Full older style driving licence	
Benefit book	Recent bank statement from another bank or building society
Student identity card	
National insurance card plus a payslip, P60 or P45	Recent credit card statement
	Recent council tax bill or payment book
HM Revenue and Customs Notice of Coding	
Alternatives that might be acceptable:	**Alternatives that might be acceptable:**
Letter from someone of standing – eg, a doctor or teacher, who knows you	Local council or housing association rent card or tenancy agreement (but not a private tenancy agreement)
If under 18, introduction from a parent or guardian who is an existing customer	Vehicle registration document
Letter from the Department for Work and Pensions inviting you to open a Post Office card account	Vehicle licence renewal notification
	Car insurance certificate
	Letter from the Universities and Colleges Admissions Service (UCAS)
	Student Loans Company award letter
	University/college offer letter or letter of acceptance or enrolment

Note: you must produce one document from each list. You cannot use the same document for both identity and address.

If you do not have any of the documents listed in the table, banks can accept alternative forms of proof – eg, a letter from a doctor or teacher who has known you a long time. Branch-level staff are often unaware of this and unclear about what sorts of alternative proof are acceptable. If you have problems of this sort, ask to speak in private to the manager or another person who is authorised to deal with exceptional cases.

The money laundering regulations were revised during 2007. As a result, you might not need to provide any proof of your identity and address if you take out a pre-payment card with a reasonably low limit or certain savings accounts where payments in are made via your current account or basic bank account.

The bank may run a credit check (see p134) before accepting your custom. This is not necessary if you are applying just for a basic bank account (or could be offered one), since a basic account includes no loan facilities and little risk of going overdrawn. Unfortunately, some banks have standard new customer procedures and do not think to waive the credit check where it is not needed. If your application is turned down on credit history grounds, point out to the bank that you should still be eligible for its basic account if it has one. If necessary, ask to discuss your needs in private with the manager.

A bank does not have to offer you an account and you do not have an absolute right to have one. However, if you feel your request to open an account has been unreasonably turned down, you should complain (see p61).

Switching accounts

Once you have an account, it would be easy to stay with the same bank year after year, even though another might offer a better deal or better service. Switching to a new account is, however, straightforward.

From 1 November 2009, banks are required to comply with Financial Services Authority rules (see p61) which require that account switching should be carried out promptly and efficiently. The broad procedure for switching is as follows.

- Contact the new bank to open an account. Say that you are switching accounts. The new bank will explain the transfer process to you and tell you how long it is likely to take. The new account should be up and running within 10 days.
- The new bank will ask your old bank for information about regular payments that are to be transferred.
- Your old bank must provide the new bank with details of your standing orders and direct debits within three working days of receiving the request from the new bank.
- Keep both accounts open while the transfer takes place.
- Once the new account has fully taken over, ask your old bank to close the old account.

- If any mistakes or delays during the transfer trigger bank charges (eg, you go overdrawn because your wages go into one account but payments are still being drawn from the old account), the charges will be cancelled.

If you have access to the internet, visit a comparison website such as www.uswitch.com for more information.

Closing an account

To close an account, contact your bank. You may be asked to confirm your request in writing. The process should take only a few days. Return plastic cards and unused cheques to the bank and tell them where to send the balance of the account (including interest that has built up but not yet been paid out).

If your bank asks you to close the account, it will normally give you at least 30 days' notice.

8. **Regulation and complaints**

To do business in the UK, a bank must be authorised by the Financial Services Authority (FSA), which has responsibility for ensuring that the bank is solvent and prudently run and operates proper complaints procedures. Authorised banks and building societies are covered by the Financial Services Compensation Scheme, which may replace your money if the firm becomes insolvent (see Chapter 10).

In the past, the FSA has not regulated how banks handle their business with customers. Instead, most UK banks agreed to comply with a voluntary Banking Code. This set out standards of good practice, and a bank's failure to follow the Code would have been evidence you could use to support a complaint.

Following the global financial crisis that started in 2007, all aspects of the regulation of banks came under review. Among the resulting changes, the voluntary Banking Code was replaced from 1 November 2009 by FSA rules setting out how banks should conduct their business with customers. The FSA rules broadly replicate the former Banking Code requirements. See http://fsahandbook.info/FSA/html/handbook/BCOBS.

If you are not happy with something your bank has done or failed to do, first contact the bank in the normal way – ie, at the branch or call centre you usually deal with. If you are still not happy, say that you want to make a formal complaint. The bank should tell you how to do this. If not, check the bank's entry on the FSA Register, which includes contact details for complaints. If the bank still does not resolve the matter to your satisfaction, consider taking your case to the Financial Ombudsman Service (see Appendix 2).

For more information about how you are protected through the regulation of financial firms and what to do if you have a complaint, see Chapter 10.

Bank and payment scams

Be on your alert for these common scams and do not get caught out.

Cheque overpayment fraud. You sell something through an advert or online auction. The buyer sends you a cheque for more than the agreed price and asks you to pay back the surplus. After you have transferred the money, you will find the buyer's cheque bounces. Do not accept an overpayment, however plausible the story. Return the cheque and insist on a new one for the correct price. Do not send the goods until you are sure the payment has cleared.

Advance fee fraud. You receive a letter or email, telling you about money stuck in a country abroad, often after the overthrow of a government or other dramatic event. You are offered a mouth-watering slice of the money if you will agree to the funds being transferred through your account. You may have to send money upfront to cover costs, which you will never see again. You will be asked for your bank account details. Expect your account to be cleaned out. Do not fall for these bogus tales.

Bank charge cold callers. Riding on the back of the current investigation into excessive overdraft charges (see p57), fraudsters may phone or email alleging they are from a firm or even the Government's Office of Fair Trading and will help you claim back bank charges – all they need are your bank details. Once again, expect your account to be cleaned out.

Phishing. You receive an email claiming that you need to verify or update your security details for a bank account or payment service. Click on the link provided and you will be directed to a bogus website where you can helpfully give the fraudsters the information they need to dip into your account. Do not respond to emails like this and report them to the bank concerned and www.banksafeonline.org.uk.

Trojans. You receive an email with a plausible tale and invitation to click on a link or open an attachment. This enables the fraudsters secretly to install software on your computer. In some cases, merely previewing the text of an email enables malicious software to be installed. Typically, the malicious software could be a keystroke logger that records your passwords when you visit genuine websites, such as your online bank, and sends the information by internet to the fraudsters. Treat emails with suspicion. Do not preview them, click on links or open attachments unless you are confident they are from a trustworthy source. Make sure your computer is protected by a firewall and up-to-date anti-virus software.

Card skimming. Your debit or credit card details are copied when you use them to make a payment or to draw cash from an ATM. The details are used to make fraudulent purchases, often abroad. Do not let your card out of your sight when making payments and do not use an ATM if anything about it seems odd or suspicious. See p48 for more tips on using your cards safely.

Notes

1 Department for Work and Pensions,
Family Resources Survey 2007/08, DWP,
2009

2 Department for Work and Pensions,
Family Resources Survey 2007/08, DWP,
2009

3 BACS, *Household Bills Solved, Thanks to
Direct Debit*,
www.thesmartwaytopay.co.uk/family-
life/managing-bills.asp, accessed 5 July
2009

4 HM Treasury, *Financial Capability: the
Government's long-term approach*, 2007

1. Managing your everyday money
5 Department for Work and Pensions,
Press Release, 13 November 2008

Chapter 4

Saving

This chapter covers:
1. When to save or invest (below)
2. Saving versus investing (p73)
3. Special schemes to encourage saving and investing (p76)
4. Types of savings products (p81)
5. Types of investment (p95)
6. Regulation and complaints (p116)

Basic facts
- Around half of British households have a savings account with a bank, building society or National Savings and Investments.[1]
- Choosing to buy an item on a year's credit instead of saving up for it could easily add 10 per cent to its price (see p66).
- Nearly two-fifths of households have at least one individual savings account, including one in four households with an income under £100 a week.[2]

1. When to save or invest

Motives for saving and investing

There are three main reasons for saving and/or investing.

- **As insurance**. You put money aside in case you might need to pay for something in future. For example, you can build up an emergency ('rainy-day') fund to help you out if your car or house needs urgent repairs or an essential piece of equipment breaks. You might accumulate a larger fund if you want enough to cover lost earnings for a few months in the event of losing your job or being off work sick without pay.
- **An opportunities fund**. This is similar to the insurance motive but to cover treats rather than emergencies. If you have some money you can draw on at short notice, it makes it possible to buy a bargain when you see one or accept an invitation to join friends for a holiday.

- **To pay for future consumption**. This happens when you save up to pay for something specific, such as a car, holiday or wedding, and when you save up to cover general spending in a specific phase of life, such as going to university or retirement. You may be saving to finance your own future consumption or that of someone else – eg, your children or grandchildren.

Alternatives to saving and investing

Insurance

If you are saving mainly for the insurance motive (see p64), the alternative might be to take out insurance instead. For example, you might take out house contents insurance to cover some types of loss of, or damage to, your possessions, or income protection insurance to cover lost earnings. There can be problems with this approach, including:

- insurance is not available to cover some things, such as normal maintenance to your home, car or other possessions;
- insurance typically has many conditions and exclusions, so it might not pay out in situations where you thought you would be covered;
- some types of insurance are often poor value for money – eg, extended warranty insurance to cover the breakdown of household appliances;
- other types of insurance may give you value for money, but can be too expensive for many people.

Where insurance does provide cover, however, generally it can pay out as soon as the policy is in place. If you rely on your savings, something bad might happen before you have built up enough savings to cover the event.

State benefits

If the insurance motive is your main reason for saving, you need to be aware of any state benefits for which you might be eligible. They could affect the amount you decide to save. For example, you might be able to claim employment and support allowance (see p296) if you cannot work because of illness. If your income is low, you might question whether your own savings could provide any more than you could get from your state pension and/or means-tested benefits. However, you should be wary of relying on state benefits because:

- you cannot be sure that you will be eligible at the time you need them;
- some payments from the social fund are discretionary and so you may not receive anything;
- the amounts paid are fairly low and might not pay you enough to cover the costs you face;
- in some cases, there is a waiting period before you receive any help – eg, most people on means-tested benefits have to wait 13 weeks from the start of their claim before getting help with their mortgage interest (see p311).

Cost of borrowing instead of saving

	If you borrow or save over one year			If you borrow or save over two years			If you borrow or save over three years		
	Monthly repayment if you borrow	Amount you would have to save each month	Total extra cost of borrowing	Monthly repayment if you borrow	Amount you would have to save each month	Total extra cost of borrowing	Monthly repayment if you borrow	Amount you would have to save each month	Total extra cost of borrowing
Borrow at no cost Borrow at 0% and save at 2%	£41.67	£41.22	£5.34	£20.83	£20.41	£10.24	£13.89	£13.47	£15.11
Borrow cheaply Borrow at 10% and save at 2%	£43.86	£41.22	£31.64	£22.97	£20.41	£61.60	£16.03	£13.47	£92.28
Borrow expensively Borrow at 25% and save at 2%	£46.92	£41.22	£68.42	£26.07	£20.41	£135.88	£19.23	£13.47	£207.41

Note: this table shows the extra you might pay for something with a cash price of £500 if you borrowed, rather than saved, to buy it. It assumes that the cost of the item does not change during this time.

Chapter 9 explains the rules for the main benefits and tax credits (other than pensions) and the amount you might be able to claim. See Chapter 6 for details about state pensions.

Borrowing

If you are saving either to take advantage of unexpected opportunities or to finance some specific spending, the main alternative is to borrow instead. If you cannot afford to save, this might be the only option open to you.

Borrowing lets you bring your spending forward, but at a cost, since you have to pay interest on the money you borrow. Chapter 5 looks at different ways of borrowing, the costs, and the pros and cons of each. The table on p66 gives some examples of the extra amount you might pay for something if you were to borrow rather than save up for it, assuming the price of the item you are buying does not change.

In general, borrowing makes sense only if:
- you cannot afford to save;
- you cannot wait to save up because you need the item now and it would take too long to save – eg, if you need to replace your car in order to get to work;
- the price of the item is likely to rise so that the savings you make today outweigh the cost of borrowing – eg, an item in a sale. Conversely, if the price is likely to fall, which tends to be the case with computers and other consumer electricals, you could be better off saving up;
- it is genuinely free or cheap. Sometimes shops offer '0 per cent credit' but you need to check the small print to make sure you really do get free credit (see Chapter 5);
- it lets you invest in your future financial wellbeing – eg, a student loan to finance a period at university (see p123); *or*
- you realise you will pay over the odds by borrowing to buy now but you feel the cost is worth it and you know you will be able to repay the credit within a reasonable time.

Selling

The final alternative to saving up is to sell something either now, so that you can buy immediately instead of waiting, or in the future to fund your spending when the need arises. To fund future spending you might plan on, say, using an equity release scheme (see p162) to provide yourself with income in retirement.

Government impact on saving and investing

In some areas, the Government attempts to influence your decisions about saving by offering incentives. These are used, for example, to encourage you to:

- build up an emergency/opportunities fund – eg, the Saving Gateway scheme (see p76);
- save for retirement – eg, many types of pension schemes and plans (see Chapter 6);
- build up savings and investments generally – eg, individual savings accounts (ISAs) (see p76);
- build up an opportunities fund for your child – eg, child trust funds (see p80).

The Government's approach is not simply paternalistic. Its policies also target other aims, such as reduced government spending, since without your own emergency fund or retirement savings you might need to claim means-tested state benefits.

Means-tested benefits (see Chapter 9), while not intended to help people who have their own resources to fall back on, are generally structured so as not to discourage a modest amount of savings. For example, the means test usually disregards savings up to at least £6,000 (and considerably more in some circumstances).

Your ethics and beliefs

Your choice of savings and investments may be affected by your ethical stance or religious beliefs. For example, earning interest is not permitted under *Shariah* law, making ordinary bank and building society accounts unsuitable (see pp95 and 115).

Who should think about savings and investments

Saving and investing are important at all stages of life. Depending on the events affecting you, different strategies and considerations will be suitable.

Relationships

If you get married, form a civil partnership or start living with someone, you might want some joint savings – eg, to build up an emergency fund or to buy a home. You should review the size of any emergency fund to see if it adequately matches the needs of your life as a couple. If your relationship breaks down, any joint savings and investments will have to be split between you. If you suspect your ex-partner might be planning to leave with your share, see a solicitor. If you receive a lump-sum settlement on divorce, you need to decide how to invest it and might want advice from an independent financial adviser (see Chapter 2).

Lone parents

It can be especially hard to make ends meet if you are bringing up a family on your own, so setting aside some savings may be a struggle. However, an emergency fund provides a valuable safety net when things go wrong (eg, if your washing machine or car breaks down), so try to build up some savings if you can. The table below shows how saving just £2 a week could quickly mount up to a useful sum. If you are getting certain state benefits, the Saving Gateway could be ideal for you when it starts in April 2010 (see p76).

If you save £2 a week for:*	Your savings could grow to:	
	Savings account	Saving Gateway account
Six months	£52	n/a
One year	£105	n/a
18 months	£158	n/a
Two years	£212	£317

*Assumes your savings earn 2 per cent a year interest after tax (2.5 per cent gross).

Young people

Usually, it is very tax efficient for a young person to build up her/his own savings and investments because everyone – even a child – can have a certain amount of income and capital gains each year tax free (see Chapter 8). However, if a parent gives her/his child money to save (or investments) and it produces more than £100 of income (eg, interest) a year, all the income is taxed as the parent's income not the child's. So, unless the income is no more than £100, the child's own personal tax allowance is wasted. The £100 limit applies per parent per child, so if both parents gave money or investments, the child could have up to £200 income a year without a problem.

A way around the limit is to choose from the handful of investments that are exempt from the rules. They are:
• child trust funds;
• National Savings and Investments (NS&I) children's bonus bonds;
• friendly society plans.

Cash individual savings accounts are *not* exempt. The table on p70 compares these options.

Capital gains of any amount always count as the child's, not the parent's. Another way around the £100 limit is to invest parental gifts to produce capital growth rather than income – eg, in a growth unit trust.

Investments for young people exempt from the £100 limit from parental gifts

	NS&I children's bonus bonds	Child trust fund	Friendly society plan	Invest for capital growth
Savings or investment?	Savings	Either	Investment	Investment
Is it risky?	No	Can be – you choose	Yes – you choose how much	Yes – you choose how much
How is it taxed?	Tax free	Tax free, except income from shares and share-based investments which are taxed at 10%	Tax free, except income from shares and share-based investments which are taxed at 10%	Tax free assuming child has unused capital gains tax allowance (see Chapter 8)
Charges	None	Up to 1.5% of fund if stakeholder; otherwise, could be higher	Often high in proportion to amount invested	Varies – can be high
When can child have the money?	Anytime, but no later than age 21	18	Usually after 10 or more years – you choose the term	Could be anytime but depends on investments you choose

Redundancy

If you find yourself redundant and have previously built up an emergency fund, you may now need to draw from it to cover your living expenses. However, if you have received some redundancy money you could use some of this to start or top up your emergency fund. To work out how much you need, estimate how long you might be between jobs and add a few months to be on the safe side. This money should be invested in a bank or building society account for easy access.

A redundancy lump sum might give you the opportunity to do something completely different – eg, retrain for a new career or start a business. While considering your options, set the money aside in a safe place. At this stage, avoid long-term commitments such as investment-type insurance policies (see p111) which will penalise you heavily if you want your money back early. Until you know what you want to do, stay flexible and stick to short-term savings, such as bank and building society accounts. If you are certain that you can put some money away for the longer term, consider, for instance, unit and investment trusts and, perhaps, ways of topping up your pension (see Chapter 6).

Older people

A common goal in later life is using savings and investments to provide an income. It may be tempting to leave money in the relative safety of a bank or building society. However, in the difficult economic climate following the 2007 global financial crisis, most high street savings accounts offer returns close to zero. Shop around for higher returns from post and internet accounts or by agreeing to leave your money for a fixed period.

Another problem with savings accounts is that they are vulnerable to inflation (see p74). Over the years, as retirement progresses, your capital and income will tend to buy less and less each year. One option could be to put some of your money into other investments, such as corporate bonds, that may offer a better return, but these do involve additional risks (see p99). Another possibility is to choose inflation-proofed investments, such as NS&I index-linked savings certificates (see p91).

Saving in a difficult economic climate

In 2007, a global financial crisis hit the world. This not only affected high finance, but has also had a big impact on ordinary savers and investors.

In September 2007, the UK experienced its first bank run in over 150 years, with customers queuing outside Northern Rock Bank to draw out their savings in fear they would be lost if the bank collapsed. Savers who had been tempted by high interest rates offered by Icelandic banks, such as Icesave and Kaupthing Edge, found their accounts frozen. To restore confidence in the system, the UK Government quickly gave assurances that no British savers would lose their money and boosted the compensation scheme that protects depositors with banks and building societies (see Chapter 10).

Although the immediate bank crisis was dealt with, the aftermath remains. Banks were weakened and reluctant to lend to households and businesses. This pushed many economies, including the UK, into recession with the economy shrinking rather than growing, unemployment rising and stock markets tumbling. Many people have compared what has happened to the Great Depression of the 1930s. To try to prevent a repeat of the 1930s, some governments, including the UK, have used extreme economic measures. In the UK, this has included cutting the Bank of England base rate to just 0.5 per cent. This base rate is important as it works throughout the economy and influences all the other interest rates, such as those offered on savings accounts and the cost of mortgages. Such low interest rates are good news for those borrowers who, for example, have seen their monthly mortgage repayments drop. But low interest rates mean many savers are getting virtually no return at all on their money. With stock markets also very volatile, it is hard to know what saving and investing strategies to choose. You should consider the following points.

- If you do not need the savings (eg, as an emergency fund or to provide income), consider using them instead to pay off any debts. The interest rate on many forms of borrowing, such as credit cards, has not fallen much, if at all. So you will save yourself more by clearing these debts than you could earn by putting the money in a savings account.

- Now might be a good time to buy long-lasting items, such as a new car or an extension to your home, or to invest in your education or training. You may be able to take advantage of competitive prices during the recession and you will give up relatively little interest by using your savings in this way.
- Do not leave your money in a savings account with a low rate. Many high street banks have followed the Bank of England's lead and cut the interest rates they offer savers close to zero. Not all accounts offer such meagre returns, so you should shop around for accounts offering a better deal. For example, at the time of writing, many instant access accounts were paying around 2.5 per cent a year compared with, say, 0.05 per cent from a deposit account with one of the big banks. Check the Compare Products tables published by the Financial Services Authority and comparison websites such as www.moneyfacts.co.uk.
- If you will not need your money back soon, consider accounts and bonds where you leave your money invested for a fixed period – eg, one to five years. At the time of writing, these accounts offered 4 to 5 per cent.
- Make use of your ISA allowance (see p78). That way you avoid an already low return being reduced further because of tax.
- If you are tempted by products that offer a better return than a savings accounts with a promise of getting you capital back in full, check the terms and conditions very carefully. These products are never risk-free. You should only invest if you understand the nature of the risks involved and are happy to accept them.

2. Saving versus investing

There are no hard and fast rules about what is meant by 'saving' and 'investing' but, in general:
- **saving** means putting your money into products where there is no risk of losing your capital (unless the provider were allowed to fail, which is considered unlikely). It includes accounts offered by banks and building societies and National Savings and Investments (NS&I) products;
- **investment** tends to mean products where there is some inherent risk of losing your capital.

This is a useful distinction because savings are suitable if you can invest only for the short term (eg, less than five years), will need your money back at a set time, or would feel uncomfortable taking any risk with your capital. By contrast, investments are appropriate for the long term, provided you are prepared to take some risk in order to have the chance of a better return. For more about this trade-off and a general outline of the factors to consider when choosing products, including savings and investments, see Chapter 1.

Managing risk

There are four main types of risk which you may need to weigh up.

- **Capital risk** is the risk of losing some of your original money.
- **Inflation risk** is the risk that, although you may get your capital back in full, its buying power will have been reduced because of inflation. Similarly, the risk that the buying power of any income from your investments declines over the years because of inflation.
- **Shortfall risk** is the risk that your savings or investments do not grow by enough to meet a specific target, such as producing a sufficient lump sum to pay off a mortgage or a large enough fund to provide a comfortable retirement income.
- **Interest risk** is the risk that you will lose out because of a change in interest rates – eg, a fall in rates will reduce your income if you have money saved at a variable rate. On the other hand, you cannot benefit from a rise in rates if you are locked into a fixed rate of interest.

It is easy to fall into the trap of looking only at capital risk but if you stick to 'safe' investments such as savings accounts you considerably increase both inflation risk and shortfall risk if you are investing for the medium to long term (five to 10 years or longer). The table on p74 shows how even a low rate of inflation can seriously reduce the buying power of your money over time, especially when interest rates are also low. In the example shown, although it is assumed that the interest rate on savings is 2.5 per cent, for a basic-rate taxpayer this is just 2 per cent after tax. With inflation also assumed to be 2 per cent a year, the savings with net (after-tax) interest reinvested only just maintain their buying power and do not grow at all in real terms. This is even more of a problem if you are drawing off the return as an income rather than investing it. The table shows, for example, that after 10 years, £20 a year net income would buy only the same as £16 today if inflation averaged 2 per cent a year, and the £1,000 a year in the account would be worth only the same as £820 today.

The table on p75 gives an example of how much you would need to save each month to build up a target amount – in this case £100,000 over 25 years (perhaps to repay a mortgage loan). As you can see, if you stick to low-risk/low-return savings, you might not be able to afford to save enough.

However, the slump in the stock market that started in 2007 is a reminder that capital risk is very real. If you put all your money into higher risk/higher return investments, like shares, you might get a handsome return, but, equally, you could make a significant loss if you have to cash in when share prices are low. This last point is important: with an investment like shares, you only make a capital gain or loss when you eventually sell the investment. If you are a long-term investor and the stock market falls, you may make a loss on paper, but provided you do not have to sell at that point in time, it is not a real loss. Provided share prices recover before you need your money back, the temporary paper loss is not relevant to you.

How inflation reduces the buying power of your money

Number of years your money is invested	If you reinvest the net interest[i]		If you draw the net interest as income[i]			
	Amount in your account	Buying power of money in your account[ii]	Amount in your account	Buying power of money in your account[ii]	Amount of income	Buying power of your income[ii]
1	£1,020	£1,000	£1,000	£980	£20	£20
2	£1,040	£1,000	£1,000	£961	£20	£19
3	£1,061	£1,000	£1,000	£942	£20	£19
4	£1,082	£1,000	£1,000	£924	£20	£18
5	£1,104	£1,000	£1,000	£906	£20	£18
6	£1,126	£1,000	£1,000	£888	£20	£18
7	£1,149	£1,000	£1,000	£871	£20	£17
8	£1,172	£1,000	£1,000	£853	£20	£17
9	£1,195	£1,000	£1,000	£837	£20	£17
10	£1,219	£1,000	£1,000	£820	£20	£16
11	£1,243	£1,000	£1,000	£804	£20	£16
12	£1,268	£1,000	£1,000	£788	£20	£16
13	£1,294	£1,000	£1,000	£773	£20	£15
14	£1,319	£1,000	£1,000	£758	£20	£15
15	£1,346	£1,000	£1,000	£743	£20	£15
16	£1,373	£1,000	£1,000	£728	£20	£15
17	£1,400	£1,000	£1,000	£714	£20	£14
18	£1,428	£1,000	£1,000	£700	£20	£14
19	£1,457	£1,000	£1,000	£686	£20	£14
20	£1,486	£1,000	£1,000	£673	£20	£13

[i] Assumes your money earns 2 per cent interest a year after tax has been deducted (2.5 per cent gross).

[ii] The amount of money today that would buy the same, assuming that prices are rising by 2 per cent a year.

Amount you would need to save each month to build up £100,000 over 25 years

	Lower risk/lower return		Higher risk/higher return	
Yearly interest rate before tax	2.5%	5%	7%	9%
Yearly interest rate after tax	2%	4%	5.6%	7.2%
Amount you would need to save each month	£257	£196	£156	£123

The trick is to balance the various risks by spreading your money across a range of savings and investments when you are investing for the long term and shifting to safer investments as the time approaches when you will need your money back.

Broadly, there are four 'asset classes' as shown in the table on p76. As a long-term investor, you should normally choose some savings and investments from each class, so that, if one type performs badly, this hopefully will be offset by better performance from the others. This strategy will tend to reduce your overall return a bit, but this is the trade-off for the reduction in risk. Some unit trusts and similar investments give you a ready-made mix of investments from different asset classes.

There are no set rules about how much you should put into each asset class. Some people suggest that the amount you have in share-based investments should be inversely proportional to your age, so if you are 30 you should have 70 per cent (in other words, 100 per cent minus 30) of your money in share-based investments; if you are 80 just 20 per cent. But this is simplistic. If your basic needs are all covered and you have a lot of money, you might be happy to put proportionately more into higher risk investments. If you are unhappy about taking risks, you should invest proportionately less. It is a difficult decision – consider getting help from a financial adviser (see Chapter 2).

Within each asset class, you can reduce risk further by having a spread of different investments. For example, if you are investing in shares, do not pick just one company. Instead, choose shares from a range of different companies. If you invest through a unit trust or similar investment, you get a stake in a ready-made spread of different companies' shares.

When you are within, say, five to ten years of needing your money back, you can lock in gains and reduce your exposure to falls in the stock market by gradually shifting away from the higher-risk assets such as shares and property into the lower-risk assets, such as bonds and cash. Shifting assets in this way is sometimes called 'lifestyling'. You need to apply the strategy flexibly. For example, if the stock market is already low at the time you would normally start to move out of shares and into cash, making the shift could mean locking in losses. You might decide to put off shifting out of shares until the stock market recovers. However, you need to be aware that this is not a risk-free decision, since the stock market could fall further instead of recovering.

The main asset classes

Lower risk/lower return		Higher risk/higher return	
Cash	**Bonds**	**Property**	**Equities**
eg, bank and building society accounts, NS&I products, *Shariah-compliant* accounts, such as *Mudaraba*	eg, gilts, corporate bonds, *Shariah-compliant* bonds (*Sukuk*)	eg, unit trusts, real estate investment trusts and similar funds investing in commercial property, such as offices and shops	ie, shares in companies and share-based investments, such as many unit trusts and investment trusts

3. **Schemes to encourage saving and investing**

The Government is keen to encourage certain types of saving and investing and has set up a number of special schemes to do this. Often, government schemes work as 'wrappers' that offer either tax or cash advantages but let you choose how to save or invest the money inside the wrapper. See pp81 and 95 for details of the particular types of savings and investments mentioned here.

Saving Gateway

What it is and how it works

This scheme, which has been tested by the Government since 2002, is due to be launched nationally from April 2010. It is designed to encourage people of working age on a low income to build up savings and develop a savings habit. Having some savings to fall back on in an emergency makes it less likely that a household will have to resort to expensive debt.

Under the Saving Gateway scheme, you make regular savings into an account with a bank, building society or credit union for a period of two years. In addition to earning interest, you get a bonus, called a maturity payment, funded by the Government, at the end of the two-year term. During the two years, you pay in up to £25 a month and can withdraw part or all of your money at any time. Within these general rules, providers may set their own terms and conditions, such as restrictions on withdrawals. Both interest and the maturity payment are tax-free.

The maturity payment adds 50p for each £1 of the highest balance you achieve (excluding interest) during the two-year term. For example, if you pay in the maximum £25 each month and make no withdrawals, your highest balance excluding interest would be 24 x £25 = £600, so you would get a maturity payment of £300.

At the end of two years, The Saving Gateway account closes but you can roll over the proceeds (including the maturity payment) into an individual savings account (ISA) (see below).

In the event of death before the completion of the two-year term, your Saving Gateway account is closed and the proceeds become part of your estate. The proceeds still include a maturity payment, but this will usually be less than it would have been had the account run for the full two years.

Who should consider a Saving Gateway account

You are eligible for a Saving Gateway account if you are entitled (either on your own or with someone else) to:

- tax credits provided your household income is below a set amount (£16,040 in 2009/10);
- income support;
- jobseeker's allowance;
- employment and support allowance;
- incapacity benefit;
- severe disablement allowance;
- carer's allowance.

For details of these benefits, see Chapter 9.

Once opened, you can carry on with the account until it matures, even if you stop claiming benefits.

When the scheme starts in 2010, you will get a letter inviting you to open an account and containing your Saving Gateway reference number. You will have three months from the date on the letter to open the account with any of the providers taking part in the scheme. You can transfer your account at any time without charge to another provider if you want to.

A Saving Gateway account is in the name of just one person – it cannot be held jointly with someone else. You can only have one Saving Gateway account during your life.

Everyone who has the opportunity to do so should consider opening one of these accounts. The maturity payment from the Government gives a big boost to your savings. Even ignoring any interest, the maturity payment alone gives you a return equivalent to nearly 50 per cent a year – far more than you can get from other form of saving.

Individual savings accounts

What they are and how they work

ISAs were introduced in April 1999 and the Government has now said that they will continue indefinitely.

An ISA is a wrapper into which you can put various savings and investments. The return from them is then partially or completely tax-free, depending on the type of investments you choose. There are two different components that can go into an ISA as shown in the table.

The savings and investments you can put in an individual savings account and how they are taxed

Component	Type of savings and investments you can put in it	How the savings and investments are taxed
Cash	Savings products like accounts from banks, building societies, National Savings and Investments (NS&I) and *Shariah*-complaint equivalents – eg, *Mudaraba*.	Interest is tax-free.
Stocks and shares	Many types of shares, corporate bonds and *Shariah*-compliant equivalents (*Sukuk*), gilts, unit trusts, open-ended investment companies, investment trusts, investment-type life insurance and similar investments.	Dividends from shares and distributions from share-based unit trusts and similar investments are taxed at 10 per cent.[3] Other income is tax-free. Capital gains are tax-free.

You have a new ISA allowance each tax year (see below) and you can choose how to use it. You can invest in:

- **stocks and shares.** You can put up to the whole £7,200 in 2009/10 (£10,200 from 6 October 2009 for people aged 50 and over and from 2010/11 for everyone else) into that component; *or*
- **cash.** You can invest up to £3,600 in 2009/10 (£5,100 from 6 October 2009 for people aged 50 and over and from 2010/11 for everyone else) in the cash component and, if you like, the remainder of your allowance in the stocks and shares component.

Your individual savings account allowance

- Each tax year, you have an ISA allowance. It is up to you whether you use it, but any allowance not used by the end of the tax year is lost – it cannot be carried forward to another year.
- The overall allowance in 2009/10 is £7,200 or, from 6 October 2009, £10,200 for people aged over 50 at the time they make the investment. You can invest all of this in stocks and shares or you can split it between the cash component (up to £3,600 or, from 6 October 2009, up to £5,100 for people 50 and over) and, if you like, the rest in stocks and shares.
- From 2010/11, the overall allowance increases to £10,200 for everyone, of which you can put up to £5,100 into the cash component, with the rest in stocks and shares.

- The allowance refers to the amount you originally invest regardless of any withdrawals. For example, if you are eligible to put £5,100 into a cash ISA, pay in £2,000 and then withdraw £500, you still have just £3,100 allowance left for the year (not £3,600).
- You can switch money already invested in the cash component to the stocks-and-shares component but not vice versa.
- When Saving Gateway accounts and child trust funds mature, the proceeds can be rolled over into an ISA without affecting your annual ISA allowance for the year.

You cannot create the ISA wrapper yourself; you have to go to an ISA manager. In practice, the providers of the savings and investments will double up as ISA managers and often offer products ready-wrapped in an ISA. So, for example, a bank, building society or NS&I will offer a range of accounts, including an ISA account. Similarly, if you are looking at unit trusts, some may come ready-wrapped as a unit trust ISA. But other ISA managers (eg, fund supermarkets and stockbrokers) let you choose which unit trusts, shares and other investments to put within your ISA.

Personal equity plans (PEPs) were a forerunner of stocks and shares ISAs. From 6 April 1999, no new personal equity plans (PEPs) can be sold but you can continue to hold any PEPs you had before this date. To simplify the administration of PEPs, since 2008/09, they have all been automatically converted to stocks and shares ISAs.

Who should consider an individual savings account

In general, you have to be 18 to be eligible for an ISA, but you can have a cash ISA from age 16. Whether or not they are a good choice depends largely on your tax position.

- **Non-taxpayers**. ISAs offer tax advantages. You cannot benefit from these if you are a non-taxpayer. However, sometimes cash ISAs offer a higher return than other types of bank and building society accounts – in that case, even a non-taxpayer might be better off choosing the ISA. You might be a non-taxpayer now but expect to pay tax in future – eg, if you are a student, since ISAs continue indefinitely, it is worth using your ISA allowance each year to build up maximum tax-free savings for later. If you expect eventually to cash in or sell an investment with a profit that exceeds your annual capital gains tax allowance (£10,100 in 2009/10 – see Chapter 8), it might be worth investing in it through an ISA.
- **Basic-rate taxpayers**. Cash ISAs and stocks and shares ISAs that invest in corporate bonds and gilts, offer a completely tax-free return. Provided any extra charges for the ISA do not come to more than the tax saved, choosing an ISA rather than investing in the same investments without the ISA wrapper should be a good idea. The income from shares, share-based unit trusts and similar investments is taxed in the same way whether you invest through an

ISA or without the ISA wrapper, so it is only worth choosing the ISA if it will save you capital gains tax (see Chapter 8).

- **Higher rate taxpayers**. Investing through an ISA will save you tax. Any charges for the ISA are unlikely to be high enough to wipe out this advantage.

Child trust funds

What they are and how they work

Child trust funds are accounts for every child born on or after 1 September 2002 with free money from the Government. Once you have registered for child benefit, the Government sends you a voucher for £250 (£500 if your family is on a low income), with which to open your child's child trust fund account. The Government pays in another £250 (£500) when the child reaches age seven and is consulting on a further top-up at age 11. Anyone else (eg, parents, other relatives and friends) can add to the child's account up to an overall maximum of £1,200 a year.

The aim of the child trust funds is twofold: to ensure that every young person eventually starts adult life with some money to help them, and to educate children about money, supported by linked activities at school. In September 2009, for the first time children will start to receive their age seven top-up from the Government. Schools will hold special lessons to coincide with this event to stimulate children's interest in their child trust fund and in savings more generally.

A child trust fund matures when the child reaches 18. At that stage, the young person can withdraw the money and use it for any purpose s/he likes. If s/he wants to carry on saving, the child trust fund can be automatically rolled over into an ISA.

You open the child trust fund account by giving the voucher, or the details from it, to one of the many providers (see www.childtrustfund.gov.uk for a list). You must complete an application form, though some providers let you do this by phone or internet. To comply with the money laundering requirements (see p58), you may be asked for proof of your identity and address, but since late 2007 providers no longer have to ask for these details. If you do not invest your child's voucher within 12 months, the Government will automatically open an account for your child.

There is a choice of ways to invest: in a savings account like a bank or building society account (credit unions can also offer these), or in an account investing on the stock market. All child trust fund managers have to offer a stakeholder account which has capped charges (no more than 1.5 per cent a year of the value of the fund) and invests initially in a range of stock market investments, shifting to lower risk savings as the account approaches maturity. If the Government opens the account for your child, it will always choose a stakeholder account. Child trust finds are flexible, so you can switch provider and/or account type at any time.

While the fund is invested, the savings and investments in it are taxed in the same way as ISAs (see p78). This means that income from shares and share-based investments is taxed at 10 per cent, but other income and gains are tax-free. There is no tax to pay when the young person cashes in the child trust fund.

Any income and gains building up within the child trust fund will not affect the family's eligibility for state benefits or tax credits.

Who should invest in a child trust fund

A child trust fund is not for short-term saving. However, it could be suitable if you want a long-term investment in order to build up a lump sum for your child that s/he can use after reaching age 18. All eligible children have a child trust fund because the Government automatically opens the account for your child if you do not. The key question is whether you should add any of your own money to the account, assuming you can afford to.

Everyone, even a child, has tax allowances. This means the first slices of income (£6,475 in 2009/10) and gains (£10,100 in 2009/10) are tax-free, so the tax treatment of child trust funds does not generally offer the child any immediate advantage over other savings or investments. However, if you are a parent, income from money you give your child may be taxed as your own (see p69), but will not be if you invest for your child in a child trust fund (or certain other investments). This will not be an important consideration if your income is too low for you to pay tax. At age 18, when the child trust fund matures, the proceeds can be rolled over into an ISA and so may eventually increase the tax savings your child can make when s/he is an adult.

You might feel reluctant to take risks with your child's money and so be drawn to a savings-type child trust fund. Bear in mind that 18 years is a long-term investment and, in general, share-based investments have tended to produce better returns than savings over the long term.

Some providers give you the option to invest your child's money on an ethical basis – eg, in funds that avoid alcohol, tobacco, the arms industry and so on or pursue good human rights or climate-related practices. One provider (The Children's Mutual) offers a *Shariah*-compliant child trust fund.

Pensions

The Government encourages saving for retirement through a range of tax reliefs and, with some types of pension, a bonus if you pay little or no tax (see Chapter 6).

4. **Types of savings products**

With all the products described in this section, there is no capital risk (unless the provider goes out of business, in which case you will probably be eligible for compensation – see Chapter 10). This means you get back all the money you originally invested.

To choose and open any of the accounts listed below, follow these steps.

- Choose the type of account you want by checking the descriptions below. Accounts vary mainly on the basis of access (how easily and quickly you can get your money back), how you invest (lump sums or regular payments), minimum investment, how the return is paid (lump sum or regular income) and tax treatment.

- Shop around for the highest interest rates. The best rates are often offered by phone and internet accounts. Check out the Compare Products tables published by the Financial Services Authority, lists in the personal finance sections of newspapers and comparison websites such as www.moneyfacts.co.uk. Bear in mind the limitations of comparison websites (see p8) and use two or three sites rather than relying on just one.

- Consider how you want to run an account. With some phone and online accounts, you also need a current account or basic bank account (see Chapter 3) which is the only channel for paying into and withdrawing money from the savings account. If branch-based, make sure there is a branch convenient for you to use. If you want to be able to make withdrawals at cash machines, choose an account with a cash card.

- To open, visit a branch (or post office for National Savings and Investments (NS&I)), phone or fill in an online application form. You will need to provide proofs of identity and address in the same way as for current accounts (see p58).

Annual equivalent rate

The interest you get from a savings account is expressed in a standard way that takes into account not just how much you get, but when you get it. The sooner you receive the interest, the sooner it can be reinvested to earn more. So interest paid or credited, say, monthly, is worth more to you than interest paid yearly. The annual equivalent rate (AER) reflects this.

You can directly compare the AER for one account with the AER for another. The higher the AER, the better the return on offer.

If the account pays interest at a variable rate (ie, an interest rate that can rise or fall), the AER is based on the rate currently being paid. If interest rates change, the actual return you get will be different from the AER. If an account pays a fixed interest rate, the AER shows the return you will actually get.

Instant/easy access accounts

What they are and how they work

Instant/easy access accounts (including NS&I easy access savings accounts and investment accounts) are savings accounts where you can get your money back at any time without giving notice. However, there might be a daily limit on the amount you can withdraw – eg, £250 or £300 a day. Some accounts give you a plastic card letting you withdraw money at cash machines. Some accounts are operated by post, phone or internet; others are branch-based. The NS&I accounts can be operated through post offices.

Money in your account earns interest at a variable rate. Normally it is paid to you or credited to your account with tax at the basic rate already deducted. Higher rate taxpayers have extra tax to pay. Starting rate taxpayers can claim back some of the tax. Non-taxpayers can either claim back the tax using Form R40 or arrange to be paid without any tax deducted by completing Form R85 (see p355). NS&I interest is paid gross.

There may be a minimum investment but with many accounts this is just £1. However, it is common for higher rates of interest to be paid on larger balances (called 'tiered interest'). Subject to the minimum, you pay in *ad hoc* amounts and lump sums when you like.

What they cost

There are no explicit charges. The costs faced by the provider will be reflected in the interest rate offered.

Useful for

- Emergency fund.
- Opportunity fund.
- Managing day-to-day money if you do not need current account features (see Chapter 3).
- Teaching children to manage money – some accounts are designed for children and offer incentives, such as money boxes and magazines.
- Short-term saving.

Providers

Banks, building societies and NS&I.

Pitfalls and what to watch out for

- Your account may become uncompetitive or even superseded (see below) so be prepared to check rates regularly and move your money to get a better return.
- Inflation reduces the buying power of your money.
- If interest rates fall, your money earns less.

Non-taxpayers and starting rate taxpayers

The interest from many savings accounts and bonds is paid with tax at the basics rate already deducted. If you are a non-taxpayer, you can arrange to have your interest paid gross (without tax deducted). To do this, fill in Form R85 which you can get from the provider or, if you prefer, download from the 'Find a form' service on the HM Revenue and Customs website (www.hmrc.gov.uk). Give or send the completed form to the provider.

If you have paid tax on your savings interest but you are a non-taxpayer or a starting rate taxpayer, you can claim back the overpaid tax. To do this complete Form R40 from your tax office or the 'Find a Form' service on the HM Revenue and Customs website. Send your completed form to your tax office.

See Chapter 8 for more details.

Superseded accounts

From time to time, providers bring out new accounts which often offer better interest rates than those being earned by existing savers, and existing accounts might be closed to new investors. Under new rules due to apply to banks, building societies and credit unions from 1 November 2009 onwards, providers must provide appropriate information to their customers in good time, in an appropriate form and in clear language so that they can make informed decisions. This includes information about the different services offered by the provider that share the main features of the service you have. However, it is a good idea for you to check regularly (at least once a year) to make sure you are still getting a good return and to switch accounts if necessary.

Cash individual savings accounts

What they are and how they work

These are savings accounts which are often instant/easy access (see p82) but are also available as notice accounts or bonds (see p87). Accounts are operated by branch, phone, post or internet. Most cannot be operated through cash machines.

These accounts are inside an individual savings account (ISA) wrapper (see p77), so the interest they earn is tax-free. Interest is usually variable but some accounts offer a fixed rate.

There may be a minimum investment (eg, £100 with NS&I's cash ISA) but with many accounts the minimum is just £1. However, it is common for higher rates of interest to be paid on larger balances (called 'tiered interest'). Subject to the minimum, you pay in *ad hoc* amounts and lump sums as and when you please. The maximum investment allowed under the tax rules is £3,600 in 2009/10, increasing to £5,100 from 6 October 2009 for people aged 50 and over and from 2010/11 for everyone else.

What they cost

There are no explicit charges. The costs faced by the provider will be reflected in the interest rate offered.

Useful for

- Emergency fund if you choose instant/easy access.
- Opportunity fund.
- Short- to medium-term saving, especially if you are a taxpayer.

Providers

Banks, building societies and NS&I.

Pitfalls and what to watch out for

- Your account may become uncompetitive, so be prepared to check rates regularly and move your money to get a better return.
- Inflation reduces the buying power of your money.
- If interest rates fall, money invested at a variable rate earns less.

Credit union accounts

What they are and how they work

Credit unions are mutual organisations owned and run by their members for their members. Usually the people running the credit union are all unpaid volunteers. Members have a 'common bond' – eg, they all live in the same area, belong to the same church, or work for the same employer or in the same industry. From a date yet to be announced (but likely to be late 2009), a single credit union can have members covered by a number of different common bonds – eg, a geographical area, members of specified housing associations and employees from particular firms. Traditionally, credit unions offer savings accounts and cheap loans, but, increasingly, larger credit unions are offering other financial services, such as basic bank accounts and various types of insurance. Usually, you can borrow only once you have built up a reliable record of saving. Therefore, savings accounts normally require you to pay in regularly every week or month, although the minimum payment may be very low. Savings technically earn a dividend rather than interest. Although the dividend is taxable, it is paid gross (without any tax deducted). From a date yet to be announced (likely to be late 2009), credit unions will be able to offer interest-paying accounts as well.

Useful for

- Emergency fund.
- Opportunity fund.
- Providing the discipline of setting money aside regularly.
- Providing access to cheap loans if you need them.

What they cost

There are no explicit charges. The costs faced by the provider will be reflected in the interest rate offered.

Providers

Credit unions. You can join only if you are eligible under the terms of the particular credit union's common bond(s). For a list of local credit unions, see www.abcul.org or ask your local authority.

Pitfalls and what to watch out for

- Restrictions on the maximum return on your savings are being removed, but it is likely that many credit unions will still pay less than you would get with a bank or building society.
- Inflation reduces the buying power of your money.

Christmas savings schemes

What they are and how they work

Many Christmas savings schemes are not really savings products at all. They are pre-payment schemes. You save a small sum each week or month which you cannot get back as cash and in return receive high street vouchers, a food hamper or other goods as Christmas approaches. Often your savings are collected by a local representative who calls at your home.

Following the collapse of a scheme called Farepak in 2006 (see p87), some credit unions and other providers now promote schemes specifically aimed at Christmas savings. Typically, these require you to pay regular sums into an account. Some lock your money in until Christmas approaches with no earlier access, but you can then get your money back in cash. The Post Office and some credit unions let you load your savings onto a plastic card that can be used to buy goods at specified high street stores.

- -

Savings stamps

The Post Office operates multi-purpose savings stamps which can be used to pay for any products and services available through post offices, such as paying household bills, buying travel or car insurance, gifts and so on.

- -

What they cost

There are no explicit charges.

Useful for

Spreading the cost of Christmas.

Providers

Pre-payment schemes: hamper companies, supermarkets and local schemes offered by small retailers and clubs. Savings accounts: credit unions, the Post Office and some banks.

Pitfalls and what to watch out for

- In 2006, the hamper company Farepak collapsed, causing 150,000 people to lose most of their Christmas savings. Because this was a pre-payment scheme, there was no protection, as there would have been for a savings account. The Government worked with the hamper industry to set up a voluntary protection scheme, under which customers' payments are held in a separate account operated by an independent trustee. Make sure that any national scheme you join belongs to the scheme and be aware that small, local schemes are unlikely to be covered.
- Savings with a pre-payment scheme do not earn interest, the goods you get might be more expensive than you could purchase them elsewhere, and hampers might include items you do not want.
- Savings schemes let you draw your savings as cash, so you might be tempted to spend the money on something else.
- There are alternative ways of saving for Christmas that may be more appropriate – eg, because they are more flexible or offer more protection. For more information visit www.oft.gov.uk/savexmas.

Notice accounts

What they are and how they work

These are savings accounts where you can get your money back without losing interest only if you give advance notice that you want to make a withdrawal. The notice period varies according to the account you choose but is typically 30, 60 or 90 days. Some accounts let you have your money back without giving the required notice, but you then lose some interest.

Some accounts are operated by post, phone or internet; others are branch-based.

Money in your account earns interest at a variable rate. Normally it is paid to you or credited to your account with tax at the basic rate already deducted. Higher rate taxpayers have extra tax to pay. Starting-rate taxpayers can claim back some of the tax. Non-taxpayers can either claim back the tax using Form R40 or arrange to be paid without any tax deducted by completing Form R85 (see p355). There may be a minimum investment (eg, £100, £250, £2,000 or more). However, with many accounts the minimum is just £1. It is common for higher rates of interest to be paid on larger balances (called 'tiered interest'). Subject to the minimum, you pay in *ad hoc* amounts and lump sums as and when you please.

What they cost

There are no explicit charges. The costs faced by the provider will be reflected in the interest rate offered. However, you lose interest if you withdraw money without giving the required notice.

Useful for

Short- to medium-term saving.

Providers

Banks and building societies.

Pitfalls and what to watch out for

- Your account may become uncompetitive or even superseded (see p84), so be prepared to check rates regularly and move your money to get a better return.
- You might unexpectedly need your money back at short notice – some accounts do not allow this; with others you lose interest.
- You might expect to earn a higher rate of interest by agreeing to a notice period, but often you can get as good or better rates with an instant/easy access account (see p82).
- Inflation reduces the buying power of your money.
- If interest rates fall, your money earns less.

Term accounts and bonds

What they are and how they work

Term accounts and bonds (including NS&I guaranteed growth bonds) are savings accounts where you agree to leave your money invested for a set period – eg, one, two or five years. With some, you can get your money back earlier but then lose some or even all of the interest. With others, you cannot get your money back early.

Money in your account earns interest, usually at a fixed rate. Normally it is credited to your account with tax at the basic rate already deducted. Higher rate taxpayers have extra tax to pay. Starting-rate taxpayers can claim back some of the tax. Non-taxpayers can either claim back the tax using Form R40 or arrange to be paid without any tax deducted by completing Form R85 (see p355).

Note that, even though you may not be able to have the money until the end of the term, you are liable for tax each year as interest is credited to your account.

These accounts are for lump-sum investments and there is a minimum investment (typically £500, £1,000 or more – £500 with the NS&I bond). Often larger investments can earn higher interest. Some bonds pay a higher rate of interest each year you leave your money (called '**escalator bonds**').

What they cost

There are no explicit charges. The costs faced by the provider will be reflected in the interest rate offered. If early withdrawal is allowed at all, you lose some or all of the interest.

Useful for

Short- or medium-term saving, depending on the term you choose.

Providers

Banks, building societies and NS&I.

Pitfalls and what to watch out for

- You might unexpectedly need your money back at short notice – some accounts do not allow this, with others you lose interest.
- Inflation reduces the buying power of your money.
- If other interest rates rise, you could find yourself locked into an uncompetitive return.

Monthly interest and income accounts

What they are and how they work

Monthly interest and income accounts (including NS&I guaranteed income bonds and income bonds) are savings accounts where interest – which is usually variable – is paid to you at regular intervals, often monthly. With some accounts, you must have a current account, basic bank account (see Chapter 3) or other savings account into which the interest can be paid.

Many accounts let you have your capital back at any time without giving notice. With others, there is a notice period or loss of interest. With NS&I guaranteed income bonds (but not the income bonds) you have to invest for a fixed number of years and there is a 90-day interest penalty for withdrawing your money early.

Money in your account earns interest, usually at a variable rate. However, the NS&I guaranteed income bonds pay interest rate at a fixed rate.

Normally, interest is paid to you or credited to your account with tax at the basic rate already deducted. Higher rate taxpayers have extra tax to pay. Starting-rate taxpayers can claim back some of the tax. Non-taxpayers can either claim back the tax using Form R40 or arrange to be paid without any tax deducted by completing Form R85 (see p355).

Often, there is a minimum investment – eg, £500 with the NS&I guaranteed income bonds. Some accounts pay higher rates of interest on larger balances (called **'tiered interest'**).

What they cost

There are no explicit charges. The costs faced by the provider will be reflected in the interest rate offered. However, with some accounts, you lose interest if you withdraw your money without giving notice.

Useful for

Providing you with income.

Providers

Banks, building societies and NS&I.

Pitfalls and what to watch out for

- Your account may become uncompetitive or even superseded (see p84) so be prepared to check rates regularly and move your money to get a better return.
- Inflation reduces the buying power of both your capital and your income (see p74). This will be a particular problem if you are relying on the income to fund your day-to-day living expenses over a long period.
- If interest rates fall, your money earns less, unless the account offers a fixed rate.

Regular savings accounts

What they are and how they work

These are savings accounts into which you pay a set sum each month. The minimum is usually £10 to £50 a month and there may be a maximum – eg, £500 a month. Usually, you lose some interest if you do not keep up the payments for a minimum period or you miss too many payments.

Many accounts let you have your capital back at any time without giving notice. With others, there is a notice period or loss of interest. In general, you are restricted to a limited number of withdrawals each year – eg, just one or two. If you go over this limit, you either lose some interest or the account is closed.

Money in your account earns interest, usually at a variable rate. Normally, interest is paid to you or credited to your account with tax at the basic rate already deducted. Higher rate taxpayers have extra tax to pay. Starting-rate taxpayers can claim back some of the tax. Non-taxpayers can either claim back the tax using Form R40 or arrange to be paid without any tax deducted by completing Form R85.

What they cost

There are no explicit charges. The costs faced by the provider will be reflected in the interest rate offered. However, with most accounts you lose interest if you do not keep to the conditions concerning payments and withdrawals.

Useful for

- Building up an opportunity fund with some added discipline to stop you dipping into the money too readily.
- Short- to medium-term saving, if you need some extra discipline to make you save.

Providers

Banks and building societies.

Pitfalls and what to watch out for

- Make sure you are getting a higher interest rate than from, say, an instant access account (see p82) in return for agreeing to the restrictions on paying money in and drawing it out.

- Some accounts quote a very high interest rate for a short period (eg, one year) but limit the amount you can save each month. Such rates can be attractive if you genuinely want to save monthly but not if you are really a lump-sum investor. For example, if you invest £250 a month (£3,000 over a whole year) at 10 per cent you would earn around £160 in interest, but this is little more than the £150 you would get by investing a lump sum of £3,000 at the outset for 5 per cent.
- Inflation reduces the buying power of your money.
- If interest rates fall, your money earns less.

National Savings and Investments certificates

What they are and how they work

These are savings accounts where you invest for a set term (two, three or five years, at the time of writing) during which you earn interest either at a fixed rate or, in the case of index-linked certificates, at a rate linked to changes in the retail prices index. Interest, which is tax-free, is credited each year and paid out at the end of the term.

On any money you withdraw within the first year, you get no interest at all. If you withdraw after this, but before the end of the term, you lose some of the interest.

What they cost

There are no explicit charges. The costs faced by the provider are reflected in the interest rate offered. However, you lose interest if you withdraw your money early.

Useful for

- Short- to medium-term saving, depending on the term you choose.
- Protecting your money against inflation if you choose index-linked certificates.

Provider

NS&I.

Pitfalls and what to watch out for

- Inflation reduces the buying power of your money, unless you choose the index-linked option.
- If other interest rates rise, you may find yourself locked into an uncompetitive return.

National Savings and Investments children's bonus bonds

How they work

These are savings accounts where anyone over the age of 16 may invest money for a person under the age of 16. The bonds have a set term of five years, during which they earn tax-free interest at a fixed rate plus a fixed bonus at the end of the term. At the end of each five years you can automatically leave the money reinvested for a new five-year period at whatever fixed rate and bonus then applies.

Interest is not treated as your income if you are a parent making the investment for your own child (see p69).

On any money withdrawn within the first year, you get no interest at all. If you withdraw after this, but before the end of the term, you lose some of the interest.

What they cost

There are no explicit charges. The costs faced by the provider are reflected in the interest rate offered. However, you lose interest if you withdraw your money early.

Useful for

Building up a fund of savings for a child over the medium term.

Provider

NS&I.

Pitfalls and what to watch out for

- Inflation reduces the buying power of the money.
- If other interest rates rise, the child may be locked into an uncompetitive return.

Guaranteed equity bonds

How they work

These bonds, which are examples of 'structured products' (see p115), are designed to give you the chance of sharing in the higher returns that stock market investments tend to offer but without the risk of losing your capital, which is inherent in shares and share-based investments (see p101).

They are savings accounts where you invest for a set term (eg, three, four, five or seven years) during which you earn interest at a rate linked to changes in share prices (measured by changes in, for instance, the FTSE 100 Index). If share prices fall over the term, you just get your capital back and no interest.

Interest is credited to the bond with tax at the basic rate already deducted. Higher rate taxpayers have extra tax to pay. Starting-rate taxpayers can claim back some of the tax. Non-taxpayers can either claim back the tax using Form R40 or arrange to be paid without any tax deducted by completing Form R85 (see p355). You become liable for tax only when the bond reaches the end of its term. Some of these bonds are available within an ISA wrapper (see p77), in which case the interest is tax-free.

In general, you cannot get your money back before the end of the term. However, a few providers do let you have:

- a loan secured against the bond, which itself continues until maturity; *or*
- your money back early but you might then get back less than you originally invested.

What they cost

There are usually no explicit charges. The costs faced by the provider are reflected in the interest rate offered. A few providers charge an arrangement fee.

Useful for

- Short- to medium-term saving, depending on the term you choose.
- The chance of a stock market-linked return without the risk of losing your capital.

Provider

Banks, building societies and NS&I.

Pitfalls and what to watch out for

- It is easy to confuse these bonds with other guaranteed equity products (see p115) which do not protect you from losing your capital.
- You cannot usually get your money back early. Where you can, you may no longer be protected from losing your capital.
- If the stock market falls, you get no interest at all.
- Even if the stock market rises, you usually get only a proportion of the growth in share prices (eg, 75 to 95 per cent) and you do not get any of the income you would normally get from investing in shares (see p101) or unit trusts (see p104).
- These bonds are called 'guaranteed' and aim to return your capital in full but, in the event of the organisation providing the underlying guarantee going bankrupt, you could lose some of your capital. Only NS&I (a government agency) is able to provide a complete guarantee because in the final resort it is backed by taxpayers' money. With other bonds, the underlying guarantee usually comes from a bank or other large financial institution. Although, generally, the risk of such institutions defaulting or going bankrupt is considered very small, the collapse of the investment bank Lehman Brothers (which provided the underlying guarantee for some bonds of this type) in 2008 showed that this can happen and, when it does, savers do not necessarily get their money back.

Premium bonds

What they are and how they work

These are NS&I accounts where, instead of earning interest, you have the chance each month to win prizes in a draw. Prizes, which are tax-free, range from £25 up to £1 million. In July 2009, for each £1 invested, you had a one in 36,000 chance of winning a prize. The table below shows the number of prizes you could expect to win in a year if you had average luck (although you could do better or worse than average).

You can choose whether to have prizes paid out or automatically reinvested.

The minimum investment is £100 as a lump sum or £50 a month if you opt for the 'regular purchase scheme'. The maximum is £30,000, including any reinvested prizes.

You can withdraw your capital at any time without notice, but it takes about seven working days for the money to reach you.

Number of premium bond prizes you can expect to win in a year with average luck

Value of holding	£1,000	£5,000	£10,000	£20,000	£30,000
Expected number of prizes a year	0.33	1.67	3.33	6.67	10

What they cost

There are no explicit charges. The costs faced by the provider are reflected in the amount of money in the prize fund.

Useful for

Remote chance of winning a life-changing amount of money.

Provider

NS&I.

Pitfalls and what to watch out for

- Inflation reduces the buying power of your capital.
- You are gambling with the interest you would otherwise have earned by putting your money into a savings account. There is no guarantee that you will win any prizes at all, so the gamble might not pay off.
- The odds of winning the £1 million monthly jackpot is very small indeed: just 1 in 41 billion each month per bond in mid-2009 (compared with, for example, one in 14 million for each main Lotto draw).
- Even with average luck at winning prizes, you might be able to get a better return for your money elsewhere. In July 2009, the prize fund was equivalent to a return of 1 per cent a year on the total amount invested in premium bonds. This is tax-free, so a basic-rate taxpayer would need taxable interest of 1.25 per cent to be left with 1 per cent after tax and a higher rate taxpayer would need 1.67 per cent. At the time of writing, you could easily get a better return from the highest paying savings accounts.

Ethical savings

As well as meeting their own financial goals, many savers would like to put their savings to some wider good for society or the environment. If this applies to you, consider a bank or building society that follows an ethical policy.

Co-operative Bank has had an ethical policy since 1992. It bases the policy on its customers' views. For example, it does not invest in businesses which are involved in the arms trade, uncontrolled genetic modification, tobacco trade, currency speculation, which fail to uphold human rights, or whose policies are bad for ecology, the environment or animal welfare. It seeks to support businesses which have fair trade policies, or which are involved in social enterprise or sustaining the environment.

Ecology Building Society is 'dedicated to improving the environment by promoting sustainable housing and sustainable communities'. To this end, it lends to fund energy-efficient housing, renovation, small-scale and ecological enterprise and low-impact lifestyles.

Smile internet bank is part of the Co-operative Bank and is covered by its ethical policy described above.

Triodos Bank lends only to organisations which have social aims, benefit the community or develop individual talents, such as charities, community projects, social businesses and environmental projects.

These banks and building societies generally do not offer the best rates of interest, so you may need to be prepared to sacrifice some return for following your principles.

Shariah-compliant savings. Under Islamic (*Shariah*) law, interest (*Riba*) is prohibited and so too are dealings involving pork, alcohol, gambling, pornography or anything else illegal under Islamic law. Islamic banking works on the principle of profit sharing (and loss sharing) instead of interest. For example, with a *Mudaraba* contract, your money is invested on your behalf and you receive a share of any profits the investment makes. In the UK, *Shariah*-compliant banking and savings products are offered by, for example, the Islamic Bank of Britain, HSBC Amanah Finance and Lloyds-TSB. Despite the rapid growth of *Shariah*-compliant products, Islamic scholars are divided on how well banks can really meet the requirements of *Shariah* law. *Shariah*-compliant products are open to non-Muslim customers as well as Muslims and could be a suitable choice if you are looking for ethical banking and investments.

5. Types of investment

There is a huge range of investments available. Many are variations on a theme; others are new, complex and suitable only for sophisticated investors. This section describes the main investments that most investors are likely to consider. In general, you should be wary of complicated investments or variations that deviate too far from these broad mainstream products – make sure you fully understand how they work and what they offer before you commit yourself and bear in mind that if it sounds too good to be true, it probably is.

With all investments, risk and return are inseparably linked (see p72). If you are offered a high return with no risk, be very suspicious. The prospect of a high return always involves taking extra risks, so make sure you have identified those risks and are comfortable taking them.

Choosing the right investments can be difficult, so consider getting financial advice (see Chapter 2).

With all investments, if you are a new customer, you will need to provide proofs of identity and address in the same way as for current accounts (see p58).

Annuities

What they are and how they work

You exchange a lump sum for an income either for life (called a **'permanent** or **lifetime annuity'**) or for a set period (a **'temporary annuity'**). The payments normally stop when/if you die. With a 'joint-life last-survivor' annuity, the payments continue until the second of two people has died.

For annuities you buy with a pension fund, see Chapter 6. This section considers annuities you choose to buy with other money – they are called **'purchased life annuities'**.

You cannot normally get your capital back as a lump sum, but part of the income you receive is treated as return of your capital. The rest is treated as savings income and only that part is taxable. The capital element is tax-free. However, some annuities (**'with guarantee'**) do guarantee to pay out for at least a minimum number of years (eg, five or ten years), even if you die before that then. And others (**'capital protected'**) will pay out the balance of your capital if you die before you have received as much in income as you originally invested.

Normally income is paid to you with tax at the basic rate already deducted. Higher rate taxpayers have extra tax to pay. Starting-rate taxpayers can claim back some of the tax. Non-taxpayers can either claim back the tax using Form R40 or arrange to be paid without any tax deducted by completing Form R85 (see p355).

For each £10,000 of capital you invest, the **'annuity rate'** tells you how much income a year you will get when the annuity starts. The amount of income you get is set at the time you buy an annuity. With a **'level annuity'**, the income is fixed at one amount and does not change. With other types of annuity, the income changes, usually once a year – eg, increasing by a set amount (**'escalating annuity'**) or in line with inflation (**'RPI-linked'**). Some annuities (**'investment-linked'**) pay an income linked to the performance of a fund of investments.

The level of income from an annuity depends in part on the return the annuity provider can get from investing your capital for the required period and is linked to the return from gilts (see p98). With a permanent annuity (payable for the rest of your life), the level of income depends heavily on the life expectancy for an average person of your age and sex, because, the longer you live, the longer the period over which the annuity has to pay out. The level of income might be increased if you are not expected to live as long as average – eg, because you are ill or smoke).

What they cost

There are no explicit charges. However, the costs the provider incurs are reflected in the annuity rate offered. The annuity rate also usually reflects commission payable to an adviser. However, the commission may be rebated if you instead pay an adviser by fee. See Chapter 2 for more information on how to pay for advice.

Useful for

- Providing you with income either for life or a set period.
- Using in conjunction with other investments. For example, temporary annuities provide a stream of regular payments that can be used to pay the premiums for a life insurance policy.

Providers

Insurance companies.

Choosing and buying

Different providers offer different rates and specialise in different types of business, so it is important to shop around. An independent financial adviser (see Chapter 2) can help you do this. Alternatively, check out the comparative tables published in the personal finance pages of newspapers and by organisations such as Moneyfacts. Bear in mind the limitations of comparison websites (see p8) and use two or three sites rather than relying on just one.

Once you have decided on the provider, approach the company directly or get your adviser to sort out the paperwork. Payments should be made directly to the annuity provider not the adviser.

Pitfalls and what to watch out for

- Make sure you understand that you cannot get your capital back as a lump sum. So, once you have invested, there is no going back.
- The more options you build into your annuity, the lower the income you get. For example, if you want a capital-protected annuity, your income will be lower than from an annuity with no capital protection. If you want an escalating annuity, the starting income will be much lower than for a level annuity.
- Do not buy without shopping around. The difference between the best and worst rates on offer is significant and the choice you make at the outset will permanently affect your future income.

Gilts (British Government stocks)

How they work

These investments typically offer you an income plus a capital gain or loss. They are loans to the Government at a fixed interest rate and mostly for a fixed term, but you do not have to keep the loan until the Government pays you back. Instead, you can sell it on the stock market. You invest either by buying directly from the Government when the gilts are first issued or through the stock market. There is a wide choice of different gilts with different terms and interest rates. The return from gilts is usually modest, reflecting the fact that gilts are deemed to be very safe investments because the UK Government is considered unlikely to default on its debts.

The interest from gilts is taxable but usually paid without any tax deducted (though you can opt to have tax at the basic rate already deducted). Any capital gain you make is tax-free. Taxable income and gains must be declared either through your tax return or PAYE coding review form (see Chapter 8).

What they cost

At any time, the stock market price at which you can buy a gilt is slightly higher than the price at which you can sell. This **'spread'** is, in effect, a cost you pay.

In addition, you pay dealing charges when you buy and sell gilts that have already been issued. There are no dealing charges if you buy directly from the Government when a gilt is newly issued. Dealing charges vary.

Example of dealing costs when you buy or sell gilts[4]

You trade this amount of gilts:	Commission	Minimum charge	Examples
You buy up to £5,000	0.7%	£12.50	Buy £500 of gilts, pay £12.50. Buy £3,000, pay £21.
You sell up to £5,000	0.7%	None	Sell £500, pay £3.50. Sell £3,000, pay £21.
You buy or sell more than £5,000	£35 plus 0.375% of excess over £5,000	£35	Buy or sell £6,000, pay £38.75.

Useful for

- Providing you with income if they pay a high rate of interest.
- Spreading risk. By investing some of your money in gilts, you can balance them against higher risk investments (such as shares) and so reduce the overall risk of your total investment portfolio.
- Gilts that pay a low rate of interest can be used to invest for a tax-free gain.

Providers

Gilts are issued by the UK Debt Management Office (DMO – see Appendix 2). You can buy and sell gilts through a stockbroker or through the DMO. The latter is likely to be cheaper if you are buying and selling small amounts.

Choosing and buying

Gilt prices and returns are published daily in some newspapers, such as *The Financial Times* and *The Times*. They are also available on many websites, including that of the DMO (see Appendix 2).

Which gilts you choose depends on your financial aims. For example, if you are looking for income, consider gilts that pay high interest. If you want to spread your money across a range of different gilts, you might do better to look at unit trusts instead (see p104).

Pitfalls and what to watch out for

- If you buy a gilt and hold it for its full term, you know at the time you invest exactly what return you will get – your return is fixed and guaranteed. If you have to sell before then, you do not know in advance at what price you will be able to sell and so your return is no longer fixed.
- Typically, if you choose gilts paying high interest, you will make a capital loss if you hold them for the full term or sell before then. In effect, you are swapping some of your capital for an income.
- Inflation reduces the buying power of the income from and capital invested in conventional gilts. However, you can buy index-linked gilts. With these, both the interest you get and the amount that is paid back at the end of the term are increased in line with inflation.

Corporate bonds

What they are and how they work

A corporate bond is a loan to a company. Instead of keeping the loan until it is repaid, you can sell it on the stock market. While you hold the bond, you usually receive interest and this is normally at a fixed rate, but there are many variations.

Corporate bonds are similar to gilts except you are lending to a company not the Government. Unfortunately, companies sometimes default and fail to repay their debts, so corporate bonds are not as safe as gilts. This should be reflected in the return, so you would expect a corporate bond to offer a higher rate of return than a similar gilt. Rating agencies code companies according to how risky they seem to be. The companies that are deemed to be the safest are given scores like 'AAA'. But even some very solid, well-established companies (like Barings Bank and, more recently Bradford and Bingley) have defaulted in the past.

The interest from corporate bonds is taxable but paid without any tax already deducted. Gains from most bonds quoted on UK stock markets are tax-free.

What they cost

At any time, the stock market price at which you can buy a corporate bond is higher than the price at which you can sell. This **'spread'** is, in effect, a cost you pay.

In addition, you pay dealing charges when you buy and sell bonds that have already been issued. These are similar to the charges for gilts (see p98) but vary from one firm to another.

Useful for

- Bonds paying higher interest are useful for providing you with income.
- Spreading risk. By investing some of your money in bonds, you can balance them against higher-risk investments (such as shares) and so reduce the overall risk of your total investment portfolio.
- Bonds paying low or no interest can be used to invest for a tax-free gain.

Providers

You buy and sell corporate bonds through a stockbroker.

Choosing and buying

Corporate bond prices and returns are published daily in some newspapers, such as *The Financial Times*. They are also available on websites, particularly those of stockbrokers.

Which bonds you choose depends on your financial aims. For example, if you are looking for income, consider bonds with a high interest rate. If you want to spread your money across a range of different bonds, you might do better to look at unit trusts instead (see p104).

Pitfalls and what to watch out for

- You may be tempted to buy bonds offering seemingly high returns, but, in general, the higher the return the greater the risk that the company might default and that you might lose money.
- If you are looking at variations, make sure you understand the risks involved. For example, convertible bonds give you the option to exchange your bonds for shares in the company and often behave more like shares (which are more risky) than bonds. 'Junk bonds' typically pay no interest at all and you hope to make a large capital gain by buying cheaply and selling them on for more, but the risk of default is high.
- If you buy a conventional corporate bond and hold it to redemption, you know at the time you invest exactly what return you will get. If you have to sell before redemption, however, you do not know in advance at what price you will be able to sell and so your return is no longer fixed.
- Typically, if a bond offers a high rate of interest, you will make a capital loss when the bond is repaid or you sell. In effect, you are swapping some of your capital for an income.

Shares (also called 'equities')

What they are and how they work

When you hold shares in a company, you are a part-owner of the company along with all the other shareholders. You do not have to be an owner permanently because you can sell your shares to someone else. Finding a buyer is easy if, as is the case with all public companies, the shares are quoted on a stock exchange.

A stock exchange is a permanent marketplace where shares are traded every working day. You do not usually deal directly with the market, but instead place your order with a stockbroker. The price at which a company's shares are bought and sold in the market place moves up and down according to the number of people wanting to buy and sell. So, if there are lots of buyers and not many sellers, the share price will tend to rise. But if there are lots of sellers and few buyers, the price will tend to fall.

The return you get from holding shares depends on how the company's fortunes fare and comes in two forms.

- **Dividends.** You share in the profits the company makes if it pays out an income in the form of dividends, usually paid at six-monthly intervals. Not all companies pay dividends. if they do, with **'ordinary shares'** the amount paid generally varies from year to year. With **'preference shares'** the amount is fixed but paid in full only if the company has made enough profit.
- **Capital gain (or loss).** You generally also hope to make a capital gain from shares by eventually selling them at a higher price than that at which you bought them. If the price has fallen, you will make a loss.

There are all sorts of factors that affect a company's share price. If the company is expected to do well in the future, lots of people might want to invest, which tends to push up the share price. If the prospects for the economy look good, investors may want to buy shares in lots of different companies, so the stock market as a whole might rise. Looking at the last 100 years or so, over the long term (eg, 10 years or more), shares have tended to give investors a significantly better return than safer investments, such as savings accounts, gilts and corporate bonds. However, this has not been true over the last decade because of the severe crash in the stock market from 2007.

Over shorter periods, the shares can fall sharply, so it is important that you can leave your money invested in order to ride out dips in the stock market.

Individual share prices may fall, even when the stock market as a whole is doing well. If a company runs into trouble, its share price might never recover. If the company goes out of business, its assets have to be used to settle its debts and what is left – if anything – is shared out between the shareholders. There is often more than one type of share and the different types are treated differently when a company goes bankrupt. People who hold 'preference shares' get their money back before any other types of shareholders. People who hold 'ordinary shares' (the most common type of share) are last in line and so most likely to lose some or all of their money. At most, you stand to lose all the capital you invested in the shares, assuming the shares are **'fully paid'**. If they are **'partly paid'** you have been paying for the shares by instalment and you can be called on to pay any instalments that are still outstanding.

To guard against the risk of losing all your money if a company fails, spread your money across the shares of several different companies, preferably in different industries and sectors of the economy so that bad events in one area will not affect all your shares. To spread your risks even further, consider investing in the shares of companies in different countries so that you are not tied to the fortunes of a single economy.

Dividends are paid with tax at 10 per cent already deducted. Only higher rate taxpayers have any extra tax to pay. Non-taxpayers cannot reclaim the tax. Capital gains are taxable, but may be covered by your yearly tax-free allowance or other reliefs. See Chapter 8 for details. Capital gains are tax-free and higher rate taxpayers have no further tax to pay if the shares are held through an individual savings account (ISA) (see p77).

What they cost

At any time, the stock market price at which you can buy a company's shares is higher than the price at which you can sell. This 'spread' is, in effect, a cost you pay. The spread is small for the shares of big, popular, well-established companies, such as Barclays, Boots, Tesco and Vodafone, but it can be large for the shares of small or unpopular companies.

In addition, you pay dealing charges when you buy and sell shares. These vary from stockbroker to stockbroker but, typically, you might pay around 1.5 per cent of the value of the shares for a deal up to, say, £7,000. The cheapest dealing charges tend to be from online brokers or postal dealing services and might be just a flat fee of around £10 to £15. Alternatively you may have to pay a flat monthly or quarterly fee with perhaps one or two free trades per charging period. Dealing charges are higher if you opt for a service which includes advice from your broker (see Chapter 2).

When you buy shares (but not when you sell), you must also pay stamp duty at 0.5 per cent of the value of the shares. On sales and purchases over £10,000, you might also be charged a small 'PTM levy' or 'compliance charge' that goes towards the cost of the Panel on Takeovers and Mergers (PTM), which regulates share dealings. If you hold shares through an ISA, there may be extra charges for the ISA.

Although you can hold your shares directly yourself, it is generally more convenient to hold them through a **'nominee account'**. This means a broker holds the shares on your behalf, collects the dividends and passes them on to you, and deals with the general administration of the shares. Depending on the terms of your contract with the provider of the nominee account, you may lose some shareholder rights – eg, to vote, attend annual meetings, receive shareholder incentives and/or the option to have dividends automatically used to purchase more shares. When you come to sell the shares, this is done directly from the nominee account within the normal settlement period allowed (three working days). By contrast, if you hold your shares directly, you will need to post your share certificate or deliver it in person, which usually takes longer than three days and you normally have to pay extra for this non-standard service. Some brokers charge you for using their nominee account, so you must check the charges and weigh them up against the advantages of the nominee account.

Useful for
- Capital growth over the long term (eg, 10 years or more). Because companies as a whole generate economic growth, buying their shares lets you participate in the increasing wealth of a nation over time.
- Income, if you choose shares that pay relatively high and steady dividends – eg, shares in gas, electricity and water companies, shares in well-established firms, most preference shares.
- Gambling, if you choose shares in new or growing companies. If your hunch is right and the company gets established, you could make a hefty gain. If you are wrong, you could lose all your money.

Providers
Buy and sell through a stockbroker.

Choosing and buying
Share prices and other information are published daily in many newspapers. They are also available on websites, particularly those of stockbrokers.

Which shares you choose depends on your financial aims (see above). If you need help choosing, get advice from a stockbroker or an independent financial adviser (see Chapter 2). If you want to spread your money across a range of different shares, you might do better to look at unit trusts or investment trusts instead (see p104).

Pitfalls and what to watch out for
- Shares are not suitable if you can invest only for the short term (fewer than five years) or you will need your money back at short notice. Medium-term investors (five to ten years) should be cautious about investing in shares since, following a sharp fall in the stock market, it may take many years for share prices to recover fully.
- Shares are risk investments, so you could lose some or all of your money. However, there are steps you can take to reduce the risks – eg, spread your money across the shares of several companies, invest only part of your money in shares and the rest in cash, bonds and property (see p75).

- If you are investing for income, bear in mind that with most shares dividends are not guaranteed and may fall or be missed altogether.
- Dealing charges make buying and selling shares expensive, especially if you are trading fairly small amounts. If you want a spread of different shares and have less than around £20,000 to invest, unit trusts (see below) and investment trusts (see p108) will normally be a more cost-effective choice.
- Owning shares can be complicated. Companies get taken over, offer investors new shares, split or consolidate their existing shares, and so on. You may be called upon to make some complicated decisions. To avoid this, consider unit trusts instead (see below).
- Because capital gains from shares are taxable (and you can claim tax relief for losses), you need to keep a detailed record of your share purchases, sales, takeovers, and so on over the years so that you can work out any eventual tax bill. You can avoid this task if you hold your shares through an ISA (see p77).

Unit trusts and open-ended investment companies

What they are and how they work

A unit trust is a professionally managed fund invested in a large spread of different shares, bonds and/or other investments, depending on the type of unit trust you choose. An open-ended investment company is essentially the same as a unit trust but structured in a slightly different way. By investing in a unit trust, you automatically have a stake in a ready-made investment portfolio.

The fund is notionally divided into units and you invest by buying units. The overall size of the fund varies because, as more investors join, new units are created and more investments added to the fund. As investors leave, units may be cancelled and investments in the fund sold.

There are several advantages to choosing a unit trust.

- **Cost**. This is a lower-cost way of having a spread of different companies' shares and/or other investments than holding the shares directly.
- **Administration**. You do not have the complications of buying, selling and holding shares directly – eg, finding a stockbroker and dealing with takeover bids.
- **Investment decisions**. A professional manager deals with all the details about which shares or other investments to hold and when to buy and sell them. You just have to choose a unit trust that meets your financial aims.

For most small investors (and certainly those with less than £20,000 to invest), unit trusts or similar investments such as investment trusts (see p108) will be a cheaper, more convenient way to invest in the stock market for the long term.

The return you get from a unit trust may be in two forms.

- **Income (called 'distributions')**. This is usually paid out or credited to your holding at six-monthly intervals.

- **Capital gain (or loss).** You make a gain if you can sell your units at a higher price than you paid for them. If the unit price falls, you make a loss. The price of the units directly reflects the value of the investments in the fund.

Some trusts specialise in producing income, others in giving you growth. Different unit trusts invest in different sorts of investments and offer different combinations of risk and return. In general, the more specialist the underlying investment fund, the greater the risk.

Examples of different unit trusts

Type	How it is invested	Level of risk
UK gilts	At least 90 per cent in gilts.	Least risky
Cautiously managed	Range of assets. No more than 60 per cent in shares. At least 50 per cent in UK or European assets.	
UK equity and bond income	Between 20 per cent and 80 per cent in UK gilts and corporate bonds. Between 20 per cent and 80 per cent in UK shares. Maximum 20 per cent in non-UK assets.	
UK all companies	At least 80 per cent in UK shares.	
Far East, including Japan	At least 80 per cent in Far Eastern shares, of which no more than 80 per cent is in Japanese shares.	Most risky

Capital gains are taxable, but may be covered by your yearly tax-free allowance or other reliefs.

Distributions from unit trusts investing in shares are paid or credited with tax at 10 per cent already deducted. Only higher rate taxpayers have any extra tax to pay. Non-taxpayers cannot reclaim the tax. Capital gains are tax-free and higher rate taxpayers have no further tax to pay if the shares are held through an ISA (see p77).

Distributions from unit trusts investing mainly or completely in gilts and/or corporate bonds are paid or credited with tax at the basic rate already deducted. Higher rate taxpayers have extra to pay. Starting-rate taxpayers and non-taxpayers can reclaim some or all of the tax deducted. Distributions and gains are tax-free if you invest through an ISA (see p77). See Chapter 8 for more information about tax.

What they cost

Unlike direct investment in shares, gilts and corporate bonds, there are no dealing costs when you buy and sell units. However, there are various charges built into the investment itself.

- **Front-end charge (also called an 'initial charge')**. Typically, this might be up to 5 per cent of the money you invest. However, some unit trusts have no charge but may instead make an exit charge (see below). The front-end charge is reduced or waived if you buy through a 'discount broker' or 'fund supermarket' (see p107).

- **Bid-offer spread**. At any time, the offer price at which you can buy a unit is usually higher than the bid price you could get by selling. The difference is called the spread. It often incorporates the front-end charge but may also account for another 1 or 2 per cent more of the amount you are investing. Some unit trusts and all open-ended investment companies do not have a spread and are called 'single-priced'.

- **Annual charge**. This is the amount the manager takes for running the fund and is typically up to 1.5 per cent a year of the value of your investments. In 2009, some **tracker funds** (see p108) with much lower charges of around 0.15 per cent a year were launched and this may encourage other funds to cut their charges.

- **Fund expenses**. These are seldom explicit, but they reflect the value of the investments in the fund, and therefore your units, after deducting costs such as dealing charges when investments in the fund are bought and sold and payments to custodians who keep the investments safe. Look out for a measure called the 'total expense ratio' (TER) which combines the annual charge and some of these fund expenses (but not dealing costs). The TER for most trusts is between 1 and 2 per cent a year of the value of your investment.

- **Exit charge**. With some unit trusts – particularly those where there is no front-end charge – there is a deduction from the money you get back if you sell within, for instance, five years.

Useful for

- Convenient way to invest in stock market investments, such as bonds and shares, without the complications of holding such investments directly.
- In particular, it is often much easier to invest overseas via a unit trust than directly.
- Capital growth over the medium to long term (five or 10 years or more). Medium-term investors (less than 10 years) should be cautious about investing in share-based unit trusts.

- Income if you choose units that pay out distributions ('distribution units') rather than those which automatically reinvest them ('accumulation units'). Some unit trusts specialise in providing a high level of income. These include many unit trusts investing in gilts and/or bonds, as well as some share-based trusts.
- Spreading risk. For example, share-based unit trusts give you a stake in a ready-made portfolio, typically of 100 or so different companies. Some unit trusts give you a mix of different assets by investing in, for instance, shares and bonds. You can spread risks further by investing in a selection of different trusts.

Providers

Unit trust management companies, agents tied to a management company (eg, some banks and building societies), discount brokers, fund supermarkets and financial advisers (see Chapter 2).

Choosing and buying

Unit trust prices and other information are published in some daily newspapers such as *The Financial Times* and *Daily Telegraph*. Information is also available from the Investment Management Association and many websites (see Appendix 2). The Financial Services Authority publishes tables comparing unit trust ISAs.

If you have already decided on a particular unit trust, you can buy units directly from the unit trust management company or a firm acting as its tied agent, although buying through a discount broker or fund supermarket will normally be cheaper. A few unit trust management companies offer share exchange schemes where you can swap your direct holdings of companies' shares (eg, shares you acquired through a privatisation or a building society demutualisation) for units in the unit trust.

A fund supermarket is a website where you can pick and choose from a wide range of unit trusts and buy at knock-down prices (because the front-end charge is usually slashed or waived altogether). Discount brokers are similar but often operate by phone or post as well as the internet.

If you are not sure which trusts to choose, buy through an independent financial adviser who can also help you make your decision (see Chapter 2).

You can invest either in lump sums or through regular savings. The minimum investment is usually around £25 or £50 a month or lump sums starting at £250 or £500.

Pitfalls and what to watch out for

- Unit trusts are stock market-linked investments. Their value can go down as well as up, so you might lose some of your capital.
- Different unit trusts offer different combinations of risk and return. Make sure you understand the risks involved. For example, where a unit trust invests in

shares quoted on a foreign stock exchange, there is usually the added risk of exchange rate movements (though some fund managers use special techniques to remove this risk).

- If you invest for a high income, there is usually less scope for the value of your units to grow and they may even fall in value. So you will be sacrificing some of your capital in exchange for income.
- With trusts investing in gilts and bonds, the value of your capital can go up and down. You do not invest for a fixed return as you would if you invested directly and held the gilt or bond until redemption.
- Charges vary greatly from one trust to another and according to the route by which you buy. Bear in mind that a trust with high charges will have to work harder than a low-charging trust to give you the same return. Ask yourself what (if any) extra benefits you are getting if you pay higher charges.
- Do not be seduced by past performance. There is no evidence that a trust which has performed well in the past will continue to do so in the future. However, there is some evidence to suggest that a trust which has performed badly in the past might continue to do badly, so you might want to avoid the worst performers.

Active v passive

An actively managed investment fund is one where the fund manager selects the shares (or other investments) that make up the fund and decides the best time to buy and sell. Often the fund manager is trying to beat the stock market as measured by an index, such as the FTSE 100. In **absolute return funds**, the manager is trying to achieve at least a set target return (regardless of what happens to the stock market). Generally, charges are higher for active funds because you are paying for the work done by the fund manager and also usually for frequent buying and selling of the investments in the fund.

The alternative is a passive investment fund, also called a **tracker fund** or **index fund**. The fund is set up to mimic the performance of a stock market as measured by an index (or sometimes some other index – eg, to reflect the performance of the art market). Because the manager is not trading often or doing lots of research to find winners, the charges for these funds tend to be much lower. The cheapest are often exchange traded funds which are similar to unit trusts, but you buy and sell shares in them on the stock market.

Investment trusts

What they are and how they work

Like unit trusts (see p104), investment trusts give you a stake in a ready-made portfolio of shares and/or other investments and there is a wide choice of different investment funds. However, the structure of investment trusts is different.

An investment trust is itself a company quoted on a stock exchange and you invest by buying shares in the investment trust company. The number and type of shares is generally fixed when the investment trust company is first launched. This means that, although the value of your shares is heavily influenced by the value of the investments in the underlying fund, it is also affected by demand for and supply of the investment trust shares themselves.

The value of the investment fund divided by the number of investment trust shares is called the 'net asset value' per share. It is common for the price of a trust's shares to be lower than the net asset value (in which case the shares are said to be trading at a discount). You might think that makes the shares look like a bargain, but there is no guarantee that the discount will disappear in future. Equally, if the shares are priced above the net asset value (ie, trading at a premium), they are not necessarily expensive and the premium will not necessarily disappear in future.

An investment trust investing in a particular type of investment fund is generally more risky than a comparable unit trust because, unlike a unit trust, the investment trust can borrow money to invest in its fund. The ability to borrow magnifies both gains and losses – an effect called '**gearing**'.

Gearing was a problem for some investment trusts during the stock market crash between 2000 and 2003 because it exacerbated their losses. Investment trusts had a bad press a few years ago because some had been investing in each other's shares, creating a vicious cycle where as one trust's shares fell in value, they dragged down the value of other trust's shares and so on. However, not all investment trusts were affected and many remain sound investments. Before you invest, check the level of risk carefully since this will vary from one investment trust to another. The greater the level of borrowing and the greater the extent to which a trust invests in the shares of other trusts, the higher the risk.

The choice of investment funds available through investment trusts is similar to the range of unit trusts available – see p105 for some examples. The return you get may be:

- **income in the form of dividends**. These are the same as for any other type of share (see p101);
- **capital gain (or loss)**. You make a gain if you can sell the shares at a higher price than you paid. But if the share price has fallen, you make a loss.

Some investment trusts ('**split capital trusts**') offer different types of share to suit different investors. '**Income shares**' receive dividends but little or no capital growth. Holders of '**capital shares**' receive the bulk of any capital growth when the trust is wound up on a pre-set date.

Income and gains from investment trusts are taxed in the same way as other shares (see p101).

Real estate investment trusts and property authorised investment funds
Real estate investment trusts are a special type of investment trust that invests in a portfolio of commercial and/or residential property. Unlike other investment trusts, the

company running the portfolio does not pay any tax on income and gains from properties held in it.

Property authorised investment funds are very similar except they are unit trusts. Tax is deducted only once the income and gains are paid out to you and depends on your personal tax situation. You receive income in the form of property income distributions from which tax at the basic rate (20 per cent in 2009/10) has been deducted. If you are a non-taxpayer or starting-rate taxpayer, you can claim back all or part of this tax. If you are a higher rate taxpayer, you have extra to pay. Distributions and gains are tax-free if you invest through an ISA (see p77) or a pension scheme (see Chapter 6). See Chapter 8 for more information about tax.

What they cost

The costs are like those for shares (see p102). However, you may also be able to buy directly from the investment trust management company, in which case dealing charges may be lower because the company can pool your purchase with that of other investors and so get a discount for buying in bulk.

Some investment trust management companies also offer share exchange schemes where you can swap your direct holdings of companies' shares (eg, shares you acquired through a privatisation or a building society demutualisation) for shares in the investment trust.

Useful for

- Convenient way to invest in stock market investments, such as bonds and shares, without the complications of holding such investments directly.
- In particular, it is often much easier to invest overseas via an investment trust than directly.
- Capital growth over the long term (10 years or more).
- Income if you choose income shares.
- Spreading risk. An investment trust may give you a stake in a ready-made portfolio of, say, 100 or so different companies. You can spread risks further by investing in a selection of different trusts.

Providers

Investment trust management companies, stockbrokers, a few fund supermarkets and financial advisers (see Chapter 2).

Choosing and buying

Investment trust prices and other information are published in the share price section of some daily newspapers such as *The Financial Times* and *The Times*. Information is also available from the Association of Investment Companies and many websites (see Appendix 2).

If you have already decided on a particular investment trust, you can buy shares directly from the management company or through a stockbroker.

If you are not sure which trusts to choose, get advice from a stockbroker or independent financial adviser (see Chapter 2).

As with other shares, you usually invest a lump sum and dealing charges can make small sums uneconomic. However, most management companies operate regular savings schemes, letting you economically invest as little as around £25 a month and *ad hoc* lump sums as small as £250.

Pitfalls and what to watch out for

- Investment trusts are stock market investments. Their value can go down as well as up, so you might lose some of your capital.
- Different investment trusts offer different combinations of risk and return. Make sure you understand the risks involved. Assessing risk can be difficult, so consider getting financial advice (see Chapter 2).
- Do not be seduced by past performance. There is no evidence that a trust which has performed well in the past will continue to do so in the future. However, there is some evidence to suggest that a trust which has performed badly in the past might continue to do badly, so you might want to avoid the worst performers.

Investment-type life insurance

What it is and how it works

Like unit and investment trusts, investment-type life insurance offers you a stake in a ready-made portfolio of shares and/or other investments, but this time within the wrapper of a life insurance policy.

Using a life policy offers two main advantages over unit or investment trusts.

- With a unit-linked policy, you can easily, and often cheaply, switch from one investment fund to another within the policy. By contrast, switching unit trusts may involve selling one trust and buying another with all the various charges and administration involved. However, some unit trusts and many open-ended investment companies are structured so that you can easily switch between funds.
- With a with-profits policy, you get a spread of different assets and to some extent you are insulated from the impact of falls in the stock market (but not necessarily from a large or prolonged fall). There is no other investment that gives you quite the same features. The return you get is largely based on the performance of an underlying fund of investments. The fund hopefully grows and some of that growth is paid out or credited to you and the other investors in the form of bonuses (called 'reversionary bonuses' or 'annual bonuses'). The rest of the growth is kept in reserve for periods when the fund performs badly. You are not guaranteed to get annual bonuses and the amounts vary from year to year. In general, provided you keep the investment until it matures, once an

annual bonus has been added to your investment, you keep it. If you cash in the investment early, a special charge might be deducted from what you get back. This is called a 'market value reduction' (MVR) or 'market value adjustment' (MVA) and it takes back some of the annual bonuses you have already had. When your investment matures, you get a 'terminal bonus' which can be a large part (up to, for instance, half) of your total return from the investment. The terminal bonus is based on the growth of the fund over the time you held the investment that was held in reserve rather than being paid out. If the fund has a run of bad years, the terminal bonus will be reduced. You are not guaranteed to get a terminal bonus and the amount that investors get can be very different from one year to the next.

However, the way investment-type life insurance is taxed (see below) is a drawback for most investors. Other drawbacks are high charges (see p113), inflexibility and complexity. Many policies commit you to a set term or to saving regularly and, if you cash in, stop or miss payments, charges often reduce your return. The structure of these investments is often complicated so that it is hard to understand how they work, the risks involved or the full impact charges might have.

You invest by paying regular premiums or a single premium into the life policy. Part of your premium may be used to buy life cover (ie, to pay out at least a minimum sum if you die) but often the life cover is just a token amount. The bulk of your money is invested either on a with-profits or unit-linked basis (see p111).

You get your money back either when the policy matures or if you cash it in. Many policies give you a very poor return if you cash them in during the early years. There are two main types of policy.

- **Endowment policy.** This is designed to run for a set period (called the 'endowment period') – often, at least 10 years. This is the type of policy you may have taken out to pay off a mortgage (see Chapter 5). At the end of the period, the policy matures and pays out a lump sum. The size of the lump sum depends on investment performance over the endowment period.
- **Whole life policy.** In theory, this is set up to run for your whole life. However, it builds up a cash-in value and some policies are designed as bonds to be cashed in after a minimum period of, for instance, five years.

Investment-type life insurance comes in many different forms. Some policies are for regular saving, some are for lump-sum investment. Some aim to build up a nest egg, others to pay out an income.

The taxation of life insurance policies is complicated and poorly understood. Often there is no tax for you personally to pay on the proceeds from a policy, but this does not make the return tax-free. In most cases, you pay no tax because the insurance company has already paid tax on both income and gains made by your invested money. The company will usually have paid tax at higher rates than you personally would have paid and you cannot claim back any of the tax already deducted. Only two types of life policy offer tax advantages: insurance policies held through ISAs (see p77) and those held through certain types of friendly society plan (see below). For details of how life insurance policies are taxed, see Chapter 8.

Tax-efficient friendly society plans

Friendly societies are mutual organisations that offer life insurance products that, in the main, are the same as those offered by life companies. However, friendly societies may also offer tax-efficient plans.

These are usually set up as regular savings endowment policies lasting at least 10 years. The maximum you invest is limited (to £25 a month or £250 a year in 2009/10). Your money is invested on either a with-profits or unit-linked basis (see p111) and builds up tax-free, except that any dividends or similar share-based income added to your fund has had 10 per cent tax deducted, which cannot be reclaimed. This favourable tax treatment is basically the same as the way ISAs and child trust funds are taxed.

However, when choosing a plan, check the charges carefully. Because the maximum you can invest is fairly low, any flat-rate charges reduce heavily your return.

What it costs

Charges vary from one policy to another but typically if you invest on a unit-linked basis you may have to pay:

- **administration charge/policy fee**. Deducted from your premiums before the remainder is invested;
- **unit allocation**. The percentage of your remaining premium that will be used to buy units. This might be 95 per cent, meaning £95 out of every £100 is invested. Do not be too impressed by allocation rates over 100 per cent. If you pay a premium of £100, deduct a policy fee of £5 and then have a 102 per cent allocation, this means 102 per cent x £95 (£96.90) is invested;
- **capital units**. Some of your premium might be used to buy these. Their only distinction is that they have a higher than normal annual management fee, so are just an obscure way of charging you extra;
- **bid-offer spread**. At any time, the price at which you buy units is higher than the price at which you can sell them back. This is, in effect, another charge;
- **annual management fee**. Usually around 1 per cent a year of the value of your investment;
- **other fund charges**. Other charges (eg, dealing charges for buying and selling investments in the fund) are deducted from the value of the investments in the fund and so are hidden charges;
- **surrender charges**. If you cash in your policy before maturity, often an extra charge will be levied.

If you have invested on a with-profits basis, a policy fee is usually deducted and there are likely to be surrender charges. The other costs are not explicit but help to determine the level of bonuses you get.

Useful for

- Capital growth if you choose a policy designed for growth, but generally, unless you are a higher rate taxpayer, you could invest in a similar but more tax-efficient way by choosing, say, unit trusts.
- Income, if you are currently a higher rate taxpayer. Many life policies have a special feature that allows you to take an income now but put off any tax bill until the policy eventually matures. See Chapter 8 for details.
- Reducing risk, if you invest on a with-profits basis. Although your return is still linked to the stock market, the smoothing of returns may help to protect you from falls in the market.
- Regular saving, if you need some discipline to make you stick to your intentions. But life policies are generally not tax-efficient unless you are a higher rate taxpayer, so consider instead a regular savings account (see p90), unit trust savings scheme (p104) or investment trust savings scheme (see p108).

Providers

Life insurance companies and their tied agents (eg, many banks and building societies) and financial advisers (see Chapter 2).

Choosing and buying

Information about the investment funds underlying unit-linked policies is published in the managed funds section of some daily newspapers such as *The Financial Times* and in specialist magazines such as *Money Management*. Information is also available on some websites (see Appendix 2).

If you have already decided on a particular life company, you can invest direct with that company or through its tied agent. If you are not sure which to choose, get advice from an independent financial adviser (see Chapter 2).

Pitfalls and what to watch out for

- The return on insurance policies is linked to the stock market, so you could lose some of your capital.
- Be aware that policies designed to provide an income are not as safe as bank and building society income accounts (see p89). With life policies, whether or not you get all of your capital back depends on stock market performance.
- These products are often complicated. Before you invest, make sure you understand how they work, what risks are involved and when these risks might materialise.

- Insurance salespeople, tied agents and independent financial advisers are usually paid a fairly generous commission by the life company when they sell you these policies. Be aware that this might influence the salesperson or adviser to recommend a policy when possibly other investments would suit you better.
- Be aware that with most policies the company has already paid tax that you cannot claim back. Unless you are a higher rate taxpayer, you can usually get a more tax-efficient return from other competing investments, such as unit trusts.
- Be aware that, with some policies, if they mature after you reach age 65 you might lose 'age allowance', which would push up your tax bill for the year (see Chapter 8).

Structured products

These let you share in the higher returns the stock market tends to offer but aim to reduce the risk of losing your capital. Many are called guaranteed equity bonds, guaranteed income bonds or guaranteed growth bonds. Only the savings-based guaranteed equity bonds described on p92 give you a reasonably firm guarantee that you will not lose any capital at all. Other guaranteed equity investments are more complicated and give you a degree of protection but no guarantees. There are basically two types.

Unit trust protected funds. These are a type of unit trust (see p104). Typically, your investment is divided into three-month periods and you choose a level of capital protection. With a '100 per cent fund', at the end of each three months you get back at least the amount you had invested at the start, plus a proportion of any increase in a stock market index. With, for example, a '95 per cent fund', you are guaranteed to get back only at least 95 per cent of your starting capital but you get a bigger proportion of any increase in the stock market index. You could lose heavily if the index fell – eg, if you invested £10,000 and the index fell heavily for two quarters in a row, you might get back only 95% x 95% x £10,000 = £9,025 (a fall of 9.75 per cent over six months).

Life insurance guaranteed equity investments. These are investment-type life insurance policies (see p111) set up as bonds with a fixed term of, say, five years. You can get your money back earlier but surrender charges then reduce your capital. Provided you invest for the full term, you aim to get your capital back in full, plus any increase in the value of an underlying investment fund or a stock market index to which the bond is linked. But with many of these bonds, full return of your capital is guaranteed only if the stock market index does not fall by more than a certain amount (eg, 25 per cent) over the term. If the index falls by more, your capital shrinks dramatically in line with the drop in the index.

Ethical and Shariah-compliant investing

If you invest directly in shares or bonds, you can choose which companies to support with your money. But if you invest through a professionally managed fund – as you do when you choose unit trusts, open-ended investment companies, investment trusts, investment-type life insurance or pension plans – you have placed the choice in the hands of the fund manager. It is possible that your money might be used to buy the shares of companies involved in, say, the arms trade or tobacco industry, or with a poor human rights record. If you want to avoid this, you can. There are now a wide range of funds available that invest your money on an ethical basis.

The basis used varies from one fund to another. Some use negative criteria to screen out unsuitable companies. Others use positive criteria to seek out companies that actively improve society or protect the environment. Some funds use both criteria.

Many listings of unit trusts, investment trusts and managed funds now include a section headed 'ethical investing'. You can find out about the ethical policies pursued by contacting the management company concerned and from the Ethical Investment Research Services.

For information about funds which comply with Islamic law, contact the Institute of Islamic Banking and Insurance (see Appendix 2).

6. **Regulation and complaints**

All organisations involved in offering savings and investments in the UK must, by law, be authorised by the Financial Services Authority (FSA). Provided you deal only with authorised firms, you are protected in certain ways – the firm should be solvent and honestly run, you should have access to proper complaints procedures and, if the worst happens, you may be eligible for compensation. You can see whether a firm is authorised by checking the FSA Register (see Appendix 2).

The FSA also lays down detailed rules governing how investment firms deal with their customers. For example, you have a right to know who you are dealing with, what type of service they can give you, and a right to clear information about products in a set format that helps you compare one product with another. These rules apply to the investment business of all types of firms, including, for example, banks and building societies.

For details about the FSA rules and how they protect you, see Chapter 10.

In the past, the FSA has not had rules on how savings providers deal with customers. Most banks, building societies and National Savings and Investments agreed voluntarily to abide by a voluntary code of practice, the Banking Code. However, from 1 November 2009, the Banking Code was replaced by FSA rules. These set out, for example, the requirement that you receive adequate and timely information about the products in which you are interested.

If you have a complaint about a savings or investments product or advice you were given, complain first to the firm concerned. If it does not deal with your complaint satisfactorily or does not respond within a reasonable time, you can take your case to the Financial Ombudsman Service (see Chapter 10).

If a savings or investment firm goes out of business owing you money, you may be eligible for redress from the Financial Services Compensation Scheme (see Chapter 10).

Savings and investment scams

Be on alert for these common scams and do not get caught out.

Boiler rooms. You get a phone call out of the blue from a firm selling you shares, fine wine or other investments that promise superb returns. You invest and receive reports on how well your investments are doing. You will typically be persuaded to buy more. When you want to cash in your gains, the firm vanishes. Experienced investors are more often caught by this scam than novices. Be very wary of doing any business with a firm that cold calls you. Always check the FSA Register to make sure firms are authorised. Report scams to the FSA Moneymadeclear helpline or the police.

Pump and dump. Emails and chatrooms sing the praises of a genuine company, usually small and relatively unknown. More and more investors pile in pushing up the price. When it reaches a good height, the scammers, who planted the tips and rumours in the first place, pull their money out for a large profit. The share price tumbles leaving everyone else with a loss. Do not be taken in by tips from dubious sources especially about obscure companies.

Ponzi scheme. This is a type of pyramid scheme. The deal looks sound but money put in by later investors is used to pay a return to the early investors and provide a lavish lifestyle for the operator. Eventually the scheme collapses and all but the early investors lose their money. If a deal sounds too good to be true, avoid it. Make sure any firm you deal with is FSA-authorised.

Affinity fraud. A fraudster joins a church or club where people tend to know and trust each other. After a while, s/he passes on a great investment tip to members. The fraudster seems to have done well, so members gratefully take up the offer. The fraudster and the money vanish. Regardless of who gives you a tip or how well you think you know them, do not part with money without checking out any investment opportunity thoroughly and ensuring that you are dealing with an FSA-authorised firm.

Notes

1 Department for Work and Pensions,
   Family Resources Survey 2007/08, DWP,
   2009
2 Department for Work and Pensions,
   Family Resources Survey 2007/08, DWP,
   2009

3. Schemes to encourage saving and investing
3 This type of income was tax free before 6
   April 2004.

5. Types of investment
4 Debt Management Office, *Gilt Purchase
   and Sale Service*, www.dmo.gov.uk/
   index.aspx?page=Gilts/
   Retail_Brokerage, accessed 27
   September 2009

Chapter 5

Borrowing

This chapter covers:

Basic facts

- In April 2009, British people were borrowing £1.5 trillion (£1,459,200,000,000). Over £1.2 trillion of this was mortgages and other loans secured on their homes; £232 billion was credit card and other consumer credit debt.[1]
- The average household buying a home with a mortgage spends 29 per cent of its after-tax income on housing.[2]
- In 2007, 1.9 billion purchases were made using credit cards, with an average value of £63.22.[3]
- The number of people turning to individual voluntary arrangements in England and Wales was 39,116 in 2008 compared with a rate of 6,000 to 7,000 five years earlier.[4]

1. When to borrow

Motives for borrowing

There are three main reasons for borrowing.

- **To spend more than you otherwise could.** Especially if you are on a low income, you may feel you have no choice but to borrow to make ends meet, but be very wary of this course of action. It is not sustainable in the long run. If you are continually spending beyond your means, borrowing can get out of control and you may run into debt problems. If this happens, see p167 for steps you can take to get your finances back on track.

- **To bring forward spending** so that you can buy something now instead of having to wait. There are often good reasons for doing this – eg, to cope with a financial emergency such as urgent car repairs, or to take advantage of a special offer that will not be available for long. Another example is buying a home – borrowing to buy makes sense since you would have to pay for somewhere to live if you waited many years until you could afford to buy outright.

- **To boost your future income or wealth** – eg, by borrowing to buy a car to get to work or taking out a student loan that lets you invest in your own education or training so that, hopefully, you will have a higher income in the future. Similarly, you might borrow to start a business. You should always weigh up the risks carefully. Do not borrow to put money into high-risk investments or very risky business ventures – if you lose money on the investment or venture, you will still have the problem of repaying the loan.

Alternatives to borrowing

Saving

If you can wait, you could save up to buy later instead of borrowing to buy now. Unless you expect the price of the item to rise, the advantage of saving is that you will pay less for it because you avoid the interest and other charges involved in borrowing and you also earn interest on the amount you save. See the table on p66 for a comparison of saving versus borrowing.

Benefits and tax credits

Before borrowing to meet a financial crisis – eg, if your washing machine needs to be replaced, first check that you are claiming all the benefits for which you are eligible. In 2005/06, for example, it is estimated that up to 1.71 million pensioners were not claiming the pension credit to which they were entitled.[5] If you are already claiming certain benefits, see whether you can get a loan or grant from the social fund. See Chapter 9 for information about benefits and tax credits.

Selling

If you are determined to buy an item now, you may have other things you no longer use or could manage without that you could sell to raise the money you need.

Cut down

One obvious way to avoid borrowing is not to buy so much. This will not be an option if you are borrowing to meet basic needs – see p167 for suggestions on how to cope with problem debts.

Sustainable borrowing

The golden rule is to borrow only if you have a clear plan for repaying the loan.

- Work out a budget by looking at the income you have coming in and your expenses. Subtract the expenses from your income. Any amount left is the money you have available to repay any borrowing. If the amount is zero or less, you could:
  - create some extra income – eg, by taking on extra work;
  - trim your spending – eg, by cutting out luxuries and non-essential items;
  - decide not to borrow (see p120 for alternatives); *and*
  - (but this is not recommended) borrow, but run the risk of debt problems (see p167).
- When working out whether you can keep up the repayments, make an allowance for possible increases. For example, repayments might increase at any time if you have a variable rate loan, or they might rise later on if you have chosen a loan with an initial fixed-rate period or a low-start deal.
- If available, consider types of borrowing that are designed to give you a bit of leeway in making repayments. For example, with student loans, repayments start only when you earn at or above a minimum income, and a flexible mortgage can help you cope in the short term with crises such as losing a job.

Who should think about borrowing

Relationships

If you marry, form a civil partnership or start living with someone, you may want to borrow – eg, to buy a home or household items. It is important to be aware that, with joint loans, each of you is 'jointly and severally' liable for the whole debt. So, whatever any private agreement you have with your partner, if s/he does not keep up with the repayments, you will have to pay them instead. Be particularly wary of taking out loans secured against the family home – if you or your partner cannot keep up the repayments, you could lose your home.

If you relationship breaks down, as a top priority, cancel any joint credit cards and ask your bank to freeze any joint bank account to prevent your partner running up or increasing an overdraft. A joint home may need to be sold and any mortgage paid off. You may need a new mortgage to buy your own home. Newly separated or divorced people – women in particular – may experience difficulty obtaining financial products if previously their ex-partner dealt with the couple's financial affairs. As a result, you might have no credit history. See p134 for ways to deal with this. Nevertheless, a bank should still be willing to offer you a basic bank account (see Chapter 3). Fuel companies may insist that you either pay by direct debit or use a pre-payment meter. Having at least a basic bank account means you can choose the direct debit option, which will be cheaper.

Lone parents

Money may be especially tight when you are bringing up a family on your own, so it is particularly important to budget carefully and avoid debt problems. If you need money in a crisis and you are on state benefits, check if you are eligible for a loan from the social fund (see Chapter 9).

Students

Tuition fees

The system for financing students starting university changed radically from 2006 onwards. Under the new system, students usually have to pay tuition fees each year but can take out student loans to cover these. However, the precise arrangements depend on where you normally live and where you study.

If you normally live in **England or Northern Ireland**, wherever in the UK you study, you may be charged tuition fees. These can be up to £3,225 a year in 2009/10 in England, Wales and Northern Ireland, but less in Scotland. You can apply for a student loan to cover the full amount of your fees.

If you normally live in **Wales**, wherever in the UK you study, you may be charged tuition fees up to £3,225 a year (in 2009/10) and can apply for a student loan to cover the full amount of your fees. If you study in Wales, in 2009/10 you can get a non-repayable grant (£1,920 in 2009/10) towards your fees, which is available regardless of your family income and reduces the amount you need to borrow. However, the grant is being abolished for students starting courses from 2010/11 onwards and replaced with an extra student loan.

If you normally live in **Scotland** and you study in Scotland, you do not normally pay tuition fees. If you study elsewhere in the UK, you pay up to £3,225 a year (in 2009/10) and can take out a student loan to cover this.

Student grants, bursaries and scholarships

If your household income is low, you may qualify for a grant or bursary to help towards your living costs while at university. Once again, the precise arrangements depend on where you normally live.

If you normally live in **England**. You may qualify for a maintenance grant of up to £2,906 (in 2009/10). Each £1 of maintenance grant you get reduces by 50p the amount of maintenance loan you can have (see p123). So if you get the full grant of £2,906, the maximum loan you can have is reduced by £1,453. You can get the full maintenance grant if your household income is £25,000 or less and no grant if household income is £50,020 or more. In between these limits a reduced grant is paid;

If you normally live in **Northern Ireland**, you may qualify for a maintenance grant up to a maximum of £3,406 (in 2009/10) with the first £1,792 replacing the student loan. The grant is means tested and you will get the full amount only if your household income is £18,820 or less. If your household income is above

£40,238, you get no grant at all. If it is in between those limits, you get a reduced amount;

If you normally live in **Wales** and your household income is low, you may qualify for an Assembly learning grant of up to £2,906 in 2009/10. There are also bursaries for Welsh students studying in Wales which are means tested.

If you normally live in **Scotland**, you study in Scotland and your household income is low, you may qualify for a young students' bursary (up to £2,640 in 2009/10) which replaces part of any student loan (see below).

Other grants to help with living costs are available for students who are eligible for means-tested benefits, such as income support and housing benefit. Typically, you will be eligible if, for example, you are a lone parent, a student couple with children or if you are disabled and on a low income. You might also qualify for extra grants if, for example, you are caring for children. Individual universities and colleges usually also have a range of bursaries and scholarships for low-income students and others. These grants, bursaries and scholarships do not affect the amount of student loans you can get.

There are various schemes to encourage a supply of graduates to fill certain types of public sector job which you might qualify for if you are training to be a teacher, doctor, dentist, nurse, midwife or certain other health professional, or social worker.

For more information, see www.direct.gov.uk and the contact details in Appendix 2.

Student loans

You can apply for a student loan to cover the full amount of your tuition fees. In addition, you can apply for a student loan for maintenance (ie, to cover the cost of books, travel, accommodation, food, clothes, and so on). The amount of loan you can have depends on your household income and is reduced if you qualify for a maintenance grant. Parents are generally expected to make up any shortfall, but there is no compulsion to do so and it is now common for students to take part-time work to support themselves while studying.

Maximum student loans for maintenance in 2009/10

	England	Northern Ireland	Wales	Scotland
Studying in London	£6,928	£6,643	£6,648	£4,625
Studying elsewhere in the UK	£4,950	£4,745	£4,745	£4,625
Living at parent's home (London or elsewhere)	£3,838	£3,673	£3,673	£3,665

Note: you may get less than the maximum depending on your household income and whether you qualify for maintenance grants and bursaries. A reduced amount is available for your final year.

You only start to repay your student loans after you have finished your course. Repayments start once your income exceeds a set threshold (£15,000 a year since April 2005). You repay an amount equal to 9 per cent of your income over the threshold. Repayments are collected automatically by your employer through the PAYE system or through self-assessment if you are self-employed (see Chapter 8). Any amount left unpaid after 25 years is written off.

Interest on student loans is charged at a rate equal to inflation. This is usually much lower than the rate charged on other forms of borrowing.

Redundancy

If you receive a lump-sum redundancy payment, you could use some of this to repay part or all of your outstanding loans, in particular your mortgage. This could help substantially to cut your monthly expenses. Watch out for early redemption fees, however, which typically apply during the first five years of a mortgage. Bear in mind that, once a lump sum has been used to pay off a loan, it is gone. You might prefer to keep some capital to give yourself more flexibility to respond to new opportunities.

Older people

Many people find themselves 'asset rich, income poor' in older age. In particular, although your income might be low, you might own a valuable home. One way to improve your finances could be to move home, downsizing to somewhere less expensive and using the cash released to top up your income. If you do not want to move home, an equity release scheme (see p162) could be an option. However, be wary of equity release if you are eligible for means-tested state benefits, such as pension credit and council tax benefit (see Chapter 9). The cash or income you release could reduce the benefits you can claim, leaving you no better off, or even worse off. Get advice from your local Citizens Advice Bureau or housing advice centre before going ahead. See Appendix 2 for contact details.

2. **Overview of credit**

The cost of borrowing

You normally pay interest on the amount you borrow and, with some types of borrowing, there is an arrangement fee and possibly other charges. Watch out for various types of insurance bundled in with the loan (see p125).

You may see interest-free credit offers – check the small print to make sure there are no hidden charges and shop around to make sure you are not paying more for the goods or services than you would if you bought elsewhere.

For most types of borrowing, the lender must tell you the annual percentage rate (APR). This is a standardised way of expressing the cost of borrowing. The

APR takes into account the interest and other charges that you *must* pay and also the timing of these payments. It does not include charges that you might pay only in certain circumstances – eg, if you paid off the loan early or you opted to include insurance that is not a compulsory part of the deal.

The timing of payments is important because, in effect, the earlier you have to make them the more you pay for the loan or, put another way, the less you get for your money. As an example, consider two loans each for £1,000 and both charging you £200 interest. With one, you have to pay back £100 every month; with the other, you pay back nothing until the end of the year when you pay off the full £1,200 in a single lump sum. The second loan is the cheaper deal because you have the use of the full amount of borrowed money for longer. It may not necessarily be the better deal for you, however, because you might find it easier to manage monthly repayments rather than finding a large lump sum in one go.

You can use the APR to check whether a deal looks cheap or expensive. Using APRs to help you compare products is straightforward: the higher the APR the more expensive the borrowing. So a loan with a low APR is cheaper than one with a higher APR. But you should also look at the repayments you will have to make – there is no point choosing a cheap deal if you would not be able to manage the monthly payments. You may be able to reduce the payments by opting to borrow over a longer period, but bear in mind that this will increase the total you have to pay back (see the table below).

Example of how much you might pay back each month and in total

How long you borrow for (the term)	5 years	10 years	15 years	20 years	25 years
Your monthly payment	£21.94	£13.99	£11.61	£10.59	£10.08
Total paid back	£1,316	£1,679	£2,090	£2,541	£3,025

Note: assumes you borrow £1,000 at an interest rate of 12 per cent a year

Credit and insurance

You can take out insurance that will make your interest payments (but not any capital repayments) if you are unable to work because of illness or losing your job. This insurance is called by a variety of names: payment protection insurance (PPI), loan payment protection insurance, credit insurance, accident sickness and unemployment cover and, in the case of mortgages, mortgage payment protection insurance. Typically, such insurance pays out for a maximum of one or two years. Whether or not it is worth having depends on the type of borrowing involved, the cost of cover and the small print of the policy. An investigation by the UK's Competition Commission found that PPI has been widely mis-sold in the past. New rules are being phased in to protect consumers (see p127), but you should still be wary when considering this product.

The type of borrowing

You might be able to keep up the payments on a small loan without the need for insurance. If the loan is unsecured, you might decide that there is not much the lender could do if you had to suspend the payments temporarily (see p168).

The picture is different if you have a mortgage or other loan secured on your home. If you do not keep up the payments you could lose your home, so insurance could be worth having. If you cannot work, you might be eligible for benefits to cover some or all of your mortgage interest payments but, in most cases, you do not receive help during the first 13 weeks of your claim (see Chapter 9). Therefore, you might consider taking out insurance to cover that period. However, the Government has set up a number of schemes to help homeowners during the financial crisis that started in 2007 (see p152).

The cost of cover

Loan and mortgage payment protection insurance can be expensive. For example, in mid-2009, the monthly repayments for a £5,000 unsecured personal loan over three years were £158 a month. Including loan payment protection insurance, the costs rose to as much as £186 a month – an extra £28 a month or £1,008 over the full term of the loan.[6]

Rather than paying for PPI monthly, you might be offered a single premium deal where you pay one lump sum to provide cover for the whole loan. In the past, some policies did not offer a refund of any of the single premium if you paid off the loan early. From spring 2007 onwards, under an agreement between the Financial Services Authority (FSA) and PPI providers, refunds must be given if you pay off the loan early. This agreement applies to both new and existing PPI policies – if you have an existing policy, the provider should write to you to explain how refunds will be dealt with.

If you decide to take out loan or mortgage payment protection insurance, you usually do this when you start the loan or mortgage but you can take out cover later. The lender can usually arrange cover, but you will often get a better deal by shopping around – consult an insurance broker (see Appendix 2).

The policy small print

Before taking out loan or mortgage payment protection insurance, it is vital to check that the policy suits your particular circumstances and will pay out if needed. In particular, check the exclusions set out in the policy wording. For example, the unemployment cover often does not apply if you work on a casual basis or on temporary contracts. Some policies do not cover the self-employed or part-time workers, and the illness section usually will not cover spells of not being able to work because of a 'pre-existing condition' (in other words, a health problem you already had before you took out the policy) and may exclude claims related to common conditions, such as back problems and mental health. Some policies have age limits – eg, no cover beyond age 65.

The Competition Commission investigation found that the claims ratio (the proportion of total premiums paid out in claims) was extremely low for PPI at around 14 per cent compared with, for example, 78 per cent for car insurance.

Mis-selling of payment protection insurance

Lenders and advisers are often keen that you should take PPI out for two reasons. Firstly, it reduces the risk of the lender losing money if you cannot keep up the repayments and, secondly, the lender or adviser usually earns a commission payment from the insurer for every policy it sells. The Competition Commission found that between 50 and 80 per cent of the premium you pay for this insurance is paid as commission to the lender that sold you the policy. It is not usually compulsory to take out insurance as a condition of a loan. However, prior to the investigation, some lenders automatically gave you a quote including insurance or implied that your chances of getting a loan were improved if you took up the PPI. You could unwittingly end up paying heftily for insurance you did not want.

As a result of the Competition Commission investigation, the sale of single PPI has already been banned and a package of measures is being introduced to protect consumers. This includes the following.

From April 2010:
- marketing material you get about PPI must include a clear statement of the cost expressed as the monthly cost for each £100 of cover, so that you can easily compare the insurance on offer with other deals available;
- if you ask, the insurance provider must tell you the provider's claims ratio – ie, the proportion of the premiums paid by customers that are paid out in claims. This will give you some measure of the value for money offered by the policy;
- you must be provided with a personal quote, setting out the main terms of the cover and the cost.

From October 2010:
- it has been proposed that there will be a ban on the sale of PPI at the time you take out a loan or within seven days. Under the proposals you can be given a quote and the lender may then contact you when the seven days are up. This breathing space is to give you time to think and to shop around for competing deals, although, you can initiate the purchase before the seven days are up. However, providers have legally challenged these proposals and, at the time of writing, it is unclear whether they will go ahead;
- the sale of single premium PPI will be banned.

In the meantime, be aware that you do not have to take out PPI. Ask for a quote without insurance and stand your ground if a salesperson tries to pressurise you to take out cover you do not want.

Different ways to borrow

The table below summarises the main types of credit available and when they might be useful. The flowchart on p135 aims to help you decide what sort of credit might best suit your needs.

Different ways to borrow

Type of credit	Guide to typical cost	Main features	Useful for	Where from
Affinity card (donation card)	Moderate to expensive	Credit card (see p129) where a donation is made to a specified charity, good cause, football club or other organisation when you take out the card and each time you use it. See p139.	Not that useful. Usually you can get a better credit card deal by shopping around. If you want to support a particular organisation, arrange your own separate donations.	Banks, building societies, through charities and clubs
Authorised overdraft	Cheap to moderate	Borrowing for any purpose. Feature of a current account. Very flexible: provided you stay within the agreed limit, you choose how much and when to borrow and repay. See Chapter 2.	Borrowing for a fairly short period.	Your own bank
Bond committee and partnership scheme	Cheap	Informal community organisation. Usually you agree to pay a set amount each week or month to a centralised fund. You can then borrow from the fund.	Borrowing cheaply over the short to medium term.	Your local community – eg, churches and community centres

Type of credit	Guide to typical cost	Main features	Useful for	Where from
Catalogue buying	Expensive	You buy by mail order, selecting items from a home shopping catalogue and spreading payment over many months. As well as paying interest on the amount you borrow, prices may be higher than you would pay if you shopped around. See p148.	Spreading cost of household items (eg, clothes and gifts) if your budget is tight – often fairly small payments are accepted.	Catalogue companies
Community development finance institution	Cheap to moderate	Loans and investment finance mainly for small businesses and community projects, but also some individual loans, in deprived areas with the aim of fostering regeneration. Average loan to individuals is £600.	Many uses – eg, home improvements, start-up capital for a business, back-to-work loan. Will often consider business ventures that mainstream lenders are not interested in.	Community development bank, community development loan fund, community development venture fund and similar bodies
Credit card	Free to expensive	Plastic card you can use to make purchases (and draw cash from cash machines, though this is costly). Very flexible: provided you make the minimum repayments each month, you choose how much and when to borrow and repay. See p139.	Convenient way to pay. Free very short-term borrowing, provided you pay off the balance each month. Cheap way to borrow for a short period. Tends to be expensive if you borrow long term.	Banks, building societies, and through charities and clubs

Type of credit	Guide to typical cost	Main features	Useful for	Where from
Credit union	Cheap to moderate	Loan for any purpose from a mutual self-help group. You have to be a member and might have to first build up some savings. Larger credit unions offer a wider range of services, which may include loans without the need to build up savings first. See p164.	Manageable borrowing over the short to medium term. Willing to consider applicants with no or a poor credit history. Borrowing from some credit unions might enable you to build up a credit record so that later you are eligible to borrow elsewhere.	Credit union
Doorstep lender	Expensive	Small loans (typically up to £500) for any purpose. Convenient because you can make small weekly repayments collected from your home and lender might be flexible if you have problems with repayments, but the total you pay back is very high. Avoid unauthorised lenders (loan sharks) who are very expensive and often use threatening tactics to recover their money.	Spreading costs if your budget is tight and coping with an unexpected expense. Available even if you have no or a poor credit record. From mid-2007 onwards, can enable you to build up a credit record so that later you are eligible to borrow elsewhere.	Home credit companies

Type of credit	Guide to typical cost	Main features	Useful for	Where from
Free overdraft	Free	Borrowing for any purpose. Feature of some current accounts, particularly for students and new graduates. Many current accounts have a small, free overdraft. See Chapter 2.	Supporting yourself while studying or training. Letting you draw the last few pounds from your account at a cash machine. A buffer if you accidentally go overdrawn.	Your own bank
Hire purchase	Moderate	Similar to a personal loan, but taken out to buy a specific item and you do not own the item until you have made the final payment. See p148.	Buying expensive items, such as a car, and spreading the cost over, say, three years.	Finance company but often arranged by shop where you buy
Illegal lender (loan shark)	Very expensive	Unauthorised lenders may seem the only option if you are finding it hard to borrow elsewhere, but they are very expensive and use threatening tactics. Be aware that illegal lenders have no rights in law to get their money back from you. See p137 for more details and help available.	Not useful. Do not borrow this way.	
Life insurance loan	Cheap	If you have an investment-type life insurance policy (see p111) invested on a with-profits basis, you may be able to borrow against the cash-in value of the policy. Use the money for any purpose. See p165.	Medium- to long-term borrowing.	Life company with which you have a policy

Type of credit	Guide to typical cost	Main features	Useful for	Where from
Lifetime mortgage	Expensive	Borrow to raise cash for any purpose or extra income. Type of equity release scheme where you take out a mortgage secured against your home. The mortgage is not repaid until you die (or move permanently into a care home).	Older people who need to raise a lump sum or boost their income.	Selected banks and specialist companies, through a financial adviser
Mortgage	Cheap to moderate	Loan secured against a property – eg, your home.	Buying your own home. Buying another property – eg, a second home or buy-to-let property. Long-term loan for any other purpose – eg, home improvements, school fees.	Banks, building societies, specialist lenders, through a broker
Rent deposit scheme (bond scheme)	Free	The scheme provider guarantees to compensate your landlord if you cause damage to the property or fail to pay your rent. In other words, no money changes hands unless there is a problem. You have to repay any money that is paid out to the landlord. Usually the guarantee lasts for the first 12 months of your tenancy. Alternatively, a few schemes lend you the money to pay the deposit yourself and you repay it gradually from, for instance, your wages or benefits.	Paying the deposit required when you rent private accommodation.	Some local councils, housing associations, churches, community groups and other voluntary organisations
Secured personal loan	Cheap to moderate	Loan for any purpose secured against your home	Debt consolidation, but think carefully – if you cannot keep up the payments you could lose your home. Medium-term borrowing for any purpose.	Banks and building societies (not necessarily your own), finance companies

Type of credit	Guide to typical cost	Main features	Useful for	Where from
Social fund loan	Free	Loans from the Government available if you are claiming certain benefits, usually repayable over a maximum of 18 months. They are paid from a cash-limited fund, so even if you have a good case you might get less than you ask for or nothing at all. See Chapter 9.	Budgeting loans are intended to help you meet a lump sum expense for, for example, furniture, home repairs, or expenses of getting a job. Crisis loans are intended to meet an urgent, short-term need where there is a risk to health or safety.	Through Jobcentre Plus
Store card	Expensive	Plastic card you can use to make purchases but only in a particular shop or range of shops. See p144.	Not useful. Expensive way to borrow.	Shop where you can use the card
Student loan	Cheap	Loan you take out to cover living costs and, from 2006, tuition fees while at university. Repayments start only after graduation and when your income exceeds £15,000 a year. See p166.	Supporting yourself at university.	Through your local authority
Unauthorised overdraft	Expensive	Spending more money than you have in your current account, without your bank's permission. See Chapter 2.	Not useful. Expensive way to borrow and you bank will require you to repay what you owe quickly.	Your own bank
Unsecured personal loan	Moderate to expensive	Loan that can be for any purpose or, where arranged by a retailer, loan to buy a specific item such as electrical goods or double-glazing.	Medium-term borrowing.	Banks and building societies (not necessarily your own), finance companies, 'doorstep' lenders

How much can you borrow

In general, it is up to you to decide how much you can afford to borrow (see p121). Lenders want to be sure they will get their money back so will check your creditworthiness, but these checks are often scant and you may find it easy to get more credit than you can afford. Think carefully before signing up for any new credit. Bear in mind that, with a secured loan, the lender can get its money back by selling whatever the loan is secured against – usually your home. This protects the lender who may, therefore, be even less concerned about checking your creditworthiness and whether you can afford the loan. With mortgages used to buy a home, lenders *must* consider whether you can afford the loan, though the rules do not say how this should be done. Many lenders limit the loan to a given multiple of your income as a rough guide to affordability, but others look more closely at your income and existing spending and commitments.

Are you creditworthy

Most lenders make checks before deciding whether to lend to you and, if so, how much they will charge. The checks take two main forms.

- **Credit scoring.** When you apply for credit, you will be asked lots of questions – eg, about your age, marital status, income, existing credit cards and whether you own your home. The lender assigns a score to each of your answers. If your total score is above a certain amount, you get the loan. If you score less, you might be turned down or you might be offered a loan on different terms – eg, a lower amount or at a higher interest rate. You might be turned down by one lender but welcomed by another. This is because different lenders specialise in different types of business and so seek out different types of customer. The credit scoring system each lender uses is designed to identify the type of customer the lender wants.

- **Credit reference.** Almost every UK adult is on the database of at least one of the three credit reference agencies – Equifax, Experian and Callcredit. Your file contains publicly available information, such as your name and address taken from the electoral roll and any county court judgments, and usually also information lenders have agreed to share with each other about how you handle credit. This latter information shows what loans you have, whether you have made payments on time, whether you missed any and, if payments were late, how late they were. When you apply for credit, the lender will run a check on your file. Checks made during the last two years or so are also recorded on your file, so lenders can see if you have made a lot of recent credit applications. The credit reference agency does not decide whether or not you get a loan and it does not have blacklists. The information it provides is purely factual and it is up to the lender to decide how to use it.

If you are turned down for credit

If you ask, a lender is unlikely to tell you precisely why you were turned down, but may give you a rough idea and must tell you if it checked with a credit

Which sort of credit could you use?

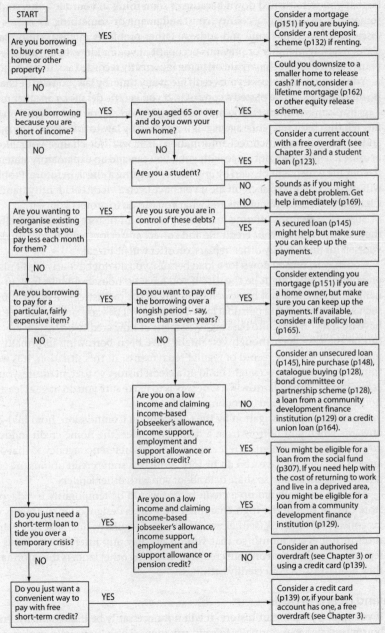

START

Are you borrowing to buy or rent a home or other property?
— YES → Consider a mortgage (p151) if you are buying. Consider a rent deposit scheme (p132) if renting.

NO ↓

Are you borrowing because you are short of income?
— YES → Are you aged 65 or over and do you own your own home?
— YES → Could you downsize to a smaller home to release cash? If not, consider a lifetime mortgage (p162) or other equity release scheme.

NO ↓ (Are you borrowing because you are short of income?)

NO ↓ (Are you aged 65 or over and do you own your own home?)

Are you a student?
— YES → Consider a current account with a free overdraft (see Chapter 3) and a student loan (p123).

NO → Sounds as if you might have a debt problem. Get help immediately (p169).

Are you wanting to reorganise existing debts so that you pay less each month for them?
— YES → Are you sure you are in control of these debts?
— NO → Sounds as if you might have a debt problem. Get help immediately (p169).
— YES → A secured loan (p145) might help but make sure you can keep up the payments.

NO ↓

Are you borrowing to pay for a particular, fairly expensive item?
— YES → Do you want to pay off the borrowing over a longish period – say, more than seven years?
— YES → Consider extending you mortgage (p151) if you are a home owner, but make sure you can keep up the payments. If available, consider a life policy loan (p165).

NO ↓ (Do you want to pay off the borrowing over a longish period...)

Are you on a low income and claiming income-based jobseeker's allowance, income support, employment and support allowance or pension credit?
— NO → Consider an unsecured loan (p145), hire purchase (p148), catalogue buying (p128), bond committee or partnership scheme (p128), a loan from a community development finance institution (p129) or a credit union loan (p164).
— YES → You might be eligible for a loan from the social fund (p307). If you need help with the cost of returning to work and live in a deprived area, you might be eligible for a loan from a community development finance institution (p129).

NO ↓

Do you just need a short-term loan to tide you over a temporary crisis?
— YES → Are you on a low income and claiming income-based jobseeker's allowance, income support, employment and support allowance or pension credit?
— YES → You might be eligible for a loan from the social fund (p307). If you need help with the cost of returning to work and live in a deprived area, you might be eligible for a loan from a community development finance institution (p129).
— NO → Consider an authorised overdraft (see Chapter 3) or using a credit card (p139).

NO ↓

Do you just want a convenient way to pay with free short-term credit?
— YES → Consider a credit card (p139) or, if your bank account has one, a free overdraft (see Chapter 3).

reference agency. The lender is required to tell you which agency it used. It may be that you were turned down because of something in your file – this could be something major like a county court judgment or something as minor as a discrepancy in your name and address. Other problems might be information about a family member or previous occupant at your address being included on your file or a loan you have paid off being incorrectly recorded as still outstanding.

You have the right to see your credit file at any time. By law, you can be charged no more than £2 to be posted a copy of it. If you get the details by another means – eg, by phone or internet, you may be charged more. If you find an error on your file, tell the credit reference agency. It is required by law to investigate the matter and to remedy any incorrect information. If it will not change your file (eg, because a lender does not agree with you), you can add an explanatory statement to your file which will be seen by any lender running a check in future. Problems will also occur with your credit file if you have been a victim of identity fraud. See Chapter 10 for more about this and what you can do to protect yourself.

Steer clear of firms offering to 'repair' your credit history for a fee. Legally, all they can do is check your credit file and correct any errors, which you can do for yourself for just £2. Any other 'repairs' on offer will be illegal.

You may be turned down for a loan because you do not have any credit history on your file. This might be the case if you have no household bills in your own name and you have not borrowed from any of the mainstream lending sources, such as credit cards and personal loans. Lenders will be wary simply because they have no data on which to base an assessment of how creditworthy you are. This can be the case even though you might have been borrowing informally and maintaining a steady record of regular repayments. In this situation, it is worth thinking about how you might build up a credit history so that, in future, you can access more forms of borrowing. One way is to make sure you do have at least one household bill registered in your name.

Following an investigation by the Competition Commission, from mid-2007 onwards when you borrow from a doorstep lender (the home credit industry), your record of repayments is recorded with a credit reference agency so that other lenders can see you have a credit history. Similarly, some credit unions use credit reference agencies and so share data about you with other lenders.

Another way to build up a credit record would be temporarily to take out a store card or one of the high-charging credit cards designed for customers who are considered high risk (see below). Use the card regularly, but make sure you pay it off in full every month so that you do not pay any interest. The loans and repayments will appear on your credit record giving other lenders the information they need to assess your creditworthiness.

Paying over the odds

If you have a poor credit history, it will not necessarily be impossible for you to borrow but you will normally have to pay more. This also usually applies if you have no credit history – eg, because you are young and just starting your financial life, or newly divorced and your partner had handled all the finances.

At one time, mainstream lenders were simply not interested in people with a poor credit record, but these days some offer loans or credit cards with a range of interest rates that vary according to your credit standing – eg, a customer with good standing might pay under 10 per cent a year whereas someone with a poor record might be charged double or more.

If one operates in your area, a better option would be to join a credit union (see p164). You will normally have to build up some savings first, but can then borrow at a rate which is limited by law to no more than 2 per cent a month (26.8 per cent a year), though many charge a lot less. Some credit unions offer instant loans, without your having to build up any savings first.

If you cannot borrow from a mainstream lender or a credit union, you might have little choice but to turn to more expensive sources, such as 'doorstep' lenders. These are companies that typically make weekly visits to your home to collect your repayments. You can usually pay back in small instalments, but the overall cost of borrowing this way is extremely high – interest rates of 600 per cent a year or more are not uncommon.

At all costs, avoid borrowing from unregulated loan sharks who charge even more and often use threatening tactics if you cannot keep up your payments.

Illegal lenders (loan sharks)

It is a criminal offence for anyone to lend money without having a licence to do so. There is an online public register you can consult to check if someone who is offering to lend you money is licensed (see Appendix 2). If s/he is not, do not do business with her/him and report her/him to the police or your local trading standards office.

Illegal lenders are commonly called 'loan sharks' because of the rough tactics they use to get money from you. Typically, they might insist on taking valuable documents, such as your passport, cash card or Post Office card as 'security' and you might be forced to make direct debit payments into a loan shark's bank account. Loan sharks charge you an extremely high rate of interest, give you little or no paperwork when you take out the loan and no receipts for your payments, and add 'fines' or penalties without warning for late payments. They are likely to harass, threaten, intimidate and even be violent if you do not pay up.

At first, you might not realise you are dealing with an illegal lender. Many loan sharks operate in an informal way and may be introduced to you as a 'friend of a friend'. They seem very plausible and as if they are genuinely helping you out at a difficult time. Do not be embarrassed if you are taken in – many people are. If you are in debt to a loan shark, you may feel alone and frightened, but there is help.

Loan sharks are breaking the law and can be fined and sent to jail. You are not breaking the law – you are the victim of a crime. Moreover, the debt you owe is not legally enforceable – ie, there are no legal steps an illegal lender can take to get the money back. There are specialist illegal money lending teams throughout the UK who can investigate and arrest illegal lenders. They can also offer you advice and support. You can contact the illegal lending teams directly on a round-the-clock, confidential national hotline (Tel: 0300 555 2222). Alternatively, if you contact any of the free, independent debt advice agencies such as a Citizens Advice Bureau, Community Legal Advice (England and Wales only), Consumer Credit Counselling Service, Money Advice Scotland or National Debtline, they can put you in touch with the specialist teams. See Appendix 2 for contact details.

For more information about illegal lending and what help is available, see www.direct.gov.uk/stoploansharks.

3. **Plastic cards**

Types of card

There are lots of ways to pay with plastic but they do not all involve borrowing.

Which plastic lets you borrow?

Type of card	What it is	Can you borrow?
Cash card, debit card*	Issued with many current accounts (see Chapter 3). Not a form of borrowing.	No
Cheque guarantee card*	Issued with some bank accounts (see Chapter 3). Not a form of borrowing, but if you use it to back a cheque for which you do not have enough money in your account, you could get into debt.	No
Charge card	A card that lets you pay for things but you must pay off the full balance every month – eg, the original American Express and Diners Club. Not a form of borrowing.	No
Reward card	Card you present when shopping on which points are recorded which you can later exchange for gifts or use to pay for shopping. Not a form of borrowing.	No
Pre-payment card (purse card)	You load up the card with cash before you can use it, or buy it ready-loaded, so not a form of borrowing. Some cards have a very specific use – eg, in electricity meters, at canteens, or to make phone calls. Others are more general (see Chapter 3) and can be used anywhere you would use a cash or debit card.	No

Credit card	Way of borrowing, though you can choose to pay off the full balance every month.	Yes
Affinity card (donation card)	Type of credit card, therefore a way of borrowing.	Yes
Store card	A way of borrowing. Most work like credit cards; a few work in a different way – see p144.	Yes

Note: with a current or basic bank account, you usually you get just one card that has one or more of the following functions: cash card, debit card and/or cheque guarantee card.

Credit cards

How they work

You have a plastic card which you can use to pay for goods and services in shops and other outlets that accept the card. Credit cards are very widely accepted throughout the UK and many countries abroad.

When you use the card, the amount you spend is added to your account. You have a credit limit which specifies the maximum you may run up on the account.

Each month, you are sent a statement showing the amount outstanding on the account and the minimum you must pay off. The minimum is usually around 3 per cent of the outstanding balance or £5 – whichever is higher. You can choose to pay off more if you like. If you do not pay off the full balance, you are charged interest (see below). The interest charge often comes to more than the minimum you must pay off each month, so if you make only the minimum payments, your credit card debt is likely to grow even if you are not making any new purchases.

You can also use your credit card to get cash from cash machines and *bureaux de change*, but there is an extra charge for this (see below).

What they cost

A few cards charge an annual fee – eg, £10 or £20. But there are so many cards without any fee that you can easily avoid this charge.

Using a credit card to make purchases is free if you pay off your outstanding balance in full each month. In effect, you are getting interest-free credit from the day you make a purchase to the date you pay off the balance – this period can be up to 59 days depending on the details of how the card works.

If you do not pay off the balance in full by the required date, you are charged interest on the money you have borrowed and this is added to your next statement. Different card companies use different methods but, for example, interest might be charged from the date of each purchase up to your next statement date. Some statements show the amount of interest that will be added next month if you make only the minimum repayment this month. The interest rate varies greatly from one card to another – in mid-2007, rates from under 10 per cent up to 40 per cent were on offer. With some cards, the rate of interest you are offered depends on your credit standing (see p134).

The rate of interest charged if you use a credit card to get cash is usually higher (eg, 1 to 10 per cent more depending on the card) than the rate charged for purchases and the interest is charged even if you do pay off your balance in full. In addition, there is usually a handling fee for cash withdrawals of around 1 to 2 per cent of the amount withdrawn.

If you use a credit card abroad, there is usually an extra fee – called an 'exchange rate loading' – of 1.75 to 2.75 per cent of the value of the transaction. On the other hand, the exchange rate used to convert your transaction into £s is usually competitive because the card company is changing money in bulk.

You face extra charges if you miss a monthly payment or go over your credit limit. Following an investigation into excessive charging by the Office of Fair Trading (OFT), such charges should be in line with the administration costs the card provider incurs. The OFT has said that a charge in excess of £12 will be presumed unfair unless the card provider can prove otherwise.[7]

Many cards offer a low or zero per cent rate on a balance you transfer from another credit card. The zero rate typically lasts for a set period (eg, six months) after which it reverts to the normal rate for purchases. However, you will not necessarily get the benefit of the low or zero rate for the full six months because with many cards whatever you pay off each month is usually used first to reduce the transferred balance before being set against any new purchases. Watch out for an 'exit charge' if you decide on a further transfer to another card.

Useful for

- Convenient way to pay, especially if you are buying at a distance (by phone, post or internet).
- Short-term (up to 59 days) interest-free credit provided you use the card only for purchases and you pay off the balance in full each month.
- Cheap short-term borrowing (up to several months) provided you shop around for a card with a low interest rate.
- Indefinite interest-free borrowing if every six months or so you shift the outstanding balance on your card to a new card offering a zero per cent rate on balance transfers. To get the full benefit of the zero per cent rate, pay off only the minimum each month, use a different card for any new transactions and choose cards with no exit charge.
- Extra protection, since the card issuer is liable along with the retailer if something goes wrong with the goods or services you are buying (see p173). This protection applies when you are using your card in the UK and also abroad or buying (eg, by internet) from a firm based abroad.

Example of a credit card statement

Last month Mrs Walters paid off her bill in full.

Mrs Walters paid of her bill in full last month, so there is no interest to be added to this statement.

Spenditcard

Customer services: 0870 000 0 000

Card reference: 0987 6543 2109 8765

Account holder: Mrs Joan Walters

www.spenditcard.co.uk

Account details

Date	Transactions	Amount
14 Nov	Specsavers, Yeovil	£132.99
17 Nov	Marks & Spencer, Yeovil	£21.99
17 Nov	Boots, Yeovil	£12.07
17 Nov	W H Smith, Yeovil	£56.97
23 Nov	Morrison, Wincanton	£78.77
24 Nov	Ask, Yeovil	£29.30
7 Dec	Interest charge 7 December	£0.00
7 Dec	**New balance**	**£332.09**

Account summary

On 7 December 2008

Previous balance	£105.68
Payments received	£105.68
New transactions	£332.09
New balance	£332.09

Payment due

Minimum payment	£9.96
Payment date	3 January 2009
Purchase APR	16.9%
Cash APR	20.9%
Next month's estimated interest	£3.96

Credit limit

Current limit	£1,000
Available credit	£609.45

(this may reflect recent transactions not included on this statement)

If Mrs Walters pays off the full £332.09, there will be no interest to pay on the items on this bill. But if she does not pay off the full balance, interest will be charged at this rate.

The bill this month is £332.09.

Mrs Walters must pay off at least £9.96 this month (3% of £332.09). The payment must be made by 3 January.

If Mrs Walters pays off just the minimum £9.96, she will be charged interest on the items on this month's statement. The interest would be £3.96 and would appear on next month's statement.

Providers

Banks, building societies and organisations that choose to brand a card – eg, clubs, charities, newspapers and car manufacturers.

Choosing and applying

Decide how you will use the card. If you will pay off the bill in full every month, the interest rate does not matter. Choose a card with a long interest-free period and no interest provided you pay off the full balance. If you expect to borrow, choose a card with a low interest rate. Avoid cards with an annual fee. See p140 for other features you might want to consider.

For information about different cards, see the comparative tables published in the personal finance sections of newspapers, personal finance magazines and websites, and by specialist firms such as Which? and Moneyfacts. Bear in mind the limitations of comparison websites (see p8) and use two or three rather than relying on just one. The Financial Services Authority's Moneymadeclear Compare Products tables are due to include credit cards from some time in 2010.

Literature about a credit card must include a summary box, which gives you key information about the card, such as the interest-free period, interest rate and other charges, in a standard way so you can more easily compare one card with another.

Phone the card company for an application form, apply online or, if applicable, in person at a branch. You will need to fill in a detailed application form, which will probably be used as the basis for credit scoring (see p134), and the lender will run a credit reference check (see p134).

Pitfalls and what to watch out for

- If you pay your bill late, even if you pay off the full balance, you will be charged interest, which will be added to your next statement. You may also be charged a fixed fee for late payment. If you normally pay the bill in full, but tend to be disorganised, make sure you choose a card with a low interest rate.
- Credit cards are an expensive way to get cash – and this includes getting foreign currency from a *bureaux de change*. Try to use an alternative.
- It is very easy to get credit cards, and card issuers often raise your credit limit without consulting you first. Do not get carried away by the availability of all this credit. Make sure you keep your spending within the limit you can afford. If you do run into problems, get help (see p167).
- It can be difficult to work out how much in total you are paying in interest.
- Plastic cards are prone to fraud (see Chapter 10).

Credit card cheques

If you have a credit card, you may find the issuer sends you unsolicited blank cheques inviting you to use them to pay for anything you like up to a certain value (eg, £3,000) which is additional to your normal card limit. If you use the cheques, the amount spent is added to your credit card account and paid off in the normal way. Be very wary of these cheques for the following reasons.

They are expensive. You make repayments in the normal way for your credit card, so these cheques are not a good way to borrow unless you will quickly pay back the full amount owed. In addition, they are usually treated like cash withdrawals so you pay a higher rate of interest than on purchases and there is an extra handling charge – eg, 2 per cent of the amount for which you write out the cheque.

There are better ways to borrow a lump sum. See the flowchart on p135 for suggestions on how to borrow for a particular, fairly expensive item.

They may tempt you to borrow when you cannot afford to. To avoid this, tear up the cheques as soon as you get them and ask your card issuer not to send any more.

They are insecure. To guard against anyone else fraudulently using the cheques, make sure you destroy them by shredding them, tearing them up or burning them.

In July 2009, the Government announced plans to ban card companies from sending out these unsolicited cheques from a date yet to be announced. You will be able to opt in to receiving them if you want to.

Credit card perks

Credit cards frequently offer you a range of add-ons, but very few of them are worth having. Some examples include the following.

Cashback. When you use the card, you earn cash – typically 0.5 to 1 per cent of the amount you spend on the card – which is credited to your account. Although you must spend quite a lot for even a small cashback, this is a perk worth having provided the card has all the other features you want.

Card protection. You have a single number to call to report and cancel cards which are lost or stolen. This is a useful facility though you can buy card protection yourself for around £15 a year. In addition, you are not liable for misuse of a lost or stolen card although this perk is of no real value since both the law and the Financial Services Authority rules protect you anyway (see p61).

Points schemes. You 'earn' points when you use the card which can be redeemed for goods or services from a catalogue, but you need to spend a lot to get enough points, the range of goods and services is limited, and there may be restrictions – eg, short breaks in hotels but only between certain dates.

Air miles. Similar to points schemes, but you spend the points on flights. Might be good if you fly a lot but you can often get cheap flights anyway – eg, by booking on the internet.

Purchase protection insurance for, say, 100 days to cover damage, loss or theft of something you have bought with the card. If you have house contents insurance, you probably have this cover anyway.

Extended warranty for, say, two years for certain items you have bought with the card. Typically covers things like electrical goods which are unlikely to break down in the first few years anyway (see also p224).

Travel accident insurance. Pays out a lump sum if you suffer a specified injury while travelling and you paid for your tickets by credit card. This is no substitute for full travel insurance, which is what you really need to cover the risks while on holiday or away on business. A few of the cards aimed at wealthier customers offer full travel insurance, but watch out for high annual fees for these cards.

Emergency cash while abroad if your credit card is lost or stolen, but your travel insurance normally covers this.

Affinity cards (donation cards)

How they work

These are credit cards and work as described above. However, an affinity card is linked to a named organisation – eg, a charity or a football club. When you first take out the card, the issuer makes a donation to the organisation of, for example, £10 or £15. Each time you use the card, a further small donation is made – typically 0.25 per cent of the amount you spend – eg, 25p if you spend £100.

What they cost

See credit cards, above. Interest rates tend to be higher than for the best-buy ordinary credit cards. Some have a particularly high rate if you use the card to get cash.

Useful for

*   Showing your support for a particular organisation.

Providers

Banks, building societies and the organisations involved.

Choosing and applying

See credit cards on p142.

Pitfalls and what to watch out for

*   Not a very effective way of giving to the charity or other organisation. Instead, get a best-buy ordinary credit card and, out of what you save, arrange your own donations. If the organisation is a charity, you can do this tax efficiently through the Gift Aid scheme (see Chapter 8).
*   Other drawbacks are as for ordinary credit cards (see p142).

Store cards

How they work

Most work like credit cards (see p139) except that you can use them only for purchases in certain shops. However, some are budget cards and, with these, you agree to make a set minimum payment every month – eg, £25. You can then make purchases up to a multiple of that amount – eg, 24 x £25 = £600.

As a store card holder, you may get certain perks, such as previews of sales and discounts on some or all of your purchases.

What they cost

Most store cards are very expensive. For example, the interest rate may be up to 20 per cent more than for a best-buy credit card.

Useful for

- Convenient way to pay, but only if you would shop in those shops anyway and you do not use the card to borrow – in other words, you pay off what you owe in full every month.
- Too expensive to be useful as a way to borrow.

Providers

The shops where you can use the card.

Choosing and applying

If you want a store card, get details from a participating shop. You can usually apply and qualify for discounts on your purchases straight away.

Pitfalls and what to watch out for

- Very expensive.
- Other drawbacks are as for credit cards (see p142).

4. **Personal loans**

How they work

You either shop around for a loan which is paid into your bank account and you then spend or use as you like, or a retailer from whom you are buying something specific arranges a personal loan for you from a finance company. When arranged by the retailer, you may have to pay part of the price straight away as a deposit and just borrow the balance.

The loan is a lump sum which you pay back with interest, normally by making regular monthly payments of a fixed amount over a set term – eg, one, three, five or seven years.

Personal loans may be secured or unsecured (see Appendix 1).

What they cost

You may have to pay an arrangement fee up front but the main cost is the interest you pay. The rate of interest you are offered may depend on your credit standing (see p134). Interest is worked out on the decreasing balance. This means the repayments are designed so that, if you pay the same amount each month, the whole loan including the interest will be paid off by the end of the term. However, since you are paying off some of the capital each month, the amount you owe is falling (ie, your balance decreases) and the amount of interest you are charged takes this into account. The table below gives an example of how this works.

Example of a decreasing balance loan

Month	A Outstanding balance of loan at start of the month	B Monthly payment made	C Interest charged this month (% of A)	D Capital paid off this month (B−C)
1	£1,000	£91.05	£13.89	£77.16
2	£922.84	£91.05	£12.82	£78.23
3	£844.61	£91.05	£11.73	£79.32
4	£765.29	£91.05	£10.63	£80.42
5	£684.87	£91.05	£9.51	£81.54
6	£603.33	£91.05	£8.38	£82.67
7	£520.66	£91.05	£7.23	£83.82
8	£436.84	£91.05	£6.07	£84.98
9	£351.86	£91.05	£4.89	£86.16
10	£265.70	£91.05	£3.69	£87.36
11	£178.34	£91.05	£2.48	£88.57
12	£89.77	£91.05	£1.25	£89.77
Total paid		£1,092.60	£92.57	£1,000

Note: assumes £1,000 borrowed over 12 months at an interest rate of 18 per cent a year.

The loan is normally for a set term. If you decide to pay off the loan early, there is usually an early repayment fee (which effectively gives the lender some of the interest it has otherwise lost by the payments stopping early). This fee is worked out according to a formula. If you want to know how this works, ask the lender for an explanation or get the free leaflet *Repaying Your Loan Early* from the Finance and Leasing Association (see Appendix 2).

Loan payment protection insurance (PPI – see p125) is optional. Do not unwittingly buy this cover if you do not want it. If it is not clear whether the quote includes insurance, check and if necessary ask for a quote excluding cover. New rules concerning the sale of PPI are being introduced during 2010 (see p127).

Useful for

- Buying expensive items, such as a car, furniture or home improvements.
- Replacing more expensive debts – eg, paying off a long-term credit card debt. Secured personal loans are especially useful for cutting the monthly cost of outstanding debts, but be aware that if you do not keep up the payments you could lose your home (see p168).

Providers

Many people turn first to their own bank, but you can shop around and borrow from any bank, building society or finance company. The Post Office also offers loans. Doorstep lenders are another option, but consider this route only if you cannot borrow from other, cheaper sources.

If a shop or salesperson can arrange a loan for an item you are buying, check whether it would be cheaper to shop around for your own loan and then pay cash for the item.

Choosing and applying

Check the comparative tables produced by specialist organisations (eg, Moneyfacts) and in the personal finance sections of newspapers and many personal finance websites.

To apply, contact the lender or, if applicable, ask in the shop offering credit. You will need to fill in a detailed application form, which will probably be used as the basis for credit scoring (see p134), and the lender will run a credit reference check (see p134).

Pitfalls and what to watch out for

- You choose at the outset the length of time you will take to repay the loan. Bear in mind that, the longer the term, the less you will pay each month but the more you will pay overall (see p124).
- It is an inflexible way to borrow because there is usually a charge if you decide to pay off the loan early.
- If you have a secured loan, it is crucial that you can keep up the monthly payments. If not, you could lose your home (see p168). If you run into problems, get help immediately (see p167).
- Bear in mind that loan PPI is usually expensive and full of exclusions (see p125). Lenders often automatically include the cost of insurance in a quote, but you do not normally have to take out this cover. Ask for a loan quote excluding cover.
- If your credit standing is poor or you have no credit history (see p134), personal loans are expensive. You might be able to borrow from, for example, a credit union instead.

- Avoid loan sharks – your debt problems will only become worse. Instead, get help (see p137).
- Some retailers offer 'zero per cent finance'. This means you are allowed to spread your payments for an item, but pay no interest on the balance outstanding. The offer may be a genuinely cheap way to buy, but check the details carefully – eg, whether the cash price is higher than you would pay elsewhere, whether you have to pay a large deposit, and what happens if you do not pay off the full amount by the end of the zero per cent period (interest might then be charged right back to the date of purchase).
- Watch out for deals that are quoted in months – make sure you understand how many years it is for.

5. **Hire purchase and conditional sale**

How it works

Hire purchase (HP) is a common way to buy expensive items, such as a car. The retailer from whom you are buying arranges the HP deal for you through a finance company with which the retailer has an agreement (or, less commonly, you shop around yourself to find a finance company). You agree to make regular monthly payments of a fixed amount over a set term – eg, one, two or three years.

Superficially, an HP agreement looks like buying with a personal loan (see p145) and you might confuse one for the other. But there are two important differences.

- **Ownership**. Although you can use the item straight away, it does not belong to you until you have made the final payment. If you do not keep to the terms of the agreement (eg, you miss a payment) the finance company (which has, in effect, bought the item from the retailer) can take the item back. There may be other conditions you must stick – eg, in the case of a car, ensuring that it is comprehensively insured and that you keep it in good condition. There may also be an annual mileage restriction. In reality, you are hiring the item during the term and have an option to buy it (usually for a nominal sum) when the agreement comes to an end.
- **Changing your mind**. Since you do not own the item until the end of the HP term, you can cancel the deal at any time and return the goods. This is useful if you can no longer afford the payments, the novelty of the item has worn off or a better model is launched. However, you are responsible for paying all the instalments due up to the time you cancel and the finance company can by law usually write into the agreement a requirement that, including amounts already paid, you pay at least half the purchase price in total.

Conditional sale is very similar to HP and is commonly used for car purchase. Under a typical agreement, having paid a deposit, you pay the outstanding amount by fixed monthly instalments. However, there is no final option to buy as under HP. Under a conditional sale, the car automatically passes into your ownership when the last instalment has been paid. As with HP, if you voluntarily cancel a conditional sale agreement before the end of the full term, you must return the goods and will usually be required to bring your total payments up to at least half the purchase price.

What they cost

Your regular payments are really rent for the use of the item, but they are set to reflect the cash price of the item plus interest. The finance company bears little risk because it can always take the goods back if you do not stick to the agreement, so the 'interest' may be lower than it would be for an unsecured personal loan used to buy the same item.

Bear in mind that, if you cancel the deal, you must usually have paid at least half the purchase price of the item (see above).

Useful for

Buying an expensive item like a car and cheaper than taking out an unsecured personal loan.

Providers

Retailer where you are buying an item. Alternatively, having chosen an item, you can approach a finance company directly and ask it to give you an HP agreement.

Choosing and applying

You have little choice if you use a retailer's own HP deal. If you shop around, contact several finance companies for quotes. (Finance companies tend to be the same organisations that offer personal loans and most high street banks have a finance arm.)

You must fill in an application form and you may be subjected to credit scoring and credit referencing (see p134), but you may be able to get HP even if you have been turned down for a personal loan because, in effect, the lending is secured against the item you are buying.

Pitfalls and what to watch out for

- Check the conditions of the deal – eg, you may be required to take out insurance or have the item regularly serviced.
- If you break the conditions, the finance company can take back the item even if you have paid nearly all the instalments. If you have paid one-third or more of the total due under the agreement, the company must have a court order to do this.

- If the company formally terminates your agreement, you will be liable for the full amount due under the agreement as if it had continued to the end, less what you have already paid and less the amount the company gets back from selling the goods.
- You usually must have paid at least a minimum amount before you can cancel the agreement.
- If you voluntarily surrender the agreement, the company can still require you to pay a sum equal to half the total amount due under the contract, less what you have already paid (including any deposit) and should have paid. In addition, you must pay any arrears and extra if the goods are damaged.
- You cannot sell the item until you have made the final HP instalment.

Personal contract plans: an alternative to hire purchase

When buying a car, there are various ways to pay: cash; personal loan; conditional sale; HP or a personal contract plan (PCP). With a PCP, you pay a deposit and then monthly payments for, say, three years. At the end of this time, you could:

- stop the payments and give back the car;
- make a large lump-sum payment (called a 'balloon payment') and the car becomes yours;
- assuming the car is worth more than the balloon payment would be, use the difference as a deposit on a new car.

The advantage of a PCP is that the monthly payments are lower than for conditional sale or HP. However, the total cost tends to be higher than conditional sale or HP because the size of the final balloon payment means you are, in effect, borrowing more.

Gap insurance

By law you must have car insurance (see Chapter 7). If you have comprehensive cover, your insurance should pay out for any loss or damage to your own car. In the worst case, your car might be a complete write-off or stolen and not recovered. However, your insurance normally pays only the second-hand value of the car at that time and this may be less than you need to buy a replacement or to pay off any outstanding car loan or purchase deal. Gap insurance is designed to cover the shortfall. There are restrictions – eg, the maximum payout is limited (eg, to £10,000) and the policy lasts only, for instance, the first three or five years of a car's life. Bear in mind that many comprehensive car insurance policies will pay for a brand new replacement if your car is written off or stolen in the first year of its life. You can buy gap insurance through car dealers, but it usually costs less if you go to an insurance broker (see Appendix 2).

6. **Mortgages**

Renting versus buying a home

Sixty-nine per cent of British households own their own home (33 per cent outright and 36 per cent with the aid of a mortgage).[8] Home ownership, however, is neither affordable nor the best option for everyone. Both home ownership and renting have advantages, but also drawbacks.

	Advantages	Drawbacks
Home ownership	Freedom to use your home as you like.[i]	High buying costs
		Maintenance costs.
	Freedom to decorate and adapt it as you like.[ii]	Cost of insuring the home.
		Hard to move quickly – eg, for your work.
	Live rent-free once mortgage paid off.	Ties up your capital.
	Tax-free capital gain if value of your home rises.	You could lose money if the value of your home falls.
	May give you enough capital to buy progressively better homes.	
Renting	Easy to move – eg, for work or if the neighbourhood deteriorates.	Landlord may restrict the way you use your home.
	Landlord is responsible for maintenance.	Landlord may restrict the way you decorate and adapt your home.
	Landlord is responsible for insuring the building.	You may miss out in being able to afford to buy if house prices rise.
	Freedom to invest any capital in more flexible investments.	Rent is 'dead money' which cannot help you get a better home later.

[i] Subject to any restrictions imposed by a mortgage lender – eg, on lodgers, and any restrictive covenants in your deeds.
[ii] Subject to planning permission, buildings regulations and other legal constraints.

Deciding whether you can afford to buy means looking not just at the monthly outlay but also the upfront costs of buying. These include a deposit, valuation and legal fees and stamp duty land tax (see table on p152).

5

Stamp duty land tax on property purchase in 2009/10

Price of property	Tax rate[i]	Example
Up to £175,000[ii]	0%	No tax
£175,001 to £250,000	1%	On £176,000 home, £1,760
£250,001 to £500,000	3%	On £300,000 home, £9,000
Over £500,000	4%	On £600,000 home, £24,000

[i] Applies to whole price not just the excess over the threshold.

[ii] Until 31 December 2009. From 1 January 2010, the 0% band is due to revert to 'Up to £125,000'.

Since the global financial crisis which started in 2007 and the subsequent fall in house prices, lenders have become more cautious and you are unlikely to be able to borrow the full cost of a home. Typically, you will be expected to have a deposit of at least 10 per cent of the value of the home and to get the best mortgage deals you might have to have a much bigger one – eg, of 40 per cent.

A very important consideration when deciding whether to rent or buy is security of tenure. If you rent from a local authority or housing association, you will usually have a long-term lease. If you are renting in the private sector, it is more common to have a six-month lease, although typically this may be rolled over and renewed for further periods. The main problem with tenure arises if your landlord does not own the property outright but is buying it with a buy-to-let mortgage. The recession and fall in house prices caused by the 2007 global financial crisis has put pressure on many buy-to-let landlords. If your landlord cannot keep up the mortgage payments, the lender will normally repossess and sell the property in order to get the loan back. As a tenant, you have no contract with the lender, no rights to stop this process and could find yourself evicted with very little notice. At the time of writing, the Government is in the process of changing the law so that tenants in this situation with have the legal right to two months' notice to leave. In the meantime, opening any mail that arrives at your home for the landlord may at least give you some advance warning.

Government help for homebuyers during the financial crisis

The global financial crisis which started in 2007 triggered a recession in many countries around the world, including the UK. A feature of recession is rising unemployment. Job loss is therefore a key reason for homeowners to run into problems keeping up their mortgages payments, with a real risk of their homes being repossessed. To avoid a steep rise in the number of people losing their homes, the Government has introduced a number of special schemes.

A protocol with lenders. Lenders have agreed that they will use repossession as a last resort. Therefore, if you run into mortgage problems, your lender should explore a full range of options which might include, for example, extending the term of your mortgage (which would reduce the monthly payments – see the table on p156), deferring the interest for a period and adding it to your outstanding loan and, if necessary, giving you time to sell your home yourself (in which case, you are likely to get a better price than if it sold quickly by the lender on repossession). If your lender does not follow the protocol, you should raise this with the court if repossession action is started and the court will take this into account. You can also complain to the Financial Ombudsman Service (see Chapter 10).

Support for mortgage interest. If you lose your job and your savings are low, you may be entitled to means-tested state benefits (see Chapter 9). The benefits may cover interest (but not capital repayments) on your mortgage but you could not get this help until you had been on benefits for 39 weeks. This waiting period has been cut so that help now starts 13 weeks after the start of your claim.

Mortgage Rescue Scheme. This may help if your home is being repossessed and so you will become homeless and will have to apply to your local authority for accommodation. There are two types of help: shared equity or mortgage-to-rent. Under the shared equity version, a housing association pays off part of your mortgage so that your monthly payments are reduced and, in return, the housing association takes over legal ownership of part of your home. This means when you eventually sell, the housing association will take part of the proceeds. Under the mortgage-to-rent version, you sell your whole home to the housing association, which uses the proceeds to pay off your mortgage. Instead of paying a mortgage you then pay rent to the association. Rent is charged at a subsidised rate so your outgoings should be less. This scheme applies in England, although similar schemes operate in the rest of the UK.

Homeowners Mortgage Support Scheme. This could apply if you have an unexpected temporary drop in your income, cannot meet your mortgage payments and your lender has agreed to be part of the scheme. The lender may agree to let you defer your interest payments for up to two years. You will have to make good the missed interest later on when your income recovers.

For details of these schemes, contact your local authority, your lender or any of the free, independent debt advice organisations listed in Appendix 2 – eg, Citizens Advice Bureau, Community Legal Advice (England and Wales only), Consumer Credit Counselling Service, Money Advice Scotland and National Debtline.

Sale and rent back schemes

A number of private firms claim to be able to help you if you run into mortgage problems by offering sale and rent back schemes. You agree to sell your property to the firm, but have the right to carry on living there as a tenant. This sounds similar to an equity release scheme (see p162), but in fact is very different. Sale and rent back schemes have a number of serious flaws that were highlighted in a study by the Office of Fair Trading.[9] Problems arise because:

- you will be offered a knock-down price for your home, which often means you get very poor value from the deal;
- even though you sold at a discount, you are still charged a full commercial rent as a tenant;
- the big selling feature of these schemes is that you can stay in your own home but, in fact, the tenancy agreement is usually only for six- or 12-months. After that, the landlord may raise the rent substantially or even not renew the lease at all. So you have no security of tenure;
- the landlord usually buys property with a mortgage. If the landlord cannot keep up the mortgage payments and the home is repossessed, you have no right to stay.

These problems were considered so acute, that the Government rushed through legislation to bring sale and rent back schemes within the scope of Financial Services Authority (FSA) regulation from mid-2009. Initially, only a skeleton set of rules apply, with full regulation due from 2010. From mid-2009, all firms offering these schemes must be authorised by the FSA (which will mean firms being able to demonstrate that they are doing business in an honest and professional manner). Firms must treat customers fairly, ensure the schemes they offer are suitable given your circumstances and offer proper complaints procedures.

Ordinary mortgages

How they work

A mortgage is a loan secured against your home and most often used to buy the home (but it can be used for other purposes – see p159). Homes are costly items, so you usually arrange to pay off the mortgage over a long period (typically up to 25 years), which keeps the monthly payments to a manageable level.

All mortgages work in one of two ways.

- **Repayment** (also called 'capital and interest'). Each monthly payment pays off both the interest due and part of the capital. Provided you make all the agreed payments, the whole loan is paid off by the end of the mortgage term.
- **Interest only**. Your monthly payments cover only the interest on the loan and none of the capital. At the end of the mortgage term, you pay off the capital in a single lump sum. This means you need to plan where the lump sum will come from (see below).

If you do not keep up the monthly mortgage payments as agreed or, in the case of an interest-only loan, pay off the capital in full at the end of the term, the lender can take possession of your home and sell it in order to get back the money you owe.

Paying off an interest-only mortgage

With an interest-only mortgage, the amount you borrow stays the same throughout the whole mortgage term and you pay it off in a single lump sum at the end. You choose where the lump sum will come from.

One possibility would be to sell the property. This could be feasible if it is a buy-to-let investment, but there are always the risks that you will not be able to find a buyer or that the sale proceeds will be less than the amount of the outstanding loan.

Selling is not be feasible if it is your home and you need to continue living in it, so the main option is to save regularly during the mortgage term to build up the lump sum you need. In effect, you are hoping to invest for a higher return than the rate of interest you are paying to borrow and this is likely only if you choose investments whose return is linked to the stock market (see Chapter 4). The main investments used are:

– endowment policy. This is a sort of investment-type life insurance (see p111). Endowment mortgages could have been a sensible choice up to the mid-1980s, but the tax and investment climate then changed. Despite that, endowment mortgages continued to be sold for many years. However, for most people, they are not now a good choice;

– individual savings account (ISA). Savings in an ISA build up partly tax-free (see p78). The maximum you can save this way is limited to £7,200 a year from 2009/10, increasing to £10,200 from 6 October 2009 for people aged 50 and over and from 6 April 2010 for everyone else;

– personal pension. Personal pensions benefit from various tax reliefs (see Chapter 6), including taking one-quarter of your pension fund as a tax-free lump sum. You could earmark the lump sum to pay off your mortgage. A big drawback is that this might leave you short of money to fund your retirement.

With all stock market investments, there is a risk that your money will not grow as well as you had hoped. In addition, unless you invest on a with-profits basis (see p111), the value of your investment might fall rather than rise. So there is no guarantee that your savings will build up enough to pay off your mortgage in full. It is essential that you check the progress of your savings regularly (eg, once a year) and increase the amount you are saving if it looks like there could be a shortfall. If you are not happy with this risk, choose a repayment mortgage instead.

What they cost

The main cost of a mortgage is the interest you are charged. However, there are also other costs (see p158).

Your monthly payments depend on the type of mortgage you have (repayment or interest only), the mortgage term and the interest rate. For example, the table on p156 shows that, if the interest rate was 6 per cent a year and you have a 25-year repayment mortgage, you can expect to pay about £6.44 a month for each £1,000 you borrow. So for a £50,000 mortgage you would pay around 50 x £6.44 = £322 a month.

With a repayment mortgage, the interest is worked out on a decreasing balance basis by assuming that the current rate of interest applies throughout the mortgage term. In practice, the rate is likely to change and every time it does the monthly payment is recalculated (though for convenience some lenders alter the amount you pay just once a year, which is called the 'gross profile' method of paying).

With an interest-only mortgage, the interest is a percentage of the capital, which stays the same throughout the mortgage term.

How much you might pay each month for your mortgage

Interest rate per annun	Repayment mortgage with a remaining term of:						Interest-only mortgage*
	5 years	10 years	15 years	20 years	25 years	30 years	Any term
1%	£17.09	£8.76	£5.98	£4.60	£3.77	£3.22	£0.83
2%	£17.51	£9.19	£6.43	£5.06	£4.24	£3.69	£1.67
3%	£17.95	£9.65	£6.90	£5.54	£4.74	£4.21	£2.50
4%	£18.39	£10.11	£7.39	£6.05	£5.27	£4.77	£3.33
5%	£18.84	£10.59	£7.90	£6.59	£5.84	£5.36	£4.17
6%	£19.29	£11.08	£8.43	£7.16	£6.44	£5.99	£5.00
7%	£19.75	£11.59	£8.97	£7.74	£7.06	£6.65	£5.83
8%	£20.22	£12.11	£9.54	£8.35	£7.71	£7.33	£6.67
9%	£20.70	£12.64	£10.13	£8.99	£8.38	£8.04	£7.50
10%	£21.18	£13.18	£10.73	£9.64	£9.08	£8.77	£8.33
11%	£21.67	£13.74	£11.35	£10.31	£9.79	£9.52	£9.17
12%	£22.17	£14.31	£11.98	£11.00	£10.52	£10.28	£10.00

Note: this table shows the monthly payment for each £1,000 you borrow worked out as if the interest rate applied for the whole of the remaining term.

*To this you must add the cost of savings you make to build up a lump sum to pay off the capital at the end of the term.

You can choose what type of interest deal you want.

- **Standard variable rate.** This is the lender's basic interest rate. It is variable and tends to move up and down in line with interest rates in the economy as a whole. Usually it is not the best choice, but might be the only option if you are interested in, for example, a cashback deal (see p157) or an all-in-one mortgage (see p157).
- **Discounted rate.** This is a variable rate which is a set percentage below the lender's standard variable rate for a set period – usually the first one to five years of the mortgage. This keeps your mortgage payments low in the early years when money may be tight, but you need to make sure you can cope with a jump in payments once the discounted period is over.
- **Base rate tracker.** This is a variable rate that is a set percentage above the Bank of England base rate and so moves up and down in line with changes in that rate (usually within 30 days of the change in the rate being tracked). Typically, the tracker period lasts for a set time and you revert to the standard variable

rate when the tracker period ends. A base rate tracker is designed to ensure that you get the full benefit of any fall in the base rate. However, with some deals there is a floor (eg, 2 per cent) below which your mortgage rate will not fall, even though the Bank of England base rate may be lower. In mid-2009, the base rate was 0.5 per cent.

- **Capped rate**. This is a variable rate that is, however, guaranteed not to go above a certain level even if interest rates generally continue to rise. Often the rate is also 'collared', which means it will also not fall below a certain level even if rates generally go lower. The advantage is that, although your monthly payments go up and down, you know they will not go above a certain amount which helps you to budget.

- **Fixed rate**. The interest rate is set at one level for a specified period. Typically, this might be two to ten years, but a few lenders offer longer fixed terms. The big advantage of a fixed rate is that you know exactly how much you will have to pay each month, which makes it easy to budget. The drawback is that you will not benefit from any fall in interest rates generally.

- **Cashback deal**. Strictly, this is not an interest rate deal but you should weigh it up alongside the interest rate. With a cashback, you usually pay the standard variable rate (see above), but at the start of the mortgage you receive a cash lump sum – eg, 3 to 5 per cent of the amount you are borrowing. It is up to you how you use the money – eg, you could use the money to furnish your new home or put it in a savings account and use it to help pay your monthly mortgage payments during the first few years or if interest rates go up.

Mortgage variations

Flexible mortgage. You are allowed to vary your monthly repayments and sometimes even to take a repayment holiday. Interest is usually worked out daily, so you immediately get the effect of increasing your repayments or paying off an extra lump sum. Being able to reduce or miss payments can help you cope with temporary financial situations – eg, a drop in income while on maternity leave or switching jobs.

All-in-one (off-set) mortgage. You have your current account and possibly also a savings account with the mortgage lender. You pay the standard variable rate on the mortgage, but before the interest is worked out the balances in your current and savings accounts are deducted from the outstanding mortgage. The current account and savings account earn no interest as such, but because they reduce the amount on which mortgage interest is charged, they are effectively earning the mortgage rate. Moreover, because you do not pay tax on the loan interest saved, the 'return' on your savings is tax-free. A drawback of having your current account and/or savings with the same provider as your mortgage is that, if you run into problems making your mortgage payments, the lender might automatically use your current account and/or savings to pay off the arrears.

Right-to-buy mortgage. This is a mortgage you use to buy a council home (or a home which was previously owned by the council but transferred to another social landlord) and which you have rented for at least two years. You can use an ordinary mortgage from any lender, but some lenders offer special right-to-buy mortgages where, for example, you can add legal and valuation fees to the loan instead of paying upfront and can borrow even if your credit history (see p134) is poor. They are useful if you cannot get a standard mortgage, but tend to be expensive.

Self-certification mortgage. Usually a lender requires proof of your income before agreeing to give you a mortgage. However, if you cannot provide proof – eg, you run a small business and do not have audited accounts or a large part of your income is from a variable source such as commission, some lenders offer mortgages where you do not need to give the usual proofs. However, you generally pay a higher than normal interest rate for such loans. The FSA is proposing that these mortgages should be banned in future.

Other costs

If you have an interest-only mortgage, the largest additional cost is the amount you save each month to build up a lump sum to pay off the capital at the end of the mortgage term.

A mortgage is secured on the property so the lender needs to know that the property is valuable enough to cover the whole loan. Therefore, you must have the property valued and there is a charge for this, typically around £300 or so. (You can choose to have a more complete survey of the property, which you arrange yourself and which costs more.) You normally employ a solicitor or conveyancer to deal with the paperwork associated with the mortgage, which again costs several hundred pounds. As a special offer, lenders might waive the valuation fee and/or pay your legal fees up to a certain amount.

You may have to pay an arrangement fee (sometimes called a 'booking fee') when you apply for a mortgage. This is most common with fixed- and capped-rate deals.

If you are borrowing a large amount relative to the value of the property (eg, more than 90 per cent of its value) you may have to pay a high lending charge (also called a 'mortgage indemnity premium' or 'mortgage indemnity guarantee'). This is a one-off premium for insurance that protects the lender, but not you, if the property has to be sold to repay the loan. If the sale proceeds are too low to pay off the loan in full the shortfall is made up by the insurance. But the insurer can then try to recover the shortfall from you. The high lending charge can be added to your loan and paid off over the mortgage term – although convenient, this pushes up the total cost of the insurance.

The lender will insist that you have buildings insurance in case your home is damaged or destroyed (see Chapter 7). You may have to arrange this through the lender or, if you are allowed to choose your own insurance, the lender might charge an administration fee for checking the policy is suitable.

A particular mortgage deal may come packaged with other types of insurance – eg, home contents insurance, life insurance (see Chapter 7) and/or mortgage payment protection insurance (see p125).

If you pay off your mortgage in the early years or during the period of an interest rate deal, you must usually pay an early repayment fee (also called an 'early redemption fee'). This might be up to, say 5 per cent of the amount paid off or six months' interest. With some mortgages, the fee is levied even after an interest rate deal has finished – eg, you might have a discounted rate for two years, but face an early repayment fee for five years.

If you pay off your full mortgage at any other time, there is usually a deeds fee (also called a 'sealing fee') to cover the administration and legal work involved with ending the mortgage.

Useful for

- Buying your home.
- Buying a second property – eg, a holiday home or buy-to-let property (ie, a property you let out to bring in a rental income and hopefully also make a capital gain when you sell the property).
- Paying for expensive items, such as home improvements or helping children with the cost of university. You must be happy to repay the money over a long period, which will mean you are paying more in total than you would with a shorter-term loan (see p124).
- Replacing existing debts so that your monthly payments are lower.

Providers

Banks, building societies, specialist mortgage lenders and mortgage brokers.

Choosing and applying

Check out the tables comparing mortgages produced by, for example, the Financial Services Authority, Moneyfacts and other comparison websites. Bear in mind the limitations of comparison websites (see p8) and check out two or three rather than relying on just one. Many websites have interactive software to help you narrow down the choice. Tables are also published in the personal finance sections of newspapers and personal finance magazines. Either shop around yourself or enlist the help of a mortgage broker (see Chapter 2).

When you have a shortlist of mortgages, approach the lenders directly or through your broker (at a branch, by phone or online). Whenever you enquire about a particular mortgage, you must be given a key facts illustration which sets out the important features of the mortgage deal in a way which makes it easy for you to compare one mortgage deal with another.

Check the details of each mortgage deal and, if you choose one, consider asking for a mortgage promise. This is a document stating that the lender agrees in principle to give you a loan of a certain amount. Having a mortgage promise may give you the edge when making an offer on a property because it shows you are a serious buyer and that you have funding in place.

When you have found a property (or immediately if you are remortgaging), complete the lender's detailed application form. The lender will seek a credit reference (see p134) and normally requires proof of your earnings (eg, a recent P60, letter from your employer, or audited accounts if you are self-employed). The property must be valued and, provided both you and the property are suitable, you will normally be offered the mortgage.

Although a mortgage is a long-term loan, you do not have to keep the same deal for the full mortgage term. From time to time (eg, every five years or whenever a special interest rate deal comes to an end), check whether you would pay less by switching to a different lender. You need to weigh up whether the resulting drop in your monthly payments will outweigh the costs of switching (valuation fee, legal fees and any early repayment charge on paying off the old mortgage).

Pitfalls and what to watch out for

- A mortgage is secured on your home. If you do not keep up the repayments, you could lose your home.
- Do not borrow more than you can afford. Consider your income and existing spending to judge how much you can afford. Do not forget other costs such as insurance premiums, stamp duty and maintenance.
- If the mortgage interest rate is low for the first year or so, make sure you can cope with the increase in payments once the special deal ends.
- Watch out for penalties if you want to pay off the mortgage early. Be aware that, with some special interest deals (discounted or fixed rates), penalties extend beyond the period of the deal, making it expensive to switch to a cheaper lender.

Shared equity mortgages

How they work

Shared equity mortgages are schemes to make buying a home more affordable. You take out a mortgage that helps you buy part of the home, but you rent the rest. So, each month, your home-related expenses include mortgage payments and rent. Typically, you can buy between 25 and 75 per cent of the home. Many schemes are flexible and offer you the option of 'staircasing', which means increasing (or decreasing) the proportion of the home you own. With most, you can increase your ownership up to 100 per cent of the property. Each extra share you buy is valued according to the market price of the home at that time. When you want to sell, the scheme provider may have the option to nominate the person who will buy, but otherwise it is just the same as selling any other home. You benefit from any increase in the part of the home you own, but not the part you rent. Many shared-equity mortgages are part of government programmes to encourage homeownership – eg, New Build HomeBuy, which gives priority to existing social tenants and public sector key workers (such as people working for the police and in hospitals) and Social HomeBuy to help existing social tenants buy part or all of their current home (or an alternative offered by their landlord) at a discounted price.

What they cost

The total mortgage payment plus rent are normally a lot lower than the cost of a mortgage to buy the whole home because the Government generally subsidises the rent you pay under the scheme.

You might be offered a 100 per cent mortgage for the share you are buying or you might need to find a small deposit (eg, 5 per cent of the value of the share you are buying). Mortgage costs are as for ordinary mortgages (see p155).

Useful for

- Buying your own home when you cannot afford an ordinary mortgage deal.

Providers

Registered social landlords and some developers.

Choosing and applying

With some schemes, you have to be nominated by your local authority from the housing waiting list. With others, you can apply direct. You are not normally eligible if you can afford to take out an ordinary mortgage to buy the whole home.

You pay rent to the landlord. The mortgage part of your scheme is provided by a bank or building society in the same way as an ordinary mortgage.

Pitfalls and what to watch out for

- As with an ordinary mortgage, a shared equity mortgage is secured on your home. If you do not keep up the repayments, you could lose your home.
- Do not borrow more than you can afford. Consider your income and existing spending to judge how much you can afford. Do not forget other costs such as insurance premiums, stamp duty and maintenance.
- If the mortgage interest rate is low for the first year or so, make sure you will be able to cope with the increase in payments once the special deal ends. Similarly, if you choose a variable rate mortgage, make sure you would be able to cope if the rate increased.

Islamic (*Shariah*-complaint) home finance

How they work

Shariah law prohibits interest to be charged or received. Therefore, Islamic home finance is arranged on an alternative basis, most commonly as *Ijara* (leasing) with diminishing *Musharaka* (equity). You typically buy, for instance, 20 per cent of the property and a bank buys the remaining 80 per cent. You pay rent to the bank during the term of the agreement. You also make regular capital payments that each buy a further slice of the home from the bank, until you own the whole home. Another option is *Murabaha* (purchase and resale) where the bank buys most of the property you want and immediately resells it to you at a higher price. You own the whole home immediately, but pay the bank in instalments over an agreed period. It is also important that the home finance provider is not using its money for any purposes prohibited under *Shariah* law, such as investing in industries concerned with alcohol, pork or gambling.

What they cost

You will usually be required to put down a larger deposit (eg, 20 or 30 per cent of the purchase price) when buying with Islamic home finance than with an ordinary mortgage.

Useful for

- Muslims and others who do not wish to pay interest.
- As an alternative to an ordinary mortgage for anyone, regardless of their religious beliefs.

Providers

A handful of UK banks – eg, the Islamic Bank of Britain, HSBC Amanah Finance, Lloyds TSB.

Choosing and applying

Direct to the provider or through a mortgage broker (see Chapter 2).

Pitfalls and what to watch out for

- Do not enter an agreement for more than you can afford. Consider your income and existing spending to judge how much you can afford.
- Do not forget other costs such as insurance premiums, stamp duty and maintenance.

Equity release schemes

How they work

These allow you to raise money from your home to use for any purpose while retaining the right to continue to live in it. There are two main types of equity release scheme.

- **Lifetime mortgage.** You take out a mortgage against your home. Typically, you do not make any monthly interest or capital repayments. Instead, interest is 'rolled up' and added to the outstanding loan balance, which is paid off only when you no longer need the home (usually on death or on moving permanently into a care home).

- **Home reversion scheme**. This does not involve mortgages (but is included here for comparison). You sell part or all of your home to the reversion company. You get cash now and also become a tenant with the right to remain in your home for as long as you need to, either rent-free or for a peppercorn rent. The home is sold when you die or move permanently into a care home and the reversion company then takes its share of the sale proceeds.

Both schemes can provide either a lump sum or an income. Although income can be provided by investing the lump sum, it is often more tax-efficient to draw a regular pattern of small lump sums.

What they cost

The amount owed on a lifetime mortgage can grow at an alarming rate when interest is added as the example in the table below shows. So your estate will end up paying back a lot more than you originally borrowed. With a home reversion scheme, the firm usually has to wait many years to get anything back from the deal and this is reflected in the amount it will give you for the part of the home you sell – eg, you might sell 60 per cent of your home but receive only 30 per cent of the home's value. So, with equity release, you will never receive the full value of the part of the home you give up. How much of the value of your home is left to pass on to your heirs will depend on the amount you borrow or sell and also how house prices change in future. There are also other costs involved, such as legal fees, arrangement fees, and ongoing costs of insurance and maintenance.

How the amount owed under a lifetime mortgage might grow

	Interest rate per annum					
	5%	6%	7%	8%	9%	10%
Mortgage term (years)						
1	£52,500	£53,000	£53,500	£54,000	£54,500	£55,000
5	£63,814	£66,911	£70,128	£73,466	£76,931	£80,526
10	£81,445	£89,542	£98,358	£107,946	£118,368	£129,687
15	£103,946	£119,828	£137,952	£158,608	£182,124	£208,862
20	£132,665	£160,357	£193,484	£233,048	£280,221	£336,375
25	£169,318	£214,594	£271,372	£342,424	£431,154	£541,735

Note: the amount borrowed is £50,000. The table shows the outstanding balance after interest on the loan has been added as the mortgage term progresses. Interest is then charged on the loan plus interest – a process called 'compounding.'

Useful for

- Raising a lump sum or extra income if you have no other sources and do not want to move home.

- Some advisers suggest using equity release schemes to reduce inheritance tax on your estate at death. However, you could end up simply transferring money to the provider rather than HM Revenue and Customs with no real gain for your heirs.

Providers

Lifetime mortgages from banks and building societies. Home reversion schemes from specialist firms.

Choosing and applying

This is a complex area, so get advice from an independent financial adviser. If you are considering a home reversion scheme, it is also essential to get independent advice from a solicitor working for you, not the reversion company.

Pitfalls and what to watch out for

- Be very clear that an equity release scheme will not give you full value for the part of your home that you give up. The only way to extract the full value would be to downsize by selling your home and buying somewhere cheaper.
- With a lifetime mortgage, make sure it comes with a no negative equity guarantee, so that the outstanding loan can never exceed the value of your home.
- With a home reversion scheme, any increase in the part of the home you have sold benefits the reversion scheme provider not you. On the other hand, the provider would also bear any loss on that part of the home if house prices fell.
- Before going ahead, consider discussing your intentions with people who might expect to inherit from you, so that they understand the situation.
- Be very wary of using an equity release scheme to increase your income if you are eligible for benefits. The lump sum or income raised is likely to reduce the benefits you can claim.
- Income from some types of equity release scheme could have a disproportionately large impact on the tax you pay. Ask your adviser to consider this and to recommend a suitable type of scheme.

7. **Other types of credit**

Credit union

A credit union is a mutual self-help organisation owned and run by its members and regulated by the Financial Services Authority (FSA). The members must all have a common bond, such as living in the same area, working for the same employer, or belonging to the same church. From a date yet to be announced (but likely to be by the end of 2009), a single credit union may combine members covered by more than one common bond.

The rules vary, but normally you must save with the credit union for at least three months before you are allowed to borrow. However, some credit unions now make immediate loans even if you have not yet built up a record of saving. Your savings may earn interest. This is currently technically a dividend paid at the discretion of the credit union only if funds are available, although the rules are due to change so that credit unions will in future be able to offer accounts that pay contractual interest. Some credit unions pay only a low rate of return or no dividends at all. You do not have to save regularly but can pay in *ad hoc* amounts as and when you can afford to.

The maximum loan you can have by law is £5,000 plus the amount you have saved. Individual credit unions may set a lower limit. The maximum interest you can be charged on the loan is 2 per cent a month (26.8 per cent a year). This limit applies even if you have a poor credit history. If you have a good credit history or good record of saving, you are likely to be charged less than 2 per cent. Credit unions rely on the common bond to foster a sense of mutual responsibility between members, so borrowers are less likely to fail to make the repayments as they fall due.

You usually have to repay the loan within three years if it is unsecured and seven years if it is secured.

To find out if there is a credit union you could join, or for information about how to start one, contact the Association of British Credit Unions Limited.

Life insurance loan

If you have a with-profits life insurance policy, which has built up a cash-in value, you could cash it in to raise some money, but charges mean the amount you get back may be poor value (see p113). An alternative may be to take out a loan secured against the value of the policy.

Some personal loan providers (see p145) offer life insurance loans. So too might the insurance company with whom you hold the policy.

You cannot normally borrow against the value of a unit-linked life insurance policy (see p111) because, unlike a with-profits policy, if stock markets fall you can lose some or all of the cash-in value that has built up.

Student loan

If you are studying at university, you can take out a student loan each year to help towards your living costs and, since 2006 in England and Wales, to cover your tuition fees. If your home and place of study are both in Scotland, there are no tuition fees. See p122 for details of the support available for students.

There is no interest on the money you borrow. Instead, the amount you owe is increased each year in line with inflation. This makes student loans a relatively cheap way to borrow.

You start to repay student loans only after your course has ended and then only if your income exceeds a set threshold (£15,000 in 2009/10). Your repayments are set at 9 per cent of your income above the income threshold. You can pay off more if you like, but do not do this if you would then have to borrow from a more expensive source (eg, a credit card or mortgage).

For information, contact the relevant student finance helpline if you live in England, Wales or Northern Ireland, or the Student Awards Agency for Scotland. Alternatively, visit the Department for Business, Innovation and Skills student support website (www.dius.gov.uk).

Zopa

Usually when you borrow, you do so through an institution like a bank or a credit union whose business is transferring money from savers to people who want to borrow. Zopa is a 'social lending' website (http://uk.zopa.com) that brings savers and borrowers together to trade directly with each other. Because there is no institution involved needing a profit, potentially both savers and borrowers can get a better deal. If you want to borrow, you have to fill in an online application form which includes details of your address, spending, bank account and employer. You must have an income of at least £12,000 a year and are not eligible if you have outstanding debt problems. You are credit scored and your loan application is assigned to one of four risk-related categories. Savers (ie, the people who lend) indicate what category of loan they are interested in making and how much interest they want. Borrowers can compare the loan deals on offer before deciding which to take up.

Pay-day loans

According to a survey by Abbey Banking in 2008, two-thirds of British people run out of cash each month. On average their funds run out five days before pay day. This gap is met by the pay-day loan business which makes relatively small, short-term loans designed to tide you over until your next pay cheque. They are convenient, but expensive – you typically pay back around £25 for every £100 you borrow. Because you are borrowing over a short period (anything from a few days up to a month), the true cost of these loans is extremely high – eg, over 1,700 per cent a year. If you need to roll over the loan for a further month, the amount you owe escalates rapidly because you then pay charges on the charges. Pay-day loans are available through high street cash shops and online. To qualify, you must be an employee and have a bank account.

Pawnbrokers

Pawnbrokers are another source of short-term loans, typically used to ease a temporary cash flow problem. You can borrow from £5 up to many thousands usually for a period of six months, although you can repay the loan early at any time. There are no credit checks because pawnbrokers only provide secured loans. You hand over to the pawnbroker an item against which the loan will be secured – eg, in the vast majority of cases, this is something made of gold, a piece of jewellery or a watch. The pawnbroker values the item and this determines the maximum loan you can have. For example, if you offer an item with a second-hand value of £1,000, you might be able to borrow up to £500. Monthly interest is added to the loan. At the end of six months, if you have not already paid off the loan and redeemed your item, you can:

- repay the loan with interest and get your item back;
- pay the interest, but roll over the loan for a further period;
- pay back nothing and the pawnbroker sells the item in order to recover the loan and interest. If the loan was for no more than £75, the pawnbroker keeps any surplus. If the loan was for more, the pawnbroker must pay any surplus to you.

Even though the loans are secured (so the risk to the pawnbroker is low), interest rates are fairly high – eg, around 8 per cent a month (which is equivalent to an annual percentage rate of over 152 per cent). Many pawnbrokers operate from high street shops that often double up as jewellers and may offer other services, such as cashing cheques for a fee for people without bank accounts. You can also deal with online pawnbrokers, in which case, the security is sent and returned by post.

8. **Dealing with debt**

Your rights and responsibilities

When you borrow money, you enter into a contract with the lender. You are required by law to be given a written agreement setting out the terms and conditions.

The main obligation on you is to make the agreed repayments on time. If you fail to do this, you are in breach of the contract and the lender has the right to try to get its money back. The steps it can take to do this depend on the type of loan and what it is for – see the table on p168. As shown, some of the steps would have a very serious impact on you, especially if you might lose your home or have essential services cut off. Therefore, it is important that you seek help as soon as you realise you have a problem keeping up the repayments.

What can happen if you do not pay money you owe

Type of debt	What the lender can do to recover its money	Is this a priority debt? (see p169)
Your rent	Take you to court to recover the rent owed. Evict you to stop any more rent going unpaid.	Yes
Your mortgage	Repossess your home and sell it to raise the money to pay off the loan.	Yes
Other loans secured on your home	Repossess your home and sell it to raise the money to pay off the loan.	Yes
Fuel bills	Take you to court to recover the money owed. Cut off your gas or electricity to stop the amount owed increasing.	Yes
Telephone bill	Take you to court to recover the money owed. Cut off your telephone to stop the amount owed increasing.*	Yes, if a telephone is important to you
TV licence	You can be fined and/or sent to jail and your possessions seized to pay the arrears and fines.	Yes
Council tax	Take you to court. You can be fined and/or sent to jail and your possessions seized to pay the arrears and fines.	Yes
Other taxes	You can be fined and your possessions seized to pay the arrears and fines. You could be declared bankrupt.	Yes
Magistrates' court fines	You can be sent to prison and/or your possessions can be seized to pay the arrears.	Yes
Hire purchase payments (eg, for a car)	Take back the goods.	Yes, if the goods are important to you – eg, if you need a car
Water bills	Take you to court to recover the money owed. Water companies are not allowed to cut off your supply.*	No

| Credit card debts, unsecured personal loans, overdrafts | Take you to court to recover the money owed. Refuse you any further credit. If you owe money to the bank where you have a current account or basic bank account, the bank may take money from the account to pay off what you owe to the bank. This can be a problem if there are more important debts to be paid off first, so you may need to open a new basic bank account with a different bank. | No |

*Note: some fuel and water suppliers have set up charities which can make grants to help vulnerable customers cope with utility debts and provide help getting their finances back on track. Contact the fuel or water supplier for details.

If you have a debt problem

For help dealing with a debt problem, contact:
- a Citizens Advice Bureau;
- Community Legal Advice (England and Wales only);
- Consumer Credit Counselling Service;
- Money Advice Scotland;
- National Debtline.

See Appendix 2 for contact details.

For further information about dealing with debt, see CPAG's *Debt Advice Handbook*.

If you are in debt, you should do the following.
- **Stop borrowing more**. To remove temptation, cut up your credit and store cards.
- **Work out how much you can afford to pay each week or month to clear your debts**. Do this by making a note of all your spending over a week and then preparing a budget, listing all your income and expenditure. See what spending you could cut back on. Make sure you are getting all the income to which you are entitled. See Chapter 9 for information about benefits and tax credits.
- **Prioritise your debts**. Give top priority to debts with unacceptable consequences – eg, your rent or mortgage (so you can avoid losing your home), fuel bills (so you will not be cut off), a car loan if your car is essential for travel.

- **Put your available money towards paying off the priority debts**. Spread what is left over across the non-priority debts, such as your credit card, unsecured personal loans and overdraft. Even if the amount you can pay each non-priority lender is small, they are likely to accept what you offer because their only alternative is to go to court and the court is likely to order you to pay similarly small amounts.
- **Contact each lender**. Explain the problem and state how you intend to pay off what you owe. Ask the lender to freeze your debt while you repay the backlog by foregoing any new interest charges. It is best to negotiate in writing so that you have a clear record of what is agreed and cannot be persuaded to pay more to any creditor than you can afford.

The free, independent debt advice agencies will help and advise you on all these stages. In particular, they will help you work out a budget and a plan for clearing your debts and, if you want, can negotiate with your creditors on your behalf.

Debt management companies

You will see advertisements, for example, in newspapers and on television, for firms that can help you sort out your debts. You generally make a single monthly payment to the company, which then negotiates with your creditors on your behalf and handles your payments to each one. You should avoid these companies because of:

- **charges**. Typically, the whole of your first monthly payment goes to the debt management company with none of it being used to reduce your debts. Out of each subsequent payment, around 15 per cent is taken by the company in charges. You could get the same service free of charge from any of the organisations listed above;
- **poor service**. For example, many of these companies have a reputation for being sloppy when working out your budget, failing to take all priority debts into account and failing to negotiate a freeze in interest while you pay off what you owe.

Debt consolidation

Private companies offer to consolidate your loans by replacing all your debts with a single loan. The aim is to reduce the amount you pay each month for all your debts and this is achieved by replacing unsecured borrowing, such as credit cards and personal loans, with a single loan secured against your home. For this reason, the advertisements will mention 'homeowners only' or similar words. Be very wary of going down this route. Bear in mind that you could lose your home if you fail to keep up the payments on a secured loan.

Other solutions

There are a range of other options for dealing with your debts. With these, you do not deal direct with your creditors yourself but must go through an official process and usually there are fees or charges. The options available in England, Wales and Northern Ireland are described below. Different arrangements apply in Scotland.

- **Debt relief order (DRO).** This is a relatively new arrangement available since 6 April 2009 and designed to help you if your income is low and you have few assets. You apply through an intermediary – eg, one of the free independent debt advice agencies listed on p169, such as a Citizens Advice Bureau or National Debtline. The arrangement covers all your eligible debts and lasts for 12 months. During the 12-month period, you make no payments (unless your circumstances change, in which case the arrangement may be reassessed) and your creditors cannot take any action against you. At the end of 12 months, any remaining debt is written off. You may be eligible for a DRO, if your income after essential spending is £50 a month or less, you have no more than £300 in savings, and your debts total no more than £15,000.

- **Administration order.** There is a legal provision available if you have debts of less than £5,000 in total and at least one county court judgement against you. It allows you to make a regular monthly payment into the court, which then make *pro rata* distributions to all your creditors. During this process, all creditors are prevented from adding interest or taking any further legal action against you.

- **Individual voluntary arrangement (IVA).** This is a legally binding agreement to pay off an agreed proportion of your debts (eg, 25p to 40p in the £1) through regular payments over a set period (typically five years), after which the remaining debts are written off. Provided you keep up the agreed payments, you should not lose your home or job.

- **Bankruptcy.** Trustees are appointed to take over handling your financial affairs. They can sell the assets you own, including your home if you own it, in order to pay off as much of your debts as possible. Bankruptcy usually lasts for 12 months, after which any remaining debts are written off. Bankruptcy may prohibit you from, or make it impossible to carry on doing, certain jobs, such as being a company director or manager, a Member of Parliament, local councillor, solicitor or accountant.

DROs, IVAs and bankruptcy must be administered by an insolvency practitioner or other official. The fee for a DRO is £90, but IVAs and bankruptcy may cost several thousands of pounds and will be deducted from the money you have available to clear your debts. A DRO, IVA or bankruptcy will also affect your ability to get credit, both during the term of the agreement or bankruptcy and for six years after, during which time the arrangement continues to be shown on your credit reference agency files. For example, you may find it impossible or very expensive to get a mortgage or other loans, and utility companies may insist on a deposit and payment via a pre-payment meter.

For more details, see CPAG's *Debt Advice Handbook*.

Debt remedies in Scotland

Debt arrangement scheme (DAS). To be eligible for a DAS you must have more than one debt and there must be no trust deeds or bankruptcy orders against you. You draw up a plan to pay off your debts, as described on p169, but you apply through an approved money adviser for the plan to be recognised as a DAS. Your creditors must then stop any action to recover the debts and interest on them is frozen. You make a single monthly payment to an approved distributor who deals with your creditors. When you go to any of the free, independent money advice agencies listed on p169, they can suggest whether a DAS would be suitable and pass you on to a DAS-approved money adviser. A DAS is free through some approved money advisers, but others charge.

Trust deed or protected trust deed. This is a legally binding arrangement with your creditors. Your assets, including your home, are passed to a trustee whose aim is to pay off as much as possible of what you owe. If the trust deed is 'protected', the creditors cannot start any new action against you, in particular bankruptcy proceedings. You are discharged from the deed after three years. The main advantages of a trust deed over bankruptcy are that you are not banned from certain types of job or holding public office and, in theory, you can still apply for credit (although in practice you are unlikely to find sources willing to lend to you).

Bankruptcy. In Scotland this often called 'sequestration' and bankruptcy orders are administered by the Accountant in Bankruptcy. Otherwise, arrangements are similar to those for the rest of the UK.

9. **Regulation and complaints**

Most types of lending, including pawnbroking, are controlled by the Consumer Credit Act 1974 and Consumer Credit Act 2006, which set out, for example, the way credit is advertised, information you must be given before and after entering into a loan agreement, and some safeguards against being charged exorbitant rates of interest (though you can still legitimately be charged very high rates if your credit standing is poor).

Under the 1974 Act, if a credit card is lost or stolen and misused, the maximum loss you are liable for is £50 (regardless of whether you have taken reasonable care to look after the card and its security details).

The 1974 Act also requires that, where you use a credit card to pay for something costing more than £100 and up to £30,000, the card issuer is equally liable with the retailer if something goes wrong – eg, the goods are faulty or the firm goes out of business before supplying you with the goods or service. This is often referred to as 'equal liability'. Try to get your money back from the retailer but, if that does not succeed, claim from the card company.

The Financial Services Authority (FSA) regulates advice about most mortgages used to buy a home, lifetime mortgages and home reversion schemes. Comprehensive rules apply to the way lenders and advisers do business with customers. These include a requirement that you be given a key facts illustration setting out the important details of any mortgage or equity release scheme you are interested in so you can compare one deal with another. You can check whether a lender or adviser is authorised to do this sort of business and is covered by the rules by checking the FSA Register (see Appendix 2).

Many lenders abide by a code of practice operated by the Finance and Leasing Association (FLA). The code sets out standards of good business practice when dealing with customers and requires members to have proper complaints facilities. Contact the FLA for a copy of its code. Many equity release scheme providers belong to a trade body, Safe Home Income Plans, which requires members to abide by its own code of practice in addition to the FSA rules.

If you have a complaint, first contact the lender or, if applicable, the broker who gave you advice. If the firm does not deal with your complaint satisfactorily, take your case to the Financial Ombudsman Service.

For more information about how you are protected when you borrow and about making a complaint, see Chapter 10.

Borrowing scams

Be on your alert for these common scams and do not get caught out.

Credit repair. Steer clear of firms offering to 'repair' your credit history for a fee. Legally, all they can do is check your credit file and correct any errors, which you can do for yourself for just £2. Any other 'repairs' on offer will be illegal.

'Self-cert' mortgages. If you opt for a self-certification mortgage, do not be tempted to lie about your income. (In the past, some unscrupulous brokers have encouraged customers to do this.) Not only could you end up being unable to keep up the payments, you will also be guilty of fraud and could be fined or get a prison sentence.

Debt management companies. If you have problem debts, do not go to a debt management company. It is selling its own products and services, so will not necessarily look at the full range of options open to you. Moreover, you will pay a large fee to the company and this reduces the amount available to clear your debts. Get independent and free advice from a Citizens Advice Bureau, Community Legal Advice (England and Wales only), the Consumer Credit Counselling Service, Money Advice Scotland or National Debtline. See Appendix 2 for contact details.

Notes

1 Bank of England, *Lending to Individuals: April 2009*, Statistical Release, 2009
2 Department for Communities and Local Government, *Housing Statistics: live tables*, Table 901, www.communities.gov.uk, accessed 27 September 2009
3 UK Payments Administration Ltd, *Plastic Cards in the UK and How We Use Them in 2007*, www.apacs.org.uk, accessed 16 July 2009
4 Insolvency Service, *Statistical Release: insolvencies in the fourth quarter 2008*, www.insolvency.gov.uk, accessed 16 July 2009

3. **Plastic cards**
5 Department for Work and Pensions, *Income-related Benefits Estimates of Take-up in 2007/08*, Office for National Statistics, 2009
6 Moneyfacts, *Moneyfacts*, 2009
7 Office of Fair Trading, *OFT's Action on Credit Card Default Charges*, 2006

6. **Mortgages**
8 Department for Work and Pensions, *Family Resources Survey 2007/08*, DWP, 2009
9 Office of Fair Trading, *Sale and Rent-back: an OFT market study*, OFT, 2008

Chapter 6

Pensions

This chapter covers:
1. Saving for retirement (below)
2. State pensions (p184)
3. Pension savings (p190)
4. Occupational pensions (p192)
5. Personal pensions and stakeholder schemes (p195)
6. Other benefits from pension schemes (p199)
7. Annuities and income drawdown (p200)
8. Pitfalls and what to watch out for (p205)
9. Keeping track of your pensions (p209)
10. Regulation and complaints (p209)
11. Future changes: personal accounts (p212)

Basic facts

- If you rely on state pensions and benefits for your retirement income, in 2009/10, you will have £130 a week (single person) or £198.45 (couple) to live on.[1]
- The richest fifth of pensioner households had an average income of £512 a week (single) or £1,206 (couple) between 2005 and 2008. At least half of this came from occupational pensions, personal pensions and other investments.[2]
- Starting early makes pension savings more manageable. For example, to provide yourself with £1,000 a year of pension payable from age 65, you might need to save around £20 a month if you start at age 25, or £60 a month if you start at age 45 (see p178).
- In 2007, 53 per cent of men and 58 per cent of women working full time belonged to an employer's pension scheme.[3]

---

1. Saving for retirement

The need to save for retirement

On average, retirement might last 20 or 30 years or more, and providing an income for such a long period is expensive. Normally, the only realistic way of building up enough pension is to save regularly throughout all or a large part of your working life.

Throughout your working life, you normally pay national insurance (NI) contributions. These qualify you for a pension from the state scheme (see p184). The table below shows how much state pension people received in 2007/08.

How much pensioners get from the state[1]

	Single people		Couples	
	% of pensioners getting this type of income	Average £ per week for those receiving it	% of pensioners getting this type of income	Average £ per week for those receiving it
State retirement pension[i]	96%	£108	93%	£157
Means-tested benefits[ii]	42%	£68	18%	£64

[i] Including other benefits, such as bereavement benefits, for which you qualify by paying national insurance contributions.

[ii] Pension credit, housing benefit, council tax benefit and social fund grants.

Most people would prefer a bigger income than this, which means saving extra for retirement. The main ways to do this are as follows.

- **An occupational pension** scheme offered by your employer. Your employer normally pays a large part of the cost of providing your pension and these schemes benefit from tax advantages. See p192 for details.
- **A personal pension**. Usually you bear the full cost of providing your pension (though some employers will pay into your personal scheme). These also benefit from tax advantages. See p195.
- **Other investments** suitable for long-term saving (such as unit trusts, perhaps investing through an individual savings account). See Chapter 4.

The advantages of using an occupational scheme or personal pension are:
- you get tax relief, usually up to your top rate of tax, on your own contributions;
- any contributions paid by your employer count as a tax-free perk of your job;
- the invested contributions build up partially tax-free (dividend and similar income is taxed at 10 per cent, but other income and gains build up tax-free);
- at retirement you can take part of your savings as a tax-free lump sum (but the rest must be used to provide taxable pension).

However, there might be little point in saving extra if it would provide you with only a small amount of additional pension. This is because, under current rules, anyone aged 60 or over who has less than a certain amount of income is entitled to claim means-tested pension credit (PC) to bring their income up to a minimum level. See Chapter 9 for more information on PC and on the gradual increase in the minimum age for claiming it that applies from April 2010 onwards. If you can build up only a small amount of pension, you may simply be displacing benefits that you could otherwise have claimed.

If you can afford to save something for retirement, you might be unwise to let the availability of PC influence your pension savings too heavily. There have been many changes to the state pension system over the years and PC might have changed or disappeared by the time you retire.

How much do you need to save

The income you might need

Many financial advisers suggest you should aim for a retirement income equal to two-thirds or half of your pre-retirement income. This is a very rough-and-ready rule and it is better to think about how much income you might actually need in retirement. Your spending patterns could be very different from when you are working – eg:

- work expenses, such as commuting, lunches and smart clothes might be saved;
- income tax may be lower, particularly because from age 65 you qualify for a higher personal allowance (see Chapter 8);
- NI and pension contributions will probably disappear altogether;
- housing costs may be lower if you have been buying your own home with a mortgage, which may be paid off by retirement;
- family costs may be lower if your children have finished education and left home. On the other hand, you might want to help support grandchildren;
- health costs might be higher if you develop health problems with increasing age;
- home-related costs, such as fuel bills, might increase if you spend more time at home. On the other hand, insurance premiums might fall to reflect a lower risk of burglary where someone is in the home most of the time;
- travel and holiday costs might rise if you go on more trips, but could fall since you can go away at off-peak times.

Use Part 1 of the calculator on p179 to note down your estimate of how much income you might need in retirement. Do this in today's money – do not worry about inflation between now and retirement because the calculator takes this into account later on.

How much pension you might already get

In Part 2 of the calculator on p179, write down the amount of pension you are already on track to get from any schemes and plans into which you already pay. You can get this information:

- for state pension, from a retirement pension forecast from The Pension Service (see Appendix 2) or a 'combined benefit statement' from your occupational scheme or personal pension, if you have one. These combined statements are still fairly new and not all schemes and plans provide them. They show not just your expected pension from the scheme or plan but also your expected state pension based on the NI contributions you have paid and those you expect to pay between now and retirement;
- for a current occupational pension (see p192), from the benefit statement you normally get each year. The statement must show in today's money the pension you can expect at retirement if you carry on paying in as now. This is the figure to use in the calculator on p179 if you expect to carry on in the same or an equivalent job until retirement;
- for current personal pension(s) (see p195) from the statement(s) you get each year. This shows the pension you can expect at retirement in today's money if you carry on paying in as now;
- for old occupational and personal pensions you no longer pay into, from the statement you get each year. These show in today's money the pension you can expect at retirement assuming the pension is left to accumulate until then.

Add up all these amounts and subtract the total from your target retirement income. If you are left with a number bigger than zero, you need to save an additional amount to stand a good chance of getting the retirement income you want. Use Part 3 of the calculator and the table below to work out roughly how much extra you need to save through a pension scheme or plan. If you use other types of savings or investments, different tax treatment means you may need to save more.

Instead of using the paper-based calculator below, Age Concern-Help the Aged has produced an interactive CD-ROM called MoneyTrail to guide you through the same process (see Appendix 2).

How much you need to save each month for every £100 a year of pension

Years until chosen retirement age	Man retiring at age:					Woman retiring at age:				
	55	60	65	70	75	55	60	65	70	75
5	£44	£36	£30	£24	£20	£45	£39	£33	£27	£21
10	£20	£17	£14	£11	£9	£21	£18	£15	£12	£10
15	£12	£11	£8	£7	£6	£13	£11	£9	£8	£6
20	£8	£7	£6	£5	£4	£9	£7	£6	£5	£4
25	£6	£5	£4	£3	£3	£6	£5	£5	£4	£3
30	£5	£4	£3	£3	£2	£5	£4	£3	£3	£2
35	£4	£3	£2	£2	£2	£4	£3	£3	£2	£2
40	£3	£2	£2	£2	£1	£3	£3	£2	£2	£1
45	£2	£2	£2	£1	£1	£2	£2	£2	£1	£1
50	£2	£2	£1	£1	£1	£2	£2	£1	£1	£1

Note: this assumes:

– tax relief at the basic rate is added to amount shown;

– the amount you pay in is increased once a year in line with price inflation;

– price inflation averages 2.5 per cent a year;

– investment return is 7 per cent a year;

– charges are 1.5 per cent a year for the first 10 years and 1 per cent a year thereafter;

– the fund is used at retirement to buy an annuity whose income changes each year in line with inflation.

Pension calculator

£ each month in today's money

Part 1: how much income are you likely to need in retirement?
Expenses:
Food and non-alcoholic drink
Household items
Personal spending and clothes
Smoking, alcohol and luxuries
Household bills – fuel, telephone, council tax, water
TV licence, pay TV costs
Rent or mortgage
House buildings and contents insurance
Home repairs and maintenance
Everyday travelling – car insurance, servicing, petrol, bus and train fares
Holidays
Health-related costs – prescription charges, long-term care insurance premiums
Other
Total monthly spending =
Total monthly spending x 12 = **total yearly spending**   Box A ☐

Before-tax income required:
Multiply A by the appropriate factor:
    If A is £11,500 or below, factor = 1.0
    If A is £11,501 – £21,000, factor = 1.1
    If A is £21,001 – £40,000, factor = 1.2
    If A is £40,001 – £53,000, factor = 1.3
    If A is £53,001 or more, factor = 1.4

=   Box B ☐

Part 2: how much pension might you already get?
State pension
Current occupational pension
Current personal pension(s)
Old occupational and personal pensions
Monthly total =
Monthly total x12 = **yearly total**   Box C ☐

Part 3: how much extra do you need to save?
Your pension shortfall:
B – C = **your pension shortfall**
(if less than zero, insert 0)   Box D ☐

Your savings factor:
Using the table on p178, find the age for someone of your sex
nearest to that at which you plan to retire. In the left-hand column,
find the number of years until you reach that age. The
corresponding figure is your **savings factor**.   Box E ☐

Suggested extra you need to save:
$$\frac{D}{100} \times E =$$ Box F ☐

To improve your chance of retiring on the income you need, you
should try saving this much extra each month.

Note: assumes you pay in this amount and tax relief at the basic rate is added by the
pension provider. With some arrangements, you pay in the total sum and claim tax relief
separately. If you are a higher rate taxpayer, you can claim extra relief, so the overall cost
to you will be less than the amount shown. Assumes you increase the amount you save
once a year in line with inflation.

When you plan to retire

As the table on p178 shows, the earlier you plan to retire, the more you need to
save. This is because you cut short the time over which you can build up a pension
and the pension has to be paid out for longer, assuming you have an average
lifespan. The earliest age at which an occupational or personal pension can start
to be paid is usually 55 (from 6 April 2010, age 50 before then). Most occupational
schemes have a '**normal retirement age**', often 65. With a personal pension, you
may be asked to state in advance your target retirement age, but you can usually
change this later on.

The state pension is payable no earlier than state pension age (see below). If
you retire before then, you will have to manage without your state pension for
the first few years. Some occupational schemes are integrated with the state
scheme and provide extra pension (a 'bridging pension') until the state pension
starts.

Conversely, by retiring later, you reduce the amount you need to save. This is
because the pension has longer to build up and on average will be paid out for a
shorter time. The latest age at which you can start drawing a non-state pension is
75. State pension is also increased if you delay starting it. Alternatively, the delay
can earn you a lump sum (see p188).

State pension age

At present, if you are a man, the earliest age at which you can start receiving your state pension is 65.

Women's state pension age is being gradually raised from 60 to 65 between 6 April 2010 and 2020. If you were born between 6 April 1950 and 5 April 1955, your state pension age is 60 plus the number of months (or part-months) by which your birth date falls after 5 April 1950. For this purpose, a month runs from the sixth day of one month to the fifth day of the next.

The Pensions Act 2007 raises the state pension age for younger men and women to 68 by 2046. The increase in pension age is to be brought in in stages. If you were born:

- between 6 April 1959 and 5 April 1960: age 65 plus the number of months by which your birth date falls after 6 April 1959;
- between 6 April 1960 and 5 April 1968: age 66;
- between 6 April 1968 and 5 April 1969: age 66 plus the number of months by which your birth date falls after 6 April 1959;
- between 6 April 1969 and 5 April 1977: age 67;
- between 6 April 1977 and 5 April 1978: 67 plus the number of months by which your birth date falls after 6 April 1959;
- from 6 April 1978 onwards: age 68.

For a calculator to work out your state pension age, visit www.direct.gov.uk

Who should think about pensions

Relationships

If you are married, in a civil partnership or living together and you belong to an occupational scheme, check whether lump sums and pensions payable on death would be payable to your partner.

Private sector schemes generally treat unmarried partners in the same way as married ones. However, in the past, public sector schemes often did not pay pensions to unmarried partners. Most now do, but usually this improvement came into effect only for pension rights that you build up on or after a set, fairly recent date. This means it may be many years before your partner becomes entitled to a reasonably large survivor's pension. However, you may be able to boost the survivor's pension s/he would get by paying extra contributions now.

If you separate or divorce from your husband, wife or civil partner, you may be able to claim part of her/his pension rights or s/he may be able to claim part of yours. Particularly if you are a woman, your husband or partner may have been the higher earner and building up pension rights that were originally intended to benefit you both at retirement. On divorce, any pension rights should be taken into account in the divorce settlement and can be shared between you. A court will ensure pension rights are looked at but, if you do not involve a court or you are unmarried, it is up to you to make sure they are included. Get help from a solicitor and, if the pension rights are large, consider involving a consulting actuary.

If your relationship breaks down and you were living together without being married or in a civil partnership, you normally have no claim to your ex-partner's pension savings or pension.

Young people

Pensions take a long time to build up, so the earlier you start saving the better. Even a child can have a personal pension and anyone (eg, parents, grandparents and family friends) can pay into the scheme. The amount given is treated as net of tax relief, so tax relief at the basic rate is added to the child's scheme (even though most children are non-taxpayers). The maximum total contributions to the scheme each year are £2,880 (which comes to £3,600 with the tax relief). The contributions build up largely tax-free and eventually one-quarter of the pension fund can be drawn out as a tax-free lump sum, though the rest must be taken as taxable pension. The child cannot draw out the savings until s/he reaches 55, but this could be one of the most valuable gifts a child ever gets. If you would prefer to make gifts that a child could use a bit earlier in life, consider, for example, a child trust fund (see Chapter 4).

Redundancy

If you are facing redundancy and you are aged at least 55, or younger but in poor health, you might consider taking early retirement. Normally, early retirement means your pension is significantly lower than it would have been had you carried on until the normal pension age for your scheme. Try negotiating with your employer to see if your redundancy package could include an enhanced pension. Bear in mind that you will have to manage without your state pension until you reach state pension age.

Older people

Many people ease into retirement gradually from work – eg, by reducing their hours or switching to part-time work. Changes in the law have increased the scope for doing this.

On 1 October 2006, new laws came into effect making it illegal to discriminate in the workplace on the grounds of age. The legislation protects people of any age, including young workers, but is particularly important for older people who want to carry on working for as long as possible. Under the new law, it is generally illegal for an employer on the grounds of age to:
- refuse to employ you;
- dismiss you;
- refuse you training;
- deny you promotion;

- give you worse terms and conditions than other employees;
- retire you before age 65 (or an earlier age if your employer has an earlier normal retirement age that can be justified as necessary).

Your employer must give you at least six months' notice of your retirement date (either when you will reach 65 or earlier if there is a justifiable earlier normal retirement age at your workplace) and, if you want to, you can apply to carry on working beyond that date. Your employer must consider your request, but can turn you down and does not have to give reasons.

Changes to pension legislation in 2006 may also help you to carry on working if you want to. Since April 2006, if your employer and your pension scheme rules allow it, you can start to draw your pension while still working. This could make it possible, for example, to work part time and top up your income with pension.

Going to live abroad

If you are a British national, you and your family have the right to move freely around the European Economic Area (EEA) (see p353) to take up employment, work as a self-employed person or to provide or receive a service. While in another EEA state, you are entitled to the same social support as nationals of that country. Contributions you have paid in the UK can help you qualify for benefits, including state pension, in other EEA countries and in some situations you may still receive UK benefits. For more information, see the free Department for Work and Pensions (DWP) booklet SA29, *Your Social Security Insurance, Benefits and Health Care Rights in the European Community and in Iceland, Liechtenstein and Norway.*

If you retire to another EEA country, you continue to receive any UK state retirement pension, including annual increases.

Since June 2002, Switzerland also participates in the EEA arrangements, although it is not an EEA member.

If you retire to a non-EEA country, you continue to receive any UK state pension but, in many cases, not the yearly increases to the pension during the time you are abroad. This applies, for example, if you go to live in Australia, Canada, New Zealand or South Africa. Before moving abroad, contact the DWP to check what agreements, if any, exist with the country in which you intend to live or work and see the free booklet GL29, *Going Abroad and Social Security Benefits,* available from the DWP.

Occupational and personal pensions can also be paid to you abroad. Bear in mind that the foreign currency value of a pension denominated in sterling will go up and down as the exchange rate changes. For example, if you retire to France and the value of the pound falls against the Euro, your pension will buy less in France than it did before.

2. State pensions

Basic pension

The main state retirement pension is the basic pension. Broadly, everyone who has paid or been credited with enough national insurance (NI) contributions of the right type during their working life gets this pension.

'**Working life**' means the years from the one in which you reach age 16 up to the last full year before you reach state pension age. For this purpose, a year means the period from 6 April to the following 5 April. You pay NI contributions while you are working. You are credited with contributions in various situations if you are unable to work. The table on p185 summarises when you are likely to build up your entitlement to state pension. See Chapter 8 for more information about NI contributions.

Anyone reaching state pension age on or after 6 April 2010 will get the full basic pension (£95.25 a week for a single person in 2009/10) provided you have contributions or credits for 30 years of your working life (usually 44 years for a man and 39 for a woman reaching state pension age before then). The pension is reduced *pro rata* if you have fewer years, so that one year's worth of contributions buys about £3.18 a week of basic pension at 2009/10 rates. The reduction in the number of years needed for a full pension from 6 April 2010, and other changes to the state system being brought in at the same time, mean that many more people, especially women who often have broken work patterns because of caring responsibilities, are eligible for their own full basic pension.

From 6 April 2010, wives, husbands and civil partners can build up their own state pension as described above. Alternatively, they can claim a pension based on their partner's NI record of contributions and credits. The maximum pension based on a partner's record is £57.05 a week at 2009/10 rates. This is reduced in line with your partner's own pension if s/he has not paid or been credited with enough contributions during her/his working life to qualify for the full amount. From 6 April 2010, you must be over state pension age to qualify for a pension based on your partner's contributions and it is paid directly to you, counting as your own income. Before 6 April 2010, this type of pension could only be claimed by a woman relying on her husband's record. Partners who cohabit without being married or in a civil partnership cannot claim this type of pension.

At present, all state retirement pensions are increased each year in line with price inflation unless Parliament decides otherwise. Under the Pensions Act 2007 measures, from a future date (originally expected to be April 2012 but subject to the Government being able to afford the improvement), the basic pension will be increased in line with earnings inflation (which tends to be 1 to 2 per cent a year higher than price inflation).

Building up a state pension[i]

Your situation	National insurance contributions paid or credited	Do these count towards the basic state pension?	Do these count towards the state additional pension?
Employee earning less than the 'lower earnings limit' (£95 a week in 2009/10)	No contributions No credits	No	No
Employee earning at least the lower earnings limit but less than the 'primary threshold' (£110 a week in 2009/10)	No contributions Credits	Yes	Yes
Employee earning at least the primary threshold	Class 1 contributions at the full rate *or*	Yes	Yes
	Class 1 contributions at the married women's reduced rate[ii]	No	No
Self-employed person	Class 2 contributions *or*	Yes	No
	No contributions if your profits are below the 'small earnings exception' (£5,075 in 2009/10) and you have opted not to pay contributions *and*	No	No
	Class 4 contributions	No	No
Employee earning less than lower earnings limit or self-employed with profits below the small earnings exception but getting working tax credit	Credits	Yes	No
Unemployed, claiming jobseeker's allowance and available for work	Credits[iii]	Yes	No

Your situation	National insurance contributions paid or credited	Do these count towards the basic state pension?	Do these count towards the state additional pension?
Claiming employment and support allowance (or incapacity benefit)	Credits[iii]	Yes	Yes
Claiming statutory maternity, paternity or adoption pay, or maternity allowance	Credits	Yes	No
Not working and caring for children under age 12 (or age six if you reach state pension age before 6 April 2010) for whom you get child benefit	Credits	Yes[iv]	Yes[iv]
Not working, caring for someone who is elderly or disabled who gets certain disability benefits or you get carer's allowance	Credits	Yes[iv]	Yes
Aged 16 to 18 and still at school or in higher education	Credits	Yes	No
Aged 18 or over and undergoing an approved training course (but not including going to university)	Credits	Yes	No
Not working, under state pension age but older than the state pension age for women	Credits[v]	Yes	No
Other situations, such as being at university, taking time off to travel, keeping a home but without caring responsibilities	No contributions No credits	No	No

Your situation	National insurance contributions paid or credited	Do these count towards the basic state pension?	Do these count towards the state additional pension?
	Class 3 contributions (voluntary)	Yes	No

[i] This table reflects the rules as they stood in 2009/10. Different rules applied in some earlier periods. The rules are complicated and this table can give only a broad outline. For more detail contact HM Revenue and Customs.

[ii] This is a lower rate of contributions which some married women and widows have opted to pay. (The option is no longer available, but you can continue with it if you had already opted to pay at the reduced rate at the time the option was abolished.) The intention was that these women would pay less, qualify for few benefits in their own right and rely instead on their husbands. In addition to losing the right to pay contributions towards your own state retirement pension, you also do not qualify for any NI credits towards the pension if you are off work because of maternity, incapacity or unemployment.

[iii] To qualify for credits and, depending on the benefit you are claiming, there may also be a condition that you have paid some contributions within the last two years.

[iv] For people reaching state pension age before 6 April 2010, these credits (home responsibilities protection) do not (like other credits) fill gaps in your record. Instead, they reduce the number of years you need to qualify for a given level of pension.

[v] These credits will disappear once the pension age for women is the same as that for men (from 6 April 2020 onwards).

Additional state pension

The additional state pension was introduced from 1978 and was originally called the state earnings-related pension scheme (SERPS) but changed from April 2002 to the state second pension (S2P).

Only employees earning more than the lower earnings limit could build up SERPS. So you could not build up SERPS if you were self-employed or not working for any reason. As the name suggests, the amount of pension you built up was linked to your earnings. The more you earned on average over your working life since 1978, the larger the SERPS pension you could get. S2P is similar to SERPS, but with the following differences.

- **Low earners get an improved pension**. Employees earning at least the lower earnings limit (£95 a week, equivalent to £4,940 a year, in 2009/10) up to the 'low earnings threshold' (£13,900 in 2009/10), are treated as if they have earnings equal to the low earnings threshold, so they build up a bigger S2P pension than they would have done had their actual earnings been used.
- **Carers get a pension**. If you are not working because you are caring for a child

under 12 (or six for people reaching state pension age before 6 April 2010) for whom you get child benefit or caring for someone who is elderly or disabled and you qualify for carer's allowance, you build up S2P pension as if you had earnings equal to the low earnings threshold.

- **Long-term sick and disabled people** build up S2P as if they had earnings equal to the low earnings threshold, provided they have also spent at least one-tenth of their working life in the workforce.
- **Flat-rate pension.** From 6 April 2009 onwards, the maximum earnings on which S2P is based (called the 'upper accruals point' or UAP) has been frozen at £770 a week (£40,040 a year) instead of being raised each year as previously. This means that eventually the low earnings threshold (which is still increased annually) will catch up with the UAP. When that happens, S2P will be a flat-rate pension – ie, everyone will get the same amount regardless of their earnings.

Note that employees earning less than the lower earnings limit and self-employed people are still not eligible for S2P. The table on p185 summarises when you are likely to build up S2P.

The maximum pension a high earner could build up through SERPS/S2P is quite generous (over £150 a week for someone retiring in 2009/10). In practice, most high earners have 'contracted out' of the S2P. 'Contracting out' means you give up some or all of your S2P and instead build up a pension through an occupational scheme or a personal pension – see p205 for more about this. As a result, the average amount is only around £36 a week[5].

Other state pensions
- **State graduated pension.** An earlier additional scheme for employees that ran from 1961 to 1975. Any pension you built up is fairly small (under £10 a week) and you might have been contracted out, which means you built up a pension through an occupational pension scheme instead.
- **Over-80s addition.** Anyone getting the basic state pension qualifies for an extra 25p a week from age 80.
- **Over-80s pension.** If you do not qualify for a basic state pension, from age 80 you might qualify for this non-contributory pension (of £57.05 a week in 2009/10). If this is your only income, you are likely in any case to be getting pension credit (see p306), so your overall income might not change.

Increasing your state pension

Deferring your pension to earn extra

You do not have to start receiving your pension as soon as you reach state pension age. Instead, you can defer its start, in which case you get extra pension when it does start or, if you prefer, you can take a lump sum. If you have already started to receive your pension, you can stop the payments and earn extra pension in the same way, but you can do this only once. You must put off the whole of your state pension, including any additional or graduated amounts as well as the basic pension. If you are a man and your wife is claiming a pension based on your NI contribution record, under current rules her pension must also be deferred.

You can defer your pension for a minimum of five weeks and for as long as you like. You earn a pension increase equivalent to 10.4 per cent for each year of deferment or a lump sum with the amount deferred earning interest at 2 per cent above the Bank of England base rate. Both the pension and lump sum are taxable. However, the whole lump sum is taxed only at the highest tax rate you were paying on the rest of your income and so does not push you into a higher tax bracket. For example, if your top rate of tax is 20 per cent (the basic rate from April 2009), the whole lump sum will be taxed at 20 per cent, even if it takes you over the threshold at which 40 per cent tax normally starts. Also, you can opt to put off drawing the lump sum until the year after your pension starts. This would be worth doing if your income, and so your top tax rate, are expected to fall in the following year. The table below shows the extra pension or lump sum you might earn.

Examples of the extra pension or lump sum from deferring your state pension

Number of years you defer your pension	Weekly increase for each £10 of deferred pension	Lump sum for each £10 of deferred pension*
1	£1.04	£527
2	£2.08	£1,066
3	£3.12	£1,620
4	£4.16	£2,187
5	£5.20	£2,768
10	£10.40	£5,900

*Worked out assuming interest of 2.5 per cent a year on the pension deferred. Rate is variable and may change during the period you are deferring your pension.

Filling gaps in your contribution record

If you take a break (eg, to study or travel), this will normally create a gap in your NI record, which could reduce your eventual pension. You may be able to boost your pension voluntarily by paying Class 2 or 3 NI contributions to plug the gap. There is a time limit for doing this, which is normally six years but may be longer for people reaching state pension age before 6 April 2015. See Chapter 8 for details. Bear in mind that anyone reaching state pension age on or after 6 April 2010 needs a record of only 30 years in order to qualify for the full basic pension. This means someone with a working life of 49 years (state pension age of 65) can have gaps totalling up to 19 years without losing any basic pension, so, in this case, it might not be worth paying voluntary contributions.

Switching from the married women's reduced rate contributions

Until 1977, married women could opt to pay Class 1 NI contributions at a reduced rate on earnings above the lower earnings limit or not pay Class 2 contributions at all. If they did, they gave up the right to their own state pension (and various other benefits) and instead relied on claiming a pension based on their husband's NI record.

Although this option has been abolished, women who had already chosen this option in 1977 can continue with it. Since then, NI rules have changed and you might be better off paying NI contributions at the full rate, especially if you are an employee on relatively low earnings. If you earn more than the lower earnings limit (£95 a week in 2009/10 or £4,940 a year) but less than the primary threshold (£110 a week in 2009/10 or £5,715 a year), switching means you will pay no contributions at all but you will be building up entitlement to both basic and additional pensions. For more information, see HM Revenue and Customs website at www.hmrc.gov.uk/faqs/women_reduced_rate.htm. If you do not have internet access, contact your tax office (see Appendix 2) and ask for a copy of the relevant web pages to be sent to you.

Paying contributions if you are self-employed with small profits

If your profits are below the level at which you have to pay Class 2 NI contributions (£5,075 in 2009/10), you might be tempted to save money by opting not to pay. This could be a false economy. For a small outlay (£2.40 a week in 2009/10) Class 2 contributions count towards the state basic pension and also towards some other benefits including employment and support allowance (see Chapters 8 and 9).

---

3. **Pension savings**

The state pension is unlikely on its own to give you the retirement lifestyle you want and it is therefore essential to save extra. The Government encourages you to do this by giving special tax treatment for savings made through 'registered pension schemes'. These include, for example, occupational pension schemes, personal pensions and stakeholder schemes. The main tax incentives are:

- **tax relief on contributions** each year up to 100 per cent of your UK earnings or £3,600, whichever is greater. This contribution limit applies to the total you pay into all the pension schemes you have or to which you belong;
- **tax relief on the savings as they grow**. If a pension fund is invested in shares, the income is taxed at 10 per cent, but the rest of the income and gains from investing in a pension fund are tax-free;
- **tax-free lump sum when you start your pension**. You can usually opt to take up to one-quarter of your pension savings as a tax-free lump sum. The rest must be drawn gradually as an annual income, which is taxable.

These tax reliefs are, in effect, capped through some limits on large pensions. These will affect you only if you expect to build up pensions worth more than a lifetime allowance set at £1.75 million in 2009/10 or your pension savings are likely to increase by more than an annual allowance set at £245,000 in 2009/10.

Pension contributions can be paid into a scheme for anyone under age 75. There is no lower age limit, so even a baby can have a pension scheme. The contributions do not have to be paid by the person who has the scheme – they can be paid in by someone else. For example, a parent can pay into a scheme for a child; or a working husband, wife or unmarried partner can pay into a scheme for their non-working partner. Anything paid in by someone else, other than your employer, counts towards your contribution limit for the year. Employers can pay into pension schemes for their employees and anything they pay is in addition to the contribution limit on p190.

Tax relief on contributions is given in one of three ways, depending on the type of pension scheme.

In an occupational scheme, contributions are deducted from your pay before income tax is worked out. This means you automatically get full tax relief on your contributions.

In personal pensions and stakeholder schemes, the amount you pay in is treated as a contribution from which tax relief at the basic rate has already been deducted. The scheme provider then claims the relief from HM Revenue and Customs (the Revenue) and adds it to your scheme. For example, if you want to contribute £3,600 in 2009/10 (the maximum if you have no earnings), you actually hand over £2,880. The scheme provider claims £720 (20 per cent of £3,600) from the Revenue and adds it to your scheme, bringing the total up to £3,600. Everyone gets this basic rate tax relief, even if they are a non-taxpayer or pay tax at a lower rate. If you are a higher rate taxpayer, you can claim extra tax relief through your tax return or the PAYE system (see Chapter 8).

If you have a retirement annuity contract (a type of personal pension you started before July 1988), typically you pay 'gross' contributions from which no tax relief has been deducted. You have to claim tax relief up to your top rate of tax through your tax return or the PAYE system. However, scheme providers have the option of accepting contributions using the system that applies to personal pensions as described above. Your scheme provider will tell you if this is the case.

Future changes: tax relief on contributions

In the past, everyone has received tax relief on pension contributions up to their highest rate. This means, in general, the higher your income, the more valuable the tax reliefs are. From 6 April 2011, higher rate relief will be restricted if you have an income of £150,000 or more. The higher relief will be gradually tapered away so that anyone on an income of around £180,000 or more will get tax relief only at the basic rate.

To prevent you pre-empting this change by making extra large contributions in the period before 6 April 2011, some new rules have been introduced with effect from 6 April 2009. The special rules do not affect you if your income is less than £150,000 or if your income is higher but you do not change your normal pattern of pension contributions or, although you change your contributions, the total you contribute is less than £20,000 a year. If you are caught by the special rules, you must pay a special tax charge on any contributions in excess of either £20,000 or your normal pattern (whichever is greater). This special tax charge in effect claws back any higher rate tax relief, so you just get relief at the basic rate.

4. Occupational pensions

How they work

The opportunity to join an occupational pension scheme comes as part of a job package. Usually it is worth joining because your employer pays towards the cost of building up a pension for you. Unlike many other perks of a job, whatever your employer pays into the scheme on your behalf is a tax-free benefit of your job.

Occupational schemes work in one of two main ways (although there are variations on these themes).

- **Defined benefit scheme.** You are promised a certain level of pension, usually based on your pay and how many years you have belonged to the scheme. For example, in the most common type – a final salary scheme – you might get a pension equal to one-sixtieth, one-eightieth or one-hundredth of your pay just before retirement for each year you have belonged to the scheme. For example, if you earned £32,000 a year and had been in a one-eightieth scheme for 20 years, your pension would be 1/80 x 20 x £32,000 = £8,000 a year. In most schemes you pay a set percentage of your salary towards the cost of building up the pension and your employer pays the balance.
- **Defined contribution scheme** (also called a 'money purchase scheme'). Your employer (and usually you too) pays a set amount into the scheme, often a fixed percentage of your pay. This money is invested and the resulting pension fund is used at retirement to provide you with a pension. You cannot know in advance how much pension you will get. This will depend on the amount paid in, how well the invested fund grows, how much is lost in charges, and the rate at which the pension fund can be converted to a pension (called the 'annuity rate' – see p200) at the time you start to draw the pension.

The main difference between the two types of scheme is who takes the risk. In a defined benefit scheme, the employer pays the balance of the cost needed to meet the pension promises and so bears the risk of the cost rising due, for example, to poor investment returns or people living longer than originally expected. In a money purchase scheme, you take these risks, though usually instead of paying extra costs you just end up with a lower pension.

If you work in the public sector (eg, as a teacher, in the NHS, for the emergency services or for a local authority), your pension, once it starts to be paid, is usually increased each year in line with price inflation, so it retains its value. Most other defined benefit schemes must increase your pension in line with inflation but only up to a maximum (generally 2.5 per cent a year). Money purchase schemes do not have to increase pensions being paid and it is up to you to choose whether to have increases or not (by deciding which type of annuity to buy – see p204).

Do not confuse occupational pension schemes with other pension schemes available through your workplace. An employer with five or more employees who does not offer an occupational scheme must have an arrangement so that you can start and pay into either a group personal pension or a stakeholder scheme through work. These are types of personal pension (see p195).

From 2012, a new national pension scheme of personal accounts is due to start. Employers who currently offer an occupational scheme might decide instead to rely on the new accounts or to pare back the occupational scheme so that it aligns with the new accounts. See p212 for details.

Normal pension age and retirement age

Occupational pension schemes generally have a normal pension age at which the standard benefits for the scheme are payable. If you start your pension earlier, the pension is reduced and, if you start your pension later, it may be enhanced.

Under anti-age discrimination laws that came into effect in December 2006, your employer cannot force you to retire before you reach age 65 on the grounds of your age. You have the right to ask to work on beyond age 65. Your employer must consider your request, but can turn you down and does not have to tell you the reasons. During 2010, the Government will review this default age of 65 and may decide to abolish it, in which case you may gain the right to stay in work for longer.

Since 6 April 2006, provided your employer and your pension scheme rules allow it, you can start to draw an occupational pension while continuing to work for the employer that provides the pension. As has long been the case, you can still draw your pension while working for a different employer.

Other schemes

Final salary schemes are expensive for employers and tend to be offered only by large firms and public sector employers. But many large firms are finding the cost too much and are closing schemes (see p207) and/or switching to alternatives. The main alternatives are a:

- **career average scheme**. A type of defined benefit scheme where, for each year of membership, you get a fraction of your pay averaged over the whole time you have been in the scheme. In a 'revalued career average scheme', the pay from earlier years will be increased in line with inflation before the pension is worked out;

- **cash balance scheme.** Your employer promises you a certain amount in your pension fund at retirement – say, a percentage of your pay for each year of membership – but leaves it up to you to use the fund to buy a pension. In this way, the employer is taking on the risk up to the point of retirement but you take over the risk from then on;

- **hybrid scheme.** Uses a mix of methods. For example, you might be offered the better of a pension worked out on a money purchase basis or a final salary pension. Or you might be offered a cash balance scheme to provide a core pension with, for instance, the option to add on a money purchase pension as well.

What they cost

Some occupational schemes are 'non-contributory', which means that your employer bears the full cost of providing the pension and other benefits. You pay nothing.

Other schemes are contributory. Typically, you might be required to pay in, for instance, 3 to 5 per cent of your pay. Your employer then pays the balance of the cost in a defined benefit scheme. According to a government survey, the average amount in 2007 was 15.6 per cent of employees' pay a year.[6] In a money purchase scheme, the employer pays in a set amount – typically, 6.5 per cent of your pay, according to the survey.

In a money purchase scheme, your employer might offer matching contributions. You choose how much you will pay in and your employer pays in the same again up to a limit.

There are various costs and charges involved with running a pension scheme and these are either to be paid out of the pension fund or directly by your employer.

Additional voluntary contributions

You can choose to pay in extra to boost the pension and other benefits you will get from an occupational scheme. You can do this either through an in-house additional voluntary contributions scheme offered by your employer or through your own arrangement, called a free-standing additional voluntary contributions scheme.

All free-standing schemes and many in-house schemes work on a money purchase basis, so the amount of pension or other benefits you can buy depends on:

– the amount paid in;
– how the invested contributions grow;
– the amount deducted in charges;
– annuity rates at the time you start the pension.

Some employers, mainly in the public sector, with final salary schemes used to offer in-house 'added-years schemes'. Your additional voluntary contributions bought extra years of membership and this increased the amount of pension and other benefits that you would get. Most public sector schemes no longer offer added years but instead you may be able to pay additional voluntary contributions to buy set amounts of extra pension (which are index-linked and so retain their buying power once they start to be paid).

Choosing and starting to save

Joining an occupational pension scheme is not compulsory. However, if your employer offers such a scheme, this is usually a good way to save for retirement because your employer pays part of the cost of providing your pension. The Government is proposing to introduce a new national scheme of pension accounts (see p212). Assuming the proposals go ahead, you will automatically be enrolled in either your employer's occupational scheme or the new national scheme, but with the choice of opting out if you want to.

Within two months of starting work you must be given information about any occupational scheme that you are eligible to join and this will include instructions about what to do next. If you are not given any information, contact your human resources department.

5. **Personal pensions and stakeholder schemes**

How they work

All personal pensions work on a money purchase basis, which means that contributions are paid in and invested to produce a fund which is used at retirement to buy a pension.

You cannot know in advance how much pension you will receive. This is because it depends on:
- the amount paid in;
- how well the invested contributions grow;
- the amount lost through charges;
- the 'annuity rate' at which the fund can be converted into a pension. An annuity is an investment where, in exchange for your pension fund, you get an income for the rest of your life (see p200).

You choose how to invest the pension fund – most providers offer a wide range of investment funds. At retirement, you do not have to buy an annuity from the same provider you have been saving with – you can shop around for the best rate. This option to shop around is called your 'open market option'.

By choosing the type of annuity you buy (see p201), you decide whether or not your pension should increase year by year once it starts to be paid (see p204).

Some personal pensions are **'stakeholder pension schemes'** which means they meet certain conditions including:

- **charges**. These can only be levied as a percentage of your fund (eg, no flat fees which could eat heavily into a small investment) and must not exceed a set limit (1.5 per cent a year during the first 10 years, reverting to 1 per cent a year after that);

- **minimum contribution**. This must be no higher than £20 and it is up to you when and how often you contribute. You cannot be forced to pay in regularly and there are no penalties for missing or stopping regular payments, which is particularly useful if your budget is tight or tends to vary;

- **transfers**. You can switch your accumulated fund to another stakeholder scheme or other pension arrangement at any time without penalty. Stakeholder schemes must accept transfers.

What they cost

It is up to you how much you pay into personal pensions. The more you pay in, the larger the pension you will receive. The table on p178 gives you an idea of the amount you might need to save each month to produce each £100 of pension. But there are no certainties. If investment performance is poor, charges rise or annuity rates fall, you will have to either save more to reach your target, boost your pension by retiring later than you originally planned (see p200) or accept a lower pension.

If you have arranged a plan yourself, you also organise how you want to pay in. For example, you might make regular contributions by direct debit or standing order (see Chapter 2) or you might make less frequent, lump-sum payments by cheque. If you have started the plan through your workplace, your contributions will normally be deducted directly from your pay and passed by your employer to the pension provider.

Various charges are built into personal pensions. If you choose a stakeholder scheme, charges may only be levied as a percentage of the value of your fund and must come to no more than 1.5 per cent a year for the first 10 years, falling back to 1 per cent a year after that.

If your personal pension is not a stakeholder scheme, there may also be other charges – eg, an administration fee taken from each contribution, charges if you transfer your fund to a different provider or start your pension earlier than intended. If you decide to invest your fund on a unit-linked basis (see p111), there are usually upfront charges when the units are first purchased and a yearly management charge of around 1 to 1.5 per cent of the value of your fund. If you invest on a with-profits basis (see p111), most charges are not explicit but are one factor reflected in the level of bonuses that you earn each year.

If you use an adviser to help you choose and set up your personal pension, you might pay a fee to the adviser, or alternatively s/he might get commission from the pension provider, in which case the plan's charges will already cover this. Paying for advice through commission is due to be abolished from 2012. It is proposed that, from then, you will pay a separate fee for any advice, though you may be able to arrange to pay the fee gradually in instalments deducted from your pension scheme. See Chapter 2 for details about how advisers are paid.

Choosing and starting to save

Personal pensions and stakeholder schemes are mainly offered by insurance companies. Organisations such as banks and building societies also offer them but are usually marketing the plans from their own insurance arm or acting as agents for an insurance company (see Chapter 2).

You can either go directly to a provider or take out a plan through an adviser (see Chapter 2). Your employer might offer access to a personal pension or stakeholder scheme through your workplace and might have negotiated a special deal (eg, lower charges), or be willing to contribute to the plan. Before opting for the workplace plan, compare it with other personal pensions on offer.

There are literally hundreds of personal pensions to choose from, though few are stakeholder schemes. The sort of factors you might want to consider when comparing plans include the following.

- **Flexibility**. Can you save in the way you want to? For example, are you committed to regular payments? Is there a penalty if you miss a payment? Can you pay in *ad hoc* lump sums when you want to? Is the minimum payment at the right level for you?
- **Charges**. How much will be deducted? How does that compare with the charges for other plans? If the charges are high, is there a good reason why you might accept this? Bear in mind that a plan with high charges will have to work harder to give you the same return as a plan with lower charges.
- **Choice of investment funds**. Do you want a big choice? Does the provider offer the type of fund you want (see p198)? Do not be persuaded by past performance claims. Research shows that funds which performed well in the past do not necessarily perform well in future. However, there is some evidence to suggest that funds which have performed badly in the past have some tendency to do so in future, so you might want to avoid the worst performers.

When you enquire about a particular plan, you will be given various pieces of literature. Most importantly, you will find a key facts document – you can spot it by the Key Facts logo (see p363). This document summarises the important features of the plan in a standardised way to help you compare one plan with another.

To compare different personal pensions and stakeholder schemes, use the Financial Services Authority Moneymadeclear Compare Products tables or surveys published by magazines such as *Which?* or *Money Management*. A financial adviser (see Chapter 2) can help you to choose a plan and also decide how much retirement income you might need and the amount you should save.

Pension fund investments

If you have a personal pension, stakeholder scheme or free-standing additional voluntary contribution scheme, you can decide how to invest your contributions. You might also have this choice if you belong to a money purchase occupational scheme or in-house additional voluntary contribution scheme. The choices are broadly the same as for investment-type life insurance described in Chapter 4, so may include the following.

UK fixed interest. A relatively low-risk unit-linked fund (see p111) where your money is invested mainly in gilts and corporate bonds issued by UK companies.

With-profits fund (see p111). You earn bonuses linked to the performance of an underlying fund of investments including shares, gilts, bonds and property. Some of the performance from good years is kept back to keep up the bonuses in bad years. In this way, the aim is for your investment to grow steadily.

Cautious managed. Medium-risk unit-linked fund (see p111) where your money is invested in a spread of gilts, corporate bonds and shares.

UK all companies. Medium-risk unit-linked fund (see p111) where your money is invested mainly in shares issued by UK companies quoted on the main London stock market.

Tracker fund. A type of unit-linked fund (see p111), where the value of your investment goes up and down directly in line with a particular stock market index such as the FTSE 100.

Global equities. Medium-risk unit-linked fund (see p111) where your money is invested in shares issued by companies from a spread of different countries.

UK smaller companies. Relatively high-risk unit-linked fund (see p111) where your money is invested mainly in shares issued by small UK companies which hopefully have good growth potential.

Lifestyle fund. At the start your money is invested largely in shares but as you get closer to your chosen retirement age the fund is shifted progressively more into safer investments such as corporate bonds, gilts and money market deposits (similar to bank and building society accounts). The aim is to protect the value of your fund from falls in the stock market as you approach the date on which you want to convert your fund into a pension.

Ethical funds. Within some of the categories above, such as 'UK all companies', some providers offer funds which invest on an ethical basis – eg, by not buying the shares of arms or tobacco companies or actively supporting companies with a good record on human rights. *Shariah*-compliant funds avoid companies involved in, for example, gambling, pork, alcohol and charging or earning interest. For more information, contact Ethical Investment Research Services.

Your choice of fund depends largely on the amount of risk you are willing to take to increase your chance of a higher return (see p9).

6. **Other benefits from pension schemes**

Regardless of their type, occupational schemes usually offer a package of benefits, not just a pension at your normal retirement age. Other benefits may include:
- a pension for your widow, widower or other partner if you die either before or after retirement;
- lump-sum life insurance if you die before retirement;
- an early pension if you have to retire because of ill health.

With a personal pension, it is generally up to you to decide whether you want to add other benefits. If you do, you must normally pay extra or accept some reduction in your pension. For example, if you want your plan to provide a pension after retirement for your partner if you are the first to die, you need to choose an appropriate sort of annuity (see p200) in which case the income you get from the annuity will be slightly lower. (Note that, following changes announced in December 2006, you cannot take out life insurance tax efficiently through a personal pension.)

You can generally start to receive the pension from a personal pension or stakeholder scheme at any age from 55 onwards (50 before 6 April 2010) and from any age if you have to retire early because of ill health. Usually, the earlier you start to receive the pension, the less income your fund will provide. To protect yourself from loss of income in the event of ill health, you might want to consider income protection insurance instead (see Chapter 7).

If you die before retirement, the value of your pension fund may be used to buy a pension for your survivors or passed to your heirs as a lump sum after deduction of tax at a special rate (35 per cent in 2009/10).

In order to bypass your estate (where your pension fund or life insurance payout could become subject to probate delays and inheritance tax), the occupational pension scheme administrator or personal pension provider will normally ask you to complete an 'expression of wish' form. In this, you state who you would like to receive the payment due on your death. The administrator or provider is not legally bound to follow your wishes, but will normally do so.

7. **Annuities and income drawdown**

How annuities work

If you have a personal pension, stakeholder scheme or free-standing additional voluntary contribution scheme, it is up to you to decide how to convert your pension fund into a pension. You make this decision at the point when you want the pension to start and it applies to your pension fund after taking any tax-free lump sum. You might also have this choice if you belong to a money purchase occupational scheme or in-house additional voluntary contribution scheme, or alternatively the decision might be made for you.

The main option is to use your pension fund to buy an annuity. An annuity is simply an investment where you swap a lump sum for an income, in this case for the rest of your life. You cannot get your lump sum back later (but see capital guaranteed annuities on p202) and the choice you make at the time you buy sets your future income, so it is very important to make the right choice.

The yearly income you get from an annuity depends on a variety of factors, including:

- **your age at the time you buy**. The younger you are, the longer on average the annuity will have to pay out and so the less you get each year;
- **the general life expectancy of the population as a whole.** An annuity is not just an investment, it is also a sort of insurance against living longer than average. The longer the population as a whole is expected on average to live, the lower the yearly income you are offered;
- **your sex**. Women tend on average to live longer than men and so usually get a lower yearly income than a man of the same age;
- **your health**. You may be able to get a higher than normal income if you are expected to have a shorter life than the average for someone of you age because of poor health or your lifestyle – eg, you smoke;
- **investment conditions**. The income from annuities is closely linked to the return from investments like gilts. As these returns move up and down in response to all sorts of economic factors, annuity rates will tend to move in line;
- **how much you can invest**. Some providers offer a higher income if you have a larger sum to invest or will only accept lump sums above a certain amount;
- **the type of annuity you choose**. The baseline is a level annuity which pays out the same income year after year until the investor dies. There are all sorts of variations (see the table on p201) and, in general, you pay for each variation through a drop in the yearly income you get.

Different types of annuity

Type of annuity	How it works	Example of the starting income for (a) a man aged 65 and (b) couple: man 65 and woman 60*	Comment
Single life annuity	Pays out an income for the life of a person and stops when that person dies. All the annuities below can be on either a single or joint life last survivor basis.	See below	Unsuitable if a partner could not cope financially following your death.
Joint-life last-survivor	Pays out an income until the last of two people dies. You choose whether, on the first death, the income is reduced. All the annuities below can be on either a single or joint-life last-survivor basis.	See below	Good choice if a partner depends at least partly on you financially.
Enhanced	Pays out a higher than average income to reflect your poor health or lifestyle. All the annuities below may be available on an enhanced basis.	Depends on your individual health and lifestyle	Should be considered if, for example, you smoke, are overweight, have diabetes, heart problems or other health conditions.
Level	Pays out the same income year after year. Income stops when you die.	(a) £672 (b) £576	Buying power is reduced by inflation. Poor deal if you die soon after investing.
Level with 10-year guarantee	Pays out the same income year after year. Pays out at least five years' income even if you die within the first five years.	(a) £648 (b) £576	Ensures you do not get a very bad deal if you die soon after investing.

Type of annuity	How it works	Example of the starting income for (a) a man aged 65 and (b) couple: man 65 and woman 60*	Comment
Capital guaranteed	Pays out at least as much in income as the capital sum you invested even if you die soon after investing.	No examples available. Lower income than for an annuity without this guarantee.	Ensures you do not get a very bad deal if you die soon after investing.
Escalating at 3 per cent, no guarantee	Pays out an income which is 3 per cent higher each year.	(a) £492 (b) £384	Provides some protection against inflation.
Retail Price Index-linked, no guarantee	Pays out an income which rises (and, if applicable, falls) each year in line with price inflation.	(a) £420 (b) £324	Protects the buying power of your income against inflation.
With-profits annuity	Pays out an income which rises and falls each year in line with an underlying fund of investments. You choose the starting income on the basis of the investment performance you expect. If you choose a low starting income, the chance of a fall in your future income is low or even removed altogether. The higher the starting income, the greater the risk that it will fall in future.	You choose the starting income and level of risk.	Gives you the chance of some protection against inflation, but there is also some risk that your income will fall.

Type of annuity	How it works	Example of the starting income for (a) a man aged 65 and (b) couple: man 65 and woman 60*	Comment
Unit-linked annuity	Pays out an income which rises and falls each year in line with an underlying fund of investments. You choose the starting income on the basis of the investment performance you expect. The higher the starting income, the greater the risk that it will fall in future. But even with a low starting income, there is a risk of a fall in future.	You choose the starting income and level of risk.	Gives you the chance of some protection against inflation, but there is also a major risk that your income will fall.
Short-term annuity	You use part of your pension fund to buy an annuity which pays out an income for up to five years which must end before you reach age 75. You leave the rest of the fund invested and can then use a bit more to buy another short-term annuity if you want to. Alternatively, you use the remaining fund to buy an annuity that will pay out for the rest of your life (or opt for income drawdown (see p208).	No examples available	Guards against being locked into a poor-value annuity, but you are exposed to 'mortality drag' – see p208.

*Average yearly income for each £10,000 invested. Income for couple reduces by one-third on first death.[7]

How income drawdown works

'Income drawdown' means leaving your pension fund invested and drawing an income directly from the fund instead of using the fund to buy an annuity. HM Revenue and Customs (the Revenue) sets rules about how much income you can draw out each year. They are designed to prevent your pension fund running out part way through retirement. Since April 2006, income drawdown is available even after you reach age 75 – this measure is aimed primarily at helping members of religious groups (eg, the Plymouth Brethren) who believe that annuities are unacceptable gambling on life expectancy.

A big advantage of income drawdown is that your pension fund does not die with you. On death before 75, the remaining fund can be used either to provide pension(s) for your dependant(s) or, after deduction of tax (at 35 per cent in 2009/10), passed on as a lump sum to anyone you nominate. On death after 75, the remaining fund can be used to provide pension(s) for dependants or donated tax-free to charity, but high tax rates mean it is not economical to leave your pension fund to anyone else.

Because of 'mortality drag' (see p208), income drawdown is suitable only if you are prepared to leave your pension fund invested in the stock market so that you have a reasonable chance of good investment growth, but this also increases the risk that the value of the fund might fall. Therefore, income drawdown is suitable only if you have a large (six-figure) pension fund or other sources of retirement income. For most people, annuities will usually be a more suitable choice.

What annuities and drawdown cost

The cost of an annuity is one of the factors reflected in the rate you are offered. The rate is quoted as so many £s of income a year for each £10,000 of pension fund. If you enlist the help of an adviser in choosing an annuity, you might pay a fee directly to the adviser (see Chapter 2).

If you opt for income drawdown, you are leaving your pension fund invested. There will be ongoing charges for managing the investments similar to those you were paying while building up your pension fund (see p194). The Revenue rules also require that the amount of income you draw is reviewed regularly and there are also charges for this. Charges, as well as investment risk, are another reason why income drawdown is generally suitable only if you have a large pension fund.

Choosing an annuity or drawdown

You do not have to buy the annuity from the same provider with which you have been building up your pension fund because you normally have an 'open market option' allowing you to take your fund and shop around to buy your annuity elsewhere. Do use this option. Many pension providers are not interested in the annuity market and will not offer you the best rate. If you do not shop around you could be missing out on a better deal.

You can get information about the annuities available from the Financial Services Authority Moneymadeclear Compare Products tables (www.fsa.gov.uk/tables) and specialist organisations such as Moneyfacts and many personal finance websites. Once you have narrowed down your choice, contact the annuity providers directly. Alternatively, enlist the help of an independent financial adviser in shopping around for the best deal – there are several that specialise in annuities (see Appendix 2). An independent financial adviser will be paid either by commission from the annuity provider, which will come out of your pension fund, or by a fee. From 2012, paying for advice by commission is due to be abolished. See Chapter 2.

Deciding whether income drawdown is suitable for you is complex. Get help from an independent financial adviser specialising in this area (usually the same advisers who specialise in annuities).

8. **Pitfalls and what to watch out for**

Contracting out

Contracting out means you stop building up additional state pension and instead build up a pension through a defined benefit occupational pension scheme. At present, you can also contract out and instead build up a pension through a defined contribution occupational scheme, personal pension or stakeholder scheme, but this option is due to be abolished from a date yet to be announced, but expected to be 2012.

You either pay lower national insurance (NI) while you are contracted out or part of your contributions is rebated. Any rebate is not paid to you personally. It is paid into the contracted-out pension arrangement.

Because of the way the rules work, if you are contracted out through a final salary occupational scheme, you are unlikely to be worse off than you would have been staying in the additional state pension scheme. In any case, if your occupational scheme is contracted out, this generally applies to all the members, so the only way to contract back in would be to leave the scheme, which would mean also losing the benefit of your employer's contributions.

Contracting out through a money purchase occupational scheme, personal pension or stakeholder scheme (called contracting out on a defined contribution basis) is much more uncertain. You are giving up a defined amount of pension as promised by the state scheme and replacing it with a money purchase pension, the value of which will depend on the size of the NI rebates, investment growth, scheme charges and annuity rates at retirement. Experts tend to agree that, these days, all but the youngest people are likely to be better off staying in or returning to the state scheme. But the decision is so complex and uncertain that many advisers will no longer offer advice about it. This complexity is a key reason why the Government has decided to abolish contracting out through defined contribution schemes.

Pension transfers

If you switch jobs, you can usually leave your pension behind in your old employer's scheme to be paid to you when you eventually retire. Alternatively, you can normally transfer your rights to a new occupational scheme or personal pension. Deciding what to do can be difficult and you might want to get advice (see Chapter 2).

If this is a money purchase scheme, you simply transfer the value of your pension fund. Be wary of transferring out of the old employer's scheme to a personal pension if the charges will be higher.

Final salary schemes generally give the best pension if you stay with your employer until retirement. If you leave early, your pension is worked out based on your pay at the time you leave (not at retirement) and the years of membership up to the time you leave. The resulting **'deferred pension'** must be increased in line with inflation between leaving and retirement but only up to a maximum level (2.5 per cent a year).

If you decide to transfer your deferred final salary pension, it is normally converted into a **'cash-equivalent transfer value'** – the cash sum that, if invested, would be enough to produce the pension by retirement based on assumptions about, for example, investment returns.

The cash-equivalent transfer value can then either be invested on a money purchase basis or used to buy benefits in a new employer's final salary scheme. It will usually buy fewer years of membership in a new scheme than you have given up in the old scheme because the new scheme works out what it might buy on the basis of your expected pay at retirement. Because of this, if you change jobs often, successive transfers can erode the value of your pension rights. If you expect to change jobs often, you may be better off with a money purchase pension arrangement.

The exception is where you work in the public sector. Many public sector schemes belong to a 'transfer club' and, as you change jobs, your years of membership built up in the old pension scheme count without reduction as years in the new scheme to which you transfer.

Leaving an occupational scheme without changing jobs

An occupational scheme is usually a better way to save for retirement than a personal pension because:

- your employer must normally pay a large part of the cost of the pension, but may be willing to pay little or nothing into your personal pension;

- the charges for running an occupational scheme are usually lower than for a personal pension; *and*
- all personal pensions are money purchase schemes. If you can join a final salary occupational scheme, this has the advantage of offering a pension which is set in relation to your pay near retirement so you are sheltered from much of the risk inherent in long-term saving.

Therefore, be very suspicious if a salesperson or adviser suggests you leave your employer's occupational scheme to take out and/or transfer to a personal pension instead. The switch might earn the adviser a large commission (see Chapter 2), but is unlikely to be a good move for you.

Closure of a final salary occupational scheme

A variety of factors, including the stock market crashes of 2000–2003 and 2007/08, and the fact that people are tending to live longer (life expectancy is increasing by about one to two years every decade), has pushed up the cost of final salary schemes for employers. As a result, some have decided to close their schemes. This may be done in several ways, which have different consequences for you. The scheme might be:

- **closed to new members**. Existing members can carry on paying in and building up pension but new employees are typically offered a money purchase arrangement instead;
- **closed to new and existing members**. Your pension so far continues to build up but you do not build up any more years of membership and new pension contributions go into an alternative pension arrangement;
- **wound up and all benefits secured**. If a scheme is wound up, legally it is usually bound to provide pensions only as if you had left the scheme early – ie, based on your pay at the time of the wind-up and not at retirement. So your pension is likely to be less than you had previously expected;
- **wound up with a shortfall in the scheme**. If there is not enough money in the pension fund to provide all the promised pensions, the employer must pay in extra contributions to make good the shortfall. If the employer has gone out of business, this may not be possible and you could end up with a lot less pension than you had been expecting. The law states the order in which the pension fund assets, such as they are, must be used and gives highest priority to pensions which have already started to be paid. The Government has set up a compensation scheme which partially protects pension rights in schemes that wind up and have a shortfall. For details, see Chapter 10.

It is important to keep the risk of scheme closure in perspective. Around nine million people belong to final salary schemes. About half of these are in public sector schemes, which are unlikely to close because they are essentially underpinned by tax revenues. Only a small proportion of schemes close with a shortfall in the scheme and, if this does not happen, final salary schemes generally remain the best way to save for retirement. Unlike a final salary scheme, in a money purchase scheme you have no protection from stock market falls and the effects of people living longer – these sorts of changes feed through directly to reduce your pension.

If your employer decides to close a final salary pension scheme, usually there is little you can do to stop the closure. In most cases, your contract of employment will state that you have the right to join a pension scheme but rarely does it specify a specific type of scheme. Your trade union or any other body representing staff may be able to negotiate with your employer. This will probably not stop the closure but could result in improvements to whatever scheme is on offer to replace the closing final salary scheme.

Inflation

Bear in mind that you build up your pension over a long period and it may provide you with an income over several decades. Over such long periods, even low rates of inflation reduce the buying power of your money. For example, after 20 years, £10,000 buys only the same as £6,100 today if inflation averages just 2.5 per cent a year. So you need to take inflation into account when deciding how much to save and when making choices at retirement. For example, a Retail Prices Index-linked annuity will protect the buying power of your income throughout retirement, but the starting income you get is a lot lower than for a level annuity (see p201). If you decide on a level annuity, make sure you set aside some of your income in the early years so that you can draw on your savings later to compensate for the effects of inflation.

Your dependants

If you have choices at retirement, consider how your partner or any other dependants might cope financially if you were to die first. If they rely on your income (eg, to cover household bills and other basics) choose, for instance, a 'joint-life last-survivor' annuity (see p201).

Mortality drag

A conventional annuity is basically insurance against living too long. You are pooled with lots of other people of your age and sex. Annuities are offered to everyone in the pool at a rate that reflects the fact that some will die early and their unused money then goes to help pay the pensions of people who live longer than average.

With arrangements where you leave part or all of your pension fund invested after your pension starts (ie, income drawdown, with-profits annuities, unit-linked annuities and short-term annuities) you are not benefiting from this pooling. So you lose the cross-subsidy of money from people who die at an earlier age than the average for someone of your age and sex. The loss of the subsidy adds to the cost of providing your pension and means you need to choose investments that are expected to produce a high enough return to compensate for this extra cost.

Advice versus information

Do not confuse advice and information. Stakeholder schemes are considered relatively simple and you will be given 'stakeholder decision trees' to help you decide whether they are a suitable choice for you. Your employer, a Citizens Advice Bureau or other organisation might offer to help you work through the decision trees but this does not amount to advice – it is still up to you to make the final choice. See Chapter 2 for details of the extra protection you get if you opt for advice.

9. Keeping track of your pensions

Over your working life, you may belong to many different pension schemes or take out a variety of different plans, especially if you change jobs often.

If you transfer your pension rights from a scheme or plan, you no longer have any claim on that arrangement and no need to keep in touch with it. However, if you leave your pension rights behind, they will eventually become payable when you retire, so you should keep in touch with these schemes and plans. The providers should send you regular benefit statements, but can do this only if you let them have your new address each time you move.

If you have lost touch with schemes and plans that owe you a pension, the Pension Tracing Service can help you trace the scheme or plan providers. See Appendix 2.

10. Regulation and complaints

State pension scheme

Acts of Parliament and various regulations set out how the state scheme works. From time to time, Parliament decides to change the rules.

If you have a problem concerning the state pension system, you should first contact the manager of the office you have been dealing with. This will probably be:

- a Revenue department if your complaint involves national insurance contributions. If your complaint concerns an award of national insurance credits, first read the explanatory notes included with Form CA82 *If You Think Our Decision is Wrong*; or

- an office of The Pension Service in most other cases. See its free leaflet GL22 *Tell Us How to Improve Our Service*.

If you are not satisfied with the outcome of your complaint, you might be able to take your case to the Tax Adjudicator if it concerns national insurance (NI). You might take a complaint concerning either NI or state pensions to the Parliamentary Commissioner for Administration (the 'Parliamentary Ombudsman'). You do this by contacting your Member of Parliament. See Appendix 2 for contact details.

Occupational pension scheme

Occupational pension schemes are set up as either:
- **trusts**. This is a special legal arrangement where 'trustees' are responsible for looking after the pension scheme on behalf of the members. A trust deed and scheme rules spell out how the scheme must be run and the benefits it provides. The trustees normally appoint a pensions administrator to handle the day-to-day running of the scheme; *or*
- **statutory schemes**. These are set up under Acts of Parliament and are mainly public sector schemes, such as those covering local authority employees or NHS workers. The Acts of Parliament and regulations set out the main rules about how the scheme is run and the benefits it provides. For each scheme, there is a centralised office which handles the day-to-day administration.

In addition, there are many laws and regulations covering various aspects of the way pension schemes are run and the protection offered to members in various circumstances. The Pensions Regulator is responsible for overseeing the proper running of occupational schemes. If you suspect your scheme is being poorly or fraudulently run, you can alert the Pensions Regulator, which may investigate and could take disciplinary action against the scheme. There are compensation arrangements to protect members' pensions in some circumstances (see Chapter 10).

If you have a complaint, you should initially take it to the person or office responsible for the scheme's administration. All schemes are required to have a formal complaints procedure and the administrator will tell you how to use this.

If you are not happy with the response, you can refer your case to The Pensions Advisory Service, which will try to mediate between you and the scheme and clear up any misunderstanding. If this is unsuccessful, you can take your case to the Pensions Ombudsman. See Chapter 10 for more details.

Personal pensions

Personal pensions count as a form of investment and so are regulated mainly by the Financial Services Authority (FSA). The Pensions Regulator is responsible for some aspects of stakeholder pension schemes, including ensuring that employers with five or more employees and without other suitable pension arrangements offer access to stakeholder schemes through the workplace.

The FSA has detailed rules which aim to protect investors, including requiring firms to be solvent and properly run and requirements about the information to be given to investors.

If you have a complaint, first contact the firm involved. All firms offering pensions or giving financial advice are required to have proper complaints procedures. If you are not happy with the outcome, The Pensions Advisory Service might be able to help. Alternatively, you can take your complaint straight to the Financial Ombudsman Service. There is a compensation scheme that may pay out if you lose money if an investment firm or adviser has gone out of business and you have lost money because of the firm's negligence or fraud (see Chapter 10).

Pension scams

Be on your alert for these scams and do not get caught out.

Pension liberation schemes. You cannot normally start your pension from an occupational scheme or personal pension before age 55 (50 before 6 April 2010). You may be approached by firms suggesting that they can unlock your pension so that you can access the cash in the scheme before that age. They usually do this illegally by, for example, transferring your pension rights to a fictitious employer's scheme, often based offshore, and in the process take a hefty slice (usually 20 to 30 per cent) of your pension fund. They are unlikely to explain that HM Revenue and Customs will also charge you a large amount of tax on the money taken out. As well as leaving yourself short of income when you do eventually retire, you stand to lose the best part of your savings. If anyone offers you cash for your pension, be suspicious and seek advice.

Mis-selling. Salespeople and advisers often stand to earn a substantial commission (see Chapter 2) if they can persuade you to take out a personal pension. Bear this in mind and be aware that a good adviser will not push you down this route if, say, you have the option to join an occupational scheme through your job. Bear in mind too that a stakeholder scheme might suit your needs but not be recommended by an adviser because, typically, they earn only a low commission for selling these schemes.

Baby boomer scam. With a large generation of people approaching retirement, there is plenty of temptation for scammers who offer free seminars on retirement planning. However, before you can leave, you have to face a hard sell encouraging you to use your retirement savings to buy products offered by the scammers. These may be real products (but not necessarily the best ones for you) or totally fictitious ones. Do not be lured into seminars. If you need help, choose your own financial adviser (see Chapter 2). Never invest in any product you do not understand or have not had a chance to look at thoroughly.

11. **Future changes: personal accounts**

As the population is tending to live longer and the post-Second World War baby boom generation reaches retirement, the cost to the nation of providing pensions is increasing. The Government appointed the Turner Commission to examine this problem and suggest some solutions. The Commission said there are basically three options: we must accept a poorer old age, we must work longer and/or we must save extra. As a result, the Government is introducing a package of measures aimed at encouraging us to work longer and save more. These measures are contained in the Pensions Acts 2007 and 2008. They include raising the state pension age and creating the framework for a new national scheme of personal pension accounts. The details of the scheme will come later, but these are the main features of the new national scheme.

- Employers must ensure that eligible workers are automatically enrolled in either the national scheme of personal accounts or another scheme that is at least as good.
- Workers may opt out if they want to.
- An eligible worker is aged at least 22 but under the pension age for the scheme and with earnings above a specified amount.
- Employers must pay at least 3 per cent of a worker's pay between set limits into whichever scheme the worker belongs to. This is considerably less than most employers currently pay into occupational schemes (see p194).
- The worker will have to pay in up to 4 per cent of her/his pay between set limits up to an annual maximum (£3,600 in 2005 money). Tax relief will add another 1 per cent.
- Personal accounts will provide money purchase pensions.
- It is intended that personal accounts will have lower charges than existing personal pensions and stakeholder schemes.
- Personal accounts will offer a limited choice of investment funds. There will be a default fund which is likely to be a lifestyling fund (see p198).
- The self-employed and people who are not working will be able to join the national scheme if they want to, but will not benefit from any employer contributions.

The new national scheme is expected to start in 2012, but will be phased in gradually and the full level of employer and employee contributions outlined above will not be in place until 2016. The Government hopes the new scheme will encourage people on low to moderate incomes, who currently do not belong to an occupational scheme, to start to save. But, if your income is low, you may still be caught in the trap where you get little value from your pension savings if they merely reduce the level of means-tested benefits you would otherwise be able to claim in retirement. According to research by the Pensions Policy Institute in 2007, young people on low earnings with a broken work history and people in their 40s and 50s, even with a full work record, are at medium risk of failing to get value for money from personal accounts. People who will be renting their home when they retire and have no other savings are at high risk.

Notes

1 Department for Work and Pensions, '£4 Billion Boost for Pensioners', Press Release, 2008

2 Department for Work and Pensions, *The Pensioners' Incomes Series 2007/08*, DWP, 2009

3 Office for National Statistics, *Private Pension Scheme Membership*, www.statistics.gov.uk, accessed 21 July 2009

4. Occupational pensions

5 Department for Work and Pensions, *The Pensioners' Incomes Series 2007/08*, DWP, 2009

6 Office for National Statistics, *Pension Trends*, 2009

7. Annuities and income drawdown

7 Financial Services Authority, *Moneymadeclear, Compare Products*, www.fsa.gov.uk, accessed 24 July 2009

Chapter 7

Insurance

This chapter covers:
1. The need for insurance (below)
2. Insuring items you own and buy (p221)
3. Life insurance (p238)
4. Health-related insurance (p243)
5. Your rights and responsibilities (p254)
6. Regulation and complaints (p255)

Basic facts
- One in six private car drivers claim on their insurance each year. One in 20 drivers are thought to be driving without insurance.[1]
- Out of every 1,000 households in England and Wales, 25 are burgled in a year.[2] During the current recession that started in 2008 one-quarter of households have cancelled or not renewed their contents insurance to save money.[3]
- The average cost of a travel insurance claim for someone aged 65 or over is 3.5 times larger than the average claim of the under-50s.[4]
- In 2008, 77,600 people in the UK were victims of identity fraud.[5]

1. The need for insurance

What is insurance

Insurance is a financial product which pays out money if specified events happen. The aim is to compensate for a financial loss suffered as the result of the event.

The main types of insurance

Type of insurance	What it does	For details, see:
Accident, sickness and unemployment (ASU)	Either pays out an income or pays the interest on a loan for a set period (eg, one or two years) if you are out of work because of unemployment or illness.	p244

Type of insurance	What it does	For details, see:
Car	Covers damage or injury for which you are responsible if you are involved in an accident while driving and, provided you have appropriate cover, repairs to your own car.	p221
Critical illness	Pays out a cash lump sum if you have or are diagnosed with a life-threatening condition, such as heart attack, stroke or cancer.	p246
Dental insurance	Pays the cost of private dental treatment.	p243
Extended warranty	Pays for repairs or replacement within the first few years of an item's life after the manufacturer's guarantee has run out.	p224
Funeral expenses	Type of life insurance (protection) that pays out a cash lump sum when you die, intended to be enough to cover your funeral costs.	p240
House buildings	Pays for repairs to your home, or its complete rebuilding, if it is damaged or destroyed by specified events, such as fire, flood or subsidence.	p225
House contents	Pays for repairs to or replacement of your possessions, including some fittings in your home, such as carpets, if they are lost, damaged or destroyed by, for example, theft, fire or flood.	p228
Identity fraud insurance	Pays for the costs of communication and legal action to put matters right if you are the victim of identity fraud. May also cover loss of earnings if you have to take unpaid time off work to sort the matter out. Does not cover amounts stolen from you by fraudsters.	p236
Income protection	Pays an income if you are unable to work because of illness or disability. The income usually continues until you recover or reach retirement age, whichever comes first.	p247

Type of insurance	What it does	For details, see:
Life (investment-type)	Insurance policy which builds up a cash value. Some or all of this is payable on your death, when the policy matures or is cashed in.	p111
Life (protection)	Insurance policy which pays out a specified sum on your death and is designed to protect your survivors from financial hardship. Some types also have an investment element.	p238
Loan payment protection	Type of ASU policy (see p214) taken out with a loan in order to keep up the interest payments for a while if you cannot do so because of job loss or illness.	p244
Long-term care	Pays out an income if you can no longer care for yourself. Used to pay for care either in your own home or in a residential or nursing home.	p250
Mortgage payment protection	Type of ASU policy (see p214) taken out with a mortgage in order to keep up the mortgage interest payments for a while, if you cannot because of job loss or illness.	p244
Mortgage protection	Type of life insurance (protection) which pays off your outstanding mortgage in a single payment in the event of your death.	p240
Possessions	Pays out for repairs to, or replacement of, your possessions, if they are lost, damaged or destroyed by, for example, theft, fire or flood.	p228
Private medical	Pays for treatment in a private hospital.	p254
Purchase protection	Pays out for repairs to, or replacement of, newly bought possessions, if they are lost, damaged or destroyed within, for instance, the first month of ownership.	p231
Service contract	Not strictly insurance, but similar. In return for an annual premium, you get free repairs to certain household services or appliances, such as your central heating system or drains.	p232

Type of insurance	What it does	For details, see:
Travel	Pays out when specified things go wrong with a holiday – eg, if you have to cancel unexpectedly because of health, if your personal possessions are lost or stolen while away or if you have to have treatment or fly back home because you are ill.	p233

When you might need insurance

Sometimes the law says you must have insurance. The most common example is if you drive a car on public roads, in which case you must have some insurance to pay out if you injure other people or damage their property.

Do you need insurance?

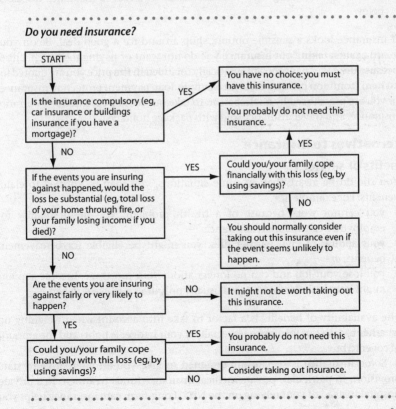

Though not a legal requirement, insurance is compulsory in some other situations. For example, if you have a mortgage, your lender will insist that you have buildings insurance to pay out if the mortgaged property is damaged or destroyed.

In other cases, it is up to you whether or not you take out insurance and you can make this decision by following these steps.

* **Step one: assess your needs**. For example, if no one is financially dependent on you, you do not normally have a need for life insurance. If you are a tenant, usually your landlord is responsible for insuring the building in which you live (but not the contents).
* **Step two: decide whether insurance is worthwhile**. Weigh up the risks you face in terms of the likelihood of an event happening, what you stand to lose if it does and whether you could withstand that loss. The chart on p217 will help you do this.
* **Step three: look at the cost of insurance and the alternatives**. Decide whether you can afford insurance and whether you are prepared to pay the price asked. In doing this, consider the alternatives to insurance discussed below.

If insurance looks a sensible option, shop around for a good deal. Be on your guard against taking out insurance you do not want or paying too much, either because the cover has been automatically included in the price you are quoted for an item (common practice with, for example, loan payment protection insurance) or you are pressurised by a salesperson to take out cover – eg, extended warranty insurance, and travel insurance sold with package holidays.

Alternatives to insurance

Benefits or services

You should be aware that, in some situations, you may be entitled to claim benefits. For example, if:

* you cannot work because of a health problem, you might qualify for employment and support allowance;
* your spouse or civil partner dies, you might be eligible for bereavement benefits; *or*
* you lose your job and can no longer afford your mortgage, income support might help with the interest (but usually only after a 13-week delay).

The availability of benefits is a factor to take into account when weighing up whether to take out insurance (especially if your budget is tight) and the amount of cover to buy.

Some insurance is specifically designed to give you an alternative to state provision. In particular, private medical insurance funds treatment in a private hospital instead of your relying on the NHS. Long-term care insurance helps you pay for care as an alternative to state funding (which may restrict your choice and involve using your savings) if you can no longer look after yourself. Neither of these types of insurance is essential – you could use the state services instead.

For information about benefits and tax credits, see Chapter 9.

Protection through your job

Employers are usually required to provide you with a minimum amount of sick pay if you are off work because of illness and often pay you more and for longer than the law requires. See Chapter 9 for details of statutory sick pay. You might get other perks through your job, such as life insurance or, if you have a company vehicle, car insurance.

Always check what you are entitled to through your job. It might remove the need for you to arrange your own insurance or reduce the amount of cover you need to buy.

Income or savings

If you are looking at a risk which would result in a relatively small loss – eg, the risk of an electrical appliance breaking down in the first few years, you might be able to replace the item or pay for repairs from your income.

If you have enough savings, you might be able to recover from a fairly large financial outlay without the need for insurance. For example, you might decide you can manage without house contents or possessions insurance if your belongings are fairly few, not too expensive to replace, and well covered by the amount you have in your savings account.

This strategy is not suitable for risks that could result in very large losses, however remote the chance of disaster seems, since there is always a small chance of the risk materialising, in which case you could face financial ruin. This will apply, for example, to any situation where you might have to compensate someone for injury caused by you or your possessions. An example of this would be a slate falling from your roof and hurting someone. If the injury was so severe that the person could not work any more, you could be sued for her/his loss of earnings, which might run to millions of pounds. To cover you against this type of risk, it is essential to have adequate insurance (called 'public liability' cover and often included as part of another policy, such as in buildings or travel insurance).

Borrowing

You might borrow the money you need to cope if something unexpected happens. Planning to do this is sensible only if you are confident that you would be able to borrow at a reasonably competitive interest rate and would have a realistic plan for paying off the debt. See Chapter 5 for information about different ways to borrow and how to manage debts.

Borrowing is not a suitable strategy for risks that could cause a very large financial loss, for the reasons outlined above.

Shopping around for insurance

With many types of insurance, you may feel confident shopping around for yourself without the help of a broker or financial adviser. Increasingly, it is common to use internet comparison sites for this purpose. Although this is a convenient way to compare a range of policies, you should be aware of the limitations of comparison websites.

- **Market coverage.** No single site covers all the providers, so you may need to check several sites and independently contact some providers to get a full picture of the market.
- **Independence.** Be aware that the website provider may receive commission when you click through from the site to buy insurance or may itself offer insurance products.
- **Different circumstances.** Price quotes are often for standardised or average people. If your circumstances are non-standard or unusual, you may find that when you contact the provider for a detailed quote that the price for you, based on your particular circumstances, could be much higher or cover might be restricted.
- **Focus on price.** These sites typically compare policies on the basis of price, but the detail of the cover may differ. If you choose the cheapest deal, you might find that it does not offer all the cover you wanted. Make sure you check the full policy wording before you buy. The FSA Moneymadeclear Compare Products tables include some insurance products and focus on key policy terms rather than price.

In 2009, a number of comparison website providers joined forces to set up the Comparison Consortium, a trade body, which tried to establish a code of good practice for its members. The code required members to:

- treat customers fairly;
- conduct their business with integrity and skill;
- ensure the comparison site is transparent and offers information that is suitable;
- manage conflicts of interest fairly;
- provide accurate prices and make clear if it is an estimate based on incomplete information;
- use customer data fairly and legally;
- operate a complaints procedure for consumers who are unhappy with the experience they had.

At the time of writing, the Consortium was no longer operating, but its code sets out standards which ideally all comparison sites should adopt.

Situations affecting insurance

Relationships

When you marry, form a civil partnership or start to live with someone, you may become financially interdependent – eg, sharing housing costs and other household bills. Consider taking out term insurance to protect each other in the event of death. Bear in mind that if only one of you is doing paid work (eg, because the other is caring for children), you may nonetheless still be financially dependent on each other and both need life cover. This is because the unpaid work of the partner at home would still have to be done in the event of the other partner's death.

When a relationship breaks down, you may no longer need life cover. But if your ex-partner will be paying you maintenance, consider taking out insurance on her/his life up to the amount of the maintenance payments to ensure the money would continue even if s/he died.

Disability

Providers of any goods and services are required to make reasonable adjustments to ensure that what they sell or provide can be accessed by people with a disability. However, insurers are permitted to refuse insurance or offer it on less favourable terms to a disabled person, but only if this is justified on the basis of relevant and reliable data. In general, this means outright refusals and blanket exclusions are unacceptable. For example, it would be unacceptable for an insurer offering a critical illness insurance to refuse to issue policies to anyone who has HIV/AIDS or to say that any claim from someone with HIV/AIDS would be turned down, but it would be acceptable to exclude from cover claims arising from these conditions (in which case someone with HIV/AIDS could still claim for unrelated conditions, such as a heart attack).

If you believe a provider of goods or services has discriminated unfairly against you because of your disability, complain to the provider. If they do not put the matter right, you can take court action.

2. Insuring items you own and buy

Car insurance

What it covers

This depends on the type of cover you choose. There are three main sorts.

- **Third party**. This is the minimum cover required by law. It pays out on claims where you or your passenger injure someone or damage someone else's property. In practice, it is unusual to take out only this cover, though it will be the default cover if, for instance, you are driving someone else's car but relying on your insurance.

- **Third party, fire and theft**. As for third party cover, but it also pays out for damage to or loss of your own car because of either fire or theft.
- **Comprehensive**. As for third party, fire and theft but also covers damage to your own car in an accident. Comprehensive policies may also come with extras, such as cover for your in-car entertainment system and a courtesy car while yours is being repaired.

Either as a feature of a comprehensive policy or as an add-on for an extra premium, you can usually have legal protection insurance which will cover the costs of solicitors and barristers if a motoring incident or dispute ends up in court.

Do you need it
By law, you must have at least third party insurance.

How it works
You take out insurance for a set period, usually a year, but insurance is available for shorter periods. There is no need to stay with the same insurer year after year. The market is very competitive, so it is worth shopping around to find the best deal.

What it costs
Normally, the premium you pay depends on a large number of factors, including the following.

- **Type of cover**. Comprehensive cover costs more than third party, fire and theft – though often not much more.
- **Where you live**. Cover for cities and towns (where theft and accidents are more common) costs more than cover for rural areas.
- **Your car**. You will pay more to insure a fast, sporty car or one which is large or expensive than a small, less powerful one. Insurers sort cars into 50 groups according to the risks involved. Car groups are published, for example, on www.parkers.co.uk and in *Parker's Guide* available from newsagents.
- **Who will drive**. In general, the premium is lower if you restrict the drivers to just you or you and one other. You will pay a lot more if a young or learner driver or someone with motoring convictions is to use the car.
- **How you use the car**. You might pay less if you drive a low number of miles each year or you do not use your car to get to and from work.
- **Where you keep your car**. You generally pay less if your car is kept overnight in a locked garage or your driveway rather than on the street.

At least one insurer is looking at using technology to log the number of miles you actually drive in order to link part of your premium to this mileage. Another offers a premium reduction to young drivers who agree not to drive at night, when young drivers in particular are more prone to accidents.

Most insurers operate a **'no claims discount'** system which means you pay a lower premium than standard at renewal if you have not made any claims within the past year. The table below shows a typical no claims discount scale, but the precise amounts vary from one insurer to another. If you switch policy, you should not lose out because the new insurer normally gives you the discount corresponding to the number of claim-free years you have built up with your previous insurer(s).

With comprehensive policies, you may have the option, for an extra premium (eg, 10 or 15 per cent more), to buy no-claims protection. This allows you to make one or sometimes two claims in a year without losing any discount.

A typical no claims discount scale

Number of years without a claim	Premium at renewal is reduced by	If one claim, discount at renewal is reduced to
1	30%	0%
2	40%	0%
3	50%	30%
4	60%	40%
5 or more	65% or 70%	50%

Since you may be reluctant to make a small claim because of the impact it would have on your no claims discount, it makes sense to opt for a voluntary excess (the first part of a claim you yourself pay) in exchange for a reduction in premium.

Choosing and buying

You can buy directly from an insurer or go through an intermediary, such as a broker. In both cases, you may be able to buy face-to-face at a high street office, by post, phone or internet. There is sometimes a discount (eg, 5 to 10 per cent) if you buy on the internet.

Some insurers (often called **'direct companies'**) specialise in dealing directly with the public, and their policies are not available through brokers. These include some supermarkets, and you can pick up information in their stores, although you apply by post, phone or internet. Most of these companies offer cover only to people with standard circumstances and might not cover you if you have special needs – eg, you have motoring convictions.

There are many insurers to choose from. To help you narrow down your choice, check out the comparisons on personal finance websites (see Appendix 2 and p8) or the surveys published from time to time by *Which?* magazine (stocked by most local libraries). Alternatively, use an intermediary, such as a broker. An intermediary can shop around for you to find a suitable policy at a good price.

Pitfalls and what to watch out for

- Watch out for compulsory excesses – the first part of a claim you must pay yourself. For example, there will usually be a large excess if a young person is to drive the car.
- If you make a claim against your policy, you normally lose some no claims discount. This happens even if someone else was to blame for the accident or other loss – it is a no *claim* discount not a no *blame* discount. If another driver was to blame, avoid losing your discount by claiming against their policy not yours.
- If you plan to drive abroad, consider a policy that includes free green cards. Many insurers charge extra each time you make a trip.
- If you pay by monthly instalments, you will usually pay more than if you pay the whole year's premium as a lump sum. If you have an accident and the car is written off, you might still have to pay some or all of any outstanding instalments.
- Most intermediaries do not check out the whole market, but deal with a limited panel of insurers, so ask how many companies they select from. Consider checking out a few direct companies yourself as well.

Extended warranty insurance

What it covers

When you buy household equipment or electrical items (eg, fridges, washing machines and computers), they usually come with a one-year guarantee from the manufacturer. Extended warranty insurance, which is sold mainly by retailers but also some manufacturers, prolongs the guarantee to cover typically the first three or five years of the item's life.

Do you need it

Not usually. This insurance is expensive and reliability testing by organisations, such as *Which?*, suggest that the probability of a new household or electrical item breaking down within the first five years is small so you are unlikely to claim. Even if you do have a problem, the cost of getting the item repaired could easily be less than the cost of the insurance.

How it works

You buy the insurance, usually paying a single premium up front, either at the time you buy the item to be insured or shortly afterwards, generally when the retailer has sent you a follow-up letter.

What it costs

This varies depending on the type of equipment to be covered and the length of the warranty, but is nearly always expensive. For example, five-years' cover for a washing machine might be around £100 and for a laptop computer as much as £400.

Manufacturers' own extended warranties are often cheaper than those sold by shops. Some manufacturers even offer free extended warranties.

Choosing and buying

You seldom choose. Shop assistants often employ hard-sell tactics to persuade you to buy. If you do not buy at the time, you will often get follow-up letters, both soon after buying and when the manufacturer's standard one-year guarantee ends.

Shops, keen to sell their own version, may fail to point out where a manufacturer offers its own extended warranty.

Pitfalls and what to watch out for

- Do not fall for the hard-sell ploys. Most modern household appliances and electrical equipment are very reliable. The chance of claiming on these policies is slim and the premium is usually excessive. You should not need this type of insurance.
- Check that cover has not been automatically included in the deal. If so, say that you do not want cover and ask for the price without it.
- Some retailers have switched from trying to sell you extended warranties to pushing service contracts instead. For example, for a yearly charge, you might be offered an 'annual check-up' for your computer and free repairs if you take your machine back to the store. As with extended warranties, think carefully about whether the benefits on offer are really worth having.

House buildings insurance

What it covers

Buildings insurance covers the fabric of your home (eg, the walls, roof, windows and doors) and its fittings, such as a fitted kitchen and bathroom suite. This insurance pays out if your home is damaged or destroyed in a variety of ways – eg, because of fire, lightning, flood, subsidence, escaping water from pipes and tanks, theft or attempted theft. It does not cover ordinary maintenance.

Buildings insurance usually also comes with extras, such as public liability insurance, to cover your responsibility as the property owner for injury caused to other people or damage to their property – eg, if a tile slips from your roof and damages a neighbour's car.

Do you need it

- Yes, if you own your home. If you are buying with a mortgage, the lender will insist that you have this cover. Even if you own your home outright, you need this insurance – very few people could afford to replace their home out of their own resources if, for instance, it was destroyed by fire.

- If you own a leasehold property, you do not normally have to buy the insurance yourself. Buildings insurance is normally arranged by the management company or other organisation that holds the freehold. You pay your share of the cost through your annual service or maintenance charge.
- You do not need to buy this insurance if you rent your home. Your landlord is usually responsible for arranging and paying for buildings insurance.

How it works

You take out insurance for a set period – usually a year. There is no need to stay with the same insurer year after year. The market is competitive, so it is worth shopping around to find the best deal.

If you have a mortgage, your lender can usually arrange buildings insurance for you and the cost is added to your monthly mortgage payments, but the lender's policy will not necessarily be the best deal. You can usually shop around and arrange your own cover but the lender will normally charge you an administration fee (eg, £25) if you do this. Occasionally, taking out the lender's insurance is part of a mortgage package and, if you choose your own cover, you will have to choose a different mortgage deal (perhaps with a higher interest rate).

Many insurers offer house insurance which combines both buildings and contents insurance (see p228) for a single premium. A joint policy can be convenient if you need to make a claim after a single event has damaged both the structure of your home and your possessions, but could be more expensive than taking out separate best-buy policies.

What it costs

The main factors influencing your premium are the following.

- **The amount of cover you need.** This is based on the cost of rebuilding your home if it was totally destroyed, including the cost of clearing the site and architects' and builders' fees. The rebuilding cost can work out to be very different from the market price at which you could sell your home. Rebuilding costs vary depending on the size of the home and the materials it is made of. The Association of British Insurers and BCIS (the trading name of the Royal Institution of Chartered Surveyors) (www.rics.org; www.bcis.co.uk) publish guidance to help you work out the rebuilding cost of your home and you can use their online calculator at http://abi.bcis.co.uk. Most policies automatically revise the building cost of your home each year in line with inflation.
- **The area you live in.** You will pay more if you live in an area prone to, for example, flooding or subsidence. If insurers think the risks are too high, you might not be able to get cover at all.

Some policies have a no claims discount, which means that your premium at renewal is reduced if you have not made any claims in the past year.

Even for policies without a no claims discount, many insurers increase your premium at renewal (or impose high compulsory excesses) if you have made a claim. Therefore, you might be better off deciding not to make small claims and instead agreeing, for a reduction in premium, a voluntary excess up to the amount below which you would not claim.

Bedroom-rated buildings policies

Instead of basing cover on the rebuilding cost of your home, some insurers offer buildings insurance cover based on the number of bedrooms your home has. The idea is to save you the trouble of working out the precise rebuilding cost. But a bedroom-rated policy still has an overall maximum on the amount you can claim, so you still need at least a rough idea of your rebuilding cost. A bedroom-rated policy could be cheaper or more expensive than a sum-insured policy, so you should check out both types.

Choosing and buying

If you have a mortgage, do not feel you have to take out the insurance recommended by the lender. Shop around to see if you can get a better deal. Some insurers will pay on your behalf any resulting administration fee imposed by the lender.

You can buy directly from an insurer or go through an intermediary, such as a broker. In both cases, you may be able to buy face-to-face, by post, phone or internet.

Direct insurers specialise in dealing directly with the public and their policies are not available through brokers. Many of these companies are not prepared to offer cover to more risky homes (eg, in a flood plain) or to people who have a history of frequent claims.

To help you narrow down your choice, check the personal finance websites (see Appendix 2) or the surveys published from time to time by *Which?* magazine (stocked by most local libraries). Alternatively, use an intermediary, such as a broker. An intermediary can shop around for you to find a suitable policy at a good price.

Pitfalls and what to watch out for

- Buildings insurance arranged by mortgage lenders is not necessarily the best deal. But if you choose your own insurance, you will probably have to pay the lender an administration fee and you might have to choose a different mortgage package.
- If you claim often, your premium at renewal might increase steeply. The alternative is to avoid making small claims, in which case you could agree a voluntary excess in exchange for a lower premium.
- Watch out for compulsory excesses – eg, you might have to pay the first £1,000 or more of a subsidence claim.

- If you buy a home in an area known for flooding or subsidence, you may find it hard, or even impossible, to get insurance.
- Take care to insure your home for the correct amount. If you are under-insured, any claim can be scaled back in proportion to the amount you are under-insured. For example, the rebuilding cost of your home is £150,000 but you insure it for only £100,000. If you make a £150 claim for damage to a bathroom fitting, the insurer might agree to pay out only £100 because you are under-insured. If you are over-insured, you will pay more for your insurance than you need.

House contents insurance and possessions insurance

What it covers

House contents insurance pays out if the furnishings of your home (including carpets, curtains and free-standing kitchen appliances) or your personal possessions are damaged, destroyed, lost or stolen. Cover is usually 'new for old' so the payout covers the cost of replacing an item with a new replacement. The basic cover applies to items while they are in your home, but you can take out an 'all risks' extension so that items are also covered outside the home – this is useful for items you take on holiday or if you want to cover a musical instrument or laptop computer.

Your contents are covered in the event of, for example, fire, lightning, flooding, escape of water from pipes and tanks, and theft. Glass fitted into furniture (including ceramic cooker hobs) and electrical equipment such as a television are normally also covered against accidental damage and, for an extra premium, you can extend accidental damage cover to other items. The policy does not cover ordinary wear and tear.

Contents insurance usually comes with extras – eg, public liability to cover your responsibilities as occupier of the home (eg, if a visitor trips on a loose carpet and injures her/himself), and cover for loss of food in a freezer if there is a power cut. Not all possessions are necessarily automatically covered – eg, you might need to pay extra to add bicycles, and there is usually a limit on the amount that will be paid out for a single item. This could be fairly low (eg, £150) so you need either to choose a policy with a higher single item limit or tell the insurer about more valuable items (eg, antiques, pictures and valuable jewellery) and pay extra to cover them.

Possessions insurance is similar to house contents insurance but covers your possessions while, for example, you are living in shared accommodation, such as a student hall of residence, or renting a furnished property. Extras are often tailored to the sort of customer – eg, policies for students may include a refund of hall fees and repayment of student loan if you unexpectedly have to give up your course.

Do you need it

Contents or possessions insurance is optional. However, most people would find it hard to manage if they lost all their possessions in a fire, so in general it is a good idea to take out this type of insurance. However, if you have few possessions, would be comfortable not replacing any that were lost, and have sufficient savings or income to replace whatever you need, you might not need this type of cover.

If you live in rented accommodation, bear in mind that your landlord does not insure the contents of your home. It is up to you to arrange and pay for suitable insurance. If you are a council or social housing tenant, you might be able to use an insurance with rent scheme (see p230).

How it works

You take out insurance for a set period – usually a year. There is no need to stay with the same insurer year after year. The market is competitive, so it is worth shopping around to find the best deal.

If you have a mortgage, your lender might offer contents insurance as part of a mortgage package. The lender's policy will not necessarily be the best deal and you can arrange your own cover but you might then have to choose a different mortgage deal (perhaps with a higher interest rate).

Many insurers offer house insurance which combines both contents and buildings insurance (see p225) for a single premium. A joint policy can be convenient if you need to make a claim after a single event has damaged both the structure of your home and your possessions, but it could be more expensive than taking out separate best-buy policies.

What it costs

The premium you pay for contents insurance or possessions insurance depends mainly on the following.

- **Level of cover**. You need to add up the value of all your possessions using the price of new replacements. The higher the total, the more you pay for cover. Often there is a minimum level of cover – eg, £30,000. Many policies automatically increase your cover each year in line with inflation.
- **Where you live**. You will generally pay more if you live in a city or town where burglary tends to be more of a problem than if you live in a rural area. The premium will also tend to be higher if other risks are greater in your area – eg, if flooding is likely.
- **Your age**. You might pay less if you are older, particularly if you have reached retirement age, since retired people tend to spend more time at home, which deters burglars.
- **Security**. You might pay less if you fit good locks to your doors and windows, have a burglar alarm and/or join a neighbourhood watch scheme.

Some insurers operate a no claims discount scheme, so you pay less at renewal if you have not made any claims during the previous year. As with buildings insurance (see p225), many insurers, even without no claims discounts, tend to increase your premium if you make even just one or two claims. Bearing this in mind, a sensible course might be to avoid making small claims and instead, for a reduction in premium, agree a voluntary excess up to the amount below which you would not claim.

Bedroom-rated contents policies

Instead of basing cover directly on the value of the contents of your home, some insurers offer contents insurance cover based on the number of bedrooms your home has. The idea is to save you the trouble of adding up the precise value of all your possessions. But a bedroom-rated policy still has an overall maximum on the amount you can claim, so you still need at least a rough idea of the total value of your contents. A bedroom-rated policy could be cheaper or more expensive than a sum-insured policy, so you should check out both types.

Choosing and buying

You can buy directly from an insurer or through an intermediary, such as a broker. In both cases, you may be able to buy face-to-face, by phone, post or internet.

Direct companies, including some supermarkets, often offer competitive premiums but only by catering for people in standard circumstances and without a history of claims. If your needs are unusual or risky – eg, you live in a high crime area or you have made several claims in the last few years, these companies might not be willing to insure you.

Check the comparison tables on personal finance websites (see Appendix 2) or the regular house insurance surveys published by *Which?* (stocked in most public libraries). Alternatively, get a broker to shop around for you.

If you live in rented local authority or other social housing, your landlord might operate an insurance with rent scheme. Typically, your landlord negotiates a standard policy available to all tenants on the same terms (regardless of the location of their particular home). The minimum level of cover allowed is often lower than for other policies (eg, £10,000), which helps to keep the premium down and is suitable if your possessions are worth less than this. The main advantage of insurance with rent schemes is that you can pay the premium on a weekly basis along with your normal rent payment. Your landlord then passes the premium on to the insurer. This can be a useful way to help you budget for the cost of insurance.

The possessions of a student son or daughter living away from home can often be covered as an extension to a parent's house contents policy. This saves the student taking out her/his own possessions insurance. Check carefully that your policy gives adequate insurance – eg, cover for possessions (such as a computer or musical instrument) while outside the student's room and while possessions are in transit between the parental home and university.

Pitfalls and what to watch out for

- Watch out for compulsory excesses (the first part of a claim that you must pay yourself).
- Since many insurers will increase your premium at renewal if you make even just one or two claims, consider agreeing to a voluntary excess in exchange for a reduction in the premium.
- Watch out for the single item limit. For example, if your £400 camera is stolen, but the single item limit is £250, you will have to pay the £150 difference.
- Insurers often treat similar items as sets and apply the single item limit to the whole set. For example, if you have 50 DVDs that cost an average of £10 each and they are all stolen, your insurer might argue that they form a set and restrict your claim to the single item limit (eg, £250) rather than the £500 payout you had expected.
- Conversely, insurers will normally pay out only for the damaged part of a set, such as a three-piece suite or matched carpets.

Purchase protection insurance

What it covers

This insurance pays out if an item you have recently bought is lost, damaged or stolen within the month or two following purchase. It is usually cover given free of charge with certain credit cards and covers items you have bought using your card.

Do you need it

Usually, no. If you have house contents or possessions insurance (see p228), the item may be covered anyway. But if the cover is free, you might as well use it. If you have to pay, do not bother.

How it works

You get the cover automatically if you have a credit card which includes it as a perk.

What it costs

Usually free.

Choosing and buying

No effort on your part is required – cover is normally part of a package of perks with some credit cards. However, this is not a valuable perk so do not choose a credit card simply to get this insurance. See Chapter 5 for guidance on credit cards.

Pitfalls and what to watch out for

Check the small print to see precisely what is covered and for how long. If you have cover through your house contents or possessions insurance, you might be required to claim against that instead.

Service contract

What it covers

Although not strictly a type of insurance, service contracts fulfil a similar function. Depending on the type of contract you choose, it covers repairs in the event of an emergency or breakdown to household services and/or appliances, such as plumbing, drainage, central heating, gas cookers, and fires and/or your electrical system. Some contracts also include an annual service.

Do you need it

The alternative is to call and pay for a repair person as and when a problem arises. A service contract relieves you of some of the trouble involved and lets you budget with more certainty.

How it works

A service contract removes much of the uncertainty about cost because you pay a yearly fee for the contract and breakdowns are normally dealt with at no further cost when they occur. The service also usually contacts the repair person for you, saving you the trouble of searching for someone.

What it costs

What you pay varies from one company to another and depends on the number of services and appliances you want to be covered. Prices range from around £40 to £150 a year.

Choosing and buying

Your gas, electricity or water service provider may send you literature about its own service. Check occasional surveys in *Which?* magazine (stocked by most public libraries) for other companies.

Pitfalls and what to watch out for

- There may be a limit on the age of appliances that the service will cover.
- The definition of emergency may be narrower than your own. Check the wording carefully so that you know in advance when you will be able to use the service.
- When you need repairs done, labour and parts are normally free but only up to a limit. The limit is usually fairly high, but if the cost came to more you would probably have little choice but to pay.

- You may have to sign up for a year at a time, often with no refund, even if you move home part way through the year.

Travel insurance

What it covers

This collects together several different types of cover that are useful when you are travelling. It usually includes at least the following.

- **Cancellation**. Pays out if you have to cancel your holiday unexpectedly because of, for instance, illness or a death in the family. Choose a policy which covers the full cost of the trip.
- **Medical emergency**. Medical treatment abroad is not usually free. Travel insurance covers the charges and, if necessary, the cost of flying you home for treatment in the UK. To guard against a worst case scenario, choose a policy which offers at least £1 million of cover in Europe and £2 million elsewhere.
- **Public liability**. Pays out if you are held liable for injuring someone or damaging property. A claim for the loss of an injured person's earnings, for instance, could be huge, so you want cover of at least £2 million.
- **Baggage**. Pays out if the possessions you are travelling with are lost or stolen. These may already be covered by your house contents insurance if you have an all risks extension (see p230), in which case some insurers will let you cancel this section of cover for a reduction (eg, 10 per cent) in the premium.

Most policies include various extras, such as a cash sum if your passport is lost, a facility for getting emergency money to you if yours is lost or stolen, and payouts if flights are delayed by more than a given time. If you intend to take part in winter sports or dangerous pursuits (such as rock climbing), you need insurance specially designed to cover these.

Do you need it

Yes. The potentially expensive disasters when travelling are:

- needing prolonged treatment abroad;
- requiring to return to the UK for treatment;
- causing injury to someone else;
- damaging someone else's property.

Any of the above could cost you many thousands of pounds, so you would be unwise to travel abroad without insurance.

Many people do not think of taking out insurance if they are holidaying in the UK but, if you are staying in a hired cottage, say, it is a good idea to have some public liability insurance in case you damage the property or its furnishings. Some letting agents will insist that you take out insurance through them unless you can show that you have a suitable travel policy.

If you are travelling in Europe, you might be tempted to rely on a European Health Insurance Card (EHIC) (see below). You should take an EHIC with you, but it is not a substitute for proper travel insurance.

European Health Insurance Card

This is a plastic card you use to get state-provided emergency treatment in countries which are members of the European Economic Area (the member states of the European Union plus Iceland, Liechtenstein and Norway) and Switzerland. It replaces the earlier E111 forms, which are no longer valid. The EHIC does not necessarily cover all of the services that you would get in the UK through the NHS and it does not include the other sorts of cover that a travel insurance policy provides (such as transporting you home for treatment, public liability, cancelled holiday or lost baggage). However, under the terms of your travel insurance, any compulsory excess applying to medical claims is often waived if you use an EHIC, so you should take with one with you.

To get an EHIC, you should get the free leaflet T5 *Health Advice for Travellers* from a post office or travel agent and complete the enclosed form. Alternatively, apply by phone or online (see Appendix 2). EHICs are free. Note that an EHIC lasts for five years at a time and you should allow seven working days from the date of your application for your first card or a replacement.

How it works

You can take out insurance either to cover a particular trip or an annual multi-trip policy which will cover all the trips you make within a year.

You can take out a policy to cover just you, you and someone else, or a whole family group. With an annual policy, it is often a good idea to choose a policy which provides cover when individual members of the group are travelling alone – eg, to cover your children if they go on school trips.

In case you need to claim for cancellation, you should take out insurance either before or at the time you book your trip.

What it costs

The cost depends mainly on the following.

- **Where you will be travelling**. Usually different premiums are charged for the UK, Europe, the rest of the world excluding USA, and worldwide, with the cost increasing as you cover more countries.
- **The length of your trip**. You pay more the longer you will be away.
- **The type of policy**. An annual policy costs more than a single trip policy from the same provider, but the difference is often not large and, if you shop around, a yearly policy from one provider might not cost any more than single trip insurance from another.

- **Sports cover**. You pay extra to include winter sports or other dangerous pursuits. You can choose annual policies that include some winter sports cover for a limited number of days each year.
- **Where you buy**. Insurance is generally expensive if you buy the cover offered by a tour operator or travel agent as part of the holiday package. You will usually pay less if you shop around for your own cover.

Age may also be a factor. Some policies charge more for, or do not cover, people over age 65. However, some others specifically cater for the over-50s – but you should still shop around to check whether you can get a better deal from a non-specialist provider.

Choosing and buying

You can buy travel insurance directly from insurers, through either specialist travel insurance brokers or non-specialist intermediaries and through a variety of other agents, including tour operators and travel agents. You can buy face-to-face, or by post, phone or internet.

Direct companies tend to offer policies which may not be suitable if you have non-standard needs – eg, you are aged 65 or over, have health problems or plan to take part in extreme sports.

If you book a holiday through a travel agent or tour operator, it cannot force you to take out its own travel cover, but generally it insists that you have cover before it will sell you the holiday. This can put you in a situation where you feel pressurised to accept the agent's or operator's cover. To avoid this, arrange insurance before you book the holiday and take a copy of the policy details and schedule with you. To narrow down your choice of policies, use the comparative tables on the many personal finance websites (see Appendix 2) or which are published from time to time in *Which?* magazine (available in most public libraries). Alternatively, use a broker.

Pitfalls and what to watch out for

- Travel insurance from tour operators and travel agents is usually expensive. Instead buy from an insurer or broker – online policies are often cheapest.
- If you plan to go abroad two or more times in a year, an annual policy is likely to work out cheaper than single-trip policies.
- Travel insurance is not '**underwritten**', so insurers rely on exclusions to control the extent of claims. With an underwritten policy, the insurer considers all the relevant facts before deciding whether to offer cover and at what price. In particular, policies will not usually pay out for claims linked to a health problem you already had before buying the insurance.
- Many policies cover people only under age 65.
- Check out the policy conditions. For example, expensive sports equipment might be covered only if it is kept with you or locked up, which might be tricky

if you are out for the whole day. If you need to claim for theft, you usually must have reported the incident to the police and have obtained a crime number.

Identity fraud insurance

What it covers

This insurance mainly covers the expenses you may incur trying to protect your identity, recover money stolen from you and refute claims against you for debts taken out fraudulently in your name if you are the victim of identity fraud. See Chapter 10 for a description of identity fraud and how you can reduce the chance of it happening to you.

The insurance does not cover any money you lose as the result of such a fraud. So, typically, it covers the cost of contacting the police, credit reference agencies and your bank and lenders by phone, fax and post. It also covers legal costs if you have to defend yourself against claims brought against you or challenge incorrect information held about you, as a result of the fraud. It may also cover earnings you lose if you need to take unpaid time off work to sort the matter out. Usually there is a maximum limit on your claims – eg, £60,000 a year. If you are a victim of identity fraud, the insurer assigns you a caseworker to give advice and suggest an action plan for you to follow, and the insurer will register you with CIFAS (see p237). There may be other add-ons, such as regular or unlimited access to your file with one or more of the three main credit reference agencies, automatic alerts if there is any change to your credit file, and a helpline to give advice on keeping your identity safe.

Do you need it

According to CIFAS (see p237), there were 77,600 cases of identity fraud in the UK during 2008, so only a small proportion (0.15 per cent) of the adult population is affected each year, although identity fraud is a growing crime. CIFAS says it takes a typical victim between three and 48 hours of work to sort it out and clear her/his name. In extreme cases, it could take over 200 hours and cost up to £8,000. The consumer organisation, Which?, advises that most people do not need this insurance and that it is expensive for what it offers. You can protect yourself from identity fraud and sort it out if it does happen with little direct financial outlay. For example:

- see Chapter 10 for tips on protecting yourself from identity fraud;
- if you are a victim of identity fraud, in most cases you should not be legally liable for any debts run up in your name and may be able to recover money stolen from you. However, this could take time and it may be difficult to prove your case. However, this insurance would only provide advice and help with legal costs; it would not replace any money lost;
- you can check your own credit reference files on a regular basis at a cost of £2 a time;

- you can contact the police, your bank, lenders and so on for the cost of a phone call or email;
- you can arrange protective registration with CIFAS (see below).

However, you might find the legal expenses aspect of the insurance useful and you might also welcome some advice and guidance.

How it works

Usually you buy the insurance through a credit card provider or other financial services provider, but you can shop around and take out your own stand-alone insurance. You get an annual policy which you renew each year.

What it costs

Identify fraud insurance typically costs around £70 or £80 a year. Usually you pay by direct debit and the policy is renewed automatically unless you cancel it.

Choosing and buying

You can choose to buy this insurance, but more often your credit card provider or other financial services provider will suggest you take out cover. One credit card includes identity fraud cover as an automatic part of the package. You may get a cheaper deal by shopping around for yourself on the internet or approaching a broker.

Pitfalls and what to watch out for

- If the identity theft occurs while you are abroad or involves the fraudulent use of your identity abroad, the provider might restrict the level of help offered.
- If you take legal action, for example, against debt collectors trying to collect debts fraudulently run up in your name, you must contact the insurer for approval before you start any action, otherwise the insurer can refuse to cover the legal costs.
- If you take unpaid leave from work to sort out the matter, you will need to provide proof to the insurer that it was necessary for you to take that leave and proof of the earnings lost.
- To check against identity fraud, you need to check the files held about you by each of the three main credit reference agencies (see p134), but you may find that the insurance provides a service linked only to one of the agencies.

CIFAS

CIFAS is a fraud prevention service to which most UK banks, credit card companies, other lenders and many other financial services providers belong. They share information about known frauds and use this to try to prevent others. One of the services offered by CIFAS is 'protective registration'. This means that when anyone applies for credit using your name, the lender concerned (assuming it is a CIFAS member, and most are) is alerted that you may be at risk of identity fraud and will make extra security checks before agreeing to advance the credit. Protective registration costs £13.80 a year. See Appendix 2 for contact details.

3. Life insurance

There are two uses for life insurance: investment (see Chapter 4) and protection – ie, providing financial support for your survivors if you die. This section focuses on life insurance used for protection.

Term insurance (protection-only)

What it covers

Term insurance pays out if you die within a set period of time (the 'term'). If you survive the term, the insurance pays out nothing. Around three-quarters of the policies available will pay out early if you are diagnosed with a terminal illness and you are expected to survive less than 12 months (or sometimes six months).

Do you need it

If anyone (eg, your partner, your children or an elderly relative) is partly or completely financially dependent on you, you should consider having insurance to protect her/him if you were to die.

Your dependants might qualify for some support from the state (eg, bereavement benefits – see Chapter 9) and you might already have some life insurance through your employment. Often life cover is provided through an occupational pension scheme.

Work out roughly how much money your dependants might need if you were to die (use the calculator below to help you do this). If there is a shortfall, consider taking out life insurance. Term insurance is generally the cheapest way to do this, but see p241.

You do not need life insurance if there is no one who is dependent on you.

Life insurance calculator

Extra lump sum your survivors need because of your death: £

Funeral expenses – eg, £2,000

Fund to cover living costs while they adjust – eg, two months' money

Repayment of mortgage and any other loans

Other (including any inheritance tax – see Chapter 8)

Total =   Box A [ ]

Lump sums received because of your death:

Benefits – eg, bereavement payment (£2,000 in 2009/10) and/or funeral expenses grant from social fund

Payout from any existing life cover through work

Payout from any other existing life policies, including to pay off mortgage or other loans

Savings and investments that could be cashed in

Other

Total =   Box B

Lump sum needed: Box C

Box A – Box B = lump sum needed
(if less than zero, insert 0)

Extra income your survivors need because of your death: £

Loss of your take-home pay, pension or benefits

Loss of their income if they would have to give up work – eg, to care for children

Loss of income from savings and cashed investments

Other lost income

Cost of extra childcare

Cost of help with jobs you used to do – eg, home maintenance, gardening

Cost of replacing perks through your job – eg, company car

Other extra costs

Total =   Box D

Extra income/expenses saved or received because of your death: £

Benefits payable on death – eg, widowed parent's allowance (see Chapter 9)

Other benefits – eg, working tax credit (see Chapter 9)

Pensions from any occupational scheme or personal pension

Earnings if survivor would start/increase work

Other extra income

Mortgage payments and other loan payments saved if loans paid off

Life insurance premiums and pension contributions saved

Living expenses saved

Other expenses saved

Total =   Box E

Income needed: Box F

Box D – Box E =
(if less than zero, insert 0)

Multiply Box F by the factor that corresponds to the length of time your survivors will need the income:*

    5 years: 4.5
    10 years: 8.1
    15 years: 10.9
    20 years: 13.1
    25 years: 14.8

Total = income needed   **Box G**

Total amount of life cover you might need
Box C + Box G =

*Assumes you would invest lump sum insurance to provide a level income and that the investment would grow at 5 per cent after the deduction of charges.

Life cover for special purposes

In some situations, you might take out life insurance to pay for something specific in the event of your death.

Mortgage protection insurance. This is a type of term insurance which pays off your outstanding mortgage balance if you die. It is useful if your survivors would carry on living in the home and would find it hard to meet the mortgage payments without you.

Funeral expenses insurance. A type of whole-life policy which pays out a sum intended to be enough to pay for your funeral. Usually the payout is fairly small relative to the premiums you pay, making this insurance poor value, and there is no guarantee that the payout will in fact be sufficient to meet the intended costs.

Insurance to pay inheritance tax bills. See Chapter 8 for how life insurance can be used in this way.

How it works

You decide how much cover you need (see above) and the term you want. For example, if you have just had a baby, you might want cover for the next 18 or 21 years until you expect your child to be independent. You also need to decide on the type of term insurance you want.

- **Level term insurance.** The insurance pays out a cash lump sum. If your survivors will need an income for many years, they will need to invest the lump sum in a suitable way – see Chapter 3 for some ideas. Your survivors might want to get some financial advice (see Chapter 2).
- **Family income benefit.** If you die, this version pays out a series of lump sums at regular intervals over the remaining term of the policy. The payments, in effect, provide your survivors with a tax-free income. To protect the buying power of the income from inflation, choose a policy where the amount paid

out is increased each year, both up to the time any claim is made and following a claim. This type of policy is cheaper than a level lump-sum policy because the longer you survive, the less the policy has to pay out. It can also be a good choice if you think your survivors would not be comfortable making choices about investing a lump sum.

- **Reducing term insurance**. Pays out a lump sum which is lower the later in the term a claim is made. Mainly used for mortgage protection policies (see p240) to cover a repayment mortgage (see Chapter 5) or to cover some types of inheritance tax bill (see Chapter 8).

- **Increasing term insurance**. Pays out a lump sum which is increased each year of the term – eg, in line with inflation or by a fixed percentage. The premium also increases but only in line with the extra cover (see below).

- **Increasable term insurance**. This gives you the option to increase the amount of cover either once a year or when specified events take place, such as the birth of a child. If you take up the option, the premium also increases but only in line with the extra cover (see below).

- **Renewable term insurance**. You have the option to take out a further policy when the original term ends. The new policy is based on your health at the time you took out the original policy even if it has deteriorated since then. This can be a useful option, firstly if you want the flexibility to cope with changing circumstances – eg, an unexpected late addition to the family, or if, to keep down costs, you originally choose a fairly short term with a view to extending the cover later when you expect to be better off.

- **Convertible term insurance**. Gives you the option to switch to an investment-type insurance policy based on your health at the time you took out the original policy. This is generally not a useful option since other types of investment may be more suitable – see Chapter 4.

Life insurance can be taken out for one person (**single life policy**) or a couple (**joint life policy**). A joint life policy may be set up to pay out on the first death or when both of you have died. To protect survivors, you normally need a policy that pays out on first death. A joint-life policy can be useful, for example, for paying off a joint mortgage, but for general protection purposes, couples may be better off each taking out a separate single life policy. This is because you may each need different amounts of insurance cover (whereas a joint life policy covers you both for the same sum), and you might split up but still need the insurance to continue – eg, to protect children.

What it costs

The premium is set at the time you first take out the insurance, but increases in line with cover if the policy allows for the level of cover to change. Many insurers also reserve the right to increase premiums if the overall level of claims due to HIV/AIDS increases significantly. The premium you pay depends on the following.

- **The amount of cover you choose**. The higher the cover, the more you must pay.
- **The term**. The longer the term, the more you pay.
- **Your age**. The older you are when you take out the policy, the higher the premium because the risk of a claim increases with age.
- **Your sex**. Women usually pay less than men of the same age, because women tend on average to live longer and so a claim is less likely.
- **Whether you smoke**. Smokers pay more because they are more likely to die than a non-smoker of the same age and sex.
- **Your health**. If poor health increases the risk of a claim, you pay more. Insurers can also take account of the health of your immediate family, if there are specific inheritable conditions, such as early onset breast cancer.

Choosing and buying

The market is competitive, so you should shop around for the lowest premium. Personal finance websites and specialist groups like Moneyfacts publish comparative tables. Personal finance magazines publish surveys from time to time.

You can approach insurers directly or use an intermediary, such as a broker, who can then shop around for you (but will not necessarily look at the whole market – see Chapter 2). There are also many agents who sell insurance, including banks and building societies, but they often sell the policies of a single company.

You can buy face to face (eg, at the high street office of a broker), or by post, phone or internet.

If you are taking out a fairly modest level of cover (eg, up to £100,000), in setting the premium the insurer might rely mainly on the answers you give in the proposal form, although it might also check your medical records. If you are applying for a large sum, the insurer may require you to have a medical examination.

Pitfalls and what to watch out for

- If you need to protect your survivors, do not be persuaded to take out investment-type life insurance – it is an expensive way to buy the cover you need. Term insurance is much cheaper.
- In general, make sure your policy is written **'in trust'**. This means the proceeds on your death would be paid directly to your survivors. If the policy is not in trust, the proceeds go into your estate where they could be subject to inheritance tax (see Chapter 8) and delays. The insurer can easily arrange for the policy to be written in trust, which normally does not cost extra. However, if your policy is to be 'assigned' to a mortgage lender (or anyone else), you cannot also put it in trust. (Assignment is a legal arrangement that transfers the right to the payout to the lender, though any excess over the amount needed to repay your mortgage would be returned to your estate.)

- For general protection needs, couples should consider each taking out separate single life policies rather than a joint life policy. With separate policies, they can each have a different amount of cover; this arrangement is more flexible should the couple split up.
- Term insurance may include critical illness cover (see p246) as an extra. Normally, the policy pays out on either the diagnosis of a critical illness or death, but not both. So be aware that if you make a critical illness claim and spend the money, for example, on your medical care, your dependants will not get any further money if you die.

4. **Health-related insurance**

Dental insurance

What it covers

The cost of private dental treatment.

Do you need it

Not if you can get treatment on the NHS, but in many parts of the country it is impossible to register with an NHS dentist, in which case, you have no choice but to pay for private treatment.

If you are a private patient, you could just pay for treatment as and when you need it. Alternatively you can take out insurance. If your teeth are in good health and you normally just have a check up and clean with no other work, pay as you go will probably work out cheaper, but you should set aside some money in an emergency fund just in case you need expensive treatment.

How it works

You pay a regular premium. There is a choice of cover – eg, emergency treatment only, emergencies and accidents, or comprehensive cover which also includes routine treatment. You might be covered for the full cost of treatment or only up to a maximum amount (in which case, you have to pay any extra).

What it costs

Cost depends on the level of cover you choose and sometimes varies with age.

Choosing and buying

Your dentist should be able to arrange cover for you or give you contact details for insurers. Some employers offer dental insurance as a perk of your job.

Pitfalls and what to watch out for

Dental problems you already have when you take out the insurance are not normally covered, so you might need to pay for a course of treatment before you become eligible for cover.

Capitation schemes. The dentist assesses your dental health and then sets an amount that you must pay each month. The payments cover you for most of the dental treatment you subsequently receive without further charge, but you may have to pay extra for very expensive treatment.

Credit schemes. You are issued with a credit card used exclusively to pay for your dental treatment. As with an ordinary credit card, you make monthly repayments and pay interest on any outstanding balance. Usually the card lets you spread the cost of treatment over a maximum of six months.

Accident, sickness and unemployment insurance

What it covers

This pays out a tax-free income for a limited time (eg, one or two years) if you are unable to work because of illness or you become unemployed. Commonly it is used to cover specific payments – eg, your monthly mortgage interest (in which case, the insurance is often called 'mortgage payment protection insurance') or other loan repayments. It can also provide income to use in any way you choose. The accident element of the cover pays out a small lump sum if, for example, you lose an eye, limb or become total disabled.

Do you need it

If your income drops because you cannot work, you might qualify for means-tested benefits (see Chapter 9). These can help with your housing costs, although mortgage interest payments are not covered during the first 13 weeks of your claim. You could lose your home if you do not keep up your mortgage payments, so it can be a good idea to take out mortgage payment protection insurance (PPI) to cover this gap. Check that the policy gives you the cover you need – see below.

You probably do not need insurance to cover most other loans, provided they are not secured on your home – see Chapter 5 for more details.

If you want insurance more generally to replace your earnings if you cannot work because of illness, consider income protection insurance (see p247), which provides more comprehensive cover.

How it works

You pay regular premiums. If the insurance is taken out with a mortgage or other loan, the cost of cover is usually added to your monthly loan payments.

There is often a delay (eg, one or two months) at the start of the policy before you can make a claim. Under the sickness section, you may need to be ill for a minimum period (eg, a month) before you can claim – though the payout might then be backdated to the start of the illness.

It is important to check the exclusions. For example, to qualify for unemployment cover, you may need to have been employed for a minimum length of time, you may need to work at least a minimum number of hours a week, and you might not be covered at all if you work on casual contracts or you are self-employed. Under the sickness section, there is typically no cover for pre-existing conditions (health problems you already had before buying the insurance).

What it costs

You pay more, the higher the payout required. Cost varies from one company to another so it is worth shopping around.

Choosing and buying

If you take out a mortgage or other loan, the lender may offer you cover. Generally, you do not have to accept the policy on offer. Some insurers and intermediaries (including brokers and some banks and building societies) offer stand-alone policies. From October 2010, it is proposed that lenders will no longer be able to sell you PPI at the time you take out a loan, but the proposal has been legally challenged and it is unclear whether it will go ahead (see p127). The Financial Services Authority's Moneymadeclear Compare Products tables include PPI. You may also find occasional surveys in personal finance magazines, such as *Which?* (available in most public libraries). Organisations, such as Moneyfacts publish surveys of personal loans and often quote repayments both with and without PPI.

Pitfalls and what to watch out for

- The unemployment section might not cover you if you have only recently started work, you work part time or casually, or you are self-employed.
- Claims arising from health problems you already had when you took out the insurance will normally be refused. Make sure you tell the person selling you the insurance if you have a pre-existing condition.
- Lenders sometimes automatically include the cost of insurance in their loan quotes (so you might not realise you are paying for cover), but will no longer be able to do this from April 2010 onwards.
- Lenders frequently offer no explanation of cover and may be reluctant to give you a policy document before you buy. It is essential, however, that you check the cover is suitable for you.
- If you paid a single premium for insurance to cover a loan, make sure you claim a refund of part of the premium if you pay off the loan earlier than expected. The sale of new single premium policies has now been banned.
- If you feel you have been unfairly sold insurance that you do not need or does not meet your needs, complain to the firm which sold you the policy and, if you are not satisfied with the response, take your case to the Financial Ombudsman Service (see Chapter 10).

Critical illness insurance

What it covers

Pays out a large lump sum if you have, or are diagnosed with, a life-threatening condition. You do not pay tax on the payout. Most policies cover the following conditions, which account for the majority of claims:

- heart attack;
- stroke;
- cancer;
- kidney failure;
- multiple sclerosis;
- coronary artery bypass surgery;
- major organ transplant.

Other conditions may also be covered, as well as permanent total disability.

You can use the lump sum however you choose – eg, to cover living expenses, pay for treatment or adaptations at home and take a holiday.

Do you need it

Probably not. Critical illness insurance does not properly target a need because it pays out for only a limited range of health problems. If your concern is lack of income if you could not work, income protection insurance (see p247) would be better because it can pay out for conditions such as back pain and stress as well as critical conditions. If you want cash to pay for private treatment, private medical insurance (see p254) might be better because it would pay for hip replacements and cataracts as well as a heart bypass.

How it works

You pay monthly premiums and, if you have a valid claim, receive a lump sum.

You can take out a policy jointly with someone else, in which case it pays out on the first claim and then cover stops. So a joint policy is useful mainly for paying off your mortgage or some other large, joint commitment.

Some policies are combined with life insurance. Generally, this means the policy pays out on the earlier of a critical illness or death. This means there is no life cover left if you have already claimed for critical illness, so you need some other source of life cover if your survivors need protection (see p238).

What it costs

The premium at the time you take out the policy depends mainly on the following factors.

- **Level of cover.** You pay more the greater the lump sum that would be paid out – £100,000 is a fairly typical level to choose.
- **Your age.** Cost increases sharply with age because the risk of having a critical illness also increases.

- **Your sex**. Women tend to pay less than men of the same age because they are less prone to critical conditions.
- **Whether you smoke**. Smokers pay up to twice as much as non-smokers because of the increased risk, in particular of heart problems, stroke and cancer.
- **Your health**. If your health is poor, or critical illnesses tend to run in your family, you will be charged more or refused cover altogether.
- **Whether the premium is guaranteed or reviewable**. With some policies, the premium is fixed for the full term. These tend to be more expensive at the outset than reviewable policies, where the premium can be increased to reflect changes in the company's overall claims experience.

Choosing and buying

You can buy either directly from an insurer or through an intermediary, such as a broker or financial adviser (see Chapter 2). Personal finance magazines, such as *Money Management* (from larger newsagents) and *Which?* (available in most public libraries) publish surveys from time to time which may help you to narrow down the choice of companies.

Pitfalls and what to watch out for

- The policy pays out only for a limited range of health problems, not for any illness or disability.
- Newer policies may include a 'future-proofing clause'. This means the policy will not have to pay out for health problems that become significantly less serious in future because of medical advances.
- Pre-existing conditions are not covered, so make sure you tell the insurer about any health problems you already have. This applies even if the insurer says it will also be checking your medical records with your GP.
- Do not be overly impressed by long lists of conditions covered. Often a shorter list, more broadly phrased, covers the same health problems.
- If total permanent disability is included, check the definition. The most comprehensive policies define it as being unable to do your normal job.
- Watch out for exclusions. For example, some policies do not cover Alzheimer's or Parkinson's diseases if diagnosed after age 60, which is when they are most common.
- Be wary of policies that pay out only a proportion of the total according to the severity of the condition you have. The payout may be much lower than you expect unless you are terminally ill.

Income protection insurance

What it covers

This pays out a monthly income to replace part of your earnings if you are unable to work because of illness or disability. The income is tax-free if you took out the policy yourself. If it comes from a group income protection scheme arranged by your employer, the income is taxable. You can also take out cover for a non-working 'houseperson' to cover the extra costs the household would incur if that person could no longer run the home, take care of children and so on. Houseperson cover is usually for a fixed sum (eg, £10,000 a year), and pays out if the person cannot perform specified physical or mental activities.

Do you need it

If you are off work sick, you may qualify for employment and support allowance statutory sick pay and/or various disability benefits (see Chapter 9), but state help is fairly low and may provide less income than you need. Your employer may run a more generous sick pay scheme and might offer an early pension if you have to retire on health grounds – check whether you could manage on these.

If help from the state and your employer (if you have one) would leave you short, you might consider taking out income protection insurance to plug the gap. If you are self-employed, you have no employer to help, so income protection insurance is likely to be even more important.

How it works

You can choose the level of income to be paid out but only up to a limit, which is usually 50 to 65 per cent of your before-tax pay. The limit applies to the payout from all your income protection policies if you have more than one, and there is usually an adjustment to the payout to take account of benefits you can claim. The aim is to make sure that, in terms of after-tax income, a claim does not make you better off than you were when working.

You can choose a policy which pays out a level income or, alternatively, one where the income is increased in line with inflation to maintain its buying power.

The income is usually paid out until you recover or reach retirement age, whichever comes first. However, some policies have a limited term and pay out for, say, a maximum of five years.

What it costs

The monthly premiums can be set in one of three ways. With guaranteed premium policies – which are now rare – you pay the same amount each month for the whole term of the policy (except for increases in line with any built-in increases in cover). Renewable policies have a limited term (eg, five years) during which the premium is set. At the end of the term, you can take out a further policy with a new premium based on your age at renewal, but generally on your health at the time you took out the original policy. Finally, there are policies with reviewable premiums, where the cost is set for an initial period (eg, five years) and then reassessed at regular intervals.

Insurers take into account many factors when setting the premium you must pay, including the following.

- **The level of cover**. You pay more the higher the income you want the policy to pay out.
- **The type of policy**. A policy where the income to be paid out increases each year will cost more than a policy paying a level income.
- **The waiting period**. There is a delay between making a claim and the payout starting. This can be as little as four weeks and as long as two years. By choosing a longer waiting period, you reduce your premiums.
- **The definition of being unable to work**. The most expensive policies pay out if you are unable to do your normal job. Cheaper policies pay out only if you are unable to do any job for which you are suited by your training and experience. The cheapest pay out only if you are unable to do any job at all. A few insurers restrict people in less skilled work to claiming only on the basis of being unable to do any job.
- **Your age**. You will pay more the older you are when you take out the policy because the likelihood of developing health problems increases with age. Cost can become prohibitive once you hit your 40s and 50s.
- **Your sex**. Women tend to make more claims than men and for longer, so they have to pay more than men of the same age.
- **Whether you smoke**. This increases the risk of health problems, so smokers generally have to pay more.
- **The state of your health**. If you already have health problems, you might be refused cover completely, be offered a policy which excludes claims linked to the existing problem and/or charged more.
- **Your work**. The more risk of your job causing health problems, the higher the premium – eg, divers will pay a lot more than bank clerks.
- **Your hobbies**. If you participate in dangerous sports, you might be refused cover, have policy restrictions and/or have to pay extra.

Choosing and buying

You can buy either directly from an insurer or through an intermediary, such as an independent financial adviser. Income protection policies are fairly complicated, so it is a good idea to use an adviser (see Chapter 2) to help you decide how much cover you need and where to buy. Personal finance magazines, such as *Money Management* (from larger newsagents) and *Which?* (available in most public libraries) publish occasional surveys which can help you narrow down your choice of policy and company.

You will have to complete a detailed application form and may need to undergo a medical examination.

Pitfalls and what to watch out for

- This type of insurance is expensive. If you need cover but cannot afford it, try to build up some savings (see Chapter 4) in an emergency fund to support you for a while in the event of being too ill to work.

- Do not choose a level of cover which is too high. If you have to claim, the payout will be restricted to a maximum percentage of your before-tax income. Paying for extra cover is a waste of money.
- Consider policies which include a **'premium waiver'** so that you do not have to carry on paying the monthly premiums while making a claim.
- Consider policies with built-in increases to prevent the buying power of the payout being reduced by inflation.
- Do not be persuaded by an adviser to take out critical illness insurance instead. Although critical illness cover is much easier to understand, and cheaper, if your priority is to replace your income if unable to work, you need the wider cover that income protection insurance offers.

Long-term care insurance

What it covers

This insurance pays out a tax-free income if you are no longer able to care for yourself and is typically aimed at people worried about failing health as they get older. The income can be used to pay care home fees or for care in your own home. This type of insurance is fairly rare in the UK. People wanting to make their own financial arrangements for long-term care more commonly use immediate long-term care plans.

Immediate long-term care plans

Immediate long-term care plans are an alternative to long-term care insurance and are taken out when you already need care. In exchange for a lump sum (which you might raise by taking out a mortgage on your home) you get an income for the rest of your life to help pay for care. The income is usually provided by an **'impaired life annuity'**. This is an annuity (see Chapter 6) which provides a higher than normal income because you are not expected to live as long as average for someone of your age. The income offered can vary greatly from one provider to another so it is important to shop around for a good deal. Usually, the income from such annuities is partially taxable but, when paid as part of a long-term care plan, it is tax-free provided the income is paid directly to the care provider.

Do you need it

This insurance, or an immediate long-term care plan, is not essential. If you have only limited income and other assets, the state will pay the cost of care should you need it and you may qualify for attendance allowance (see Chapter 9). However, insurance or a care plan can be useful in three ways.

- **Increasing choice.** If the state is paying for your care, it may be unwilling to fund either care in a home of your choice if it is regarded as too expensive, or the level of care in your own home that you would prefer. If you can pay for your own care you have a choice.

- **Protecting your assets to pass on to your heirs.** The state will pick up the full cost of care only if your income is low and your capital (savings and other assets) come to no more than a set amount (£14,000 in 2009/10 if you live in England or Northern Ireland, £13,750 if you live in Scotland and £20,750 if you live in Wales – see Chapter 9 for more details). If you have more, you will be expected to use your capital to pay for care until it reaches the set amount. Insurance may help to prevent you having to reduce your capital in this way, although you should set this against the fairly high cost of the insurance.
- **Protecting your dependants.** If you share your home with your partner or certain other dependants, your home will not be included in the assessment of your capital, so your partner or dependant will be able to carry on living there. Any amount you are required to pay towards care out of your income is also decided without taking her/his income into account, and income you jointly rely on may be split between you (see Chapter 9). However, this could still leave your partner or other dependant with too little money to meet all the household expenses. Insurance can help leave the income s/he needs intact.

How it works

You pay either regular monthly premiums or a single lump-sum premium. The insurance pays out if you are no longer able to perform, for example, two or three specified **'activities of daily living'**. The definition of this used by different insurers varies, but typically includes:

- washing/bathing;
- dressing;
- feeding;
- continence/toileting;
- mobility (moving from one room to another);
- transfers – eg, from bed to a chair.

The payout is in the form of a regular income, which can be paid either to you or directly to a care provider.

What it costs

The premium you pay depends on the following.

- **The level of cover.** Because these policies are expensive, you do not usually try to cover the full cost of care (which could easily come to over £1,500 a month if you need to move to a nursing home). Instead, you might choose cover of, say, £1,000 a month and plan to pay the rest out of your income.
- **Your age.** The older you are at the time you start the plan, the more you pay. With many plans, premiums are fixed for the first five or ten years, but may then increase.
- **Your sex.** Women pay more than men of the same age because statistics show they are more likely to need care.

- **The number of activities of daily living you must fail**. The fewer the activities you must fail in order to have a valid claim, the higher the premium you pay.
- **The waiting period**. There is normally a delay between making a claim and the income starting. Some plans let you choose how long the delay will be. The longer the waiting period, the less you pay.
- **How long the income will be paid out**. Usually, the income continues for as long as you need it (usually until you die). But some plans let you choose to limit the payout to a maximum of, for example, three, five or ten years. In exchange, you pay a lower premium.
- **Whether the income increases each year**. The cost of care tends to rise faster than inflation, so a level income will buy less and less each year. You can pay extra for an income which increases.

This type of insurance is expensive. Cost varies greatly from one insurer to another, but could range from around £15,000 to £50,000 for a 65-year-old man buying £1,000 a month of cover.

Choosing and buying

Long-term care policies and immediate care plans are complicated and the detail varies from one insurer to another. Consider getting help from a financial adviser (see Chapter 2). Personal finance magazines, such as *Money Management* (available from larger newsagents), publish occasional surveys.

Pitfalls and what to watch out for

- Do not be scared into thinking you must have either insurance or a care plan. If you cannot afford care yourself, the state must normally pay.
- Be wary of choosing a policy that limits the time over which the income will be paid out. Although cheaper, these policies are a gamble. If you survive beyond the term of the policy and still need care, you could end up in the same situation you faced before taking out insurance.

Health cash plan

What it covers

This is not insurance, but fulfils a similar role. You pay a set amount each week or month and in return can claim a cash sum if you have to go into hospital (whether NHS or privately), visit a consultant, have a dental check-up or treatment, need chiropody, have a baby or various other health-related events. Usually, you get a set amount (eg, £50) for each night of your hospital stay and a refund of part or all of your bill up to a set cash maximum if you go to, for instance, a consultant, the dentist or optician. It is up to you how you use the money.

The hospital benefit paid out is not enough to pay for private hospital treatment, so a health cash plan is not a substitute for private medical insurance.

It could be useful, however, to cover, for example, travelling costs or to help pay for childcare. Similarly, the payouts are unlikely to be sufficient to replace your earnings if your health problem keeps you off work, so a health cash plan is not a substitute for income protection insurance. But health cash plans can help you to spread the cost of general health-related expenses in the sense that, by paying a regular sum, you may qualify for some cash help when a big bill comes in.

Do you need it

Not really. If you find it hard to manage health bills, you could just pay regularly into a savings account so that you build up a cash sum to help with, for example, dental bills or if you had to go to hospital. If you find it hard to budget and save, however, the discipline of paying into a health cash plan might be useful.

How it works

Normally, these are indefinite plans that provide cover for as long as you keep up the premiums. Typically, there is a choice of levels of cover. The higher the level of cover the bigger the cash payouts, but the more you pay each week or month. You choose whether to cover just yourself or your whole family.

When you need health treatment, you pay your practitioner as normal and then send your receipt to the cash plan provider for a partial or full refund. In the case of hospital treatment, you claim a set amount for each night as an inpatient or each day as a day patient.

The range of possible payouts often looks impressive, but whether a plan is good value depends on both the likelihood of your making a claim and the restrictions in the small print that limit the number and amount of claims.

What it costs

Typically, the most basic level of cover starts at around £10 a month (£120 a year) for a single person up to around £33 a month (£400 a year) for the highest level of payouts. Usually there is a small discount for a second adult, and children might be included either free or for an additional charge. Some plans charge more for older people.

Choosing and buying

You can buy plans directly from providers, usually by phone, post or internet. Alternatively, you can take out a plan through an independent financial adviser, broker or other intermediary. Personal finance magazines and websites carry occasional articles about health cash plans, but there are no regular surveys or websites comparing them, so you will need to shop around yourself or enlist the help of an independent financial adviser or broker.

Pitfalls and what to watch out for

- Read the small print very carefully because there are usually a lot of exclusions and conditions – eg:

- there may be a delay of six months after taking out the plan before you can claim payouts – eg, for dental treatment or hearing aids;
- some plans have a 12-month delay before paying out for pregnancy;
- there is usually a maximum payout under each section;
- under some sections, only a proportion of bills might be refunded;
- you might be limited to just one claim under each section within a specified period.

- Check for age limits. Cover might stop at age 65 or 70. With some plans, you can get cover in older age but only if you started the plan before age 65 or 70.
- Think about how likely you are to claim and the amount you would be eligible to claim. Weigh this up against the premium you will have to pay. Bear in mind, for example, that in 2007 only 8 per cent of people aged 45 to 64 had been a hospital inpatient during the past 12 months and the average length of stay was eight nights.[6]

Private medical insurance

This covers the cost of private hospital treatment if you have an 'acute' illness (one which can be cured or substantially alleviated). It does not cover chronic conditions. Private health treatment is an alternative to using the NHS and might mean being treated more quickly, at a time convenient to you and in more comfortable surroundings. Private medical insurance tends to be expensive, especially as you get older, though you can reduce the cost by opting for policies with lower levels of cover. Some employers offer insurance as a perk of your job.

5. **Your rights and responsibilities**

Duty to disclose material facts

When you take out or renew insurance, you are under a duty to tell the insurer all '**material facts**'. A material fact is any information that could influence the insurer's decision about the amount it will charge you, any restrictions it might impose or whether to offer you insurance at all. But the insurer must make clear what sort of information it requires, usually by prompting you with suitable questions on the proposal form.

Similarly, if any material facts change during the course of the insurance, you must tell the insurer – eg, if you get a motoring offence or you modify your car, you should let your insurer know.

If you knowingly withhold any material facts, you are guilty of fraud and the insurer can declare the policy void, refuse any claims and recover any money already paid out. If you unwittingly fail to tell the insurer about a material fact, the insurer might refuse to pay out if a claim is related to that fact.

Terms and conditions

Make sure you read the policy document for any insurance you take out. It may contain conditions with which you must comply in order for a claim to be valid – eg, fitting locks to downstairs windows, not leaving your car unattended with the keys in the ignition and keeping your home in good repair. It may also contain important exclusions, such as no cover for pre-existing health problems, or no unemployment cover for people working fewer than 16 hours a week.

Ideally, you should read the policy before taking out the insurance so that you can check the cover is suitable. Unfortunately, the person selling you insurance does not always make it easy and you may have to wait until a policy is sent to you shortly after signing up for the cover. In that case, read the policy document straight away and, if it is not suitable, cancel the cover by making use of your statutory cancellation period (see below).

Cancellation period

With most insurance, you have at least 14 days after taking out the cover during which you can change your mind and cancel the policy with a full refund. You do not have to give any reason for cancelling.

7. **Regulation and complaints**

The Financial Services Authority (FSA) (see Chapter 10) regulates insurance companies and advisers selling insurance.

Its rules set out how salespeople and advisers must conduct business with their customers. At the start of contact, they must explain the type of service they can offer – with advice or without. Unless you are buying a very simple product, such as car or house insurance, it is best to opt for an advice service. In that case, you have better protection if the product you have bought turns out to be unsuitable later (see Chapter 2). Advisers are required to find out your needs, recommend only suitable products and consider the relevance of any policy conditions and exclusions to your circumstances and needs. You may be given a Key Facts document summarising the important policy features and conditions.

If you have a complaint about insurance, first contact the firm concerned. If you are unhappy with the firm's response, you can take your complaint to the Financial Ombudsman Service.

If an insurance firm goes out of business owing you money, you might be able to get redress from the Financial Services Compensation Scheme (see Chapter 10).

Insurance scams

Be on your alert for these common scams and do not get caught out.

Hard sell tactics. Do not be bullied into taking out cover that you do not really want. It is easy for a salesperson to worry you with scare stories of what can go wrong and how much it might cost you. Keep a clear perspective and consider what other options you have, such as help from your employer or building up an emergency fund.

Funeral expenses plans. Be especially wary of taking out life insurance to cover funeral expenses. These plans are often very poor value. You can easily find yourself in a situation where you have paid more in premiums than a funeral would cost but you lose the right to any payout if you stop paying even more in premiums.

Notes

1 Association of British Insurers, 'Crushing Blow for Illegal Motorists', Press Release, 2007
2 Home Office, *Crimes in England and Wales 2008/09*, Office for National Statistics, 2009
3 Association of British Insurers, 'Uncovered and Exposed in the Recession: one in four people cancel their home insurance', Press Release, 2009
4 Association of British Insurers, 'Age Restriction Would Lead to Higher Insurance Costs and Less Choice', Press Release, 2009
5 CIFAS, *2008 Fraud Trends*, www.cifas.org.uk, accessed 27 July 2009

4. Health-related insurance
6 Office for National Statistics, *General Household Survey 2007*, www.statistics.gov.uk, accessed 27 September 2009

Chapter 8

•••

Tax and national insurance

This chapter covers:
1. Introduction (below)
2. The main personal taxes (p260)
3. Tax on some different types of income (p271)
4. How tax is collected (p278)
5. Getting advice about tax (p280)
6. Fraud (p281)

•••

Basic facts

– In 2009, the total tax paid by the average British person was equivalent to the whole of her/his earnings for the first 134 days of the year.[1]
– It is estimated that 29.3 million people in the UK will pay income tax in 2009/10.[2]
– Inheritance tax is expected to be charged on one out of every 50 estates.[3]
– Around 8.6 million tax returns were issued in 2008/09; 5.8 million taxpayers completed their return online.[4]

•••

1. Introduction

Governments raise money through taxes in order to pay for things which society wants – eg, roads, hospitals, schools, financial support for vulnerable people such as older or sick people, emergency services, libraries and rubbish collections.

In 2009/10, UK central and local governments expect to raise £465 billion in taxes. The charts on p258 show where these taxes come from and broadly how they will be spent. Most of the Government's tax revenue comes from income tax (£141 billion), national insurance (£98 billion) and value added tax (£64 billion). The biggest area of spending is social security benefits, including state pensions (£165 billion), followed by the NHS (£106 billion) and children/education/skills (£76 billion). Acts of Parliament give the UK Government and local authorities the right to collect taxes and to impose penalties on people who refuse to pay them.

Where UK tax revenue comes from[5]

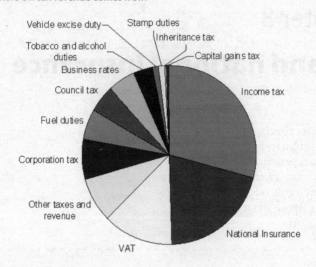

Source: HM Treasury, *Budget Report,* 2009. Projections for 2009/10

Government spending

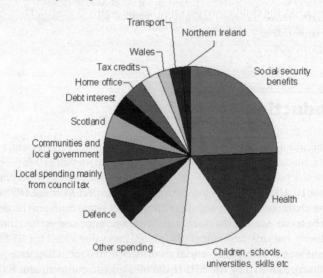

Source: HM Treasury, *Budget Report,* 2009. Projections for 2009/10

Situations affecting tax and national insurance

Relationships

Although you are taxed separately, there are some concessions in the tax system for married couples and civil partners. For example, gifts between husband and wife or civil partners are normally tax-free. This opens the opportunity to spread your joint assets tax efficiently between you.

You should make or review your will (particularly if you are unmarried) to ensure that the correct people would inherit in the event of your death and that any inheritance tax bill is minimised.

Separation and divorce have very little direct impact on your tax position. However, if, following the breakdown, you start to work or increase your hours, you might start paying tax for the first time. If you are a married woman who has been paying national insurance (NI) at the reduced rate (see p265), on divorce you cease to be eligible for this rate. You should inform your employer so that the correct rate of NI contributions can be applied.

Young people

Usually, it is very tax-efficient for a young person to build up her/his own savings and investments because everyone – even a child – can have a certain amount of income and capital gains each year tax-free. If a parent gives a child money to save (or investments) and it produces more than £100 of income (eg, interest) a year, all the income is taxed as the parent's income. So, unless the income is no more than £100, the child's own personal tax allowance is wasted. The £100 limit applies per parent per child – so if both parents give the child money or investments, s/he could have up to £200 income a year without a problem. A way around the limit is to choose from the handful of investments which are exempt from the rules. They are: child trust funds, National Savings and Investments children's bonus bonds and friendly society plans. Cash individual savings accounts are *not* exempt. See Chapter 4 for details. Capital gains of any amount always count as the child's, not her/his parent's, so another way around the £100 limit is to invest parental gifts to produce capital growth rather than income – eg, in a growth unit trust.

Students

Like everyone else, students have a tax-free personal allowance. If you are a student, your income is likely to be less than this allowance, so you either need to make sure you do not pay tax on it or remember to get a refund after the end of the tax year.

Your student loan and any bursaries are tax-free income. The main taxable income you are likely to have is interest on savings and earnings from a job. Arrange to have your interest paid gross by completing Form R85 available from the account provider or claim tax back using Form R40 from HM Revenue and Customs (the Revenue), available from www.hmrc.gov.uk. If you work only during the holidays, you can arrange to have your earnings paid without any income tax deducted by completing Form P38S and giving it to your employer. You cannot use this form if you work during term time. In this case, you will be taxed through PAYE in the normal way. If this results in you being overtaxed, you will have to claim tax back after the end of the tax year by writing to your tax office, or during the year using Form P50. The Revenue is currently consulting on ways to make it easier for students to work without being overtaxed.

Note that, in any pay period in which you earn more than £110 a week or £476 a month, you will have to pay NI and this cannot be reclaimed.

Redundancy

When you leave a job, different parts of your pay are taxed in different ways. Some are:

- tax-free. These include lump-sum compensation for an injury or disability that stops you working, compensation for the loss of a job done completely or mainly outside the UK, and some amounts paid on your behalf into a pension scheme or to buy you an annuity;
- tax-free up to a limit of £30,000. These are redundancy pay under statutory and Revenue-approved schemes, and pay in lieu of notice provided you had no contractual entitlement to it. Anything over £30,000 is taxable and your employer will usually have deducted tax under PAYE. Taking the year as a whole, this may mean that you have paid too much tax, in which case you should claim a rebate – contact your tax office;
- taxed as normal pay. This applies, for example, to payments for your services (past, present or future), including pay during your notice period (even if you do not work during your notice period) and pay in lieu of holidays.

2. The main personal taxes

Income tax

Who has to pay

Anyone – even a child – who has taxable income which comes to more than their tax-free allowance has to pay income tax.

What is taxed

Wages and salaries and the taxable value of many benefits that you get through work (see p271), profits from self-employment (see p274), interest and other income from most savings and investments (see p276), pensions, some state benefits, rents from property and many other types of income.

How it works

Tax is worked out on the income you receive during a tax year – this is the period from 6 April one year to the following 5 April. In broad terms, your income tax bill is calculated as follows.

* Add up your before-tax income (called your **'gross income'**) but exclude any income which is tax-free (see below).
* Deduct spending that qualifies for tax relief – eg, payments into an occupational pension scheme and payroll giving to charity.
* Deduct your personal allowance (see p262). This leaves your taxable income.
* Tax on this taxable income is worked out (see p263). Higher rate tax relief is given for some other types of spending that qualify for tax relief and which have already had relief at the basic rate (mainly contributions to personal pensions and charitable donations through Gift Aid).
* You can reduce the tax bill if you qualify for married couple's allowance (available only to people born before 6 April 1935 – see p262) or a few more unusual tax reliefs.

The main types of tax-free income

– Some perks you get as an employee – eg, contributions your employer makes to a pension scheme or plan on your behalf, shares through an employee share scheme, provided the rules are met, mileage allowance up to a maximum amount if you use your own transport for work, Christmas parties and similar staff entertainment within limits, canteen meals, loan of a mobile phone available for home use.
– Up to £30,000 of redundancy payments.
– Lump sum at retirement from a pension scheme or plan.
– Part of the income from an annuity (other than a pension annuity).
– Interest from National Savings and Investments (NS&I) savings certificates and children's bonus bonds.
– Premium bond prizes.
– Lottery prizes.
– Winnings from gambling (unless this is your business).
– Interest and maturity payment from a Saving Gateway account.
– Interest earned by a cash individual savings account (ISA) and cash child trust fund.
– Income other than dividends earned by investments in other types of ISA and child trust fund.
– Maintenance paid to you by your ex-husband or wife.
– Payout on death from most term insurance policies.
– Payout from most insurance policies that provide an income if you cannot work because of illness.
– Payout from most lifetime care insurance.
– Christmas bonus payable to state pensioners and winter fuel allowance.
– Pension credit.
– Working tax credit and child tax credit.

- Bereavement payment.
- War widows' and war disablement pensions.
- Income support.
- Housing benefit and council tax benefit.
- Social fund payments.
- Maternity allowance.
- Student loans, grants, bursaries and scholarships.
- Income-related employment and support allowance.
- Disability living allowance and attendance allowance.
- Money you receive for being a foster carer, within limits.

Income tax allowances in 2009/10

Allowance	Description	Amount in 2009/10	
Personal allowance	Allowance everyone gets.[i] Gives you tax relief up to your highest rate of tax. People aged 65 and over may get the higher personal allowance shown (called 'age allowance').	Under 65	£6,475
		65 to 74[ii]	£9,490
		75 or over[ii]	£9,640
Blind person's allowance	Extra allowance if you are blind. Gives you tax relief up to your highest rate.	Everyone who qualifies	£1,890
Married couple's allowance	Allowance if you are married or in a civil partnership and either you or your spouse/partner were born before 6 April 1935.[iii] Tax relief is 10% of the allowance given as a reduction in your tax bill.	Basic amount	£2,670
		Higher amount if you or your spouse are aged 75 or over[iv]	£6,965

[i] From 2010/11, people on high incomes will not get this allowance because the basic personal allowance will be reduced by £1 for every £2 by which income exceeds £100,000.
[ii] Reduced by £1 for every £2 of your 'total income' above a set limit (£22,900 in 2009/10). It is never reduced below the amount that someone under 65 gets. 'Total income' is your gross income less spending that qualifies for tax relief less personal pension contributions and less gifts to charity through Gift Aid.
[iii] Given to the husband where marriage took place before 5 December 2005. Given to the person with the highest income for marriages and civil partnerships on or after that date.

iv Reduced by £1 for every £2 'total income' above a set limit (£22,900 in 2009/10). It is never reduced below the basic amount.

Income tax rates and bands in 2009/10

Taxable income	Rate of tax paid		Maximum tax
First £2,440	Starting rate[i]	10%/20%	£244/£488
£2,441 to £37,400[ii]	Basic rate[iii]	20%	£6,992[iv]
Everything over £37,400	Higher rate	40%[v]	No limit

[i] Since 2008/09, the starting rate does not apply to 'earned income' which includes salaries, profits and pensions. Earned income is set against this band first and taxed at 20%. The 10% rate applies only to savings income and only if this band has not already been used up by earned income.

[ii] The upper limit is increased above £37,400 if you are due higher rate tax relief on contributions to a personal pension or donations to charity through Gift Aid.

[iii] Dividends and similar income are taxed at 10% (see p276).

[iv] This maximum is higher if you are due higher rate tax relief on contributions to a personal pension or donations to charity through Gift Aid, but then less of your income is taxed at the higher rate.

[v] The higher rate on dividends is currently 32.5%. From 2010/11, a new 50% tax band will apply to earned income and savings income over £150,000, with a new upper rate of 42.5% for dividend income.

Simple ways to save income tax

- If you are a couple and one of you is not using your full personal allowance, consider whether you could transfer income to that person – eg, by switching income-producing savings or employing her/him if you run your own business.
- Make sure you claim the higher personal allowance if you are aged 65 or over.
- Try to receive some of your pay in the form of tax-free perks – eg, see if your employer will pay into a pension scheme or plan for you.
- Make use of tax-free investments – eg, try to use your ISA allowance each year (see p76) and consider NS&I savings certificates.
- If you give to charity, use the Gift Aid scheme or payroll giving. You get tax relief up to your top rate.
- Paying into a pension scheme or plan also gives you tax relief usually up to your top rate. From 2011/12, this relief will be progressively reduced to just the basic rate for anyone with taxable income of £150,000 or more. In 2009/10, special rules apply to prevent people with income of £150,000 or more bringing forward contributions to beat the 2011/12 change.

- If you pay into a personal pension (including a stakeholder scheme), you get tax relief at the basic rate even if you are a non-taxpayer (see Chapter 6).
- Donations to charity through Gift Aid and personal pension contributions not only qualify for tax relief, they also reduce your total income and so can increase the amount of age allowance and tax credits you receive. See Chapter 9 for information about tax credits.

National insurance

Who has to pay

Everyone aged between 16 and state pension age who is working either for an employer or as a self-employed person, unless their earnings are very low. Employers must also pay. State pension age is currently 65 for men and 60 for women. Between April 2010 and April 2020 the pension age for women will gradually increase from 60 to 65 for women (see Chapter 6).

People not required to pay can opt to make voluntary contributions. This may be worth doing to help you build up entitlement to state retirement pension (see Chapter 6) and bereavement benefits (see Chapter 9). However, changes to the state pension (see p76) mean that people reaching state pension age from 6 April 2010 are less likely to need to make voluntary contributions.

What is taxed

Earnings from employment (but if you are an employee not the value of taxable fringe benefits) and profits from self-employment.

How it works

Some national insurance (NI) contributions help you build up an entitlement to claim certain state benefits (see Chapters 6 and 9); others are just a straightforward tax. The table below sets out the main types of contribution you might have to pay. The upper earnings limit from 2009/10 is set at the same level as that at which the 40 per cent higher rate income tax starts to be paid. From 2011/12, the primary threshold at which NI contributions start is due to be set broadly equal to the income tax personal allowance for under-65s.

National insurance contributions: classes and rates in 2009/10

Type of contribution		Who pays	How much
Class 1	Full rate	Employees earning above the primary threshold	– 11% of earnings between £110 and £844 a week; – 1% of earnings above £844 a week

Type of contribution		Who pays	How much
Class 1	Contracted-out rates	Employees earning above the primary threshold who are contracted out of the additional state pension (see Chapter 6)	If contracted out through a defined benefit scheme (see p192): – 9.4% of earnings between £110 and £770 a week (the 'upper accruals point'); – 11% of earnings between £770 and £844 a week; – 1% of earnings above £844 a week If contracted out through a money purchase scheme (see p192): – reduced rate on earnings between £110 and £770 a week – amount varies with your age; – 11% of earnings between £770 and £844 a week; – 1% of earnings above £770 a week
	Married woman's reduced rate	Some married women and widows not building up their own state benefits but relying on their husband's NI record	– 4.85% of earnings between £110 and £844 a week; – 1% of earnings above £844 a week
Class 2		Self-employed	£2.40 a week (but can choose not to pay if earnings for year below £5,075)
Class 3		Voluntary – you choose to pay to fill gaps in your NI record	– £12.05 a week; – £8.10 a week to fill gaps in 2008/09 if payment made in 2009/10

Type of contribution	Who pays	How much
Class 4	Self-employed	– 8% of profits for year between £5,715 and £43,875
		– 1% of profits above £43,875

Simple ways to save national insurance

- You do not pay NI on fringe benefits. Your employer also does not pay contributions on a few fringe benefits – eg, employer contributions to a pension scheme, childcare vouchers providing a bicycle for cycling to work. Many employers now offer 'salary sacrifice' schemes where you give up part of your pay in exchange for these.
- If you are self-employed with only low profits, you could opt not to pay Class 2 contributions. This will normally be a false economy since you can receive a lot in state benefits (eg, basic retirement pension, bereavement benefits and employment and support allowance – see Chapter 9) for only a small outlay in contributions.

Capital gains tax

Who has to pay

Anyone – even a child – who sells something at a profit which comes to more than their tax-free capital gains tax (CGT) allowance for the year. Also applies to the profit you are deemed to have made on something you give away or otherwise dispose of.

What is taxed

The profit (called the **'taxable gain'**) from things like shares, unit trusts, second homes, valuable heirlooms, and so on. But some gains are tax-free (see below).

Main items on which gains are usually free of capital gains tax

- Your only or main home. This can include a gain from selling part of your garden, provided it is not overly large.
- Items with a useful life of no more than 50 years – eg, boats and caravans.
- More durable personal belongings worth less than £6,000. This includes, for example, antiques and paintings. Special rules may limit the gain on more valuable personal items.
- Your private cars.
- British money.
- Foreign currency for your personal use abroad.

- Lottery prizes, gambling wins and premium bond prizes.
- Investments held in an ISA or child trust fund.
- Gilts.
- Most life insurance policies (but there could be income tax – see p260).
- Gifts to charities, some amateur sports clubs and some public interest bodies (such as museums).
- Gifts between husband and wife and civil partners (though there could be tax when the recipient eventually sells).
- Everything you leave on death.

How it works

The following outline assumes you are selling an item, but much the same procedure applies if you give something away or otherwise dispose of it. To work out whether any tax is due, follow these steps.

- Take the sale price of the item (called its **'final value'**).
- Find the price you paid for the item (or its market value if you were given it or inherited it). This is called the **'initial value'**.
- Subtract the initial value from the final value to give you the **'gross capital gain'** or loss.
- Deduct any allowable expenses. These are things like fees and other costs you incurred buying or selling the item, and the cost of work that enhanced the value of the item (such as restoration of a picture or adding an extension to a property). This is called the **'net capital gain'** or loss.
- Deduct any special reliefs that apply in certain situations – eg, if you are selling a business.
- Deduct capital losses on other items sold in the same year or an earlier year.
- If your gains for the year are less than your tax-free CGT allowance (£10,100 in 2009/10), there is no tax to pay.
- If the net tapered gains come to more than the tax-free CGT allowance, you pay tax at 18 per cent on the excess.

CGT was reformed from April 2008 and is now a much simpler tax than previously. However, it can still seem complicated especially if, for instance, you are selling shares or unit trusts. If you expect to have taxable gains, you may need help. If your gains will be well below the tax-free allowance, you do not need to bother with the calculations.

Simple ways to save capital gains tax

- Try to make use of your yearly tax-free CGT allowance (£10,100 in 2009/10) by, for example, having some investments that produce capital gains rather than taxable income.

• Keep a record of any capital losses you make. You can carry them forward indefinitely to reduce gains made in future tax years.

Inheritance tax

Who has to pay

Personal representatives of your estate after you have died if your estate is valued at more than the tax-free allowance. You or the recipient if you make gifts during your lifetime which are taxable. Few lifetime gifts are, however, taxable (see p270).

What is taxed

The value of your estate (everything you own including all possessions as well as money) but less any tax-free bequests, which include anything you leave to your spouse or civil partner and anything you leave to charity.

Also, some gifts (whether of money or items) that you make in your lifetime are taxable. If you pay the tax on behalf of the recipient that counts as part of the gift.

How it works

Inheritance tax (IHT) is worked out on the rolling sum of taxable gifts you have made over the last seven years. If, at any time, the rolling total comes to more than the tax-free IHT allowance for the year (£325,000 in 2009/10), tax may be due.

However, most gifts you make during your lifetime are tax-free at the time you make them (see below). The main exception is gifts to most types of trust, in which case there may be an immediate tax bill. (A trust is a legal arrangement where property is held by some people for the use by or benefit of others.) Gifts to people are tax-free when made but become taxable if you die within seven years and are called '**potentially exempt transfers**' (PETs).

For most people, the only time IHT is likely to become due is when they die. Tax is then worked out as follows.

• The value of everything you owned at the time you died is added together. This includes, for example, your home, furniture and household goods, personal possessions, car, bank accounts, savings and investments, any tax rebate due, and so on. It includes your share of things that you owned jointly with someone else.

• Deduct any debts you left – eg, an outstanding mortgage, credit card bills, income tax owed and reasonable funeral expenses.

• Deduct any bequests that are tax-free (see p270).

• Add on any gifts made in the seven years before death that were not tax-free (see p270). This includes any PETs. (These use up some of the tax-free IHT allowance and so reduce the amount of the allowance left to be set against the value of the estate).

- If the total comes to more than the tax-free IHT allowance (£325,000 in 2009/10, but see below for special rules for married couples and civil partners), IHT is charged at a rate of 40 per cent on the excess. If the total comes to less than the tax-free allowance, no tax is due.

It used to be the case that married couples and civil partners would often waste the tax-free allowance of the first of the couple to die. This was because husbands, wives and civil partners can leave their estates to each other tax-free in any case. In some cases this resulted in a large tax bill when the second of the couple died because there was just one tax-free allowance to set against the couple's remaining wealth. The situation has now changed. The tax-free allowance for a person who dies on or after 9 October 2007 may be increased if her/his spouse or civil partner died first and had not used all of her/his allowance. So the allowance can now be transferred between the couple, giving them a joint tax-free sum of 2 x £325,000 = £650,000 in 2009/10.

Most people should not worry too much about IHT because:
- since the introduction of the transferable allowance for married couples and civil partners, only one estate in 50 at death is large enough to incur a tax bill (down from around one in seven before the change);
- it is a problem for your heirs, not you;
- for many heirs, an inheritance, while welcome, is a windfall. If you think there might be tax on your estate and you do want to do something about it, consider getting professional help.

On your death, in addition to the tax on your estate, if you made any PETs within the last seven years, there may also be tax to pay on them. There could also be extra tax due on gifts on which some tax was paid at the time they were made. In both cases, the amount of tax now due is highest if the gift was made only shortly before death but reduces the longer the time that has elapsed since the gift was made. There is no tax due on gifts made more than seven years before death. Initially, the person who received the gift will be expected to pay the tax. If they cannot, or will not, your personal representatives will be expected to settle the bill out of the money in your estate. At the time of making a gift, you or the person receiving the gift could take out a seven-year insurance policy (a reducing term policy – see Chapter 7) to cover this potential tax bill.

If you give away something in your lifetime but you carry on using it or benefiting from it, the gift will not save IHT. This is called a **'gift with reservation'** and still counts as part of your estate until you stop using it or benefiting from it. Over the years, schemes have been devised to get round these rules, but, since April 2005, if you have given away something, you continue to use it and the gift is not caught by the gift-with-reservation rules, you will instead have to pay income tax each year on the value of the benefit you are deemed to receive. This income tax (called a **'pre-owned asset tax'**) may catch some arrangements where the aim was not tax avoidance – eg, if you sold part of your home to a relative or other person in order to raise a lump sum or extra income. A commercial home reversion scheme (see Chapter 5) would not be caught by this tax.

Main gifts which are free of inheritance tax

Tax-free gifts made either during your lifetime or on death:
– gifts to your husband, wife or civil partner (but only up to £55,000 if her/his permanent home is abroad);
– gifts to charity and some amateur sports clubs;
– gifts of land to housing associations;
– gifts to established political parties;
– gifts to certain national institutions and gifts of certain heritage property – eg, important paintings and historic buildings.

Other tax-free gifts during your lifetime:
– gifts up to £250 per person per year to any number of people;
– gifts of any amount made regularly out of your income that leave you able to maintain your normal standard of living – eg, gifts every birthday, premiums you pay for a life insurance policy to benefit someone else;
– gifts on marriage up to set limits – eg, £5,000 from each parent of a bride or groom;
– maintenance payments – eg, to an ex-spouse of a child under 18 or who is still in full-time education;
– any other gifts up to £3,000 each year. If you do not use the full £3,000 allowance, you can carry it forward one year (but no further), increasing your allowance that year to £6,000;
– gifts to individuals (PETs), provided you survive seven years.

Other tax-free gifts on death:
– lump-sum death benefit from pension schemes or plans, provided the trustees or provider have discretion to decide who to pay (though usually they will pay the person you nominate);
– payout from life insurance, provided the policy is written in trust for the benefit of someone other than you;
– the estate of someone killed on active service.

How you can save some inheritance tax

• Husbands, wives and civil partners can now take over any tax-free allowance unused if their spouse or partner died before them. To do this, you must have the paperwork from settling the first estate, so make sure you file these papers carefully and ensure your personal representatives would be able to find them.
• Ensure that any insurance policies are 'written in trust' so that the proceeds go directly to the person you want to benefit without becoming part of your

estate. That way the payout gets to the recipient more quickly and is not subject to IHT.

- If you are worried about IHT but most of your estate is the value of your home, there are only a few ways you might reduce a potential tax bill on death. They are full of potential pitfalls so get professional advice (see p280). Steps you might consider include:
  - giving away part of your home – eg, to your children. If you still live there, you would have to pay the new owner a full market rent for your use of the home, otherwise it would be a gift with reservation (see above) and would not save IHT;
  - giving part of your home to someone who lives there with you – eg, a carer or a grown-up son or daughter. For there to be no gift with reservation, it is essential that you do not benefit from the part of the home you have given away, so you must pay your fair share of the running costs. There could be difficulties if the person you share with later moves out;
  - assuming you are happy to spend some of your estate during your lifetime, trading down to a smaller home and spending the money released. Alternatively, you could take out a lifetime mortgage or home reversion scheme but the amount you save in tax is likely instead to go to the firm providing the scheme (see p162).
- If you have assets other than your home, you can reduce the value of your estate and a potential tax bill if you make lifetime gifts. Do not give away so much that you are left with too little to live on.

Making a will

An essential step in inheritance planning is to make a will stating who you want to receive your possessions when you die. Without a will, the law dictates how your estate is given away, giving priority to your spouse or civil partner (but not someone with whom you cohabit without being married or in a civil partnership) and children (but not stepchildren). Only by chance will the law coincide with your wishes. A will also lets you say who you would like to sort out your affairs and can speed up the administration of your estate, reducing difficulties and delays for your survivors. Wills must be precisely worded to avoid legal arguments later on, so it is best to get a solicitor to draw one up for you. A simple will can cost around £75.

3. **Tax on some different types of income**

Tax if you are an employee

Taxable pay

In general, all the earnings from your job are taxable, including salary, wages, commission and bonuses. This applies regardless of who paid you, so, for example, tips from customers and gifts from clients are also taxable. Pay that your employer is required to provide if you are ill or a parent – statutory sick pay, statutory maternity pay, statutory paternity pay and statutory adoption pay – is also taxable.

Allowable expenses and fringe benefits

As well as wages or salary, you might also get expenses and non-cash payments.

In general, if your employer is reimbursing expenses you have incurred for work purposes, the amount you get counts as taxable earnings, but you may be able to claim a compensating deduction equal to the amount you had to spend. To simplify matters, your employer might have a 'dispensation' for some expenses, in which case you are not taxed on the money reimbursed and so do not have to claim tax relief on what you spent. Some common expenses, such as mileage allowance, are tax-free anyway up to certain limits.

Fringe benefits are non-cash items that give you some personal benefit. This may be the case even if their primary purpose is to help you do your job – eg, you might have a company car in which to travel on business, but if it is also available for your private use you will be deemed to have some private benefit from the car even if you do not actually use it for private mileage.

Some fringe benefits are tax-free; some others are tax-free if you earn less than £8,500 a year (and you are not a company director). Other fringe benefits are taxable whatever your earnings. The table below gives a brief outline of some of the most common fringe benefits.

Where a fringe benefit is taxable, rules state how the benefit should be valued for tax purposes. You do not have to work this out for yourself. Your employer should deduct the correct amount of tax from your pay and after the end of the tax year should give you Form P11D or P9D showing the value on which you have been taxed. For more information, get free booklet 480 *Expenses and Benefits: a guide for tax* from HM Revenue and Customs (the Revenue) (www.hmrc.gov.uk/guidance/480.htm).

Common fringe benefits

	Tax-free	Tax-free if you earn less than £8,500 a year and are not a company director	Taxable whatever your earnings
Company car			✓
Free fuel for company car			✓
Mileage allowance if you use your own vehicle for work, up to the statutory limit	✓		

	Tax-free	Tax-free if you earn less than £8,500 a year and are not a company director	Taxable whatever your earnings
Mileage allowance over the statutory limit			✓
Company van available for private use		✓	
Financial help travelling to and from work if you are disabled and cannot use public transport	✓		
Workplace nursery	✓		
Other approved childcare paid for by your employer or childcare vouchers up to a maximum of £55 a week (in 2009/10)	✓		
Cheap or interest-free loans up to a total of £5,000	✓		
Cheap or interest-free loans that total more than £5,000		✓	
Free season ticket			✓
Free living accommodation that is necessary for, or customary in, your work, or required for security reasons	✓		
Other free living accommodation			✓
Occupational pension scheme	✓		
Private medical insurance scheme		✓	
Group income protection scheme	✓		
Moving expenses (up to £8,000 per move)	✓		
Free or cheap meals in canteen open to all staff	✓		
Christmas party and other staff entertainment up to a total of £150 a head a year	✓		
Free use of sports facilities open to all staff but not the general public	✓		
Membership of sports facilities open to the public		✓	
Loan of a mobile phone	✓		
Loans of most other things		✓	

	Tax-free	Tax-free if you earn less than £8,500 a year and are not a company director	Taxable whatever your earnings
Things your employer gives you			✓
Up to £3 a week towards additional household expenses incurred if you work at home (and more if you can prove higher extra costs)		✓	
Other personal bills your employer pays for you			✓

Adjustments to your pay

Income tax and national insurance (NI) are deducted from your pay before you get it through the pay as you earn (PAYE) system (see p278).

Your employer may make other deductions from, and in some cases additions to, your earnings, which will affect the amount in your pay packet. They include:

- **contributions to an occupational pension scheme.** These are deducted and passed to the scheme. Income tax is worked out on your earnings less these contributions, in order to give you the tax relief due;
- **contributions to other pension plans.** Contributions to a group personal pension or stakeholder scheme available through your workplace are deducted by your employer and passed to the scheme provider;
- **donations to charity using payroll giving.** You can direct that a set amount of your pay is donated to one or more charities. Your employer makes the deduction and hands it to an agency which ensures the correct sums reach each charity;
- **student loan repayments.** If you took out a student loan to fund yourself through university (see Chapter 5) and your income exceeds a set threshold (£15,000 a year in 2009/10), you are usually required to repay the loan at a rate of 9 per cent of your income in excess of the threshold. Your employer makes these deductions and passes them to the Revenue;
- **attachment of earnings orders.** Courts can direct that money you owe someone else (eg, unpaid tax or a problem debt) is paid in instalments out of your pay. Your employer makes the deductions and passes them to the court.

Tax if you are self-employed

An overview

If you run your own business as a sole trader or in partnership with others, the profits you make (or your share of them if you are a partner) count as part of your taxable income when working out your income tax bill. The situation is different if you run your own business as a company. Then your company pays corporation tax and you draw a salary as an employee and/or dividends as a shareholder. This section looks at the position only for sole traders and partners.

Once your business has been running for a few years, you are taxed on a 'current year basis' which means that tax for the tax year (6 April to following 5 April) is based on the profits for your accounting year which ends during the tax year. For example, if your accounting year runs from 1 January to 31 December, in the 2009/10 tax year you will normally be taxed on the profits you made during the year ending 31 December 2009. Different rules apply during the opening and closing years of your business.

You pay tax on your taxable profits. These are basically:

- your sales or turnover;
- *less* allowable expenses;
- *less* annual investment allowance and capital allowances.

You can also claim tax relief on losses you make in your business.

You pay tax due and also any Class 4 NI through the self-assessment system (see p278). If your business is fairly simple, you may be able to draw up your accounts and work out your tax bill for yourself. If your business is more complicated, you will probably do better to employ an accountant. This section can give only a very brief description of business taxation. For more information, contact your local Business Link (in England or equivalent organisation in the rest of the UK) or the Revenue.

Allowable expenses

You can claim tax relief on the expenses you incur running your business – eg, raw materials, stock you buy in for resale, rent for business premises, business rates, fuel and light, telephone, stationery, salaries for staff (but not what you pay yourself), bank charges and accountancy fees.

An expense is allowable only if it is incurred 'wholly and exclusively' for business – which, strictly interpreted, would exclude an expense that was partly for business and partly for private purposes. In practice, the Revenue lets you claim the business part of a joint expense provided the business element can be clearly identified. For example, you can claim for business use of your car if you keep a record of the total mileage and the number of business miles; you can claim additional household expenses if you work from home, based on the floor area or number of rooms devoted to your business.

You can claim only the cost of revenue items – basically, the cost of things that are used up in the course of trading. You cannot directly claim the cost of anything you buy that is durable – eg, buildings, machinery, office furniture, phones, copiers, computers and vans, but you may be able to claim the annual investment allowance or capital allowances.

Annual investment allowance and capital allowances

These allowances give you tax relief on the cost of buying capital items for use in your business. Every business has an annual investment allowance. This lets you write off the full cost of capital items up to a maximum of £50,000 (in 2009/10). Some types of expenditure, especially on environmentally friendly items, qualify for 100 per cent first-year capital allowances (without any maximum cash limit) and, again, this lets you write off the full cost in the year you buy the item. Where any capital spending is not covered by these allowances, you write off the cost gradually year by year through claiming writing-down allowances. Depending on the type of spending, writing-down allowances let you claim 20 per cent or 10 per cent of the balance of the cost each year.

Tax on savings and investments

The income and any capital gain you get from some types of savings are tax-free (see pp261 and 266 for some examples). The income from other savings and investments is taxable and either paid **'gross'** – ie, without any tax already deducted, or **'net'**, meaning that some tax has been deducted, although you might have more to pay. Capital gains are paid gross. The rest of this section looks at how income from the most common investments is taxed. See also Chapter 4.

Savings income paid gross

This applies, for example, to interest from National Savings and Investments (NS&I) easy access savings accounts, investment accounts and income bonds, offshore bank accounts, gilts (unless you have opted to receive net interest) and corporate bonds. You receive the interest with no tax deducted, but it is taxable at the following rates in 2009/10 if, when the interest is added to your other income, you are a:

- **non-taxpayer**: no tax to pay;
- **starting rate taxpayer**: 10 per cent;
- **basic rate taxpayer**: 20 per cent (this is called the 'savings rate');
- **higher rate taxpayer**: 40 per cent.

It is your responsibility to tell the Revenue about this income if tax is due (see p278).

Savings income paid net

This usually applies, for example, to interest from bank and building society accounts, interest from NS&I fixed-rate savings bonds, income from annuities (other than those bought with a pension fund) and distributions from bond-based unit trusts. You receive the income with tax at the basic rate (20 per cent in 2009/10) already deducted. What happens next depends on whether you are a:

- **non-taxpayer.** You can reclaim all the tax already deducted – do this using Form R40 from the Revenue (see Appendix 2). If you expect to carry on being a non-taxpayer, you may be able to arrange to receive the interest gross in future by completing Form R85 available from the provider or the Revenue (but this option is not available for the NS&I bonds);

- **starting rate taxpayer**. You are liable for tax at only 10 per cent, so you can reclaim half the tax deducted using Form R40;
- **basic rate taxpayer**. You have no further tax to pay;
- **higher rate taxpayer**. If you are a 40 per cent taxpayer, you have a further 20 per cent tax on the grossed-up income to pay. It is your responsibility to tell the Revenue about this income (see p278).

Grossed-up income

This is a term used when you receive income from which tax has already been deducted. It means the net income plus the tax deducted. For example, if you receive interest of £80 which has already had tax at 20 per cent deducted, the grossed-up income is £80 + £20 = £100 (since 20% x £100 = £20). You can work out the grossed-up income as follows: net income received x 100/(100 – tax rate).

Dividends and distributions from share-based unit trusts

You receive income with tax at 10 per cent (in 2009/10) already deducted. You cannot reclaim this tax even if you are a non-taxpayer. If you are a starting rate or basic rate taxpayer, there is no further tax to pay. If you are a higher rate taxpayer, you pay further tax, so paying an extra 22.5 per cent of the grossed-up income brings the total rate to 32.5 per cent.

Investment-type life insurance

The lump-sum payout from investment-type life insurance is normally treated as income rather than a capital gain. The insurance company has already paid tax on the income and gains from the investments underlying the policy. This is deemed to be equivalent to tax at the savings rate of 20 per cent. You cannot reclaim any of this tax even if you are a non-taxpayer or starting rate taxpayer. There is no more tax to pay if you are a basic rate taxpayer.

With most regular premium long-term policies, there is also no more tax to pay if you are a higher rate taxpayer, but with other types of policy there could be extra tax at 20 per cent of the amount you received (without any grossing up).

The payout from an investment-type life policy counts as part of your 'total income' for the tax year and so could reduce the amount of age allowance you get (see p262).

Some policies let you receive an income each year without any tax being due at the time and without affecting your age allowance at the time. Any tax (only at the higher rate) is deferred until the year the policy finally comes to an end. At that time, your age allowance could be affected.

4. How tax is collected

Pay As You Earn

If you are an employee or you receive a pension from an occupational scheme or personal pension, your employer or scheme provider will normally be required to deduct income tax (and if you are an employee, national insurance too) using the Pay As You Earn (PAYE) system before handing over each payment to you.

Your tax office tells your employer how much tax-free pay or pension you are entitled to receive each pay period and the employer or provider then uses tables or a computer program to work out the correct amount of tax to be deducted.

PAYE is used to collect not just tax on the pay or pension from that employer or provider, but also tax due on other income – eg, your state pension or interest paid gross on savings, and to give you tax relief in respect of allowances and other deductions you can claim. A few months before the start of the tax year, you should normally get a notice of coding from your tax office which shows how the amount of your tax-free pay has been worked out. If you do not agree with the calculation, you should tell your tax office and ask for a revised notice of coding.

About once every three years, you may receive a PAYE coding review form (Form P810) from your tax office. The aim of this is to update the HM Revenue and Customs' (the Revenue) information about your income from all sources and correct your PAYE tax code if necessary. The review could lead to a tax rebate or extra tax being collected. If you prefer to keep your tax affairs more up to date, you can choose instead to complete a tax return each year (see below).

If you receive income or capital gains on which tax is due, which your tax office does not already know about, you have until 5 October following the end of the tax year (eg, 5 October 2010 for amounts received in the 2009/10 tax year) to tell your tax office. You may then be sent a tax return, in which case the tax due will then be collected through the self-assessment system or PAYE (see below).

Tax returns and self assessment

If you are self-employed, a higher rate taxpayer, have untaxed investment income, receive rents or have other complications, you are likely to get a tax return each year. Tax returns are normally issued in April for the tax year that has just ended.

You get a basic return that everyone must fill in plus supplements covering different types of income or gain. Your tax office will automatically send you any supplements that it thinks you will use based on your previous tax affairs, but it is up to you to order any others that you need.

Some people get a simplified four-page tax return for people with uncomplicated tax affairs. It can be used by people with the following types of income:

- employment income with or without fringe benefits;

- self-employment income with turnover up to £30,000;
- state pension, occupational pension or some other types of pension income;
- taxable state benefits;
- rental income up to £15,000, but only from UK properties;
- taxable savings income, dividends and/or distributions from unit trusts;
- capital gains, but these must be reported on a separate form (which is the capital gains supplement from the full tax return).

The Revenue decides who should be sent the short tax return based on their tax affairs in previous years. If you are no longer eligible for the short form, it is up to you to order the full tax return instead.

Tax returns issued in April 2010 (ie, for the 2009/10 tax year) must be sent back ('filed') by 31 October 2010 if you want to send in a paper return or 31 January 2011 if you file online. There is an automatic fine (usually £100) if you miss these deadlines by more than one day.

Often you will have paid some tax during the year through two payments on account on 31 January during the tax year and 31 July following the tax year. Each payment on account normally equals half your tax bill for the previous year. Under self assessment, it is your responsibility, based on the information you give in the tax return, to work out your correct tax bill for the year and, if it comes to more than the payments on account, to pay the extra due by 31 January following the end of the tax year. If you pay the tax late, you incur interest and, if you are more than a month late, penalties as well.

If you do not want to work out your own tax bill, you could:

- file your paper tax return by 31 October. The Revenue will work out the tax bill for you and let you know how much tax is due in time for the 31 January payment deadline;
- file your tax return online. You can do this at any time up to 31 January and the software automatically and instantly tells you the amount of tax due. You cannot file the short tax return online but, if you receive the short return you can still fill in the (fuller) online tax return instead if you want to;
- get a professional to fill in and file your tax return and work out the tax for you (see p280).

If you paid more tax through payments on account than was due for the year, you will get a refund. Note that the final payment/refund on 31 January for the tax year just gone coincides with the first payment on account for the current tax year, so you will normally have something to pay in January.

If you are self-employed or a partner in a business, you must by law keep the records which back up the information you have given in your tax return until the 31 January falling five years and 10 months after the end of the tax year covered by the return. For example, for the 2009/10 tax return (received in April 2010), you need to keep your records until the 31 January 2016. If you are not in business, you must keep your records until 31 January falling one year and 10 months after the end of the tax year. For example, for the 2009/10 tax return, you keep the records until 31 January 2012. If you do not comply with these rules and cannot produce the records when asked, you could be fined up to £3,000. The Revenue might also estimate any tax it thinks you owe and, without records, you might be unable to challenge an over-estimation.

5. **Getting advice about tax**

HM Revenue and Customs (the Revenue) produces a lot of free information explaining how the tax system works. Increasingly, this is available only on its website rather than in booklet form. See the table below for a selection of the few remaining booklets available. If you do not have access to the internet, you can visit or phone the Revenue and ask for print-outs from the website. The Revenue runs a network of tax enquiry offices which can give you information and help by phone or face to face. It also operates a range of telephone helplines covering various tax topics.

If you want professional help completing your tax return but without any advice, you could use a tax preparation service (charges start at around £100 per return but more if you are self-employed). There is no legal requirement for these services to have any professional qualifications but you would be wise to choose a member of the Association of Tax Technicians (who must have passed relevant exams).

If you want more detailed help and advice, consider using an accountant. Members of the Chartered Institute of Taxation specialise in tax matters.

If you are on a low income and cannot afford professional advice, you might qualify for free help from TaxAid. Older people on a low income can also get free help from TaxHelp for Older People.

See Appendix 2 for contact details for all the above organisations.

Selection of free Revenue booklets

Booklet number	Title
IR111	*Bank and Building Society Interest: are you paying tax when you don't need to?*
IR115	*Payment for Childcare: getting help from your employer*
IR121	*Approaching Retirement: a guide to tax and national insurance contributions*
480	*Expenses and Benefits: a guide for tax*
SA/BK4	*Self-assessment: a general guide to keeping records*
SA/BK8	*Self-assessment: your guide*
SE1	*Thinking of Working for Yourself?*

| ES/FS1 | *Employed or Self-employed for Tax and National Insurance Contributions* |
| CGT1/FS1 | *Capital Gains Tax: a quick guide* |

6. Fraud

You are required by law to pay your taxes. If you earn income or make gains and do not declare them, you are breaking the law. If caught, you could face imprisonment and will have to pay fines as well as the tax due plus interest. It is also an offence to 'be knowingly concerned in the fraudulent evasion of income tax' which you will be if, for example, you agree to pay someone in cash knowing they will not declare it for tax.

Tax scams

Be on your alert for this common scam and do not get caught out.

Tax refund emails. You receive an email, seemingly from HM Revenue and Customs (the Revenue), saying you are due a tax refund. All you have to do is provide your bank or credit card details so the money can be sent to you. You will find that your bank account is empty or your card at its credit limit. The Revenue advises that it never notifies refunds by email, only by post, and letters would always come from the Revenue itself, not from any third-party firm. If you get any suspicious emails like this, forward them to the Revenue (phishing@hmrc.gsi.gov.uk) and then delete them from your computer. For more information, see www.hmrc.gov.uk/security.

Notes

1 Adam Smith Institute, *Tax Freedom Day*, www.adamsmith.org/tax-freedom-day/, accessed 31 July 2009
2 HM Revenue and Customs, *National Statistics: tax receipts and taxpayers*, www.hmrc.gov.uk/thelibrary/national-statistics.htm, accessed 27 September 2009
3 HM Revenue and Customs, 'Value Added Tax, Income Tax Allowances, National Insurance Contributions, Child and Working Tax Credit Rates 2009/10 and Other Rates', Press Release, 2009
4 HM Revenue and Customs, 'Two-thirds file Tax Returns Online,' Press Release, http://nds.coi.gov.uk, accessed 31 July 2009
5 HM Treasury, *Budget Report*, 2009

Chapter 9

- -

Benefits and tax credits

This chapter covers:
1. Benefits, tax credits and financial planning (below)
2. Benefits explained (p291)
3. How means tests work (p311)
4. Tax credits explained (p314)
5. Work, benefits and tax credits (p317)
6. Overpayments and fraud (p320)
7. Challenging decisions (p321)

- -

Basic facts

- In late 2008, 5.4 million people of working age were claiming state benefits and 4.5 million people of all ages were claiming disability benefits.[1]
- In 2007/08, up to £10.5 million of means-tested benefits were unclaimed. For example, up to 1.7 million eligible people failed to claim pension credit and up to 3.1 million eligible people failed to claim council tax benefit.[2]
- Nine out of ten families with children and 1.5 million working people without children qualify for tax credits.[3]
- In 2007/08, Citizens Advice Bureaux received over 1.5 million enquiries about state benefits.[4]

- -

1. Benefits, tax credits and financial planning

In many situations, the state provides some basic financial support – eg, if you are unable to work, or you have special financial needs because of a disability or because you have children, or to top up a low income. A wide range of benefits and tax credits are available.

Some benefits are paid only if you have limited income and capital. These are known as **means-tested benefits**. Examples are income support (IS), pension credit and housing benefit (HB). **Tax credits** are also means tested. There are two types of tax credit – working tax credit and child tax credit.

Some benefits are:
- paid if you qualify for particular means-tested benefits or tax credits. These are known as **'passported' benefits**. Examples are free school meals, health benefits and Sure Start maternity grants;
- discretionary, even if you satisfy the means test. These are social fund community care grants, budgeting loans and crisis loans, and some local authority payments – eg, for school uniforms.

See p311 for more information about how means tests work.
Non-means-tested benefits are paid to replace earnings or to provide help if you have specific needs. Normally, income and capital do not affect these benefits, although in some cases earnings and some pension payments affect the amount you can be paid. There are three types of non-means-tested benefits.
- **Contributory benefits** are paid if you (or, in some cases, your partner) have in the past paid national insurance (NI) contributions or have been credited as if you had them. Examples are contribution-based jobseeker's allowance (JSA) if you are unemployed, contributory employment and support allowance (ESA)if you are off work sick, and retirement pension. Bereavement benefits are available if your late spouse or civil partner paid sufficient NI contributions. In the case of contributory ESA, you may be able to qualify without having to have paid NI contributions if you became incapable of work when you were under the age of 20 (or 25 in some cases).
- **Non-contributory benefits** are paid whether or not you have paid any NI contributions if you have specific needs – eg, a health in pregnancy grant is paid to expectant mothers, child benefit to people with children and disability living allowance to people with disabilities.
- Some benefits are **paid by employers** to their employees. These are statutory sick pay, statutory maternity pay, statutory adoption pay and statutory paternity pay.

JSA and ESA both have two forms: contribution-based JSA and contributory ESA which you get if you have enough NI contributions and credits; and income-based JSA and income-related ESA which you may get if your income and capital are low enough, even if you do not have sufficient NI or the contribution-based element has run out. Income-based JSA and income-related ESA are means tested.

The table on pp286–289 summarise the main benefits and tax credits showing whether they are contributory, means tested or paid by employers.

Note: there are some benefits that are no longer available for new claims. However, you can continue to qualify for these if you are already getting them. These are: widowed mother's allowance, widow's pension and severe disablement allowance (SDA). In most cases, it is no longer possible to make a new claim for incapacity benefit (IB). However, you might be able to claim if you were previously entitled to IB or if you are getting IS on the grounds of disability – eg, because you are incapable of work or are registered blind.

Benefits and tax credits and the need for financial products

When planning your need for financial products, or before building up savings or taking out insurance to cover situations when you would not be able to work, you should take into account the availability of benefits and tax credits for two reasons:

- benefits and tax credits may reduce the amount of income you need from private sources and so reduce the amount of insurance or savings you need;
- income from private sources may affect the amount of benefits and tax credits you can be paid. As a result, it might not be worth building up private savings or taking out private insurance unless you can afford enough to give you substantially more than you would otherwise receive through state benefits.

When you are planning your finances (see Chapter 1) or getting advice (see Chapter 2), you and any adviser should always take any possible benefits and tax credits into account when deciding what products you might need and the amount of savings or cover you require.

Which benefits and tax credits to claim

When deciding which benefits and tax credits to claim, you should check to see:

- if you can get any non-means-tested benefits that replace earnings, such as contributory ESA or retirement pension; *then*
- if you can get any benefits because of specific needs – eg, because you have a disability or children; *and finally*
- whether you qualify for any means-tested benefits or tax credits to top up your benefit and other income.

Qualifying for some of the non-means-tested benefits may mean you are entitled to, or are entitled to a higher amount of, some of the means-tested benefits or tax credits. Remember to ask for your claims to be backdated, where applicable – in most cases, claims can be backdated only for a maximum of three months, so make your claim as soon as you realise you may be eligible. Note that if getting one of the non-means-tested benefits qualifies you for another benefit, you should claim the other benefit at the same time in order to gain maximum backdating.

Example

Carys is a lone parent. She spends a lot of her time caring for her disabled Aunt Paula who lives with her. Aunt Paula is claiming attendance allowance (AA).

Carys can claim child benefit because she has children. She can also claim carer's allowance (CA) because she is caring at least 35 hours a week for someone getting AA. She can claim child tax credit and IS to top up her income. IS is paid at a higher rate if someone is getting CA. So even though Carys's CA counts as income for IS purposes, she is better off overall.

You should bear the following in mind.

- All benefits and tax credits have a number of conditions you must satisfy – eg, you must usually satisfy residence rules and be physically present in Great Britain while claiming. In some cases, you can claim benefits while you are abroad.
- Many benefits and tax credits are affected if you (or your partner) are working (see p317).
- Special rules apply in some cases – eg, if you have to go into hospital or prison, or are resident in a care home or other special accommodation, or are a person subject to immigration control.
- Studying full time can affect entitlement to benefits. For further information, see CPAG's *Student Support and Benefits Handbook: England, Wales and Scotland* and *Benefits for Students in Scotland Handbook*.

Getting more than one benefit

You can claim a combination of benefits and tax credits. However, there are special rules – known as **'overlapping benefit' rules** – where you are entitled to more than one of certain non-means-tested benefits. You may usually only receive one of these at a time (see below for the benefits that are affected). However, it can still be worth claiming those to which you are entitled, even if they cannot be paid to you, as in some cases, entitlement allows you to qualify for, or to get a higher rate of, means-tested benefits. The rules are complicated, so if you think you might be affected, seek advice.

Benefits affected

Bereavement allowance; CA; contributory ESA; IB; contribution-based JSA; maternity allowance; retirement pension; SDA; widowed parent's allowance.

Yearly increases

Benefits and tax credits rates, and many of the thresholds for qualifying for these, are normally increased in April of each year. So if you do not qualify for means-tested benefits or tax credits currently, you may qualify when the rates go up.

Where to get more information

The benefit and tax credits rules are complex. This chapter gives only a broad overview of the main benefits you might be able to claim. For comprehensive guidance, see CPAG's *Welfare Benefits and Tax Credits Handbook*.

Tax credits, health in pregnancy grants, child benefit and guardian's allowance are administered by the HM Revenue and Customs (the Revenue). You can get information about these from the Revenue website, by contacting your local tax office or from the tax credits helpline (Tel: 0845 300 3900).

HB, council tax benefit (CTB) and help with long-term care are administered by your local authority.

Most other benefits are administered by the Department for Work and Pensions (DWP), which also publishes free information booklets. If you are of working age, you can find out about DWP benefits from your local Jobcentre Plus office. Contact The Pension Service if you are over state pension age (currently 65 for men and 60 for women, but see Chapter 6 for how this will change from April 2010).

See Appendix 2 for contact details of the above organisations.

Remember: there are strict time limits for claiming benefits and tax credits. You should claim as soon as you think you might be entitled and ask for your claim to be backdated as far as possible.

Summary of the main benefits and tax credits

Benefit or tax credit	When you might get it	Type of benefit	Taxable?
Attendance allowance	If you are 65 or over when you first claim and need help with personal care	Non-contributory Non-means-tested	No
Bereavement allowance	If your spouse or civil partner has died	Contributory[i] Non-means-tested	Yes
Bereavement payment	If your spouse or civil partner has died	Contributory[i] Non-means-tested	No
Carer's allowance	If you are regularly caring for someone who is disabled and getting attendance allowance or a specific rate of disability living allowance	Non-contributory Non-means-tested[ii]	Yes
Child benefit	If you are responsible for a child or qualifying young person	Non-contributory Non-means-tested	No
Child tax credit	If you are responsible for a child or qualifying young person	Non-contributory Means-tested	No
Council tax benefit	If you are liable to pay council tax and – your income is low; *or* – you are the only liable person and share with others who are on a low income	Non-contributory Means-tested	No

Benefit or tax credit	When you might get it	Type of benefit	Taxable?
Disability living allowance	If you are under 65 when you first claim and have care and/or mobility needs	Non-contributory Non-means-tested	No
Employment and support allowance (contributory)	If you cannot work because of illness or disability	Contributory Non-means-tested[iii]	Yes
Employment and support allowance (income-related)	If you are on a low income and cannot work because of illness or disability	Non-contributory Means-tested	No
Guardian's allowance	If you are looking after a child who is effectively an orphan	Non-contributory Non-means-tested	No
Health in pregnancy grant	If you are expecting a baby, have reached at least the 25th week of pregnancy and are receiving care from a GP or midwife	Non-contributory Non-means-tested	No
Housing benefit	If you are liable to pay rent and your income is low	Non-contributory Means-tested	No
Incapacity benefit	If you cannot work because of illness or disability	Contributory and non-contributory Non-means-tested[iii]	Yes, other than lower rate of short-term incapacity benefit
Income support	If your income is low and you fit into a specified group – eg, you are a lone parent or a carer	Non-contributory Means-tested	No, unless you are involved in a trade dispute and are claiming for a partner
Industrial injuries benefits	If you have a personal injury at work or have a prescribed industrial disease	Non-contributory Non-means-tested	No
Jobseeker's allowance (contribution-based)	If you are not in full-time paid work and are available for and actively seeking work	Contributory Non-means-tested[iv]	Yes

Benefit or tax credit	When you might get it	Type of benefit	Taxable?
Jobseeker's allowance (income-based)	If you are on a low income and are not in full-time paid work and are available for and actively seeking work	Non-contributory Means-tested	Yes
Maternity allowance	If you are pregnant or have recently had a baby	Non-contributory Non-means-tested	No
Pension credit	Guarantee credit: if you have reached the qualifying age[v] and have a low income Savings credit: if you are 65 or over and have certain income other than just the state basic pension	Non-contributory Means-tested	No
Retirement pension	If you are over state pension age (currently 65 for men and 60 for women, but see Chapter 6 for how this will change)	Contributory Non-means-tested	Yes
Social fund	Discretionary fund: grants and loans for a variety of needs Regulated fund: grants for maternity costs, funeral expenses, cold weather and winter fuel	Non-contributory Means-tested	No
Statutory adoption pay	If you have just adopted a child	Paid by employer	Yes
Statutory maternity pay	If you are pregnant or have recently had a baby or adopted a child	Paid by employer	Yes
Statutory paternity pay	If your partner has recently had a baby	Paid by employer	Yes
Statutory sick pay	If you are an employee off work sick	Paid by employer	Yes
Widowed parent's allowance	If your spouse or civil partner has died and you have dependent children	Contributory[i] Non-means-tested	Yes

Benefit or tax credit	When you might get it	Type of benefit	Taxable?
Working tax credit	If you have a low income and you: – work 16 hours or more a week and you have a child/a disability and/or you are 50 or over returning to work after a period on certain benefits; or – are 25 or over and work 30 hours or more a week	Non-contributory Means-tested	No

[i] Based on your late partner's NI record.

[ii] You are not eligible if you have earnings of more than a set amount.

[iii] Reduced if you have a pension or health insurance of more than a set amount. You do not lose your right to claim if you do 'permitted work' or you are a local authority councillor, provided any earnings or allowance do not exceed set limits.

[iv] Any earnings of yours (but not your partner's) over £5 a week (£20 in limited cases) and any private pension over £50 a week are deducted from the amount of contribution-based JSA you get. If your earnings (but not pension) exceed £64.30 a week (in 2009/10), you cease to be entitled.

[v] The qualifying age is the state pension age for women. In 2009/10, this is 60, but will start to increase from April 2010 (see Chapter 6).

Who should think about benefits and tax credits

Relationships

If you have been claiming means-tested benefits as a single person, these may be reduced or stopped when you marry, enter a civil partnership or start to live with someone, depending on your partner's circumstances, income and capital. You may acquire new rights to contributory benefits – eg, bereavement benefits on the death of a spouse or civil partner (but not an unmarried partner).

If your relationship breaks down and you become a single person again, you may become eligible to start claiming or to increase your claim for tax credits. You might also be eligible for other state benefits, especially if your income will be low.

Lone parents

As a lone parent, it may be especially difficult to juggle work and family commitments. While your children are young, you might find it hard to work at all, in which case it is important to make sure you claim any state benefits and tax credits to which you are entitled – eg, child benefit, child tax credit, IS, HB and

CTB. When you feel ready to start work, you might benefit from joining the Gateway and New Deal programme (see p319).

If you are working, you may be able to claim working tax credit (WTC) to help with childcare costs and to top up your income if it is low. Alternatively, your employer might offer help with childcare arrangements or their costs, in which case this could be a tax-free fringe benefit (see Chapter 8).

Disability and caring

If you have a disability, you may be eligible for cash help and other benefits. Eligibility for the main disability benefits (DLA and AA) depends on the nature and severity of your disability. They do not depend on your having paid national insurance contributions and they are not means tested. Regardless of your income, you have the right to ask your local authority to carry out an assessment to identify your needs and appropriate types of personal care and/or other support. If your income is low, your local authority may pay for or help to fund these services; otherwise you are normally expected to pay for them yourself.

If you are a full-time carer (caring 35 hours a week or more), you may be able to claim CA (see p293). Carers also have the right to have a needs assessment which may, for example, suggest respite care or someone to sit with the disabled person while you have a couple of hours off each week.

Older people

If your pension and any other income are low, make sure you claim any benefits to which you are entitled, such as PC (see p306), HB (see p301) and CTB (see p294).

Many people find themselves 'asset rich, income poor' in older age. In particular, although your income might be low, you might own a valuable home. One way to improve your finances might be to take out an equity release scheme (see Chapter 5). But be very wary of equity release if you are eligible for means-tested state benefits, as the cash or income you release could reduce the benefits you can claim, leaving you no better off, or even worse off. Get advice from your local advice centre, Citizens Advice Bureau or housing advice centre before going ahead. See Appendix 2 for contact details.

Living and working abroad

If you are a British national, you and your family have the right to move freely around the European Economic Area (EEA) (see Appendix 1) to take up employment, work as a self-employed person or to provide or receive a service. While in another EEA state, you are entitled to the same social support as nationals of the country concerned. Contributions you have paid in the UK can help you qualify for benefits in other EEA countries and, in some situations, you may still receive UK benefits. In general, to qualify for benefits in another EEA state, you must have worked in that country even if only for a short period.

Since June 2002, Switzerland has also participated in the EEA arrangements although it is not an EEA member. The UK also has reciprocal agreements with some non-EEA countries which give access to state support while you are (legally) working there. In most other countries, you cannot expect state help and should be prepared to support yourself. For more information, see the free HM Revenue and Customs booklet NI38 *Social Security Abroad*.

If you are claiming UK benefits, such as IS, ESA, JSA and PC, your entitlement generally ends after you have been abroad for more than a specified period. However, you can have your state pension paid to you abroad whatever the length of your stay (see Chapter 6).

2. Benefits explained

This section provides a summary of each type of benefit in alphabetical order. Note that retirement pension is covered in Chapter 6. For tax credits see p314.

Adult dependant increases

If you are getting certain benefits, you may be able to claim an increase of that benefit in respect of your spouse or civil partner, or an adult dependant who is looking after your child. These are lost if the dependant has earnings over a certain amount (which varies depending on the benefit concerned).

Adult dependant increases in 2009/10

Benefit	Weekly increase
Carer's allowance[i]	£31.70
Incapacity benefit – long-term rate	£53.10
Incapacity benefit – short-term rate (under pension age)	£41.35
Incapacity benefit – short-term rate (over pension age)	£51.10
Maternity allowance[i]	£41.35
Retirement pension (see Chapter 6)[ii]	£57.05

[i] Expected to be abolished from 6 April 2010.

[ii] Abolished from 6 April 2010.

Child additions

With many non-means-tested benefits, you used to be able to claim an extra amount if you had one or more dependent children. Most of these additions have now been abolished although some people can continue to get an increase if they were entitled to it before the abolition. If you have a child, you should claim child benefit and child tax credit (CTC – see p315).

Attendance allowance

You may qualify for attendance allowance (AA) if you are aged 65 or over when you first claim and have a severe physical or mental disability. You must need:

- frequent help with personal care throughout the day;
- continual supervision throughout the day to avoid danger to yourself or others; *or*
- repeated or prolonged supervision at night to help with personal care or to avoid danger to yourself and others.

These are known as the 'disability conditions'.
You should bear the following in mind.

- You must satisfy the disability conditions for at least six months in the two years before your award begins. However, a claimant who is 'terminally ill' (ie, who is suffering from a progressive disease from which it would not be unexpected for her/him to die within six months) should be awarded the higher rate of AA immediately. This is known as a claim under the 'special rules'.
- If you are under 65 when you first claim, you might qualify for disability living allowance (DLA) instead of AA.
- AA may be awarded for a fixed or indefinite period.
- AA does not count as income for the purposes of calculating means-tested benefits and tax credits. In fact, entitlement to AA may give rise to an entitlement to these (or higher amounts if they are already being paid).
- Your capital and income do not affect the amount of AA you can be paid.

There are two rates of AA. You get the higher rate (£70.35 a week in 2009/10) if you need care or supervision during both day and night. Otherwise, you get the lower rate (£47.10 a week in 2009/10).

Bereavement benefits

You may qualify for bereavement benefits if you are a widow, widower or surviving civil partner. There are three main types of bereavement benefit:

- **bereavement payment** – a lump-sum payment of £2,000;
- **widowed parent's allowance** – a weekly benefit paid if you are a widow, widower or surviving civil partner with at least one child, or a widow or surviving civil partner who was pregnant at the time your husband or civil partner died (£95.25 a week in 2009/10);
- **bereavement allowance** – a weekly benefit paid for up to 52 weeks if you are a widow, widower or surviving civil partner who was 45 or over when your spouse or civil partner died (between £28.58 at 45 and £95.25 a week at 55, depending on your age).

Your late spouse or civil partner must have paid national insurance (NI) contributions, unless s/he died as a result of an industrial accident or disease.

You should bear the following in mind.

- To qualify for bereavement benefits, you must usually have been under state pension age when your spouse or civil partner died (currently 65 for men and 60 for women, but see Chapter 6 for how this will change). If you were over that age, you can still qualify for a bereavement payment if your spouse or civil partner was not yet entitled to retirement pension.
- Entitlement to bereavement allowance and widowed parent's allowance ends if you remarry or enter a new civil partnership. Payment of these is suspended if you are cohabiting.
- Bereavement allowance and widowed parent's allowance are affected by the 'overlapping benefit' rules (see p285). In addition, you cannot get both widowed parent's allowance and bereavement allowance at the same time.

When you reach state pension age

When you reach state pension age (currently 65 for men and 60 for women, but see Chapter 6 for how this will change), you can no longer receive widowed parent's allowance or bereavement allowance. Instead, you may qualify for retirement pension based on your, or your late spouse's or civil partner's, NI contributions. In either case, the retirement pension you get may be boosted by your own additional state pension and part of any additional state pension your late spouse or civil partner had built up. See Chapter 6 for more about retirement pensions.

If your spouse or civil partner died after you reached state pension age, you might qualify for retirement pension based on your and her/his contribution record. In addition, you can inherit part of her/his additional state pension.

Carer's allowance

You may qualify for carer's allowance (CA) if you spend regular and substantial time (35 hours a week or more) caring for someone who is in receipt of AA the middle or highest rate of DLA care component, or constant attendance allowance in respect of industrial or war disablement. This includes if you are caring for a relative or a member of your own family – eg, your partner or child.

You should bear the following in mind.

- Strictly speaking, CA is not means tested. However, you cannot get it if you count as in 'gainful employment'. You count as in gainful employment if you have earnings above a set limit (£95 a week in 2009/10). In working this out, you use your earnings net of tax and NI and half of any pension contributions. Some care and childcare costs can also be deducted.
- You cannot get CA if you are in full-time education.
- CA is affected by the 'overlapping benefit' rules (see p285).

- If you are entitled to CA (even if this is not paid because of the 'overlapping benefit' rules), you may be entitled to a carer premium if you claim income support (IS), income-related employment and support allowance (ESA), income-based jobseeker's allowance (JSA), housing benefit (HB) or council tax benefit (CTB) or a carer's additional amount if you claim pension credit (PC). If so, you are also entitled to a £20 earnings disregard when calculating these benefits. However, CA is taken into account in full as income for these benefits.

CA is paid at a single flat weekly rate (£53.10 a week in 2009/10). You might qualify for an extra amount for an adult dependant (see p291).

Before you claim carer's allowance

If you are a carer and you get CA, any means-tested benefits of the person for whom you are caring may be affected. Your CA prevents that person receiving a severe disability premium with her/his IS, income-related ESA, income-based JSA, HB and CTB or a severe disability additional amount with her/his PC. Therefore, careful consideration must be given, or specialist advice sought, *before* you claim CA.

Child benefit

You may qualify for child benefit if you are responsible for a child or qualifying young person (a young person under 20 – or 19 in some cases – who is still your dependant – eg, because s/he is still in school). You count as responsible for a child or qualifying young person if s/he lives with you, or you contribute to her/his maintenance at a rate of at least the child benefit rate.

You should bear the following in mind.
- Child benefit can be paid whatever your income and whether or not you are in or out of work.
- Child benefit is paid in addition to other benefits and tax credits. However, for IS and income-based JSA, it counts as income if you are not getting CTC. Otherwise, it is disregarded as income for means-tested benefits and tax credits.
- You can continue to get child benefit until your child reaches 20, provided certain conditions are met. This includes if your child is enrolled on a course of full-time non-advanced education or is in approved training.

Child benefit is paid at a flat rate (£20 a week for your eldest child and £13.20 for each other child in 2009/10).

Council tax benefit

You may qualify for CTB if you are liable for council tax. Depending on your income, CTB may mean you have no council tax to pay (full CTB) or only a reduced amount. There are two types of CTB. You can qualify for:

- 'main CTB' if you satisfy the means test; *or*
- 'second adult rebate' if you are the only person liable for council tax in your home and an adult on a low income lives with you. It does not matter how much income or capital *you* have or whether you are working.

You should bear the following in mind.
- You are passported to full main CTB automatically if you are getting IS, income-related ESA, income-based JSA or the guarantee credit of PC, though you have to make a separate claim.
- If you are not getting IS, income-related ESA, income-based JSA or the guarantee credit of PC, you can qualify for main CTB if you have capital below a set limit (see p312).
- Your main CTB might be reduced if you have any non-dependants living with you – eg, a relative or friend.

Even if you do not qualify for CTB, you might qualify for a reduction in your council tax bill – eg, if you are the only adult living in your household (25 per cent reduction) and/or you have a disability for which the house has special features (in which case the property is taxed as if it is one band below its actual band). These discounts are not means tested.

Disability living allowance

You may qualify for DLA if you are under 65 when you first start to claim and have a severe physical or mental disability. DLA has two components.
To qualify for the **'care component'** you must:
- need frequent help with personal care throughout the day;
- need continual supervision throughout the day to avoid danger to yourself or others; *or*
- need repeated or prolonged supervision at night to help with personal care or to avoid danger to yourself and others; *or*
- be unable to prepare a main meal for yourself – known as the 'cooking test'.

To qualify for the **'mobility component'** you must be unable to walk, have great difficulty walking, or walking must be a danger to your life or health, or you must need supervision on unfamiliar routes.
These are known as the 'disability conditions'.
You should bear the following in mind.
- You can get one or both components if you satisfy the relevant conditions.
- You must satisfy the disability conditions for at least three months before the start of your award and be likely to continue to satisfy them for at least the next six months. However, a claimant who is terminally ill should be awarded the higher rate of DLA care component immediately. This is known as a claim under the 'special rules'.

- Children can claim DLA. They can get DLA mobility component at the higher rate from age three and at the lower rate from age five. There is no lower age limit for DLA care component, but you cannot qualify via the 'cooking test' until you are 16.
- If you are 65 when you first claim, you might qualify for AA instead of DLA (see p292). However, if you are already getting DLA when you reach 65, you can carry on getting it.
- DLA may be awarded for a fixed or indefinite period.
- DLA does not count as income for the purposes of calculating means-tested benefits and tax credits. In fact, entitlement to DLA may give rise to an entitlement to these (or higher amounts if they are already being paid).
- Your capital and income do not affect the amount of DLA you can be paid.

DLA care component is paid at three rates. You get the highest rate if you need help with care or supervision during both day and night. You get the middle rate if you need care or supervision either at night or during the day but not both. The lowest rate applies if you need limited care during the day (eg, getting up or going to bed) or you cannot prepare yourself a main meal.

DLA mobility component is paid at two rates. You get the higher rate if you cannot walk at all or walking is very difficult and the lower rate if you can walk but need supervision. The Government has said that from a future date (expected to be April 2011), people with serious sight loss will be able to qualify for the higher (rather than lower) rate DLA mobility component.[5]

Weekly rates of disability living allowance in 2009/10

Care component	
Highest rate	£70.35
Middle rate	£47.10
Lowest rate	£18.65
Mobility component	
Higher rate	£49.10
Lower rate	£18.65

Employment and support allowance

You may qualify for ESA if you cannot work because of an illness or disability – you must have what the DWP calls 'limited capability for work'. ESA replaced incapacity benefit (IB) and IS on the grounds of disability for most new claims made since 27 October 2008. If you first claimed before then, you can continue to get IB (see p301) or IS (see p302). You may be able to opt into the ESA scheme – before you do, seek advice to check whether you would be better off.

If you are an employee, you usually claim statutory sick pay (see p310) for the first 28 weeks of illness rather than ESA. If you are self-employed, you claim ESA. There are two ways to qualify for ESA.

- You qualify for contributory ESA if you satisfy the NI contribution conditions or you were under 20 (under 25 in some cases) when you first had limited capability for work. You satisfy the NI contribution conditions if you have paid enough contributions or have been credited as if you had paid them. Strictly speaking, contributory ESA is not means tested. However, the amount you get can be reduced if you have an income from certain pensions or health insurance. Moreover, although you can do 'permitted work' or work as a local authority councillor, you lose the right to claim if any earnings or allowance exceed set limits. You cannot get extra contributory ESA for your partner.
- You qualify for income-related ESA if your income and savings are low. Income-related ESA can be paid on its own or with contributory ESA. Your income (and that of your partner if you have one) affects the amount of income-related ESA you get. You may be eligible for extra income-related ESA if you have a partner.

To qualify for either type of ESA, you must be aged between 16 and state pension age (currently 65 for men and 60 for women but see Chapter 6 for how this will change from April 2010).

You cannot get ESA for the first three days of illness (called waiting days). After seven days of illness, you must supply a sick note from your doctor. You get a basic rate of ESA during the first 13 weeks of your claim, called the 'assessment phase'. During this phase, you must take part in a 'work capability assessment' which explores how your illness or disability affects your ability to work and whether it is reasonable to expect you to work. The assessment may involve completing a questionnaire and/or attending a medical examination.

After the assessment phase, you move onto the 'main phase' of ESA and get a higher allowance. As a result of the assessment, you are put into one of two groups: the work-related activity group or the support group.

If you are in the work-related activity group, you must attend a work-focused interview and are expected, with the help of a personal adviser, to prepare for and seek work that is appropriate given your degree of illness or disability.

You are put into the support group if your illness or disability is so severe that you are not expected to work. You can, if you want to, volunteer to take part in work-related activities.

During the assessment phase, contributory ESA is paid at a flat rate (£64.30 a week during 2009/10 if you are 25 or over, £50.95 if you are under 25). During the main phase, contributory ESA is paid at a flat rate of £64.30 (whether you are under or over 25). In addition during the main phase you get either a work-related activity component (£25.50 a week in 2009/10) or a support component (£30.85 a week in 2009/10), depending on the group you are in.

Income-related ESA tops up your income to a set level. You may qualify for an extra amount to help you pay eligible housing costs (see p311).

You may be able to earn a limited amount each week without it affecting your entitlement to ESA (but see p313). However, your earnings may reduce the amount of ESA you can get. You cannot get income-related ESA if your partner is in full-time paid work (see p317 for what this means). Her/his earnings affect the amount of income-related ESA you can get.

You should bear the following in mind.

- Your ESA can be paid at a reduced rate if you do not co-operate with preparing for and seeking work, but you cannot be forced to do work that is inappropriate given your state of health.
- Strictly speaking, contributory ESA is not means tested. However, if you get an income from a pension scheme or plan or an income protection insurance policy (see Chapter 7), your contributory ESA is reduced by 50p for each £1 by which this income exceeds a set amount (£85 a week in 2009/10).
- Contributory ESA is affected by the 'overlapping benefit' rules (see p285).
- You can get income-related ESA in addition to contributory ESA in some circumstances – eg, to meet eligible housing costs (see p311), if your income is low.
- You cannot get income-related ESA if you have capital over a set level (see p312).
- If you are a member of a couple, one of you claims income-related ESA for both of you.

Income-related ESA does not cover your rent and council tax, but instead you may be able to claim HB and CTB (see pp301 and 294). If you get income-related ESA, you automatically qualify for these.

Free school meals

Your children are entitled to free school meals if you receive:
- IS, income-based JSA or income-related ESA;
- CTC (but not working tax credit – WTC) and have annual taxable income of £16,040 or less in 2009/10 (or, in Scotland only, CTC with maximum WTC);
- WTC during a four-week 'WTC run-on' (see p317). In Scotland, this only applies if you get maximum CTC;
- guarantee credit of PC (in England and Wales only). In Scotland, children may qualify if you receive CTC, as above.

Also entitled are:
- 16–18-year-olds receiving any of the above benefits or tax credits in their own right;

- asylum seekers in receipt of support provided under Part VI of the Immigration and Asylum Act 1999.

Individual local authorities may make free school meals more widely available.

Guardian's allowance

You may qualify for guardian's allowance if you are entitled to child benefit for an 'eligible child'. A child is eligible if both her/his parents have died, or one has died and the whereabouts of the other is unknown, or one has died and the other has been sentenced to a term of imprisonment of two years or more or is detained in hospital by a court order.

Guardian's allowance is paid at a flat rate (£14.10 a week in 2009/10).

Health benefits

You may qualify for various benefits related to health. These include the following.

- **Free prescriptions.** You qualify if you:
  - are pregnant or have given birth in the last 12 months;
  - are under 16, or under 19 if in full-time education;
  - are aged 60 or over;
  - have certain medical conditions;
  - are undergoing treatment for cancer, the effects of cancer or the effects of cancer treatment (in England);
  - receive IS, income-related ESA, income-based JSA or the guarantee credit of PC;
  - are on a low income;
  - are an NHS hospital inpatient.

  There are also a few other situations in which you may qualify. Certain tax credit recipients are also exempted from prescription charges. Contraceptives are free for everyone, regardless of income. **Note:** prescriptions are free for everyone in Wales. This will also be the case from 2010 in Northern Ireland and from 2011 in Scotland.

- **Free dental treatment.** You qualify if you:
  - are pregnant or have given birth in the last 12 months;
  - are under age 18, or under 19 if in full-time education;
  - receive IS, income-related ESA, income-based JSA or the guarantee credit of PC;
  - are on a low income.

  There are also a few other situations in which you may qualify. Certain tax credit recipients also qualify. **Note:** NHS dental check-ups are free for everyone in Scotland and, in Wales, if you are under 25 or over 60.

- **Free sight tests.** You qualify if you:

- are under 16 or under 19 and in full-time education;
- receive IS, income-related ESA, income-based JSA or the guarantee credit of PC;
- are on a low income;
- are registered blind or partially sighted;
- have prescribed complex lenses;
- have diabetes or glaucoma or are told you are at risk of developing glaucoma, or are aged 40 or over and related to someone with glaucoma.

There are also a few other situations in which you may qualify. Certain tax credit recipients also qualify. **Note:** NHS sight tests are free in Scotland.

- **Vouchers towards the cost of glasses or contact lenses**. You qualify if:
  - you are under 16, or under 19 and in full-time education;
  - you receive IS, income-related ESA, income-based JSA or the guarantee credit of PC;
  - your eyesight changes often making your current glasses or contact lenses inadequate;
  - you are prescribed complex lenses;
  - you are on a low income.

  There are also a few other situations in which you may qualify. Certain tax credit recipients also qualify.

- **Travel to and from hospital for treatment.** You can reclaim the full cost of travelling by the cheapest means if you:
  - receive IS, income-related ESA, income-based JSA or the guarantee credit of PC;
  - are on a low income.

  There are also a few other situations in which you may qualify. Certain tax credit recipients also qualify.

- **Healthy Start food and vitamins.** This scheme provides vouchers which can be exchanged for healthy foods, such as fresh fruit and vegetables and milk. If you qualify for Healthy Start food vouchers, you also qualify for free vitamins. You qualify if you are pregnant or have a child under one (or it is less than a year since her/his expected date of birth) or are a child under four. Unless you are under 18 and pregnant, the family must be entitled to IS, income-related ESA or income-based JSA, or CTC (but not WTC) and with an annual taxable income of £16,040 or less in 2009/10. In addition, children up to age five being looked after by certain childminders, daycare providers, schools and nurseries receive free milk (this is provided by the welfare food scheme, not Healthy Start).

Health in pregnancy grant

This is a cash lump sum of £190 (in 2009/10) if you are pregnant. You can use the money in any way you like, but it is intended to help you with the costs of preparing to have your baby. You can claim once you have reached the 25th week of your pregnancy, provided you have been receiving health advice from a midwife or your doctor who usually provides you with the claim form and must fill in part of it. You get just one grant per pregnancy (even if you are expecting twins).

Housing benefit

You may qualify for HB if you live in rented accommodation and satisfy the means test.

You should bear the following in mind.

- You are passported to full HB automatically if you are getting IS, income-related ESA, income-based JSA or the guarantee credit of PC, though you have to make a separate claim.
- If you are not getting IS, income-related ESA, income-based JSA or the guarantee credit of PC, you can qualify for HB if you have capital below a set limit (see p312).
- Your HB might be reduced if you have a non-dependant living with you (eg, a relative or friend).
- HB can be paid direct to your landlord in some circumstances.
- If you are in private rented accommodation, your HB can be restricted if your rent exceeds a locally set rate based on average rents in your area. If your actual rent comes to more than the HB you get, you have to meet the shortfall.
- You can get help with some of the service charges you have to pay, but you cannot get HB for some things included in your rent, such as fuel payments and meal charges.

Housing payments (discretionary)

If you need financial assistance in addition to your HB and CTB, you might qualify for discretionary housing payments to top these up. They are paid by your local authority from a cash-limited budget, so even if you have a strong case, there is no guarantee you will receive assistance. Your local authority has the discretion to decide whether to pay you, how much and for how long.

Incapacity benefit

If you cannot work because of illness or disability and started to claim benefit before 27 October 2008, you may be getting IB. You can continue getting IB, but the Government has indicated that, at some stage, IB claimants will move onto the new ESA scheme. Before then, you may be able to switch to ESA. Before you do, you should seek advice about whether you would be better off.

The general rule is that it is no longer possible to make a new claim for IB and you have to claim ESA instead (see p296). However, you might be able to claim –

eg, if you were previously entitled to IB or if you are getting IS on the grounds of disability (eg, because you are incapable of work or are registered blind).

You must have paid NI contributions to qualify for IB unless you became incapable of work in youth (ie, before you were 20, or 25 in some circumstances).

You must be (or be treated as) incapable of work to get IB.

- If you have a regular occupation, for the first 28 weeks of your claim you are treated as incapable of work if you cannot do your normal job. This is known as the **'own occupation test'**.
- After the first 28 weeks of your claim (or from the start if you do not have a regular occupation), your capacity for work is assessed under the **'personal capability assessment'**.

Under the personal capability assessment, initially you fill in a detailed questionnaire. This is usually followed with a medical examination. You can also be 'deemed to be incapable of work' – eg, if you are a hospital inpatient.

You should bear the following in mind.

- Strictly speaking, IB is not means tested. However, unless you get the highest rate of DLA care component, if you get an income from a pension scheme or plan or an income protection insurance policy (see Chapter 7), your IB is reduced by 50p for each £1 by which this income exceeds a set amount (£85 a week in 2009/10).
- IB is affected by the 'overlapping benefit' rules (see p285).

There are three rates of IB depending on the amount of time you have been incapable of work.

- Short-term IB at the lower rate (£67.75 a week in 2009/10, £86.20 if you are over pension age) is payable for the first 28 weeks of illness (excluding the first three days).
- Short-term IB at the higher rate (£80.15 a week in 2009/10, £89.80 if you are over pension age) is payable for the next 24 weeks (with some exceptions – see below).
- Long-term IB (£89.80 a week in 2009/10) is payable after 52 weeks (or 28 weeks if you are terminally ill or you get the highest rate DLA care component). An 'age addition' is also payable if you were under age 45 when your current period of incapacity for work began.

You might qualify for an extra amount for an adult dependant (see p291).

Income support

You may qualify for IS if you are on a low income and not required to be available for work – eg, because you are a lone parent or caring for someone who is severely disabled. Note that from 26 October 2009, you cannot make a new claim for IS as a lone parent unless you have a child under 10, and this age limit will reduce to seven from 25 October 2010. If you do not fit into any of the categories of people who can claim IS, you might qualify for ESA or JSA (see p303) instead. If you are over the qualifying age for PC (see p306), you cannot claim IS and should claim PC.

You might be getting IS if you are incapable of work because you are sick or disabled. You can continue to claim IS on this basis. However, the general rule is that it is no longer possible to make a new claim for IS 'on the grounds of disability' and you must claim ESA instead. However, you might be able to claim – eg, if you were previously entitled to IS 'on the grounds of disability' or if you are getting IB.

You cannot get IS if you (or your partner) are in full-time paid work (see p317 for what this means). You can work part time and claim IS, but your earnings reduce the amount you get. However, see p318 if you are claiming IS because you are incapable of work.

You should bear the following in mind.
- You cannot get IS if you have capital over a set level (see p312).
- If you are a member of a couple, one of you claims for both of you.
- IS tops up your income to a set level. You may qualify for an extra amount to help you pay eligible housing costs (see p311).

IS does not cover your rent and council tax, but instead you may be able to claim HB and CTB (see pp301 and 294). If you get IS, you automatically qualify for these.

Industrial injuries benefits

You may qualify for industrial injuries benefits if:
- while working as an employee you have a personal injury; *or*
- you have a prescribed industrial disease contracted during the course of your employment.

You should bear the following in mind.
- You must have experienced a 'loss of faculty' and be disabled as a result of this.
- Industrial injuries benefits generally count as income for the purposes of calculating means-tested benefits. They are generally disregarded as income for tax credits. Entitlement to industrial injuries benefits may give rise to an entitlement to these (or higher amounts if they are already being paid).

Jobseeker's allowance

You may qualify for JSA if you are under state pension age (currently 65 for men and 60 for women, but see Chapter 6 for how this will change) and are available for and actively seeking work. You cannot get JSA if you (or your partner) are in full-time paid work (see p317 for what this means). You can work part time and claim JSA, but your earnings reduce the amount you get.

There are two main types of JSA.

- To qualify for contribution-based JSA you must have recently paid NI contributions.
- Income-based JSA is means tested.

A third type of JSA, joint-claim JSA, is very similar to income-based JSA. You must usually claim this type of JSA if you are a member of a couple without children and at least one of you is 18 or over and born after 28 October 1947. References in this chapter to income-based JSA are also references to joint-claim JSA unless otherwise stated.

You should bear the following in mind.

- When you claim JSA, you have to attend an interview and sign a jobseeker's agreement setting out the steps you intend to take to get back into work.
- You have to sign on regularly and tell the Jobcentre Plus office what steps you have taken to find work. You also have to attend regular interviews as required.
- You can be sanctioned – eg, if you give up a job or place on an employment scheme voluntarily or are dismissed from a job because of misconduct. If so, your JSA can be stopped or paid at a reduced rate for a period. In this case you might qualify for what are known as hardship payments. You have the right to appeal against decisions to sanction you, the length of the sanction period and whether you qualify for hardship payments.
- You can get both contribution-based and income-based JSA at the same time.
- You cannot get income-based JSA if you have capital over a set level (see p312).
- If you are a member of a couple, one of you claims income-based JSA for both of you. If you have to claim joint-claim JSA, both of you must claim.
- Special rules apply if you are 16 or 17 years old.
- Income-based JSA tops up your income to a set level. You may qualify for an extra amount to help you pay eligible housing costs (see p311).
- You can only get contribution-based JSA for 182 days. However, income-based JSA can be paid indefinitely.

JSA does not cover your rent and council tax, but you may be able to claim HB and CTB (see pp301 and 294). If you get income-based JSA, you automatically qualify for these.

Contribution-based JSA is paid at a flat rate (in 2009/10, £64.30 a week if you are 25 or over, £50.95 if you are under 25). This may be reduced if you get an occupational or personal pension or have earnings from part-time work.

Long-term care

If you have care needs you might qualify for cash help through DLA (see p295) or AA (see p292). Local authorities also administer a range of other help, such as:

- equipment and adaptations to help you cope at home;
- carers who visit to help with, for instance, getting up and going to bed;
- a sitting service to give your own carer a break;
- meals on wheels;
- day centres.

Local authorities differ on the extent to which many of these services are means tested or are available free to all. Regardless of your income and capital, you have a right to ask your local authority to carry out an **'assessment of needs'** to determine the most appropriate care plan for you.

If you can no longer manage at home, you may be offered a place in a residential or nursing home. If you are discharged from hospital into a nursing home, the NHS might be required to pay the full cost. Otherwise the cost of nursing in a care home can be met by the local authority, but you might have to pay a contribution towards the charges. In Scotland, but not the rest of the UK, personal care is also paid for by the state up to a given maximum. Help with the remaining cost of living in a care home (bed and board and, outside Scotland, personal care) is means tested, so you must pay some or all of the cost unless your income and capital are low. See p313 for information about the capital limits.

If your local authority funds your care home place, it only pays up to a standard rate. This is likely to limit your choice of home.

Direct payments, personal budgets and individual budgets

If you are eligible for help from your local social services department because you have a disability or you are a carer, you must be offered the option of receiving 'direct payments'. This means that, instead of your local authority arranging the services you need, you get a cash sum. It is then up to you to choose the provider of the services you need and contract it direct. Although this gives you increased choice and control, it can also mean added responsibilities and administration. For example, if you contract someone to come in each day to help you get up and go to bed, her/his employment status may mean you become her/his employer and are thus responsible for paying the national minimum wage and operating a payroll system to pay her/his wages and collect tax and national insurance. You can employ a payroll agency to do this and some local authorities will recommend firms.

From 2008 to 2011, local councils are required to put in place a system of personal budgets. This means funds will be allocated to an account in your name to be used to buy the social services you need. However, either you can take the funds as direct payments (cash) or you can choose the providers but leave the local authority to commission them, or a combination of both.

Individual budgets are similar to personal budgets, but combine in one account funding for care services with funding from other sources to pay, for example, for adaptations to your home, for equipment to help you live more easily at home and to help you into work. Individual budgets have been piloted in 13 local authority areas and at some stage will be rolled out nationally.

Maternity allowance

You may qualify for maternity allowance (MA) if you are pregnant or have recently given birth. If you are an employee, you usually get statutory maternity pay (SMP – see p309) but, if you are self-employed or unemployed, you can claim MA instead. You must have been an employee or self-employed for at least 26 of the 66 weeks before the week in which your baby is due. Your average weekly earnings must be at least a minimum amount (£30 a week in 2009/10).

You should bear the following in mind.

- MA is affected by the 'overlapping benefit' rules (see p285). In addition, you cannot get contribution-based JSA or statutory sick pay (SSP) if you are getting MA.
- The earliest you can claim MA is after the 15th week before your baby is due, although payment cannot begin until the 11th week before your baby is due, unless your baby is born before this.
- In some cases, it may be worth delaying a claim (if practicable) if that means you will have higher average earnings. Remember there are strict time limits for claiming.

MA is paid at the lower of a standard rate (£123.06 a week in 2009/10) and 90 per cent of your average weekly earnings. You might qualify for an extra amount for an adult dependant (see p291). It is payable for a maximum of 39 weeks.

Pension credit

You may qualify for PC if you are on a low income and you have reached the qualifying age. If you are a woman, this is pension age. If you are a man, this is the pension age for a woman born on the same day as you. The qualifying age for both men and women is currently 60, but see Chapter 6 for how this will change from April 2010.

PC is made up of a guarantee credit and, if you or your partner are 65 or over and have qualifying income over retirement pension level (eg, an occupational or personal pension), a savings credit. The guarantee credit ensures that you have at least a minimum amount to live on (in 2009/10 £130 a week if you are single and £198.45 a week for a couple). The guarantee credit tops up your income to a set level – known as your appropriate minimum guarantee. You may qualify for an extra amount to help you pay eligible housing costs (see p311).

You get 60p of savings credit for each £1 of qualifying income above a set threshold (in 2009/10 £96 a week if you are single and £153.40 for a couple) up to a maximum amount (in 2009/10 £20.40 a week if you are single and £27.03 a week if you are a couple). But you lose 40p of this credit for every £1 of total income (not just qualifying income) over your appropriate minimum guarantee. You should bear the following in mind.

- There is no capital limit for PC, but if you have capital over a certain level, you are deemed to have income from the capital.
- If you are a member of a couple, one of you claims for both of you.
- You might think it is not worth claiming PC if you are only going to get a small amount. However, it is worth making a claim because even if you only get a small award of the guarantee credit you are passported to other benefits, such as health benefits and the social fund. Even if you do not get the guarantee credit but get the savings credit you have access to payments from the social fund.

PC does not cover your rent and council tax, but you may be able to claim HB and CTB (see pp301 and 294). If you get the guarantee credit of PC, you automatically qualify for these.

Social fund

Discretionary fund

You can apply for loans or grants from the discretionary social fund. Payments are made from a cash-limited fund. If you are refused, you can challenge the decision by asking for a review. You can apply for:

- a **community care grant** to help meet the cost of starting or continuing to live independently in the community. It does not have to be repaid;
- a **budgeting loan** for specified types of expenses, such as minor home repairs or an item of household equipment. You have to repay this, usually through weekly deductions from any benefit you receive, but it is interest-free;
- a **crisis loan** to help meet an urgent need. You have to repay this, usually through weekly deductions from any benefit you receive, but it is interest free.

You should bear the following in mind.

- To get a community care grant, you must usually be getting IS, income-related ESA, income-based JSA or PC when your application is treated as made. Any grant is reduced by capital you have above £500 (£1,000 if you or your partner are 60 or over in 2009/10 – this age limit is expected to increase from April 2010 in line with the increase in women's state pension age – see Chapter 6).
- To get a budgeting loan, you must be getting IS, income-related ESA, income-based JSA or PC when a decision is made on your application. In addition, you or your partner must have been receiving one of those benefits for 26 weeks (certain breaks are disregarded). Any loan you get is reduced by capital you have above £1,000 (£2,000 if you or your partner are 60 or over in 2009/10 – this age limit is expected to increase from April 2010 – see Chapter 6).

- To get a crisis loan, you must show that you need help to meet expenses in an emergency or for rent in advance. You do not have to be getting any specific benefit to qualify. You must be likely to be able to repay the loan.

Regulated fund

This differs from the discretionary fund in that the decisions are not based on discretion. If you satisfy the rules, you are entitled to a payment. You have to be in receipt of a qualifying benefit. If you are refused a payment, you have the right to appeal against the decision. You can apply for the following payments.

- **Sure Start maternity grant.** This is a £500 lump sum payable to people on a low income to help with the costs of a new baby (expected, born, adopted or where you have a residence order or a parental order). It is available if you (or your partner) are getting IS, income-related ESA, income-based JSA, CTC of more than just the family element, or WTC including the disability or severe disability element. You can receive this grant as well as the health in pregnancy grant (see p300).
- **Funeral payment. This is a** lump sum to cover the basic costs of a simple funeral plus up to £700 to cover other funeral expenses. It can be claimed if you are responsible for the funeral arrangements and you are receiving IS, income-related ESA, income-based JSA, PC, HB, CTB, CTC of more than just the family element, or WTC including the disability or severe disability element. The payment may be recovered from any money or assets left by the person who died.
- **Cold weather payment**. This is a small payment (£8.50, but the Government has indicated that it will be £25 in 2009/10) for each week of very cold weather (with average temperatures below freezing). It is available to people getting PC, IS, income-related ESA or income-based JSA. For those getting IS, income-related ESA or income-based JSA, the benefit has to include an extra amount – eg, because of disability or because you are a pensioner, or you must be responsible for a child under five, or get CTC which includes a disability or severe disability element.
- **Winter fuel payment. This is** a lump sum payment to help you pay your fuel bills, although in practice you can spend it in any way you choose. In 2009/10 it is £250 for a single person or £125 to each member of a couple (£400/£200 if you or your partner are aged 80 or over). You must be at least the qualifying age for PC (see p306) to qualify. It is usually paid automatically.

Statutory adoption pay

You may qualify for statutory adoption pay (SAP) if you are (or have recently been) an employee and you take adoption leave. Your average gross weekly earnings must be equal to or above the NI 'lower earnings' limit (£95 in 2009/10) and you must have worked for the same employer for more than 26 continuous weeks by the end of the week in which you are notified that you have been matched for adoption.

You should bear the following in mind.

- SAP can be paid to both men and women.
- If you have a partner, s/he may qualify for statutory paternity pay (SPP – see p310).
- You cannot get contribution-based JSA while you are on ordinary adoption leave. You cannot receive SAP for any week in which you are also entitled to SSP.
- You must give your employer relevant notice and information within a strict time limit.
- Entitlement to SAP does not depend on you deciding to return to work.
- Payment of SAP can start up to 14 days before you expect your child to be placed with you. It is paid to you in the same way as your normal pay (through PAYE with tax and NI already deducted – see Chapter 8).

SAP is paid at the lower of a standard rate (£123.06 a week in 2009/10) and 90 per cent of your average weekly earnings pay. It is payable for a maximum of 39 weeks. If the adoption falls through, payment can end early.

Statutory maternity pay

You may qualify for statutory maternity pay (SMP) if you are (or have recently been) an employee and you take maternity leave. Your average gross weekly earnings must be at least equal to the lower earnings limit (£95 in 2009/10) and you must have worked continuously for your employer for 26 weeks up to and including the 15th week (called the 'qualifying week') before the week in which your baby is due.

You should bear the following in mind.

- If you do not qualify for SMP, you may be able to claim MA instead (see p306).
- If you have a partner, s/he may qualify for SPP (see p310).
- You must give your employer relevant notice and information within a strict time limit.
- Entitlement to SMP does not depend on you deciding to return to work.
- You cannot get contribution-based JSA or SSP if you are getting SMP.
- Payment of SMP can start from the 11th week before the week your baby is due (or earlier if your baby is born before this). Payments must start no later than the Sunday after your baby is born. It is paid to you in the same way as your normal pay (through PAYE with tax and NI already deducted – see Chapter 8).

SMP is paid for a maximum of 39 weeks. For the first six weeks, you get a higher rate set at 90 per cent of your average weekly earnings during the eight weeks up to the qualifying week and a further 33 weeks at the lower of a standard rate (£123.06 a week in 2009/10) and 90 per cent of your average weekly earnings.

These are the minimum amounts of maternity pay you must be given – your employer might operate a more generous scheme.

Statutory paternity pay

You may qualify for SPP if you are (or have recently been) an employee and are taking paternity leave because your partner has just given birth. You can also get SPP if you are adopting a child and your partner is claiming SAP (see p308).

You must have worked continuously for your employer for at least 26 weeks up to the 15th week before the week in which the baby is due or in the case of adoption, for at least 26 weeks up to the week in which you or your partner have been notified of a match with a child. You must also have average earnings of at least the lower earnings limit (£95 in 2009/10). You must still be employed by the same employer at the time of the birth (or at the time the child is placed with you for adoption).

You should bear the following in mind.
* SPP can be paid to both men and women.
* You cannot get contribution-based JSA while you are on paternity leave. You cannot receive SPP for any week in which you are also entitled to SSP.
* You must give your employer relevant notice and information within a strict time limit.
* Entitlement to SPP does not depend on you deciding to return to work.
* SPP can only be paid once your baby is born (or your child is placed with you for adoption) and must be paid by the 56th day after the birth (or the date the birth was originally expected if the baby is premature) or adoption. It is paid to you in the same way as your normal pay (through PAYE with tax and NI already deducted – see Chapter 8).

SPP is payable for a maximum of two consecutive weeks at the lower of a standard rate (£123.06 a week in 2009/10) and 90 per cent of average weekly earnings.

Statutory sick pay

You may qualify for SSP if you are an employee and are off work sick for at least four consecutive days. You must have average earnings of at least equal to the lower earnings limit (£95 in 2009/10). If you do not qualify for SSP, you might qualify for IS, ESA or IB (see pp302, 296 and 301).

You should bear the following in mind.
* SSP is not paid during the first three days of illness.
* You cannot get ESA or IB while you are entitled to SSP. You cannot get contribution-based JSA, SMP, SAP, SPP or MA if you are getting SSP.
* You may be able to claim IS to top up your SSP if your income and capital are sufficiently low.
* SSP is the minimum sick pay required by law. Your employer may operate a more generous scheme.

- SSP is paid to you in the same way as your normal pay (through PAYE with tax and NI already deducted – see Chapter 8).

SSP is paid at a standard rate (£79.15 a week in 2009/10) for a maximum of 28 weeks for each episode of illness. If you are still off work sick after that, you may then qualify for ESA or, in some cases, IB (see pp296 and 301).

3. **How means tests work**

There are a number of rules that are common to all the means-tested benefits. They include:
- formulae for calculating how much benefit you can get. Your entitlement is worked out by comparing your needs with your income (see p313). Help with eligible housing costs can be included with income support (IS), income-related employment and support allowance (ESA), income-based jobseeker's allowance (JSA) and pension credit (PC);
- rules for how your income and capital are calculated and what is taken into account.

Means-tested benefits have similar ways of taking account of your needs. These involve taking a basic allowance for you and your partner if you have one (or, in the case of housing benefit (HB) and council tax benefit (CTB), for each member of the family) and then adding on additional amounts to take account of extra expenses you may have because of your or your partner's circumstances (and for HB and CTB, your children's circumstances) and any eligible housing costs if you are a home owner (see below). This figure is called your **'applicable amount'** (or for the guarantee credit of pension credit (PC), your 'appropriate minimum guarantee'). Your needs are then compared with your total resources – your income and capital.

Once your needs and your income have been calculated, your benefit entitlement can be worked out. In the case of IS, income-related ESA, income-based JSA, and PC, this is done simply by deducting your income from your needs. In the cases of HB and CTB, there are more complicated formulae which also have to take into account the amount of your rent or council tax. If you have a non-dependant living with you, the amount of HB/CTB or housing costs (see below) within your IS, income-related ESA, income-based JSA or PC may be reduced.

Eligible housing costs

If you are a homeowner, help with some of your housing costs can be included in your IS, income-related ESA, income-based JSA applicable amount or your PC appropriate minimum guarantee. Costs that can be covered include help with the interest on a mortgage or eligible home improvement loan, ground rent and some service charges.

You should bear the following in mind.

- The amount you get is based on a standard rate of interest, not the rate you have to pay.
- The amount you get might be reduced if you have a non-dependant living with you – eg, a relative or friend.
- The amount you get may be reduced if your loans exceed an upper limit (£200,000 for many new claims for IS, income-related ESA and income-based JSA since 4 January 2009; £100,000 in most other cases). If you are claiming PC, the £200,000 upper limit can apply in limited cases.
- The amount you get may be reduced if your costs are considered excessive, or if you took out your loan while on IS, income-related ESA, JSA or PC (or certain periods between claims).
- Payment may be made directly to your lender.
- If you are claiming IS, income-related ESA or income-based JSA, the amount for housing costs is not usually paid until you have been claiming for a number of weeks – known as a 'waiting period' (usually 13 weeks for new claims after 4 January 2009, but it can be longer than this). If you or your partner are at least the qualifying age for PC (see p306) when you first claim, your housing costs can be included straight away. There are a number of situations when you can be treated as entitled to IS, ESA or JSA for these purposes. You should seek advice to see if these apply to you.

Capital

You cannot get means-tested benefits if your capital (together with that of your partner) comes to more than an upper limit. For PC there is no upper capital limit, but you may be deemed to have income from capital under the 'tariff income' rules (see the table below). Capital below a specified lower limit is ignored. Any capital between the two limits is deemed to produce a certain amount of income, called '**tariff income**'. This tariff income counts towards your income for the purpose of working out the benefit you get. See the table on p313 for further information.

Capital includes:
- cash;
- your balance in any current accounts and savings accounts with banks and building societies;
- the value of any National Savings and Investments products, including premium bonds;
- the value of any shares, gilts, bonds, unit trusts.

The value of your home, personal possessions or the surrender value of any life insurance policies are not taken into account.

If you own assets jointly with someone other than your partner, just your share of the capital is taken into account. This is taken to be the value of the asset divided by the number of owners, regardless of your actual share.

You cannot get around the capital limit by giving your capital away or going on a spending spree. Under what is known as the 'notional capital' rule, you can be treated as still owning the capital if it is decided that you have deliberately deprived yourself of it in order to claim benefits or increase the amount to which you are entitled.

Capital limits for means-tested benefits in 2009/10

Benefit	Lower capital limit	Upper capital limit	Tariff income
If you are under the qualifying age for pension credit:[i]			
Income support, income-related employment and support allowance, income-based jobseeker's allowance, housing benefit, council tax benefit	£6,000 (£10,000 if you live in a care home)	£16,000	£1 for every £250, or part of £250 above £6,000
If you are at least the qualifying age for pension credit[i]			
Pension credit	£10,000[ii]	No limit	£1 for every £500, or part of £500 above £10,000
Housing benefit, council tax benefit	£10,000[ii]	No limit (if on guarantee credit of pension credit) £16,000 (in other cases)	£1 for every £500, or part of £500 above £10,000

[i] The qualifying age is the state pension age for women. In 2009/10, this is 60, but will start to increase from April 2010 (see Chapter 6).
[ii] From 2 November 2009 onwards. Before this date, £6,000 (or £10,000 if you live in a care home).

Income

Each of the means-tested benefits has different rules on what income and how much of your income must be taken into account. The rules are, on the whole, more generous for PC (and for HB and CTB if you are at least the qualifying age for PC (see p306) than for the other means-tested benefits.

Most types of income are taken into account – eg:
- earnings from a job;
- profits from self-employment;
- retirement pension;
- other pensions;
- income from annuities (but less any part that pays the interest on a lifetime mortgage – see Chapter 5);
- some benefits, such as CA and bereavement allowance;
- WTC.

There are many types of income that can disregarded including some benefits – eg:
- DLA and AA;
- social fund payments;
- the £10 Christmas bonus paid to pensioners;
- for IS, income-related ESA, income-based JSA, PC, CTC and child benefit if you are getting CTC.

Earnings that can be ignored

Some of your earnings from employment or self-employment are ignored. The amount (£25, £20, £10 or £5 a week) depends on your circumstances. For ESA, there is a higher earnings disregard (£93 in 2009/10) if you or your partner are doing permitted work. The Government says that from April 2010, there will also be a higher limit for HB and CTB if you or your partner are doing permitted work. For HB and CTB, there is also:
- an additional disregard (£16.85 in 2009/10) depending on the hours you (and your partner, if you have one) work; *and*
- a childcare costs disregard (up to £175 a week for one child or up to £300 a week for two or more children), if you work at least 16 hours a week, or if you are a member of a couple, both of you do. If only one of you works, you can still qualify if the other is incapacitated, 80 or over, or in hospital or prison.

4. **Tax credits explained**

Despite the name 'tax credits', these are in fact a type of state benefit. However, the rules work differently from those for the benefits looked at in this chapter so far. Tax credits are administered by HM Revenue and Customs.

There are two types of tax credit – working tax credit (WTC) and child tax credit (CTC). Tax credits are means tested. The amount you get depends on your maximum tax credits (made up of a combination of elements – see below), your household's annual income broadly as calculated for income tax purposes (see Chapter 8) and the income threshold that applies to you. There is no limit to the amount of capital you can have, but taxable income from your capital is usually taken into account.

Entitlement, strictly speaking, depends on your annual income for the current tax year. (A tax year runs from 6 April to the following 5 April.) However, since you cannot be sure what your income for the whole year will be until after the year has ended, in practice, your tax credits are initially based on your annual income for the previous tax year. After the end of the tax year, your actual income is compared to the previous year's income and your tax credit claim is reviewed. If your actual income turns out to be lower than in the previous tax year, you receive extra tax credits. If your actual income turns out to be higher than in the previous tax year by more than £25,000, you may have to repay some of the tax credits you have had. Note that if you know that your income will be lower in the current than in the previous year, you can ask for your claim to be based on your actual income for the current year from the start.

Tax credit elements in 2009/10

Working tax credit	Maximum amount per year
Basic element (everyone gets this)	£1,890
Couple and lone parent element	£1,860
30-hour element (if you and/or your partner work at least 30 hours a week)	£775
Disabled worker element	£2,530
Severe disability element	£1,075
50+ (working 16-29 hours)	£1,300
50+ (working 30 hours or more)	£1,935
Childcare element (one child)	80% of up to £175 a week of eligible costs
Childcare element (two or more children)	80% of up to £300 a week of eligible costs
Child tax credit	
Family element	£545
Family element, baby addition (for child under one)	£545
Child element (per child)	£2,235
Disabled child element (per child)	£2,670
Severely disabled child element (per child)	£1,075

Child tax credit

You may qualify for CTC if you are responsible for a child or qualifying young person (a young person under 20 – or 19 in some cases – who is still your dependant – eg, because s/he is still in school). You count as responsible for a child or qualifying young person if s/he normally lives with you, or if more than one claim is made for the same child or young person, if you have the main responsibility for her/him.

You should bear the following in mind.

- CTC counts as income for the purposes of housing benefit and council tax benefit calculations unless you are at least the qualifying age for pension credit (see p306).
- If you are working, you may also qualify for WTC.
- The elements that make up maximum CTC are: family element; child element (one per child); disability element (one for each disabled child); severe disability element (one for each severely disabled child).
- The means test for the family element of CTC is generous. You can qualify for at least some CTC, even with a household income in excess of £50,000.
- If you have a partner, you must make a joint claim for CTC with her/him. The CTC is paid to the one who is your child's (or young person's) main carer.

Working tax credit

You may qualify for WTC if you or your partner are in full-time paid work. For WTC purposes this means at least:

- 16 hours a week, if:
  - you or your partner are responsible for a child or qualifying young person (see p315 – the rules are the same as for CTC);
  - you have a physical or mental disability that puts you at a disadvantage in getting a job;
  - you or your partner are aged 50 or over have recently started work after a period claiming certain state benefits (such as jobseeker's allowance (JSA), income support (IS), employment and support allowance (ESA) or incapacity benefit); *or*
- 30 hours a week, if you are aged 25 or over.

You should bear the following in mind.

- To qualify for WTC, you must be working or have accepted an offer of work which is expected to start within seven days. The work must be expected to last at least four weeks.
- WTC counts as income for the purposes of all the means-tested benefits.
- If you are responsible for a child or qualifying young person, you may also qualify for CTC.
- The elements that make up maximum WTC are: basic element; couple element; lone parent element; 30-hour element; disability element (one for each claimant who is a disabled worker); severe disability element (one for each severely disabled claimant); 50-plus element; childcare element (help with eligible childcare costs you pay).
- If you have a partner, you must make a joint claim for WTC with her/him. WTC (other than the amount for childcare costs) is paid to the one who is

working. If both of you are working, you can choose which of you is paid. The amount for childcare costs is paid to the one who is your child's 'main carer'.
- If you finish work, or start to work less than 16/30 hours a week, you can continue to qualify for WTC for a further four weeks – known as 'WTC run-on'.

Maximum tax credit and reduced amounts

Your maximum CTC and WTC are calculated by adding together all the elements that apply to you.

Entitlement to IS, income-related ESA, income-based JSA or pension credit acts as an automatic passport to maximum tax credits, assuming you meet the other tax credit conditions (such as the hours you work or being responsible for at least one child).

Otherwise, your income is compared to the relevant threshold (in 2009/10 £16,040 for CTC only, £6,420 if you qualify for WTC). If your income exceeds this, your maximum tax credits are reduced by 39 per cent of the excess. Note that if you have children, the family element of CTC is reduced only when your income exceeds a second threshold (£50,000 in 2009/10). The family element is then reduced by 6.67 per cent of the excess.

5. **Work, benefits and tax credits**

Entitlement to many benefits and to working tax credit (WTC) is affected by work and employment. There are a number of schemes and bonuses aimed at encouraging benefit claimants into work. See p319 for further information.

Means-tested benefits

Full-time paid work affects income support (IS), employment and support allowance (ESA), jobseeker's allowance (JSA), housing benefit (HB), council tax benefit (CTB) and pension credit (PC) in different ways.
- You cannot usually qualify for IS or JSA if you are in full-time paid work. Your partner's working hours do not affect your entitlement to contribution-based JSA, but you cannot get IS or income-based JSA if your partner is in full-time paid work.
- In general, you cannot qualify for ESA if you do any work. However, some types of work are exempt, such as genuine voluntary work and 'permitted work' which involves working for a few hours a week provided your income does not exceed set limits. Your partner's working hours do not affect your entitlement to contributory ESA, but you cannot get income-related ESA if your partner is in full-time paid work.

- Work does not affect your eligibility for HB, CTB or PC, but for HB and CTB being in full-time paid work can affect the way your income and earnings are calculated.
- If you have a non-dependant living with you who is in full-time paid work, the amount of the non-dependant deduction made from your IS, ESA, JSA or PC housing costs and from your HB and CTB can be affected.

You count as in full-time work if you work 16 hours or more a week. For IS, income-related ESA and income-based JSA (but not joint-claim JSA), your partner counts as in full-time paid work if s/he works 24 hours or more a week. Your non-dependant counts as in full-time paid work if s/he works 16 hours or more a week.

You should bear the following in mind.

- In some circumstances you may be treated as not in full-time paid work even if you are, or treated as if you are in full-time paid work when you are not.
- If you do not work the same number of hours each week, there are complicated rules for how your hours are averaged.
- You cannot qualify for IS based on your incapacity for work in any week in which you do any work (even if this is part time) unless this is work you may do while claiming – known as permitted work.
- Whether or not you are in full-time or part-time paid work, income from employment or self-employment affects your entitlement to means-tested benefits.

Tax credits

Working tax credit (WTC) is designed to ensure that you are better off financially in work than claiming benefits. You can only get WTC if you or your partner are in full-time paid work (see p316). If you normally work at least 16 (or 30) hours a week, but are off sick or on maternity, paternity or adoption leave, you might still be able to claim WTC. You might also be able to claim IS, ESA or JSA.

Other benefits

The effect of work on other benefits includes the following.

- You cannot qualify for **carer's allowance** if you are 'gainfully employed' (see p293).
- You cannot work and qualify for **incapacity benefit** or ESA in any week you actually do any work unless this is work you may do while claiming – known as permitted work.
- You must have been an employed earner when you had an accident or contracted a disease to qualify for **industrial injuries benefits**.
- You must satisfy an employment condition to qualify for **maternity allowance**.

- For **statutory sick pay, statutory maternity pay, statutory paternity pay** and **statutory adoption pay** you must be employed (not self-employed).
- You do not qualify for **child benefit** or **guardian's allowance** for a child who is aged 16 or over who does paid work for 24 hours a week or more.
- You cannot receive an **adult dependant addition** for a partner who earns more than that addition.

Moving from unemployment into work

As well as administering benefits, Jobcentre Plus also acts as an employment agency advertising job vacancies, giving advice and helping to direct people to suitable work, and acts as an information point and gateway for the very large number of government schemes designed to help people return to work. A few of these schemes are outlined below. Some are area-based and others target people on particular benefits. Generally, it is compulsory to participate in the schemes if you are receiving JSA, but optional if you claim other benefits. However, for many benefits, you (and sometimes your partner) must take part in a work-focused interview. For further information and details of the initiatives, contact your local Jobcentre Plus office.

New Deal

This is a collection of schemes designed to help you back into work if you have been receiving JSA for a period, or you are young and have a history of not being in work, education or training. You first enter a Gateway programme, during which you receive advice, and then you can join options which may involve employment, self-employment, training, education and so on with the aim of getting you into long-term, sustainable employment. If you refuse to take part in options, you can be disqualified from getting JSA for up to 26 weeks (known as a sanction).

From autumn 2009 a new Flexible New Deal programme will be introduced to replace previousprogrammes for young people and those aged 25-plus. This will involve private firms providing tailored employment and skills support, closer integration with the needs of local communities and ensuring that jobs offer ongoing progression and training. Separate New Deal programmes for people aged 50-plus, lone parents, disabled people, partners of claimants and musicians will also continue.

Subsidised employment

Claimants who are paid a wage while on a New Deal scheme or in other subsidised employment can receive WTC (see p316) to top up their pay.

Bonuses

There are a number of bonuses you might be able to get if you take up full-time paid work or increase your earnings from work and so no longer qualify for certain benefits. These are meant to give you some financial help in the first weeks after your benefit ceases.

- **Job grant** is a tax-free lump sum of £100 (or £250 for lone parents or couples with children) intended to help you with the costs of starting work – eg, travel, clothing and tools.
- If you (or your partner) return to work or increase your hours and so count as in full-time paid work, and you no longer qualify for IS, income-related ESA or income-based JSA, you might qualify for **mortgage interest run-on.** If you do, you are paid your IS, income-related ESA or income-based JSA eligible housing costs for the first four weeks after you go into full-time paid work.
- If you (or your partner) are on IS, income-based JSA, ESA, incapacity benefit or severe disablement allowance and your entitlement ends because you or your partner start work, or increase your hours or pay, you may be entitled to continue to receive the same amount of HB and CTB as you did before your entitlement ended for up to four weeks. These are known as **extended payments of HB and CTB**.

Other incentives to help you into work

The Government provides a number of other financial incentives to help you make a transition from benefits to work. These depend on where you live and whether you are in a pilot scheme area. There are a number of incentives specifically for lone parents. Ask at your local Jobcentre Plus office to see what is available.

6. **Overpayments and fraud**

If you are paid benefits or tax credits to which you are not entitled, you might have to repay the overpayment. This might be the case even if the overpayment occurred through an innocent mistake on your part. The rules on overpayments of tax credits and housing benefit and council tax benefit differ from those for other benefits.

You should always seek advice if you are told you have been overpaid benefit or tax credits. You might be able to challenge the decision that there has been an overpayment or the decision to recover the overpayment. You might be able to repay it at a reduced rate. There is also a discretionary power to waive recovery of overpayments in exceptional circumstances.

If you are found to have acted fraudulently – eg, making false statements or dishonest representations or failing to disclose a change in your circumstances which you know might affect your right to, or the amount of, benefit, you can be prosecuted. This can result in a fine and/or prison sentence. With many benefits, you can be offered the option of paying a penalty as an alternative to prosecution.

7. **Challenging decisions**

If you think a decision about your benefits or tax credits is wrong (eg, because the decision maker got the facts or law wrong, or your circumstances have changed since the decision was made), there are a number of ways you can try to get the decision changed.

- For benefits, you can seek a revision or a supersession of the decision. In some cases you have to show specific grounds. In others, you must apply within a strict time limit.
- For tax credits, you can seek a revision of the decision if your circumstances have changed or HM Revenue and Customs has reasonable grounds for believing you are entitled to tax credits at a different rate or there has been an official error.
- For both benefits and tax credits, you can appeal to the First-tier Tribunal. There are strict time limits for appealing (one month for benefits and 30 days for tax credits). You can make a late appeal in limited circumstances.

If you are considering challenging a decision, you should seek advice as soon as possible.

Notes

1 Department for Work and Pensions,
DWP Quarterly Statistical Summary,
Office for National Statistics, 2009
2 Department for Work and Pensions,
Income-related Benefits Estimates of Take-up in 2007/08, Office for National
Statistics, 2009
3 HM Treasury, *Budget 2009, Building Britain's Future*, The Stationery Office,
2009
4 Citizens Advice, *Introduction to the Citizens Advice Service 2007/08*, 2008
5 House of Commons *Hansard*, col852, 17
March 2009

Chapter 10

Protecting consumers

This chapter covers:
1. The need for consumer protection (below)
2. Regulation and legislation (p324)
3. Complaints and compensation (p329)
4. Protecting yourself against fraud (p333)

Basic facts
- In March 2009, 27,340 firms were authorised by the Financial Services Authority. In 2008/09, the Financial Services Authority imposed financial penalties on firms for misconduct totalling £27.3 million.[1]
- The Financial Services Compensation Scheme arranged £20.9 billion compensation for bank failures and £92 million in other compensation to consumers in 2008/09.[2]
- In 2007, criminals stole £535 million through card fraud. The biggest loss was from when cards were used to shop by phone and online. However, card fraud amounts to just 0.12 per cent of the value of card transactions.[3]

1. The need for consumer protection

Like many advanced economies around the world, the UK is primarily a market economy. There is a reliance on market forces to deliver the 'best' outcomes: producers bring goods and services to the market; consumers 'vote' through their purchasing behaviour so that good products and services thrive while the bad are driven out. However, in many areas, such as food, drugs, alcohol and transport, market forces can lead to undesirable or unexpected outcomes and so regulation is used to modify the way that markets work by, for example, imposing safety and competence requirements or making producers pay for unintended side effects. Financial services and products are one such area. The main features that make it undesirable to leave finance to market forces include the following.

- **Access.** Producers may be unwilling to design products that are suitable for all consumers or to sell them at prices which low-income consumers can afford. If the products and services are considered near-essential (eg, a bank account), this causes financial exclusion.

- **Infrequent engagement with the market**. With many products, such as life insurance, retirement savings and long-term care, consumers may buy only once or a few times in their life. Therefore, they have no chance to build up experience and may rely on out-of-date information handed to them by family and friends. In addition, many products are long term and so it may be many years after the initial selection and purchase before defects become apparent.

- **Complexity**. Often there are hundreds, even thousands, of competing products on offer. Consumers could not possibly evaluate them all and will look for short-cuts (such as brand name or recommendation by a friend) to help them make sense of the market and narrow down choice. This does not necessarily lead to the best choice.

- **Information asymmetry**. Often the products and services themselves are also complex and consumers may lack the time and financial capability to understand more than the basic features. This gives providers some freedom to design products and services that deliver profits to the company, but do not necessarily deliver the best outcomes for consumers. Economic theory says consumers would avoid such products, but this can happen only if consumers are aware of their poor features.

- **Ethics and crime**. By their nature, many financial products and services involve handing control of large sums of money to third parties. This creates tempting opportunities for fraudsters. Since, with long-term investment products, there is no way to predict accurately what the future outcome will be, it is hard for consumers to distinguish the bogus offers made by fraudsters from the genuine offers made by honest firms.

- **Scale**. Buying a faulty kettle or a pirated DVD may cause inconvenience and some small loss. But buying a faulty financial product or being the victim of financial crime can cause financial ruin. This is devastating for an individual or household. It is also a problem for society as a whole, which may have to provide support through the benefits system.

The above relate largely to specific firms and specific products and services, but regulation is also needed at the economy-wide level, as has been demonstrated by the global financial crisis which started in 2007. All capitalist economies rely on having a sound banking system. A key function of banks is to channel money from people who want to save to firms who want to invest and so produce economic growth. Savers with banks usually do not want to tie up their money for years or decades, whereas the firms who are investing frequently want to borrow long term. You, as a saver, are told you can have your money back at any time, but in fact it would be impossible for banks to pay back all their depositors if they all demanded their money at the same time. In normal times, this is not a problem, because only a small proportion of savers will want their money back and banks keep enough in reserve to meet these needs. But, as the run on Northern Rock Bank in September 2007 demonstrated, if consumers lose confidence in their bank, they will all turn up on the doorstep at the same time and this can cause the bank to collapse.

Therefore, an important function of regulation, in addition to ensuring that markets and firms behave competently and ethically, is to maintain consumer confidence in the system. This explains why the Government took steps to protect savers throughout the global financial crisis and why compensation schemes are an important aspect of the regulatory system.

2. Regulation and legislation

The regulators

Over time, the distinction between different financial product providers has blurred with many, especially banks, increasingly providing a wide range of different products and services. In response, eight regulatory systems, which had each focused on a particular type of financial institution, merged into a single new 'super-regulator', the Financial Services Authority (FSA). Currently, just a few areas remain outside the jurisdiction of the FSA. Following the financial crisis that started in 2007, the current system of regulation is under review and may change again in future.

The Financial Services Authority

The FSA was set up by an Act of Parliament to regulate the UK financial system, which includes all financial markets and stock exchanges and all activities which have been defined as **'regulated activities'**. These include:

- accepting deposits – eg, operating current and savings accounts;
- effecting or carrying out contracts of insurance;
- dealing in investments or arranging deals in investments;
- managing other people's investments;
- safekeeping and administering other people's investments;
- using computer-based systems for giving investment instructions;
- establishing or running unit trusts and similar schemes;
- investment advice;
- providing certain types of pre-paid funeral plan;
- offering or managing certain types of mortgage;
- issuing electronic money;
- setting up or running a credit union;
- arranging or advising on certain types of mortgage;
- arranging or advising on equity release schemes;
- arranging or advising on long-term care insurance;
- arranging or advising on general insurance (but shops selling extended warranties for the goods they sell are excluded).

Firms engaged in any of these activities must be authorised by the FSA and comply with the FSA's comprehensive *Handbook of Rules and Guidance.* Some of the rules deal with 'prudential' requirements which aim to ensure that firms are solvent and properly run. In some areas (eg, investment, mortgages and general insurance), there are conduct of business rules that set out how firms must deal with customers, including the content of advertising and the information that must be provided about products. However, increasingly, there is also a reliance on high-level principles (such as treating customers fairly). Other rules are concerned with how the FSA supervises firms and the action it can take if a firm breaks the rules.

The FSA has responsibility for ensuring that there is an independent complaints body and a compensation scheme to help consumers. These bodies are run independently of the FSA.

Unusually for a regulator, the FSA has a statutory duty to increase public awareness and understanding of the financial system. To address this, it publishes a wide range of booklets and factsheets, runs a detailed consumer website including comparative tables of selected products, operates a consumer helpline, and is increasingly involved in improving the nation's financial capability through education in, for example, workplaces and schools, and at critical lifestages, such as becoming a parent.

The Pensions Regulator

In general, occupational pension schemes are not regulated by the FSA (although if, for instance, their investments are being managed by an insurance company, that aspect does fall within the scope of the FSA).

Most of the responsibility for ensuring that schemes are properly run falls within the remit of the Pensions Regulator. As well as being able to investigate schemes and take disciplinary action, the Regulator issues codes of good practice.

The Office of Fair Trading and trading standards offices

Most loans and credit are also outside the scope of the FSA's rules (although the prudential supervision of some organisations – such as banks and building societies – that make loans is part of its remit).

Anyone offering credit must be licensed by the Office of Fair Trading (OFT). The main statutory rules governing credit are the concern of the OFT and enforced at a local level by trading standards offices (departments within local authorities).

The OFT publishes a range of consumer information leaflets and booklets and useful material on its website.

National Savings and Investments and the Treasury

National Savings and Investments (NS&I) is an executive agency of the Treasury, a government department. The Treasury is responsible for making regulations for supervising the way NS&I operates.

Voluntary regulation

Some aspects of financial products and services are not subject to rules laid down by law. In many cases, systems of voluntary regulation have been established.

It is, however, not compulsory for providers to join, so you should always check before doing business whether the firm or individual concerned has signed up to the voluntary regime. A further drawback of voluntary regimes is that they often lack teeth because, while they can withdraw membership, they cannot stop a firm from trading, as a statutory regulator can. However, bad publicity is often an effective sanction and most codes require firms to subscribe to an arbitration scheme or other independent complaints body which can direct a firm to pay compensation. Although a firm might refuse, the direction should strengthen the chance of bringing successful court action against the firm.

One of the most important systems of voluntary regulation has been the Banking Code (conduct of business rules that banks and building societies agreed to impose on themselves), but part of the aftermath of the global financial crisis is that, from November 2009, FSA rules have taken over this area of regulation. The main remaining systems of voluntary regulation are as follows.

- **Finance and Leasing Association (FLA) code.** Many finance companies, credit and store card providers and other loan companies belong to the FLA, a trade organisation. Members are required to comply with its code of practice.
- **Association of British Insurers (ABI).** This is a trade body to which most UK insurers belong. The ABI has drawn up a number of codes of business practice which members are required to observe. In addition, there are FSA rules covering this area.
- **Safe Home Income Plans (SHIP) code.** Many equity release scheme providers (whose conduct is also subject to FSA rules) belong to the trade body, SHIP, and agree to follow its code of practice. It includes a requirement, for example, that all lifetime mortgages should include a no negative equity guarantee (see Chapter 5).

The legislation

The legislation governing financial products and services has grown up piecemeal over many centuries. This section highlights only the main Acts of Parliament and secondary legislation, which are most relevant to the protection of financial consumers.

Banking Act 2009

This Act set up a permanent regime for dealing with banks that run into financial difficulties, including the ability of government to take a bank temporarily into public ownership. It formalises the Bank of England's responsibility for ensuring the health of the banking system. In addition, the Act includes measures which enable changes to be made to the Financial Services Compensation Scheme (see p331) if necessary, such as altering the way it is financed.

Consumer Credit Act 1974

This set up the system for licensing credit providers and the framework for regulating credit business. It applies, for example, to unsecured loans, hire purchase, credit cards and secured loans that do not fall within the scope of the FSA's regulation.

Consumer Credit Act 2006

This updates the consumer credit legislation, extending its scope, giving borrowers the right to challenge unfair credit agreements and bringing disputes concerning borrowing and credit within the remit of the Financial Ombudsman Service.

Data Protection Act 1998

This gives you the rights to:

- find out what personal information about you is being held on computer and in some paper records;
- correct information that is incorrect or have it destroyed (and to sue for damages if you have lost out financially as a result);
- request that your personal information is not used for direct marketing purposes;
- ask that no important decisions about you are made purely on the basis of the data using an automated process (such as computerised credit scoring);
- prevent processing of your information if this is likely to cause damage or distress.

To enforce these rights, you take up the issue first with the firm holding your data and, if unsuccessful, you can ask the Information Commissioner to step in.

Dormant Bank and Building Society Accounts Act 2008

This establishes a framework for money left untouched in bank and building society accounts for many years to be distributed and used to fund community projects. A dormant account is defined as one where there has been no customer-initiated action for 15 years or more. However, even if the money has been diverted to community use, the owner of the account still has the right to claim the money back at any time.

Financial Services and Markets Act 2000

This set up the FSA and gives it powers and responsibilities, and outlines the areas to be regulated. It is supplemented by many statutory instruments. The FSA's *Handbook of Rules and Guidance* sets out the detailed rules. The Act also set out the requirements for the Financial Ombudsman Service (see p330) and the Financial Services Compensation Scheme (see p331).

Financial Services (Distance Marketing) Regulations 2004

These regulations set out the minimum information that must be provided about a contract for most financial products before you buy and gives you the right to a cancellation period (usually 30 days for life insurance and pensions, but 14 days for other products), where you buy over the internet, by post, phone or otherwise at a distance from a provider based in the European Economic Area. They also provide that, if your debit or credit card details are used fraudulently for a distance transaction, you will be reimbursed for any loss. The regulations came into effect at different times between 31 October 2004 and 31 May 2005, depending on the type of product.

National Savings Bank Act 1971 and Savings Contracts Regulations 1969

The Act, among other matters, gives the Treasury the power to make regulations to supervise NS&I. The regulations deal with a variety of issues, including how mistakes and disputes are to be dealt with.

Pensions Act 1995

Among other measures, this set up a pensions compensation fund, now called the Fraud Compensation Fund, to compensate members of occupational pension schemes if their employer becomes insolvent and there is too little money in the pension fund to pay all the promised pensions because of fraud or theft.

Pensions Act 2004

This established the Pensions Regulator and set up a new Pension Protection Fund to compensate members of final salary pension schemes if, on or after 6 April 2005, their scheme winds up, their employer becomes insolvent or there is too little money in the pension fund to pay all the promised pensions (without any fraud or dishonesty). It also established the Financial Assistance Scheme to provide help for pension scheme members in this situation where the scheme wound up between 1 January 1997 and 5 April 2005.

Pensions Act 2007

This makes changes to the state pension system, including increasing state pension age gradually to 68, reducing the number of years of national insurance required for a full basic pension to 30, and improving state pension rights for people caring for children or elderly or disabled adults. The Act also set up the Personal Account Delivery Authority to start the process of setting up a new national pension scheme (see p212).

Pensions Act 2008

This Act extends the role of the Personal Account Delivery Authority and sets up the framework for the new national pension scheme due to start in 2012, including rules that will require employers to automatically enrol their employees in this or an alternative pension scheme.

Saving Gateway Accounts Act 2009

This sets up the Saving Gateway, including rules about who is eligible to have an account and the tax treatment. Details of how the accounts work are set out in regulations under the Act.

Supply of Goods and Services Act 1982

In most cases, a financial consumer is entering into a contract with the provider of financial products or services. This Act sets out certain implied terms in contracts, including that the supplier will carry out the service with reasonable care and skill and within a reasonable time (if no fixed period has been agreed). The Act does not apply in Scotland, but common law there has similar effect.

Unfair Contract Terms Act 1977 and Unfair Terms in Consumer Contracts Regulations 1999

The Act limits providers' ability to avoid the express or implied terms in a contract made with a consumer – eg, to exercise reasonable care or skill. The provider will not be able to rely on a standard term of the contract if it is judged unreasonable. The regulations give certain bodies, including the Office of Fair Trading, the FSA and the Consumers' Association, the powers to stop providers using unfair standard terms.

Work and Families Act 2006

Key measures in this Act are the extension of maternity leave to 52 weeks (from 26 weeks) and related extensions in maternity and paternity leave and pay. It also widens the range of people who can request flexible working to include people caring for adults as well as those caring for young children.

3. **Complaints and compensation**

What to do if you have a complaint

Your first step is to go back to the firm you were dealing with. Initially, talk to the person who has been handling your business – there might just be some misunderstanding that can be cleared up fairly easily by the person who is already familiar with your case. If that does not put matters right, ask for details of the firm's formal complaints procedure. If the firm cannot resolve the matter, you can take the complaint to the Ombudsman (see p330) or other independent body (see p331).

At each stage, make sure you keep a record of who you dealt with and what was said by both you and the firm or complaints body. If you talk on the phone, take notes during the conversation and do not forget to date your record. If you write, make a copy of your letters before you post them – most public libraries have copying facilities. Try to avoid sending original documents (such as Key Facts examples, statements and insurance policies) to the firm or complaints body – keep these safe and send copies instead. If you must send original documents, take a copy first for you to keep and post the originals by recorded delivery so that you can track their safe arrival. Try to stay calm when talking to the firm or complaints body and aim for letters that are concise and polite.

Companies' complaints procedures

These days, most financial firms are required by law, or by a voluntary code of practice to which they subscribe, to have a formal complaints procedure. If the company you are dealing with does not, ask instead to be put in touch with a senior manager.

If you are not happy with the firm's response, ask for a letter from the firm stating that you cannot reach agreement (sometimes called a **'letter of deadlock'**). Normally, you need this to take your complaint further. If the firm refuses to provide a letter or has not responded to your complaint within a reasonable time (allow eight weeks), take the complaint to the next stage regardless.

Ombudsman and arbitration

To pursue your complaint further, you could go to court (see p331), but a cheaper and speedier option is to use an independent complaints body. An advantage of this over going to court is that using an independent complaints body is normally free. If the Ombudsman or arbitrator finds in your favour, the member firm can be ordered to take steps to reimburse you or put the situation right in another way if more appropriate, such as reinstating a financial product. Maximum possible awards vary, but many of the complaints bodies can order firms to pay up to £100,000.

The main differences between the Ombudsman and an arbitration service are as follows.

- **Ombudsman scheme.** The Ombudsman can take into account good practice within an industry and any codes of practice rather than relying purely on the strict letter of the law. In most cases, the Ombudsman's decision is binding on the member firm, but not on you (so you can take your complaint to court if you want – see p331). This does not apply with the Pensions Ombudsman, where the decision is binding on both the firm and you.
- **Arbitration scheme.** This is more formal, and decisions must generally be reached strictly in line with the legal rights and obligations of you and the firm. The arbitrator's decision is binding on both the firm and you. So, when

you agree to the arbitration process, you give up your right to take your complaint to court.

All firms authorised by the Financial Services Authority (FSA) must belong to the Financial Ombudsman Service (FOS). Many others have voluntarily agreed to join. The FOS will try to resolve your dispute, provided the firm has had a chance first to set matters right. Firms which are not authorised by the FSA are often also required to belong to an independent complaints body.

If your problem concerns an occupational pension scheme, you can take your case to the Pensions Ombudsman, but first you must let The Pensions Advisory Service (TPAS) look at your case. Pension schemes are complicated and often TPAS can sort out a misunderstanding without the need for involving the Ombudsman.

Going to court

If you decide to go to court instead of using an independent complaints body or because you are unhappy with the decision of the Ombudsman, you can use the small claims track or small claims procedure if the total compensation you are seeking does not exceed:

- £5,000 in England and Wales;
- £2,000 in Northern Ireland;
- £3,000 in Scotland.

Small claims procedures are similar to arbitration. They are reasonably quick and can be cheap because you can represent yourself rather than hiring a lawyer. If your dispute is too big for the small claims track or court, going to court can be slow and costly. If you are on state benefits and/or your earnings are low, you might qualify for some free advice and help through the Legal Help Scheme (England and Wales) or Legal Aid Scheme (Scotland and Northern Ireland).

Compensation schemes

If you have lost money because of the actions (or failure to act) of a financial firm authorised by the FSA, it is up to the firm to put matters right. This might be in response to your complaint, following directions from the FOS, or as a result of an order from the FSA. Authorised firms are required to have adequate resources or insurance to cover the payment of redress. If the firm goes out of business, you might still be worse off financially. In that case, you might instead be able to claim from the Financial Services Compensation Scheme (FSCS). The table on p332 shows the maximum payout you might get, which depends on the type of product or service involved. The protection for deposits was increased following the global financial crisis that started in 2007 and other compensation limits are due to be increased and simplified from 1 January 2010.

If you are a member of any type of occupational pension scheme (ie, covering money purchase schemes as well as final salary and other defined benefit schemes), you might qualify for help from the Fraud Compensation Fund if you have lost pension or pension rights and:

- your employer has gone out of business;
- in the case of a defined benefit scheme, the scheme can meet less than 90 per cent of its liabilities to pay pensions and other benefits; *and*
- the assets have been reduced because of fraud or theft.

Any payout goes to the scheme and is then divided between the members according to an order of priority set down by law. Current pensioners come top of the list but only as far as their current pension goes – any future increases come further down the list.

Maximum payouts from the Financial Services Compensation Scheme

Type of financial product or service	Compensation payable	Maximum payout
Deposits (eg, bank and building society accounts)	100% of the first £50,000[i]	£50,000
Investments (eg, unit trusts, shares)	100% of the first £50,000 from 1 January 2010[ii]	£50,000[ii]
Long-term insurance (eg, life insurance)	90% of claim (including future benefits already declared) from 1 January 2010[iii]	No limit
Certain types of mortgage	100% of the first £50,000 (from 1 January 2010)[ii]	£50,000[ii]
General insurance (eg, car insurance, home insurance) and advice about general insurance	Compulsory insurance (eg, third party motor insurance, employer's liability insurance): 100% of claim Non-compulsory insurance: 90% of claim (from 1 January 2010)[iii]	No limit

[i] The £50,000 applies per person per authorised firm. For example, if you have a joint account, you receive up to £50,000 compensation each; if you have two accounts with banks that are part of the same group, the £50,000 limit applies to the total of your accounts with that group. For a list of which banks and brands are part of the same group, check their entry on the FSA Register (see Appendix 2). The FSA has consulted on increasing the protection for temporary high balances, such as lump sums received on house sale, inheritance and redundancy, but new rules will require European Union approval and are unlikely to be introduced before 2010.

[ii] 100% of the first £30,000 and 90% of the next £20,000 before 1 January 2010.

[iii] 100% of the first £2,000 and at least 90% of the remainder (including future benefits already declared) before 1 January 2010.

If your pension scheme was wound up on or after 6 April 2005 and your employer has gone out of business leaving an under-funded final salary or other defined benefit occupational scheme without fraud or dishonesty being involved, you may qualify for compensation from the Pension Protection Fund (PPF). If you are already drawing a pension, compensation covers the full pension plus inflation-linked increases each year up to a maximum of 2.5 per cent a year. If you are below your scheme's normal pension age, your compensation replaces 90 per cent of the pension you had built up, up to a specified maximum and it is increased in line with inflation up to 2.5 per cent a year until it starts to be paid. The maximum is set at £31,936.32 at age 65 for 2009/10 and adjusted for retirement at earlier or later ages.

If you have lost all or part of your final salary or other defined benefit pension because your scheme wound up before 6 April 2005 and your employer went out of business before 31 August 2007, you might qualify for compensation from the Financial Assistance Scheme (FAS). Compensation under the FAS is less generous than under the PPF, but has been improved as a result of several reviews and court judgments against the Government. Broadly, it replaces 90 per cent of your lost pension up to a maximum of £29,386. Once the pension starts, it is inflation-proofed up to a maximum of 2.5 per cent a year. You cannot draw your pension earlier than the original pension scheme's normal pension age (subject to a minimum age of 60 and a maximum of 65), except if you have to retire earlier because of ill health.

---

4. Protecting yourself against fraud

Using plastic cards

Plastic card fraud is big business (see p334). But the introduction of chip and PIN has changed the types of crime that fraudsters favour. Under the chip-and-PIN programme, most UK-issued plastic cards now have an embedded microchip and you authorise a transaction by tapping a PIN (personal identification number) into a keypad instead of providing a signature. This makes it much more expensive and difficult for a fraudster to use a stolen card in shops and other outlets unless they have also managed to steal the PIN. As a result, one of the fastest growing areas of fraud now is 'card-not-present fraud' where a stolen card is used to buy goods remotely by phone, mail or internet. Typically, with these remote transactions, no PIN is required.

Chip and PIN has not completely stopped the stealing and cloning of cards because stolen and fake cards can still be exported and used in countries which do not yet have chip-and-PIN technology. Often, card details are stolen by '**skimming**' (a type of counterfeit fraud). This is where a dishonest person, processing a genuine transaction, swipes your card through a small copying machine that records the details on your card's magnetic strip. The details are then sold to fraudsters who make the fake cards. Card details might also be stolen from discarded receipts or statements. It is cheap and pretty easy to copy the details stored on a card's magnetic strip, and simple for criminals to forge your signature.

Although being a victim of card fraud is unpleasant, it should not leave you out of pocket. Under the Financial Services Authority rules and, with credit cards, the Consumer Credit Act 1974, the most you would normally have to pay would be £50 and, in practice, you usually pay nothing at all. However, with debit and cash cards, you could be liable for more if the bank can show that you had acted fraudulently or been grossly negligent. For example, you would be liable if you had written your PIN on your card or told someone your PIN. The onus is on the bank to prove that you had been negligent.

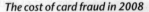

The cost of card fraud in 2008

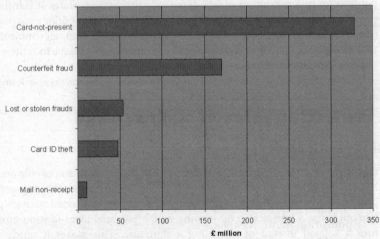

Source: UK Payments Administration

Protect yourself against card fraud

In general

– Look after your plastic cards as carefully as if they were cash.
– Check your statements as soon as you get them each month. Contact your card issuer immediately if there are any transactions you do not recognise.

- Tell the card issuer straight away if you have lost your card or you think it may have been misused.
- Never give your PIN to anyone. No honest person, bank official or policeman will ever ask you for your PIN.

When you first get your card and PIN
- Contact your card issuer within a few days if a card you expected through the post has not turned up.
- Sign your card as soon as you get it.
- You will get a slip through the post telling you your PIN. Memorise the PIN and destroy the slip.
- If you really cannot memorise your PIN, write it down but disguise the number and never carry it with your card.
- At cash machines, you can change your PIN if you want to. Choose a number that is easy to remember, but avoid any that are easy to guess (such as your birth date or phone number) or predictable, such as 1234 or 3333.

At cash machines and when paying
- Do not use a cash machine or card reader if you feel unsafe – eg, if the machine is in an isolated location or you think you might be overlooked.
- Do not use a cash machine that seems in any way unusual. Criminals sometimes fit machines with devices designed to steal cards or the information on them.
- Cancel your card immediately if it is retained by a cash machine.
- Shield the keypad with your hand or body so you cannot be overlooked when keying in your PIN (known as 'shoulder surfing').
- Do not let your card out of your sight when paying.

Identity theft

Identity theft is where someone pretends to be you, typically to run up credit debts in your name. It may take two forms.
- **Application fraud.** The fraudster uses fake or stolen documents to open card accounts in your name.
- **Account takeover.** The fraudster passes her/himself off as you, using stolen information and gets your mail redirected to a new address. S/he then reports a card as lost and requests a replacement which is sent to the new address.

Initially, you may be unaware that your identity is being used in this way, but in time, you may experience any of the following:
- rogue transactions on statements;
- bills turning up for credit and store card accounts you do not have, or for goods you have not bought;

- debt collectors arriving on your doorstep;
- being refused credit because you have a bad credit rating.

Identity theft can happen only if criminals can get hold of information about you. Unfortunately, this is becoming increasingly easier – especially if you have an unusual name. In the past, fraudsters employed techniques, such as bin-raiding (trawling through dustbins for carelessly discarded documents) and stealing post from porches, to bag snatching and housebreaking. These still happen and, if you have documents or credit cards stolen, you should assume that identity theft is likely. But, in addition, fraudsters now also use internet searching and hacking. Having obtained your name and address, often from public sources, such as the electoral role, fraudsters can piece together more data about you – eg, obtaining your birth certificate which will include your mother's maiden name. The more unusual your own name, the easier it is for fraudsters to identify and match data about you from a variety of sources.

Criminals are also adept at persuading people to volunteer sensitive information. For example, you might get a phone call (or a letter, fax or email), seemingly from an official source – eg, your bank, asking you to give personal or account details as a security check. Do not be conned.

Protect yourself against identity fraud

In general

- Dispose of receipts, statements, bills and even personalised junk mail carefully, preferably by shredding or burning. Any document giving your full name and address, whole credit or debit card numbers, or whole bank account numbers and sort codes, and whole utility bills can all be used to steal your identity.
- If it is required or suggested that you give your mother's maiden name as security information, use a fictitious name, rather than the real one.
- Do not carry around documents, credit cards or cheque books unnecessarily. They are more likely to be stolen than if they are stored securely at home. Try not to carry important documents, such as a driving licence, together with bank cards and cheque books.
- If you are away from home, store documents in, for instance, a hotel safe rather than carry them around.
- Check statements as soon as you receive them each month. Contact your card issuer immediately if there are transactions you do not recognise.
- Make a list of your regular bills and statements and the dates you expect them to arrive. If they do not turn up, assume they might have been stolen.
- Check your credit files regularly (see Chapter 5). Contact the credit reference agency if there are rogue entries on your file.
- Be suspicious if you receive an unsolicited phone call, email or fax. Do not give away any personal or account information.

- If you use the internet, be suspicious if a website does not seem quite right – it may be bogus. One ploy is for a website to offer a seemingly genuine deal. But, having keyed in your personal and card details, a message comes up to say your order cannot be processed. It is then too late, as the fraudsters already have what they want.
- Watch out for bogus emails supposedly from a bank or other organisation asking you to follow a link and key information into a website that looks genuine but is really a fake.

What to do if you think you might be a victim of identity fraud

If post you are expecting does not turn up, assume it has fallen into the hands of fraudsters. Report your suspicions immediately to the Royal Mail and ask it to check whether there have been any requests to redirect your mail to another address.

Similarly, if you have any documents or cards stolen, assume they will be used for identity fraud. Contact the card issuers immediately to cancel any cards.

Apply for protective registration. This is a service offered by CIFAS (see Appendix 2) and costs £13.80 a year. When anyone applies for credit using your details from a provider who is a CIFAS member (most are), the provider should check to see if you have an entry on the CIFAS Register. If you do, the provider is alerted to make extra security checks before agreeing to grant any credit.

Contact all three of the credit reference agencies operating in the UK. Ask to be sent monthly copies of your credit files, so that you can see straight away if someone is falsely applying for credit in your name. All the agencies let you check your file online for a fee. You have the right to correct inaccurate entries on your files – the credit reference agency concerned will tell you how to do this.

If you have identity theft insurance (see p236), contact your insurer's helpline for advice if you think you have been a victim of fraud.

Cheque fraud

Although cheque fraud is uncommon – costing around £42 million in 2008 – compared with plastic card fraud, it is just as much of a problem if you fall victim to it. Common frauds are stealing new cheque books from the post or stealing and altering cheques that have been written out.

If your cheque book is lost or stolen, provided you tell your bank immediately, you should not normally be liable for any cheques fraudulently drawn against your account. However, you could be if you do not keep to your side of your contract with the bank. Under the terms and conditions of your account, you must normally take reasonable care to prevent misuse of your cheque book. For example, you should keep your cheque book and any cheque guarantee card apart. You are also normally required to take reasonable care when writing cheques to minimise the chance of alteration or forgery.

Protect yourself against cheque fraud

- If you can, pay using a more secure method – eg, by direct debit.
- Avoid posting cheques if you can by, say, paying bills in person at your bank or a post office.
- If you do post cheques, use a plain envelope rather than the one provided.
- If you post a cheque for a large sum, check a couple of days later that the recipient has received it.
- If you are expecting a new cheque book and it does not arrive, assume it may have been stolen and alert your bank.
- Keep cheque books in a safe place and do not carry them around unnecessarily.
- Do not keep your cheque book and cheque guarantee card in the same place – eg, together in a handbag or pocket.
- When you write a cheque, do not leave gaps blank – put a line through them. If paying bills add your account number to the payee line.
- Never give anyone a blank cheque.
- Always fill in your cheque stubs and check them off against your bank statements as soon as the statements arrive. Contact your bank immediately if there are any transactions you do not recognise.

Banking and saving online

Online banking fraud is on the increase, from £23.2 million in 2005 to £52.5 million in 2008.[4] The most common type of attack is 'phishing'. This is where you get a bogus email purporting to be from your bank directing you to a fake website which can look exactly like your bank's real website. You are then asked to key in your account's security details. Other frauds use viruses (called 'Trojans') which hide on your computer, record your keystrokes, so revealing PINs and passwords, and send them by internet to the fraudsters.

Protect yourself against online banking fraud

- Do not share your account security details with anyone. If you have a shared account, each user should have their own security details.
- Try to memorise passwords, PINs and memorable dates and words. If you must write them down, disguise them.
- Do not use the same password for multiple accounts.
- Change your password regularly.
- Be wary if using a shared computer. Make sure you log off properly from your banking service so the next computer user cannot access the web pages you visited.
- Use your own computer if you can.
- Install a firewall and virus software. Subscribe to the virus software updating service.
- If you use a wireless connection, use the password feature to block other people from your service.

- Be suspicious of all emails that purport to be from your bank.
- Always key in your bank's website address. Never follow a link from an email.
- If you think you have received a 'phishing' email, forward it to reports@banksafeonline.org.uk.
- If you think you have been tricked into revealing your security details to fraudsters, tell your bank straight away.

Buying online, by phone or by post

Buying financial products and services from the comfort of your own home is very convenient, but you should take a few precautions – see below. Note that if a firm is authorised by the FSA, the regulator's rules apply whatever the medium through which you are buying.

Protect yourself when buying at a distance

In general
- Check the firm you are dealing with is authorised by the FSA. Do not just take the firm's word for it – check against the FSA Register.
- Be wary of doing business with a firm based outside the European Economic Area. There may be no protection for consumers at all.
- Be wary of dealing with a firm you have never heard of.
- If a deal sounds too good to be true, it probably is – so avoid it.
- Check out a number of different companies and competing products. Get advice (see Chapter 2) if you are unsure how to choose between them.
- Check all the paperwork you receive after signing up and store it safely.

Over the internet
- Check the website has a real-world address and phone number. Cross-check – eg, against the *Phone Book* – to make sure the contact details are genuine.
- Do not go ahead if anything seems a bit odd about the website – it might be a bogus site.
- Download the full product details and check them out before deciding whether to buy.
- Print off all information that forms the basis of the contract – if you go back later, the information might have changed.
- Make sure that you give personal and payment details only over a secure site – look for 'https' in the address bar and a locked padlock or other symbol on screen.

By phone
- Ask to be sent the full product details before deciding to buy.
- If you cannot see the product details first – eg, because you need to arrange insurance cover quickly, check the details as soon as they arrive after the deal and use your right to cancel if you are not happy with the deal.

– Do not give credit or debit card details over the phone unless you are entirely happy that you are dealing with the genuine provider. (If you are called, say you will call back and first check the number you are calling is genuine.)

By post

– Do not sign up for any old mailshot that hits the doormat. Shop around to see if it offers a good deal.

– Be wary of sending cheques and payment details through the post – they could be stolen. Consider buying by another method rather than post.

– If you do pay by cheque, see p338.

Notes

1 Financial Services Authority, *Annual Report and Accounts 2008/09*, 2009
2 Financial Services Compensation Scheme, *Annual Report and Accounts 2008/09*, 2009
3 UK Payments Administration, *2008 Fraud Figures Announced by APACS*, Press Release, www.apacs.org.uk/ 09_03_19.htm, accessed 1 August 2009

4. **Protecting yourself against fraud**
4 UK Payments Administration, '2008 Fraud Figures Announced by APACS', Press Release, www.apacs.org.uk/ 09_03_19.htm, accessed 1 August 2009

Appendix 1

Glossary

Additional voluntary contributions

Extra contributions you choose to make to boost your pension and/or other benefits from an occupational scheme.

Administration charge/policy fee

A charge taken out of each premium for investment-type life insurance before the rest is invested.

Affinity card

A credit card where the issuer gives a small sum to a specified charity or other organisation (such as a football club) when you first take out the card and each time you use it.

All-in-one (offset) mortgage

A mortgage account combined with a current account and sometimes also other accounts (such as savings accounts). The positive balance in the current and savings accounts is deducted from the balance of the mortgage and any other loan accounts, and interest charged only on the net total. In this way, your mortgage payments are reduced and your savings effectively earn the mortgage rate (a tax-free return).

All risks

Extension to house contents insurance so that items are covered even when you take them out of your home.

Annual equivalent rate

The interest you get from a savings account expressed in a standard way that takes into account not just how much you get but when you get it. (The sooner you receive the interest, the sooner it can be reinvested to earn more, so interest paid or credited, for example, monthly is worth more to you than interest paid yearly. The annual equivalent rate reflects this.) You can directly compare the annual equivalent rate for one account with that for another. The higher the rate, the better the return on offer.

Annual management charge/fee

A charge taken each year from your investment, usually worked out as a percentage of the value of your investments.

Annual percentage rate

A standardised way of expressing the cost of borrowing. The annual percentage rate takes into account the interest and other charges that you *must* pay and also the timing of these payments. (It does not include charges that you might pay only in certain circumstances – eg, if you paid off the loan early or you opted to include insurance that is not a compulsory part of the deal.) The timing of payments is important because, in effect, the earlier you have to make them the more you pay for the loan or, put another way, the less you get for your money. To see this, consider two loans each for £1,000 and both charging you £200 interest. With one, you have to pay back £100 every month; with the other, you pay back nothing until the end of the year when you pay off the full £1,200 in a single lump sum. The second loan is the better deal because you have the use of the full amount of borrowed money for longer. Using annual percentage rates to help you compare products is straightforward: the higher the annual percentage rate, the more expensive the borrowing. A loan with a low annual percentage rate is cheaper than one with a higher rate.

Annuity

A regular income payable for life (lifetime annuity) or for a set period (temporary annuity) which you get in exchange for a lump sum. Once the annuity has been bought, you cannot get your original capital back as a lump sum, and you are locked into the income agreed at the outset.

Application fraud

Form of identity theft where a fraudster obtains enough information about you to be able to take out credit cards and other financial products in your name. The fraudster runs up bills which are then charged to you.

Arbitration scheme

Scheme to help you and a firm settle a dispute which is a cheaper and faster alternative to going to court.

Arrangement fee

An up-front lump-sum charge you pay – eg, for a mortgage or personal loan.

Asset

Something you own. Savings and investments are examples of assets. They are often divided up into groups, usually called 'classes', according to the type of investment and broad level of risk involved.

Asset classes

Groupings of savings and investments according to the type of investment and the broad level of risk involved. The four main classes are:
- cash – ie, savings accounts;
- bonds – eg, gilts and corporate bonds;
- property; *and*
- equities – eg, shares, share-based unit trusts.

ATM

Stands for 'automated teller machine' and is another name for a cash machine.

Attendance allowance

State benefit for severely disabled people aged 65 or over who need help with personal care or find it difficult to get around.

Authorised firm

A financial firm regulated by the Financial Services Authority (FSA). You can check whether a firm is authorised by searching the FSA Register. If you deal with a firm which is not authorised, you are unlikely to be protected if anything goes wrong.

Automated credit transfer

Arrangement whereby money is transferred electronically from one bank (or building society) account to another without the need for a cheque or other paper instruction. Used, for example, by most employers to pay wages or salary.

Bankruptcy

Procedure whereby someone who cannot repay money s/he owes has her/his financial affairs taken over by an official who arranges to pay off as much of the money owed as possible – eg, by selling the bankrupt's assets. Bankruptcy usually lasts for a year, but is likely to affect your ability to get credit for a further six years.

Base rate

A rate of interest which is used as a reference point for setting other interest rates or which usually has a strong influence on other rates. For example, most variable rates offered on savings accounts will tend to move broadly in line with the Bank of England base rate which is set by the Monetary Policy Committee of the Bank of England. Some variable rates (called base-rate trackers) are linked directly to a base rate.

Base-rate tracker

Type of savings account, mortgage or other loan where the interest rate is linked to a particular rate of interest, such as the Bank of England base rate, and which changes directly in line with movements in that rate.

Basic bank account

Type of current account to help you manage your day-to-day money but with restricted features (no cheque book and special debit card) so that you should not be able to go overdrawn.

Basic rate taxpayer

Someone whose top rate of income tax is the basic rate (20 per cent in 2009/10).

Bereavement benefits

State benefits payable to widows or widowers.

Bid-offer spread

With unit trusts and unit-linked investments, the difference between the offer price at which you buy the units and the bid price at which you could immediately sell them. The bid price is lower, so if you sold immediately you would make an instant loss. The spread is a type of charge you pay for these investments.

Blind person's allowance

Extra tax allowance for people who are registered blind (or the equivalent where there is no registration scheme). It allows you to have more income free of income tax and gives relief up to your top rate of tax.

Bond

Name given to a wide variety of investments – eg, marketable loans to companies (corporate bond), the Government (government bond or gilt) or local authorities, some types of investment-type life insurance (such as single-premium bond), some National Savings products (such as guaranteed growth bonds), and some bank and building society products. There is no common meaning for the term, but often these are products where you would expect to invest a lump sum for the medium term or for a shorter, but fixed, period.

Bond committee

An informal community-based arrangement to provide loans.

Bond scheme

Another name for a rent deposit scheme (see p373).

The Budget

The Government's announcement, usually in March each year, of its taxation plans for the coming tax year (and sometimes subsequent tax years too). The measures can be changed by Parliament before becoming law a few months later with the passing of a Finance Act.

Building society accounts

Savings accounts (ie, deposits where the value of your original investment cannot fall) with institutions which have traditionally been 'mutual' organisations (owned by their members and having no shareholders to take a slice of any profits). Building societies can convert to become companies if enough members agree.

Buying power

What you can buy with your money, taking into account changes in prices over time. A way of measuring the effect of inflation.

Capital

The amount of money you originally invest.

Capital gain/capital loss

Capital gain is the profit you make from investing in something because of a rise in its price over the period you have held it. Conversely, a capital loss is the amount of your original money you lose because the price of the investment has fallen during the time you owned it.

Capital gains tax

A tax on the profit or gain which you make from selling (or otherwise disposing of) an asset for more than its value at the time you bought (or otherwise acquired) it. Various allowances can be set against the profit before tax is worked out, so in practice many people escape the tax.

Capital risk

The risk that you will lose money because the value of an investment you have bought falls, but also the chance that you might make money because the investment rises in value.

Capital shares

With an investment trust, a way of investing for growth over a set period.

Capital units

With unit-linked life insurance, a device for charging you extra. These units in the investment fund carry a higher than normal annual management charge.

Capitation schemes

Plan to help you pay for private dental treatment. You pay a set amount each month and then, in most cases, there is no additional charge at the time you receive treatment.

Capped-rate mortgage

A mortgage whose interest rate is variable – that is, it can be altered by the lender and tends to move in line with interest rates in the economy as a whole – except that it is guaranteed not to rise above a given level. The guarantee operates for a set time period, after which the interest rate becomes fully variable.

Carer's allowance

A state benefit you can claim if you spend a substantial amount of time looking after someone who is severely disabled.

Cashback

A lump sum you receive when taking out some types of product – eg, some mortgages. Also a scheme whereby you can draw cash from your bank account at supermarket checkouts when you pay for goods using your debit card.

Cash balance scheme

Type of occupational pension scheme that lets your employer contain the cost of providing pensions but protects you from investment risk while your savings build up, though not once retirement is reached. Your employer promises you a target cash sum at retirement and pays the balance of whatever is needed to reach that target. You then shop around at retirement with your cash to buy the best pension you can.

Cash card

Plastic card used to get cash from a current or savings account using a cash machine.

Cash equivalent transfer value

A lump sum which represents the value of your pension rights in a pension scheme. You can pay the lump sum into a new scheme in order to transfer your pension rights from one scheme to another. It will not necessarily buy the same type of benefits or benefits of the same value.

Cash individual savings account

A tax-efficient way to invest in savings accounts with banks, building societies and National Savings and Investments. The interest earned is free of income tax.

Certificate of insurance

A document, issued for example with car insurance, stating that you have the minimum cover required by law and specifying the dates between which you are covered.

Cheque

An instruction to your bank usually on a pre-printed document to transfer money from your current account to someone else's bank account.

Cheque guarantee card

Plastic card which, when presented with a cheque up to a set amount, reassures someone you are paying that the cheque will be honoured and so they will get their money. Your bank will transfer the money as directed by the cheque even if there is too little money in your account to cover it. **Note:** the cheque guarantee scheme will end in 2011.

Cheque guarantee limit

The set limit up to which a bank will honour a cheque you give someone even if there is too little money in your account to cover the cheque. To use the guarantee, you must present your cheque guarantee card to the person you are paying along with the cheque.

Child benefit

A state benefit which virtually everyone looking after a child under 16, or under 19 and in full-time education, can claim.

Child tax credit

A means-tested state benefit which can be claimed by families with children.

Child trust fund

A scheme under which the Government issues vouchers to be invested for every child born on or after 1 September 2002 and which it hopes will stimulate further saving for and by young people.

Chip and PIN

System to cut credit card fraud by requiring you to enter a personal identification number in a keypad to authorise a transaction instead of providing a signature.

Christmas savings scheme

Scheme to help you spread the cost of Christmas either by paying instalments in advance for goods or vouchers or by setting aside regular savings.

Claim

The process of requesting a payout from an insurance policy. The insurer needs to know the facts of the case, including the amount you are claiming, what it is for, and the event that caused the need for the claim.

Clearing cycle

The time taken for cheques and other money paid into a bank or savings account to be available for you to withdraw or spend. The clearing cycle has been significantly reduced for electronic payments (see Faster Payments Service on p354) but cheques continue to take several days.

Commission

Payment to a salesperson or adviser by the provider whose products have been sold, generally based on the value of the sale. You pay the commission indirectly through the charges built into the product.

Combined benefit statement

Statement from a pension scheme or pension provider showing your expected pension from the scheme or plan and also the state pension you might get at retirement based on your actual national insurance record. These statements must include estimates of your pensions at retirement in today's money.

Community development finance institution

Body established to provide grants and loans to businesses, community organisations and sometimes individuals in order to promote regeneration of a socially deprived area.

Company representative

A salesperson who can advise on and sell the products only of the one provider that employs her/him. (These might include the products of other companies that have been adopted into the provider's range.) A company representative does not give independent advice about the market as a whole.

Comprehensive cover

Type of car insurance that will pay out for damage to your own car as well as damage to other people's property and injury to other people.

Contract note

A document that records you have insurance cover. It is issued to bridge the gap until the full schedule and policy document are sent to you. In the case of car insurance, the contract note includes a temporary certificate of insurance. Also a document recording the sale or purchase of shares or other investments.

Contracting out

Giving up part or all of your state additional pension and getting instead a pension and other benefits from an occupational pension scheme, personal pension or stakeholder scheme.

Convertible bonds

Type of corporate bond which, at set dates and prices, can be traded in and replaced with shares in the issuing company instead.

Convertible term insurance

Term insurance which carries an option (for which you pay extra) to swap it in future for an investment-type life insurance policy.

Corporate bond

Loan to a company. The loan can be traded on the stock market. You receive regular interest and may make a capital gain or loss depending on the prices at which you buy and sell the stocks. There are many variations – eg, 'convertible bonds' give you the option to swap the bonds at a given future date (or dates) for ordinary shares in the company.

Council tax benefit

State benefit that pays your council tax bill for you if your income is low.

Coupon

The interest from a gilt, expressed as a percentage of the gilt's nominal value.

Credit

Can either mean borrowing money or, alternatively, the positive balance you have in a savings account.

Credit card

A plastic card you use to pay for things (and, if you choose, to get cash from cash machines) with the option to pay off the bill in instalments over a period you choose. You are charged interest on any amount you do not pay off straight away.

Credit card cheques

Cheques you receive (often unsolicited, although in 2009 the Government proposed banning this practice) from your credit card company with an invitation to use them to pay for goods and services. The value of the used cheque is then added to your credit card account and you pay it off in instalments over a period you choose. An expensive way to borrow because you are charged interest on the outstanding balance at a high rate of interest and there is usually a further charge as well for using the cheque.

Credit history

A record of how you have managed your borrowings in the past. Used by lenders to decide whether to lend to you now and, if so, what interest rate to charge.

Current account

Type of bank account you use to manage your day-to-day money.

Dealing costs

Costs you incur buying or selling something on top of the cost of the item itself – eg, the commission you pay to a stockbroker when you buy and sell shares.

Debit card

Plastic card you use to pay for things or to get cash either from a cash machine or through a supermarket cashback scheme. The amount you pay or withdraw is taken directly from the bank account to which the card is linked.

Debt relief order

Relatively new arrangement, available since 6 April 2009, designed to help people on a low income with few assets to sort out problem debts. The borrower is given a breathing space of 12 months, during which creditors cannot take any action. At the end of 12 months, the debts are written off.

Decreasing balance

With some types of borrowing (eg, personal loans and repayment mortgages), the repayments are designed so that, if you pay the same amount each month, the whole loan including the interest will be paid off by the end of the term. However, since you are paying off some of the capital each month, the amount you owe falls (ie, your balance decreases) and the amount of interest you are charged takes this into account.

Deeds fee

A charge when you pay off a mortgage to cover the legal and administrative costs the lender incurs passing the deeds of your property to you.

Defined benefit scheme

Type of occupational pension scheme where you are promised a set amount of pension at retirement, often based on your pay at that time and the number of years you have been in the scheme.

Defined contribution scheme

Type of pension scheme where a given amount is paid into the scheme by or for you but you cannot know in advance how much pension you will eventually get. This depends on the amount paid in, how well the investment grows, how much is taken out in charges and how much pension you can buy with the resulting fund at retirement.

Department for Work and Pensions

Government department responsible for state benefits and state retirement pensions.

Direct debit

Instruction to your bank to allow an organisation to take money in payment for regular bills directly from your bank account.

Direct payment

Refers to a system where disabled people and carers eligible for help from social services (such as help with personal care) receive cash and are then responsible for choosing and arranging the services for themselves.

Disability living allowance

State benefit available to people of working age who are disabled and need help with personal care or getting around.

Discounted rate mortgage

A mortgage whose interest rate is kept at a set percentage below the standard variable mortgage rate for an initial period. If this represents a genuine discount, such mortgages can be worthwhile. But with some, the difference between the normal and discounted rates of interest is added to the outstanding loan, dramatically increasing the overall cost of the mortgage.

Dividends

Income you may receive as a shareholder in a company.

European Health Insurance Card

Plastic card that is proof of your eligibility to claim emergency healthcare throughout the European Economic Area.

Employment and support allowance

State benefit available to people who are off work because of illness or disability. It replaced incapacity benefit for new claimants from 27 October 2008. You qualify for contribution-based employment and support allowance if you have paid enough national insurance contributions of the right type. You may qualify for income-based employment and support allowance if your income is low.

Endowment insurance

Type of life insurance policy which pays out either if you die within a set period or at the end of the period if you survive. Mainly used as an investment rather than a way of protecting dependants.

Equities

Another name for shares or share-based investments.

Equity release scheme

Way of raising money from your home – either by taking out a mortgage or selling part or all of the home – while maintaining the right to live there as long as you need to.

Estate

At death, everything you own less everything you owe.

Ethical funds

Investment funds which avoid investing in some companies (eg, because they are involved in activities often viewed as socially undesirable, such as gambling, tobacco or the arms trade) and/or select companies for investment because of their good policies – eg, paying fair wages to workers in developing countries.

European Economic Area

The following countries: Austria, Belgium, Bulgaria, Cyprus, Czech Republic, Denmark, Estonia, Finland, France, Germany, Greece, Hungary, Iceland, Irish Republic, Italy, Latvia, Liechtenstein, Lithuania, Luxembourg, Malta, Netherlands, Norway, Poland, Portugal, Romania, Slovakia, Slovenia, Spain, Sweden, UK.

Excess

The first amount of an insurance claim that you yourself must pay – eg, the first £100 or £500 of a claim. With a 'compulsory excess', the terms of the policy require you to pay this part of the bill yourself. With a 'voluntary excess', you agree to pay this sum in exchange for a reduction in the premium you pay.

Exchange rate loading

An extra charge made by credit card companies when you use your credit card abroad and the bill for the items purchased is translated into £s.

Exchange traded fund

An investment fund, typically constructed to track an index (for example, of share prices, such as the FTSE 1000) and which can be bought and sold on the stock market. Exchange traded funds tend to have low charges compared with other types of investment fund.

Exclusion

Something which is specifically not covered by an insurance policy – eg, some life policies do not pay out on suicide within the first year, most health insurance policies will not pay out if your claim is connected to a health problem you already had before the policy started, car insurance often does not cover drivers under 25 unless you pay an extra premium.

Exit charge

With an investment fund (such as a unit trust or unit-linked life insurance), a charge levied when you sell the investment – generally restricted to a sale within, for example, the first five years.

Extended warranty

Type of insurance that covers the cost of repairs or replacement if an item breaks down in the first few years but after the manufacturer's own guarantee has run out.

Family income benefit policy

Type of term insurance which, if you die during the term, pays out a series of tax-free lump sums to your survivor(s) over the remaining term, as if the sums were an income.

Faster Payments Service

Bank system, introduced from May 2008, which allows transactions by phone, internet and standing order (but not direct debit or cheque) to be made within two hours and often just seconds. Once a payment has been initiated using the Faster Payments Service, it cannot be cancelled.

Final salary scheme

Type of occupational salary-related pension scheme where your pension and certain other benefits depend on the amount of your pay at or near the time of retirement and the number of years you have been in the scheme.

Financial adviser

A person or firm offering advice about investments, insurance and so on. An adviser could be a company representative or tied agent selling the products of a single provider (which, however, might include the products of other companies adopted into the provider's range) or an independent adviser who can base her/his advice on all the products available on the market – you need to check which before you do business.

Financial Ombudsman Service

A single independent complaints body which covers most financial products and services.

Financial Services Authority

The single regulator responsible for most financial products and services. Its main responsibilities are banking supervision, regulating investment businesses, financial market supervision, enforcement of the rules and regulations, services to consumers and services to the industry and other regulators. Services to consumers include establishing a single Ombudsman scheme (the Financial Ombudsman Service), establishing a single compensation scheme (the Financial Services Compensation Scheme), running a consumer helpline, publishing information booklets, running a consumer website and promoting consumer understanding of financial products and services.

Financial Services Compensation Scheme

A scheme which might pay you compensation if you have lost money through the fraud or negligence of a firm, authorised by the Financial Services Authority, which has gone out of business.

Fixed rate

A rate of interest that stays the same regardless of any changes in interest rates in the economy as a whole. A fixed rate is usually offered for a set period of time, after which either your investment matures or you automatically switch to a different rate.

Flexible mortgage

A mortgage which gives you the option to make overpayments and possibly to reduce or miss payments as well.

Form R85

A form you use if you are a non-taxpayer to register with a bank or building society so that it will pay you interest without any tax deducted.

Friendly society

Similar to an insurance company, but friendly societies are allowed to offer some savings plans which are largely tax-free.

Front-end charge

A charge you pay at the time you buy or invest as opposed to charges which are spread over the lifetime of the product.

FTSE 100 Index

An average of the prices of the shares of the 100 largest UK companies quoted on the London Stock Exchange. Often used as an indicator of movements in the stock market.

Fund supermarket

An outlet – often an internet website – where you can invest in unit trusts, open-ended investment companies and sometimes investment trusts, usually more cheaply than elsewhere. Generally, you can mix and match the investments you choose to put inside an individual savings account if you want to.

Gearing

The degree to which borrowed money is invested in order to increase potential gains. However, gearing also magnifies any losses.

Generic financial advice

Guidance to help consumers make financial decisions that falls short of directing them to specific products and companies and so can be given by firms and bodies that are not authorised by the Financial Services Authority.

Gilts (British Government stocks)

Loans to central government which can be traded on the stock market. You receive regular interest and may make a capital gain or loss, depending on the prices at which you buy and sell the stocks.

Girocheque

A type of cheque often used to pay state benefits which does not have to be paid into a bank account, but can be exchanged for cash at post offices.

Global equities

Shares of companies based in different countries around the world.

Graduate account

Current account for people who have graduated from university. A common feature is that the account starts with a large free overdraft facility (usually completely used at its start if you ran up an overdraft while studying) which gradually reduces over a period of, for example, three years.

Green card

Document showing that your car insurance cover has been extended to cover driving in specified countries outside the UK for the period shown on the green card. Usually needed if you take your car abroad. Some insurers charge you extra for a green card; with others it is included within your normal premium.

Gross

Describes the interest or return from your savings or investment before any tax has been deducted. This may be the rate quoted in advertisements and product literature but, if you are a taxpayer, you will usually get less than the gross return. However, some products are tax free, in which case the gross return is the actual return you get.

Grossed-up income

The process of finding the before-tax amount which corresponds to an after-tax sum you have received. You multiply the after-tax amount by 100/(100 – tax rate).

Group personal pension scheme

Arrangement whereby an employer gives a pension provider access to its workforce for the sale of personal pensions. The pension provider, not the employer, offers and runs the pension, so it must not be confused with an occupational pension scheme. However, the employer might negotiate special terms for workers who take out a personal pension through the scheme. Some (but not many) employers contribute towards their employees' personal pensions taken out through a group scheme. A personal pension you take out this way is not tied to your job and can continue if you change jobs (though special terms and employer's contributions would probably stop).

Growth

An increase in the value of something.

Guarantee credit

Part of the pension credit payable to many state pensioners. It is the minimum amount of income that a pensioner is expected to live on. If your income from all sources comes to less, you can claim pension credit.

Guaranteed equity bonds

Various types of investment which offer a return linked to the stock market but with less risk than investing directly in shares. Some guaranteed equity bonds aim to protect you completely from losing any capital, but others do not, so make sure you understand the type of product you are buying. The extent to which you can rely on the guarantees depends on the financial strength of the organisation offering them.

Health in pregnancy grant

State benefit which provides a cash lump sum to women who are pregnant and receiving health advice from a midwife or doctor.

Higher rate taxpayer

Someone whose top rate of income tax is the higher rate (40 per cent in 2009/10). However, on dividends and similar income, higher rate taxpayers are liable at a special rate (32.5 per cent in 2009/10). From 2010/11, there will be a new, additional higher rate with a 50 per cent tax band applying to earned income and savings income over £150,000 and a new upper rate of 42.5 per cent for dividend income.

High lending fee

A charge you pay with a mortgage, which buys insurance to protect the lender (not you) against loss if you fail to keep up your payments and your home is sold for less than the outstanding amount of the loan to be paid off.

Hire purchase

A way of borrowing to buy something. Technically, you hire the goods from a finance company, paying it a regular rental fee and, after an agreed period of time, you pay a token amount to buy the goods. The goods remain the property of the finance company until the final payment, so if you do not keep up the payments, the goods are taken back.

Health cash plans

Type of product, similar to insurance, which pays out various cash sums in specified circumstances – eg, if you have to go into hospital, if you need dental treatment, if you become pregnant or if you visit a chiropractor.

HM Revenue and Customs

Government department dealing with the assessment and collection of taxes, including those on earnings, other income, profits, gains and inheritance. It also administers some state benefits, in particular tax credits and child benefit. Referred to in this *Handbook* as 'the Revenue'.

Home reversion scheme

Scheme whereby you raise money by selling part or all of your home but retain the right to continue living there rent-free or for a nominal rent for as long as you need the home.

Housing benefit

A state benefit that pays part or all of your rent if your income is low.

Hybrid scheme

Type of occupational pension scheme which works out pension and other benefits on both a salary-related basis and a money purchase basis, paying you whichever is the greater.

Ijara

A leasing contract that complies with Islamic (*Shariah*) law. When combined with diminishing *Musharaka* (see p366), the contract can be used for home purchase. For example, a bank may buy the home chosen by the consumer. The consumer then pays rent to the bank for a specified period and also regular capital sums that gradually purchase the property from the bank.

Incapacity benefit

A state benefit for people who are incapable of work because of either sickness or disability. Replaced from 27 October 2008 for new claimants by employment and support allowance.

Income drawdown

With defined contribution pensions, an arrangement whereby you draw an income at retirement direct from the pension fund instead of buying an annuity.

Income shares

With an investment trust, a way of investing for an income.

Income tax

Tax levied on most regular payments you receive – eg, earnings, pensions and income from investments.

Increasable term insurance

Term insurance where the amount of cover (and the premium) can be increased either at certain times or at given events, such as birth of a child. The extra you pay assumes that your state of health is still the same as it was when you originally took out the policy even if, in fact, it has deteriorated.

Increasing term insurance

Term insurance where the amount of cover, and the premium, automatically increase during the term either by a set percentage each year or in line with inflation. The extra you pay assumes that your state of health is still the same as it was when you originally took out the policy even if, in fact, it has deteriorated.

Independent financial adviser

An investment adviser who can consider the full range of products and companies in a market when giving you advice.

Index

An artificially constructed yardstick used to measure changes in whatever the subject of the index is or as a benchmark to which, say, investment performance can be linked or against which it can be compared. Common examples of indices are:

- **FTSE 100 Index** which tracks the performance of the share price of the 100 largest companies quoted on the London Stock Exchange;
- **Retail Prices Index** which tracks the prices of a very large basket of goods and services and so provides a measure of the cost of living.

Index-linked gilts

Loans to the Government where the amount you get back on repayment and the interest you get in the meantime are both increased in line with price inflation.

Individual budget

See 'Personal budget'.

Individual savings account

A government scheme to encourage savings by offering tax incentives. Individual savings accounts can be used to invest in a very wide range of investments through two components: cash (bank and building society accounts and National Savings), and stocks and shares (unit trusts, OEICs, investment trusts, direct investment in shares, corporate bonds, gilts and investment-type life insurance).

Individual voluntary arrangement

Procedure whereby someone who cannot repay money enters into a formal agreement to pay off an agreed proportion of their debts over a set period, usually five years. It is likely to affect your ability to get credit for a further six years.

Inflation

A sustained change in prices (or, say, earnings). A common measure of price inflation is the change in the Retail Prices Index.

Inflation risk

The risk that the buying power of your money will fall because of prices rising over time.

Inheritance tax

Tax on your estate when you die and on some gifts made during your lifetime if those gifts come to more than a given sum.

Instalments

Part-payments for something made over a period of time, usually at regular intervals.

Instant/easy-access accounts

Savings accounts where you can withdraw your money without giving any notice or losing any interest.

Insurance

Financial product that aims to compensate you for the financial loss caused by an unforeseen event. In the case of life insurance, it is often not possible to measure an actual financial loss because of someone's death, so these policies are commonly arranged to pay out a specified sum.

Interest

A payment or series of payments you get in return for lending your money to, or depositing it with, an institution. You can view it as the compensation you get for not being able to use the money yourself until it is paid back or you draw it out.

Interest risk

With an investment, the risk either that you will lose the opportunity to invest for a higher return if you are locked into a fixed interest rate, or that your return will fall if you have invested at a variable rate. Conversely, with a loan, the risk that you will be locked into paying too much if you borrow at a fixed rate or that your payments will increase if you borrow at a variable rate.

Interest yield

With gilts and corporate bonds, the interest you get as a percentage of the market price and ignoring any gain or loss you might make when the gilt or bond is repaid.

Interest-only loan

A loan where, during its term, you just pay the interest due. You do not make any capital repayments. This means, at the end of the term, you still owe the whole capital amount and must repay it in a single lump sum. You might find this lump sum by, for instance, cashing in an investment (eg, an endowment policy taken out with a mortgage) or selling the item you bought with the loan (eg, a second home or buy-to-let property).

Intermediaries

'Middlemen' who bring together customers and providers. Some are acting for providers but should give you accurate information about products and only recommend those which are suitable for you. Others (independent intermediaries) act for you and can search out the most suitable deal for you from all those on the market.

Internet account

A bank or savings account operated over the internet.

Investment trust

A company quoted on the Stock Exchange, whose business is running a fund investing in, for example, the shares of other companies or gilts and bonds. You invest indirectly in the fund by buying the shares of the investment trust.

Investment-type life insurance

Some types of life insurance ('term insurance') just pay out if you die within a set period of time and pay nothing if you survive (see Chapter 7 for more about these). Other types ('investment-type life insurance') pay out whenever you die ('whole life insurance') or when the policy matures after a set period of time ('endowment insurance') and, because a payout *must* eventually be made, they build up a cash-in value which tends to increase over time.

Investment-type life insurance has evolved and adapted so that many such policies are now designed not so much to pay out if you die but to let you use the cash-in value to provide an investment return. They do this by taking the bulk of the money you pay in premiums and investing it on either a unit-linked or with-profits basis.

Jobcentre Plus

An agency that handles the payment and administration of state benefits for people of working age on behalf of the Department for Work and Pensions and runs various initiatives to help people back into work.

Jobseeker's allowance

State benefit which may be payable to people who are unemployed. You qualify for contribution-based jobseeker's allowance if you have paid enough national insurance contributions of the right type. You may qualify for income-based jobseeker's allowance if your income is low.

Key Facts document or illustration

Document which providers of certain products, such as personal pensions, stakeholder schemes, mortgages and equity release schemes are required to give you. It sets out important information about the product in a standard way to help you understand it and to compare it easily with competing products. You can spot the document by the Key Facts logo:

Lasting power of attorney

Legal arrangement whereby you appoint someone to manage your financial affairs (and if you choose also arrangements concerning your health and welfare) should you lose your mental capacity.

Life insurance

Insurance that pays out if you die. Some sorts (investment-type life insurance) build up a cash-in value and are often used primarily as an investment rather than a way of protecting dependants.

Life insurance loan

A loan either from an insurer or another unconnected company secured against the value of an investment-type life insurance policy you have. Only with-profits policies can normally be used this way (because the value of the policy has already built up does not normally fall).

Lifestyle fund

Investment fund you use with a pension plan. While you are a long way from retirement, the fund is invested mainly in equities (shares) because these have tended to give the highest growth over the long term. As you get nearer to retirement, the fund automatically shifts into less risky investments such as bonds and cash, in order to lock in the gains you have previously made.

Lifetime mortgage

Another name for a type of equity release scheme that involves taking out a mortgage on your home in order to raise an income or lump sum.

Limit (insurance policy)

The maximum amount the insurance will pay out. This might apply to the total payout or could apply to a particular section of the policy – eg, home contents insurance normally has a limit on the amount it will pay out for a single item (eg, £250) as well as a limit on the total maximum payout to the amount you have said your possessions are worth.

Maintenance grant

Non-repayable grant available for university students from low-income households.

Mandate

A written instruction – eg to your bank.

Market value

The price of something in the open market.

Market value reduction

A charge you often incur if you transfer a pension plan before retirement from one provider to another or cash in an investment-type insurance policy early. It applies to pensions and investments invested on a with-profits basis.

Married couple's allowance

Tax allowance available to married couples if one or both were born before 6 April 1935. Tax relief is restricted to 10 per cent of the allowance and given as a reduction in the tax bill.

Material facts

Information that an insurer uses to decide whether or not to cover you and, if so, what premium to charge. You are required to tell your insurer about material facts at the time you apply for cover or if there is any change during the course of a policy. If you do not, some or all of your claims could be refused.

Maternity allowance

State benefit you can claim if you are pregnant or have recently given birth and you are not eligible for statutory maternity pay.

Means-tested state benefits

State benefits where your entitlement and the amount you receive depends on your income and savings. Designed to restrict payments only to those on low incomes and with few savings.

Minimum investment

The smallest amount you are allowed to invest. Usually it is up to the provider to set this limit and often it will be fairly high because small investments are costly to administer, but sometimes the law specifies a limit – eg, with a stakeholder pension scheme, the minimum set by the provider may not be higher than £20.

Mini-statements

A summary of recent payments in and out of your bank or building society account, usually available only through cash machines.

Money guidance

A generic financial advice service, being piloted during 2009 by the Financial Services Authority and due eventually to be available nationally. The service, which has been given the Financial Services Authority Moneymadeclear brand name, aims to deliver information, guidance and tools that are tailored to the individual to give her/him the confidence to make informed choices. If your needs are complex, the service will signpost you to an appropriate regulated adviser for more in-depth advice. The money guidance service does not recommend specific courses of action, products, types of products or providers.

Money purchase scheme

Another name for a defined contribution scheme (see p351).

Mortality drag

The extra return your investment needs to earn if you put off buying an annuity with your pension fund. The amount increases as you get older because you have lost the cross-subsidy from people who died at an earlier than average age.

Mortgage

Any loan secured against the value of your home. If you do not keep up the required interest payments and capital repayments (if applicable), the lender can take possession of your home in order to recover the amount owed.

Mortgage indemnity guarantee

Another name for a high lending fee.

Mortgage indemnity premium

Another name for a high lending fee.

Mudaraba

An investment contract that complies with Islamic (*Shariah*) law and may be used, for example, as a substitute for savings accounts (which pay interest and so are not acceptable under Islamic law). The investment is made by a skilled third party on your behalf and you share the profits or losses it makes.

Multi-tied adviser

A person or firm that advises on and sells the products of several companies.

Murabaha

A contract for purchase and resale that complies with Islamic (*Shariah*) law. May be used, for example, for purchasing a home. A bank buys the home chosen by the customer and immediately sells it to the customer at a higher price. The customer gradually pays the purchase price in instalments over an agreed period.

Musharaka

A partnership arrangement that complies with Islamic (*Shariah*) law under which you place capital with someone else (eg, a bank) and share in any profit or loss from investing the money.

National insurance

Basically, a tax on earnings from employment and profits from self-employment. Payment of enough contributions of the appropriate type entitles you to receive certain state benefits, such as a state pension, contribution-based jobseeker's allowance and contribution-based employment and support allowance.

National Savings and Investments

Savings accounts and similar investments issued on behalf of the Government.

Net

Describes the interest or return from your savings or investment after tax has been deducted. In some cases, it means tax has been deducted at a standard rate but you personally might have further tax to pay.

Net asset value

With investment trusts, the value of the investment fund divided by the number of shares. If this is more than the price you have to pay for the shares, they are said to be trading at a discount. If the net asset value is lower than the share price, the shares are trading at a premium.

No claims discount

A reduction in your premium at renewal if you have not made any claims during the past year. This is a common feature of car insurance and is also sometimes used with home contents insurance and private medical insurance.

Nominal/par value

A handy unit used when quoting the price, coupon and other details for gilts and corporate bonds.

Notice accounts

Savings accounts where you can withdraw your money only after telling the provider in advance that you intend to do this. Some accounts waive the notice period, but you then lose interest instead.

Occupational pension scheme

A scheme through which you can build up a retirement pension and other benefits run by the employer for whom you work. The employer must normally pay at least part of the cost. In a 'non-contributory' scheme, the employer foots the whole bill.

Ombudsman scheme

An independent complaints body which can try to resolve a dispute between you and a firm. It is usually free for the consumer to use and quicker than taking a case to court. Unlike a court or arbitration scheme, the Ombudsman can take into account good practice as well as the strict letter of the law.

Open-ended investment companies

Investment similar to a unit trust, but you buy shares in the open-ended investment companies. Shares are bought and sold directly from the management company at a single price and charges are shown separately.

Open-market option

With a personal pension or stakeholder scheme, your right at retirement to take your pension fund and shop around for the annuity provider that can offer you the best return.

Overdraft

The amount by which you have spent more money than you have in your current account. If you arrange the overdraft in advance, this can be a flexible and reasonably cheap way to borrow. If you overspend without asking first, it is normally very costly.

Packaged investments

In the context of the Financial Services Authority rules, this means investment-type life insurance, annuities, personal pensions, personal stakeholder pension schemes, unit trusts, open-ended investment companies and investment trust savings schemes.

Partnership scheme

An informal community-based arrangement to provide loans.

Pay As You Earn

Income tax and national insurance are deducted from your pay before you get it through this system.

Payment protection insurance

Type of insurance that continues loan repayments for a limited period if you are made redundant or you are unable to work because of illness. Also called accident, sickness and unemployment insurance.

Pension

A regular income, usually paid for life.

Pension credit

Means-tested state benefit. It has two elements: a guarantee credit to ensure a minimum level of income for everyone aged 60 or over (this age is gradually increasing in line with the rise in women's state pension age); and a savings credit to reward people aged 65 and over who have made their own savings for retirement.

The Pensions Advisory Service

A scheme, funded by the Government, to help resolve misunderstandings and disputes between pension schemes and their members or pension plan providers and their planholders. If this system of advice and conciliation fails, the dispute can be referred to the Pension Ombudsman.

The Pension Service

An agency that handles the payment and administration of state pensions and other benefits for people over state pension age on behalf of the Department for Work and Pensions.

Personal accounts

A new national pension scheme due to start in 2012. Under the scheme, employers must ensure that eligible workers are automatically enrolled in either the national scheme or another pension scheme that is at least as good, but workers may opt out if they want to. Employers must pay at least 3 per cent of a worker's pay between set limits into whichever scheme the worker belongs to; the worker will have to pay in 4 per cent of their pay between the set limits up to an annual maximum (£3,600 in 2005 money). Tax relief will add another 1 per cent. Personal accounts will provide money purchase pensions.

Personal budget/individual budget

Personal budgets are a system for disabled people and carers whereby funds are allocated to an account in their name to be used to buy the social services they need. Account holders can take the funds as direct payments (cash) or choose the service providers but leave their local authority to commission them, or a combination of both. Individual budgets are similar, but combine, in one account, funding for care services with funding from other sources for other purposes, such as adaptations to the home.

Personal identification number

A code you use in conjunction with a plastic card to access information about, and make withdrawals from, a current or savings account. To keep your money secure, it is essential that you never tell anyone your number and do not write it down in any recognisable form.

Personal loan

A way of borrowing. You get a lump sum to spend and pay it back with interest by instalments over a set period.

Personal pension

Money-purchase pension arrangement run by, for example, an insurance company, bank, stockbroker or financial advice firm. It aims to provide you with a pension at retirement and possibly other benefits. Unlike an occupational pension scheme, a personal pension plan need not be connected with a specific job.

Phishing

Type of internet fraud where you are sent an email purporting to be from your bank with a link to a bogus website where you are asked to give the security information for your account.

Phone account

A bank or savings account that you operate by phone. In the case of a savings account, you normally set up a direct debit facility between the account and your current account. The facility acts as a sort of pipe through which money flows when you want to pay money into or draw money out of the savings account.

Points scheme

With a credit card, arrangement whereby you are credited with points every time you use the card and can trade these in for goods or services when you have collected enough.

Policy

An insurance contract. You usually get a policy document setting out all the terms and conditions and a schedule which specifies the details personal to you – eg, the dates between which you are covered, any parts of the policy document which do not apply, and any particular exclusions.

Portfolio

A spread of different investments. If you invest in shares, a portfolio is a spread of shares in different companies.

Post Office card account

An account into which state benefits can be paid as an alternative to arranging for payment direct to a bank or building society account. You can withdraw cash from the account at post offices. The account has no other features – eg, no arrangements for paying bills.

Postal account

A savings account operated by post.

Pre-existing condition

A health problem you already had before you took out the policy. Insurers have two ways of dealing with this:
* **underwriting**. The insurer works out the likelihood that you might make a claim linked to the health problem. On the basis of this, the insurer might refuse to cover you at all, refuse cover just for claims linked to that problem, charge you a higher premium, or make some other adjustment to the policy;
* **moratorium**. For a set period – often two years – the policy will not pay out for any claims linked to a health problem you had within, say, the five years immediately prior to taking out the policy. Provided you have not had a recurrence of the problem or any treatment for it, the problem is covered once the set period is over.

Premium

The price you pay for insurance. Often, you are quoted a premium which is the yearly cost of cover and there may be arrangements to alter the premium at the end of each year. However, you can often arrange to pay the premium in monthly instalments. In some cases – eg, with car insurance – by paying monthly instalments, you are considered to be borrowing the unpaid part of the premium. You are charged interest on the unpaid part, which increases the cost of the cover.

Premium waiver

Option (for which you pay extra) with insurance under which your cover continues even though you are not paying the premiums because of some specified event – eg, being unable to work because of illness.

Property authorised investment fund

An investment that gives you a stake in a fund of different commercial and/or residential properties. The fund pays no tax on the income and gains from the property investments. The amount of tax you pay depends on your particular tax situation.

Proposal form

The form on which you apply for an insurance policy. It asks all sorts of questions that the insurer relies on when deciding whether to give you cover and how much to charge you. The proposal form forms part of your contract with the insurer. If you give incorrect or false information, the contract could be invalid and your claims refused.

PTM levy

Small additional charge made on large purchases or sales of shares. It is used to fund the Panel on Takeovers and Mergers (PTM), an unofficial watchdog which aims to ensure fair play for all shareholders when companies are being taken over or merging.

Public liability

A section in many insurance policies which will pay out if you are held responsible for injuring someone or damaging her/his property in your role as, say, a homeowner or occupier.

Purchase protection insurance

Insurance that pays out if items you have recently bought are lost, stolen or damaged. Often free with some credit cards but may duplicate cover you already have through your house contents insurance.

Real estate investment trust

An investment that gives you a stake in a fund of different commercial and/or residential properties. The fund pays no tax on the income and gains from the property investments. The amount of tax you pay depends on your particular tax situation.

Redemption date

Date on which a gilt or corporate bond comes to the end of its life and the loan you have effectively made is repaid.

Redemption value

The amount you get back when a gilt or corporate bond comes to the end of its life and the amount you have effectively lent is repaid.

Redemption yield

With gilts and corporate bonds, the total amount you get – ie, interest and redemption value – expressed as a percentage of the market price.

Reducing term insurance

Life insurance that pays out if you die within a set period (the term) but the longer your survive the lower the amount paid. Commonly used to pay off a repayment mortgage in the event of death.

Regular savings accounts

Accounts where you are committed to paying in at least a set amount, usually every month. If you miss more than a few payments, the interest rate is usually reduced.

Regulator

An organisation responsible for ensuring that firms observe good standards of business and for taking disciplinary action against those who break the rules.

Renewable term insurance

Term insurance which guarantees that you can take out a further term insurance policy at the end of the original term. The further policy will be based on your health at the time you took out the original policy, even if it has worsened in the meantime.

Renewal

The process of taking out a new policy immediately on the expiry of an old one.

Renewal notice

Document sent to you by an insurer with whom you have a policy warning you that your policy will soon expire and inviting you to take out a new policy at the price shown on the notice. You do not have to renew with the same insurer, but can shop around for a policy from another insurer.

Rent deposit scheme

Scheme to help low-income households get private rented accommodation either by providing the required deposit or guaranteeing to pay the landlord (who waives the deposit) if the tenant damages the rented property.

Retail Prices Index

Average of the prices of a large number of goods and services used to provide a measure of the cost of living.

Return

The total amount you gain from saving or investing your money. This might be made up of interest, income in some other form, a capital gain (or loss, in which case it reduces the return) or a mixture of any of these.

Right-to-buy mortgage

A mortgage used to buy your council home (or home which used to belong to the council but now belongs to, say, a housing association).

Sale-and-rent-back scheme

Scheme that claims to be able to help you if you run into mortgage problems. You agree to sell your home to a firm but have the right to carry on living there as a tenant. This sounds similar to a home reversion scheme (see p358) but in fact is very different. In particular, under a sale-and-rent-back scheme, you pay a commercial rent and do not have any long-term right to stay in your home.

Savings credit

A means-tested state benefit, part of the pension credit. It rewards people aged 65 or over who have made their own modest savings for retirement.

Saving Gateway

Scheme, due to be launched nationally from April 2010, to encourage people of working age on a low income to build up savings and develop a savings habit. Under the scheme, you make regular savings and, in addition to earning interest, get a bonus from the Government.

Secured loan

Most loans of this type are secured against your home and if you do not keep up the agreed payments, the lender has the right to seize ('repossess') your home and sell it in order to get the money back. A mortgage is a secured loan and so are many loans used to consolidate existing debts. Secured loans are usually cheaper than unsecured loans because the lender runs a low risk of not being able to get its money back. However, they are more risky for you because, if you run into repayment problems, you could lose your home. Think very carefully before deciding to take out a secured loan and make sure you are confident that you can keep to the repayments. Secured loans can be secured against other items of value that you own, such as a with-profits insurance policy that has built up a cash-in value.

Self-certification mortgage

A mortgage where the lender does not require proof of the earnings you say you have. Usually you pay a higher than normal interest rate for this type of mortgage. In 2009, the Financila Services Authority proposed that, in future, this type of mortgage should be banned.

Self-employed

Working for yourself rather than an employer and running your business either as a sole trader or in partnership with other people.

Share exchange scheme

Arrangement where you can swap shares you hold for a holding in a unit trust or investment trust. This usually works out cheaper than selling the shares yourself and reinvesting the proceeds.

Shared equity mortgage

Mortgage where, to keep the monthly payments down, you take out a mortgage to buy just part of your home and pay a subsidised rent to a landlord for the rest. When you sell the home, the landlord gets part of the proceeds.

Shares

Shares represent slices in the ownership of a company. Depending on the type of shares, you may have the right to vote on decisions about the running of the company and you may receive a regular share of the profits in the form of dividends. By trading shares, you also stand to make a capital gain or loss, depending on the prices at which you buy and sell.

Shortfall risk

The risk that an investment will fail to produce a target lump sum or income.

Skimming

Crime where fraudsters steal the information stored on the magnetic strip of a credit card or other plastic card and load the data onto a fake card. Criminals then spend using the card and the bills turn up on your account. Normally the maximum loss you will be held liable for is £50, and usually nothing at all.

Social fund

Part of the Department for Work and Pensions benefits system. The social fund can make grants and loans (eg, to buy essential equipment, such as a cooker) to people eligible for income support, income-based jobseeker's allowance or other means-tested benefits.

Sort code

A unique set of numbers that identifies a bank or building society. You will find it on, for example, your cheque book and bank statements. Along with your account number, you need to give the sort code to anyone who intends to pay you by direct transfer – eg, an employer paying your wages or the Department for Work and Pensions paying benefits directly to your account.

Split capital investment trust

An investment trust which has more than one class of shares, some of which receive all the income paid out by the trust, and others which receive all, or the bulk of, the capital when the trust company is wound up. The different types of shares are suitable for different types of investor, depending on whether they are seeking income or capital growth.

Spread

Term used to describe the difference between the prices at which you can buy and sell investments such as shares, unit trusts and bonds.

Stakeholder pension scheme

Pension plan introduced from April 2001. Stakeholder pension schemes are all defined contribution schemes but come in two forms: personal stakeholder schemes which work in the same way as personal pensions, and occupational stakeholder schemes which are occupational money purchase schemes that meet certain conditions. To qualify as a stakeholder scheme, a pension scheme must meet certain conditions on low charges and flexibility. This ensures that stakeholder schemes are good value products. An employer which does not run an occupational pension scheme or contribute at least a minimum amount to a group personal pension scheme must make a stakeholder scheme accessible through the workplace.

Standard variable rate

An interest rate charged by mortgage lenders on some loans and used as a reference point for setting the interest rate on some other loans, such as discounted mortgages.

Standing order

An instruction to your bank to pay a set amount each month to a specified person.

Starting rate taxpayer

Someone whose top rate of income tax is the starting rate (10 per cent in 2009/10). Since 2008/09, the starting rate applies only to savings income.

State additional pension

The state second pension and, formerly, the state earnings-related pension scheme.

State basic pension

Flat-rate pension from the state, to which you are entitled if you (or, in some cases, your spouse) pay enough national insurance contributions of the right type over your working life.

State earnings-related pension scheme

The state additional pension that you could build up between 1978 and 2002. From April 2002, you build up state second pension instead. State earnings-related pension is paid on top of the state basic pension. Employees built up entitlement to it by paying national insurance contributions on part of their earnings. However, they could contract out and build up a pension through an occupational pension scheme or personal pension instead.

State graduated pension

An old state earnings-related pension scheme which ran from 1961 to 1975. Pensions under this scheme are very small.

State second pension

A state pension paid on top of the state basic pension. It replaced the state earnings-related pension scheme from April 2002, and is designed to provide better pensions than this scheme for many people on a low income. Employees build up entitlement to it by paying national insurance contributions on part of their earnings. Some people who cannot work, because they are carers or ill, also build up the pension without having to pay. Employees can contract out of the state second pension and build up a pension through an occupational pension scheme or personal pension instead.

Statement

A document you get from time to time (eg, monthly for a bank statement, yearly for a pension statement) giving a snapshot of the value of a financial product and usually also a record of payments in and out of the account. You should check statements as soon as you get them and contact the product provider immediately if anything looks wrong.

Statutory adoption pay

A state benefit administered by your employer which you can claim when you adopt a child.

Statutory maternity pay

A state benefit administered by your employer which you can claim if you are pregnant or have recently had a child. It sets the minimum income which by law you must get in this situation. To be eligible you must earn at least a minimum amount.

Statutory paternity pay

A state benefit administered by your employer which you can claim if you take time off to care for your new child or to support the mother.

Statutory sick pay

A state benefit administered by your employer which you can claim if you are unable to work because of illness. It sets the minimum income which by law you must get in this situation. To be eligible you must earn at least a minimum amount.

Stock market

A forum where shares and some other investments are bought and sold. In the past, this used to be a physical market place but these days trading is generally done electronically using computers.

Stockbroker

Someone who buys and sells shares and other stock market investments on your behalf. The stockbroker acts as your agent, carrying out your instructions, and in return you pay her/him commission, either at a flat rate or as a percentage of the value of the deal.

Store card

Usually a type of credit card, but one which lets you buy things only in a narrow range of shops. You may get various perks – such as sale previews and discounts on what you buy – but the interest rate tends to be so high that these cards are best avoided.

Student account

A bank account aimed at students going to university. The most important feature is usually a large interest-free overdraft.

Student loan

State-sponsored loan to help you pay your living costs while at university and to pay your tuition fees.

Surrender charge

Charge if you cash in an insurance policy early which is deducted from the cash-in value.

Sweeper service

Arrangement whereby your bank automatically transfers money in your current account above a limit you specify into a savings account offered by the bank where you can earn interest. In theory it is a good idea, but you can usually get a better rate of interest on your savings by shopping around.

Tax relief

The waiving or refund of tax you would otherwise pay. For example, you get a refund of tax paid on income when it is used to make pension contributions or Gift Aid donations to charity.

Tax year

The year running from 6 April to the following 5 April. A common convention is to write the tax year from, say, 6 April 2009 to 5 April 2010 as '2009/10'.

Term

The time period over which you borrow or invest.

Term accounts and bonds

Savings accounts where you agree to leave your money invested for a set term. In exchange for this restriction, you should expect to earn a higher rate of interest.

Term insurance

Type of life insurance which pays out a cash sum (or series of cash sums in the case of a family income benefit policy – see p354) if you die within a specified period of time (the 'term'). If you survive the term, the policy pays out nothing.

Third-party mandate

An instruction to your bank to let someone operate your bank account on your behalf.

Tracker fund

An investment fund which aims to produce a return in line with changes in a particular stock market index, such as the FTSE 100.

Transfer club

Arrangement whereby years of membership you have accumulated in one public sector occupational pension scheme may be credited as years of membership in another public sector scheme when you switch jobs.

Underwriting

When you apply for some policies, the process the insurer goes through to work out the likelihood that you might make a claim. On the basis of this, the insurer might refuse to cover you at all, build restrictions into your policy, charge you a higher premium, or make some other adjustment to the contract. Not all policies are underwritten. With some, everyone gets cover at a standard price but the policy contains extra exclusions to filter out risks that the insurer is not prepared to cover. Therefore, it is essential that you check the policy wording before you buy.

Unit trust

A fund of investments in which you invest by buying units. The price of the units varies in line with the value of the investments in the fund.

Unit-linked

Describes an investment where the return you get is determined directly by the performance of an underlying fund of investments (eg, shares and bonds). It is a commonly used way of investing in the stock market.

The fund is notionally divided up into any number of units of equal value and you either own or are treated as owning a certain number of them, according to the amount of money you invested.

As the value of the units goes up and down, so does the value of your investment, so you might lose some of your original investment and/or gains you had already made as a result of earlier growth.

The more units you have, the greater your share of any income earned by the fund.

Unsecured

A loan where, if you fail to make the agreed payments, the lender does not have any automatic right to seize your home or other possessions in order to get its money back. The main step the lender can take is to go to court and the court might order you to reimburse the lender, usually in instalments over a set period and taking into account the income and essential expenses you have. However, if you do not keep up the payments ordered by the court, the creditor can ask to have a 'charge' against your home. If the court allows this, when your home is sold, the creditor gets back the money you owe out of the proceeds of the sale. Rather than waiting until you eventually move, the creditor can go back to court to request that your home must be sold.

Variable rate

A rate of interest that moves up and down – eg, in line with changes in interest rates in the economy as a whole or in line with a particular interest rate (such as the Bank of England base rate).

Whole life policy

A life insurance policy that does not have a set term but pays out whenever you die. Because it must pay out one day, it builds up a cash-in value, so this type of policy is often used as an investment.

With-profits

Describes an investment where the return you get is largely based on the performance of an underlying fund of investments. But, unlike a unit-linked investment, a with-profits investment aims to provide you with steady growth year after year, so that you can benefit from stock market returns but minimise the risk of losing either your original investment or the growth you have already been credited with in the past. The fund is usually invested in a range of different investments, such as shares, bonds and property. The fund hopefully grows as the investments in the fund make gains and earn income. Some of that growth is paid out or credited to you and the other investors in the form of bonuses (often called 'reversionary bonuses' or 'annual bonuses'), but the rest of the growth is kept in reserve. If the fund does badly and falls in value, the firm running the fund usually tries to carry on paying at least some bonus to investors by dipping into the reserves. If the fund falls for several years in a row, the bonuses may stop altogether. When your investment matures, you usually also get a 'terminal bonus' which can be a large part (up to, say, half) of your total return from the investment. The terminal bonus is based on the growth of the fund over the time you held the investment that was held in reserve rather than being paid out. If the fund has had a run of bad years, the terminal bonus will be reduced. You are not guaranteed to get annual bonuses and the amounts vary from year to year. In general, however, provided you keep the investment until it matures, once an annual bonus has been added to your investment, you keep that bonus whatever happens to the fund in future. The story is different if you cash in the investment early. Then, a special charge might be deducted from what you get back. This is called a 'market value reduction' or 'market value adjustment' and it takes back some of the annual bonuses you have already had. You are not guaranteed to get a terminal bonus and the amount that investors get can be very different from one year to the next.

Working life

For the purposes of state basic pension entitlements (see p376), working life is defined officially as the tax years from the one in which you reach age 16 to the last complete tax year before you reach the state pension age.

Working tax credit

A means-tested state benefit you can claim if you are working at least a minimum number of hours each week but your earnings are low.

Yield

A way of expressing the interest or the return from an investment as a percentage of its price. Normally, it is used for stock market investments, like bonds and gilts, whose price goes up and down. Typically, these investments offer a fixed rate of interest. Therefore, as the price rises, the yield falls and, as the price falls, the yield rises.

Appendix 2

Useful contacts

Accountant

Look in *Yellow Pages* under
'Accountants' or contact the
following professional bodies for a
list of their members in your area:

**Association of Chartered Certified
Accountants**
29 Lincoln's Inn Fields
London WC2A 3EE
Tel: 020 7059 5000
www.acca.co.uk

**Institute of Chartered Accountants
in England and Wales**
PO Box 433
Chartered Accountants' Hall
(Moorgate Place)
PO Box 433
London EC2R 6EA
Tel: 020 7920 8100
www.icaew.co.uk

**Institute of Chartered Accountants
in Ireland**
Burlington House
Burlington Road
Dublin 4
Tel: +353 1 637 7200
www.icai.ie

**Institute of Chartered Accountants
of Scotland**
CA House
21 Haymarket Yards
Edinburgh EH12 5BH
Tel: 0131 347 0100
www.icas.org.uk

Age Concern-Help the Aged

Tel: 0800 00 99 66
www.ageconcern.org.uk

Association of British Credit Unions

Holyoake House
Hanover Street
Manchester M60 0AS
Tel: 0161 832 3694
www.abcul.org

Provides information on where to
find local credit unions.

Association of British Insurers

51 Gresham Street
London EC2V 7HQ
Tel: 020 7600 3333
www.abi.org.uk

Association of Consulting Actuaries

St Clement's House
27-28 Clement's Lane
London EC4N 7AE
Tel: 020 3207 9380
www.aca.org.uk

Association of Investment Companies

9th Floor
24 Chiswell Street
London EC1Y 4YY
Tel: 020 7282 5555
www.aitc.co.uk

Association of Private Client Investment Managers and Stockbrokers
22 City Road
Finsbury Square
London EC1Y 2AJ
Tel: 020 7448 7100
www.apcims.co.uk

Association of Taxation Technicians
1st Floor
Artillery House
11-19 Artillery Row
London SW1P 1RT
Tel: 0844 251 0830
www.att.org.uk

Bank of England base rate
www.bankofengland.co.uk/
monetarypolicy

British Bankers' Association
Pinners Hall
105-108 Old Broad Street
London EC2N 1EX
Tel: 020 7216 8800
www.bba.org.uk

British Insurance Brokers Association
8th Floor
John Stow House
18 Bevis Marks
London EC3A 7JB
Tel: 0870 950 1790
www.biba.org.uk

Carer's Allowance Unit
Palatine House
Lancaster Road
Preston PR1 1HB
Tel: 01253 85 61 23
www.dwp.gov.uk

Chartered Institute of Taxation
First Floor
11-19 Artillery Row
London SW1P 1RT
Tel: 0844 579 6700 or 020 7340 0550
www.tax.org.uk

Child Trust Fund Office
Waterview Park
Mandarin Way
Washington NE38 8QG
Tel: 0845 302 1470
www.childtrustfund.gov.uk

CIFAS Protective Registration Service
Capital House
e-state
Bankhead Crossway South
Edinburgh EH11 4EP
Tel: 0330 100 0180
www.cifas.org.uk

Citizens Advice Bureau
For local Bureau, see *Phone Book* or
www.citizensadvice.org.uk
For online information:
www.adviceguide.org.uk

Communities and Local Government
Eland House
Bressenden Place
London SW1E 5DU
Helpline: 020 7944 4400
www.communities.gov.uk

Community development finance institutions

To find a member institution in your area, contact:

Community Development Finance Association
Room 101
Hatton Square Business Centre
16/16a Baldwins Gardens
London EC1N 7RJ
Tel: 020 7430 0222
www.cdfa.org.uk

Community Legal Advice

For lawyers and advice centres in your area (England and Wales only) which are able to help with, for example, debt problems and landlord-tenant disputes.
Advice line: 0845 345 4 345
www.communitylegaladvice.org.uk

Consulting actuary

For details of a consulting actuary in your area, contact the Association of Consulting Actuaries or the Society of Pension Consultants

Consumer Credit Counselling Service

Wade House
Merrion Centre
Leeds LS2 8NG
Tel: 0800 138 1111
www.cccs.co.uk

Council of Mortgage Lenders

Bush House
North West Wing
Aldwych
London WC2B 4PJ
Tel: 0845 373 6771
www.cml.org.uk

Credit reference agencies

Callcredit
One Park Lane
Leeds
West Yorkshire LS3 1EP
Tel: 0870 060 1414 or 0113 244 1555
www.callcredit.co.uk or
www.callcreditcheck.co.uk

Equifax
PO Box 1140
Bradford BD1 5US
www.equifax.co.uk

Experian
Landmark House
Experian House
Experian Way
NG2 Business Park
Nottingham NG80 1ZZ
Tel: 0844 481 8000
www.experian.co.uk

Debt adviser

See:
- Community Legal Advice
- Citizens Advice Bureau
- Consumer Credit Counselling Service
- National Debtline
- Payplan

UK Debt Management Office (DMO)

Eastcheap Court
11 Philpot Lane
London EC3M 8UD
Tel: 0845 357 6500
www.dmo.gov.uk

DMO Gilt Purchase and Sale Service
www.dmo.gov.uk/
index.aspx?page=Gilts/
Retail_Brokerage

Computershare Investor Services
PO Box 2411
The Pavilions
Bristol BS99 6WX
Tel: 0870 703 0143
www-uk.computershare.com/
investor/gilts

Department for Employment and Learning
Northern Ireland
(Student Finance Branch)
Adelaide House
39-49 Adelaide Street
Belfast BT2 8FD
Tel: 028 9025 7777
www.delni.gov.uk/studentfinance

Department for Work and Pensions
- For state pensions and state benefits if you are over state pension age, see The Pension Service.
- For most state benefits if you are of working age, see Jobcentre Plus.
- For national insurance contributions, tax credits and child benefit, see HM Revenue and Customs.

Directgov
www.direct.gov.uk

Disability and Carers Service
Attendance Allowance and
Disability Living Allowance Unit
Warbreck House
Warbreck Hill
Blackpool FY2 0YE
Tel: 08457 12 34 56
Benefit Enquiry Line: 0800 88 22 00
(textphone: 0800 24 33 55)

Education Maintenance Allowance
Tel: 0800 121 8989
England and Wales: http://
ema.direct.gov.uk/ema.html
Scotland: www.emascotland.com
Northern Ireland: www.delni.gov.
uk/index/further-and-higher-
education/ema-educational-
maintenance-allowance.htm

Ethical Investment Research Services (EIRIS)
80-84 Bondway
London SW8 1SF
Tel: 020 7840 5700
www.eiris.org

European Health Insurance Card
PO Box 1114
Newcastle upon Tyne NE99 2TL
Tel: 0845 605 0707
www.ehic.org.uk

Finance and Leasing Association
2nd floor
Imperial House
15-19 Kingsway
London WC2B 6UN
Tel: 020 7836 6511
www.fla.org.uk

Financial Assistance Scheme
PO Box 702
York YO32 9XR
Tel: 0845 601 9941
www.dwp.gov.uk/fas
www.pensionprotectionfund.org.uk/fas

Pension scheme members should
first contact their scheme.

Financial Ombudsman Service

South Quay Plaza
183 Marsh Wall
London E14 9SR
Tel: 0845 080 1800 or 0300 123 9 123
or 020 7964 0500
www.financial-ombudsman.org.uk

Financial Services Authority

25 The North Colonnade
London E14 5HS
Consumer helpline: 0300 500 5000
www.moneymadeclear.fsa.gov.uk

Comparative Tables

Tel: 0300 500 5000
www.fsa.gov.uk/tables

FSA Register

Tel: 0300 500 5000
www.fsa.gov.uk/register/home.do

Financial Services Compensation Scheme

7th Floor
Lloyds Chambers
Portsoken Street
London E1 8BN
Tel: 0800 678 1100 or 020 7892 7300
www.fscs.org.uk

Fraud Compensation Fund

Knollys House
17 Addiscombe Road
Croydon CR0 6SR
Tel: 0845 600 2541
www.pensionprotectionfund.org.uk

Pension scheme members should
first contact their scheme.

HM Revenue and Customs

- For local tax enquiry centres look
  in *Phone Book* under 'Inland
  Revenue'.

- For your own tax office, check
  your tax return or other
  correspondence or ask your
  employer or the scheme paying
  your pension.

Orderline

Tel: 0845 9000 404
www.hmrc.gov.uk.
Married women's reduced rate
national insurance contributions:
www.hmrc.gov.uk/faqs/
women_reduced_rate.htm.
Voluntary national insurance
contributions: www.hmrc.gov.uk/
nic/class3.htm

National Insurance Contributions Office

Benton Park View
Newcastle upon Tyne NE98 1ZZ
Tel: 0845 302 1479
www.hmrc.gov.uk/nic

Homebuy schemes

Homes and Communities Agency
110 Buckingham Palace Road
London SW1W 9SA
Tel: 0300 1234 500
www.homesandcommunities.co.uk

Housing advice centre

See *Phone Book* under the name of
your local authority.

Independent financial advisers

For a list of advisers in your area,
contact:
IFA Promotion www.unbiased.co.uk
Personal Finance Society
www.findanadviser.org
See also the Institute of Financial
Planning

Independent financial advisers who specialise in annuities:

The Annuity Bureau
Tel: 0800 071 8111
www.annuity-bureau.co.uk

Annuity Direct
The Innovation Centre
St Cross Business Park
Monks Brook
Newport
Isle of Wight PO30 5WB
Tel: 0500 50 65 75
www.annuitydirect.co.uk

William Burrows Annuities
Tel: 0207 484 5366
www.williamburrows.com

Institute of Financial Planning
Whitefriars Centre
Lewins Mead
Bristol BS1 2NT
Tel: 0117 945 2470
www.financialplanning.org.uk

Institute of Islamic Banking and Insurance
12-14 Barkat House
116-118 Finchley Road
London NW3 5HT
Tel: 020 7245 0404
www.islamic-banking.com

Insurance broker
- Look in *Phone Book* under 'Insurance – Intermediaries'.
- See British Insurance Brokers' Association and www.mylocaladviser.co.uk.
- To check an intermediary is authorised, contact the Financial Services Authority Register.

Investment fund websites
www.morningstar.co.uk
www.investmentuk.org
www.theaic.co.uk
www.trustnet.com

Investment Management Association
65 Kingsway
London WC2B 6TD
Information line: 020 7269 4639
www.investmentuk.org

Jobcentre Plus
For local office, check website or see *Phone Book*.
www.jobcentreplus.gov.uk

Legal help
Community Legal Advice
(England and Wales)
Advice line: 0845 345 4 345
www.communitylegaladvice.org.uk/

Legal Services Commission
www.legalservices.gov.uk/

Scottish Legal Aid Board
44 Drumsheugh Gardens
Edinburgh EH3 7SW
Tel: 0131 226 7061
Legal Aid Helpline: 0845 122 8686
www.slab.org.uk

Northern Ireland Legal Services Commission
Waterfront Plaza
8 Laganbank Road
Belfast BT1 3BN
Tel : 028 9040 8888
www.nilsc.org.uk

Local authority
See *Phone Book* under the name of your local authority.

London Stock Exchange
10 Paternoster Square
London EC4M 7LS
Tel: 020 7797 1000
www.londonstockexchange.com

Member of Parliament
- To find out who is your local MP, contact your local public library or use the search facility at http://findyourmp.parliament.uk.
- To contact your MP, write to: [your MP's name], House of Commons, London SW1A 0AA or tel: 020 7219 3000

Money Advice Scotland
For contact details of local debt advisers:
Tel: 0141 572 0237
www.moneyadvicescotland.org.uk

Money Management magazine
- Available from larger newsagents. www.ftadviser.com/moneymanagement
- Subscriptions and back issues: 020 8606 7545.

Moneyfacts
Larger public reference libraries may have copies.
Subscriptions: 0845 1689 600
www.moneyfacts.co.uk

Moneysavingexpert.com
www.moneysavingexpert.com

Mortgage broker
- www.unbiased.co.uk/find-a-mortgage-adviser
- To check an intermediary is authorised contact the Financial Services Authority Register.

Mylocaladviser.co.uk
www.mylocaladviser.co.uk

National Debtline
Tel: 0808 808 4000
www.nationaldebtline.co.uk

National Savings and Investments
Tel: 0500 007 007
www.nsandi.com

New Deal programmes
Contact your local Jobcentre Plus.

Office of Fair Trading
Consumer Direct: 08454 04 05 06
www.consumerdirect.gov.uk
www.oft.gov.uk

Payplan
Kempton House
Dysart Road
Grantham
Lincolnshire NG31 7LE
Tel: 0800 716 239
www.payplan.com

Pension Protection Fund
Knollys House
17 Addiscombe Road
Croydon CR0 6SR
Tel: 0845 600 2541
www.pensionprotectionfund.org.uk

Pension scheme members should first contact their scheme.

The Pension Service
For local office, check website or see *Phone Book*.

Tyneview Park
Whitely Road
Newcastle upon Tyne NE98 1BA
General enquiries: 0845 60 60 265
Textphone: 0800 731 7339
State pension forecast:
0845 3000 168

Pension credit application line:
0800 99 1234
International Pension Centre:
+44 (0) 191 218 7777
Pension tracing service:
0845 6002 537
www.direct.gov.uk

The Pensions Advisory Service
11 Belgrave Road
London SW1V 1RB
Tel: 0845 601 2923
www.pensionsadvisoryservice.org.uk

Pension scheme administrator (occupational pension scheme)
Usually located in your Human
Resources (Personnel) Department.
Contact details will also be in any
booklet and correspondence about
the scheme and on any pensions
noticeboard at work.

Pensions Ombudsman
11 Belgrave Road
London SW1V 1RB
Tel: 020 7630 2200
www.pensions-ombudsman.org.uk

The Pensions Regulator
Napier House
Trafalgar Place
Brighton BN1 4DW
Tel: 0870 606 3636
www.thepensionsregulator.gov.uk

Personal finance websites
There are many of these. Useful sites
include:
- www.fool.co.uk
- www.ft.com/personal-finance
- www.moneyexpert.com
- www.moneyextra.com
- www.moneyfacts.co.uk
- www.moneynet.co.uk
- www.moneysupermarket.com

- www.thisismoney.co.uk
- www.uswitch.com

Post Office
Post Office Customer Care
Freepost
PO Box 740
Barnsley S73 0ZJ
Tel: 08457 22 33 44
www.postoffice.co.uk

Royal Mail
Tel: 08457 740 740
www.royalmail.com

Safe Home Income Plans
83 Victoria Street
London SW1H 0HW
Tel: 0844 669 7085
www.ship-ltd.org

Search engines
- www.alltheweb.com
- www.altavista.com
- www.dogpile.com
- www.google.co.uk

Services Against Financial Exclusion at Toynbee Hall
28 Commercial Street
London E1 6LS
Tel: 020 7247 6943
www.toynbeehall.org.uk
See also Transact.

Small claims
Bring cases in a county court in
England, Wales and Northern
Ireland or sheriff court in Scotland.
England and Wales: www.hmcourts-service.gov.uk
Scotland: www.scotcourts.gov.uk
Northern Ireland:
www.courtsni.gov.uk

Social Security and Child Support Appeals Service

Birmingham: 0845 408 3500
Cardiff: 02920 662 180
Glasgow: 0141 354 8400
Leeds: 0113 389 6000
Liverpool: 0151 243 1400
Newcastle: 0191 201 2300
Nottingham: 0115 909 3600
Sutton: 0208 652 2366
www.appeals-service.gov.uk

Society of Pension Consultants

St Bartholomew House
92 Fleet Street
London EC4Y 1DG
Tel: 020 7353 1688
www.spc.uk.com

Solicitor

Look in *Yellow Pages* under
'Solicitors' or contact the following
professional bodies for a list of their
members in your area:

Law Society
113 Chancery Lane
London WC2A 1PL
Tel: 020 7242 1222
www.lawsociety.org.uk

Law Society of Scotland
26 Drumsheugh Gardens
Edinburgh EH3 7YR
Tel: 0131 226 7411
www.lawscot.org.uk

Law Society of Northern Ireland
96 Victoria Street
Belfast BT1 3GN
Tel: 028 9023 1614
www.lawsoc-ni.org

Stockbroker

Association of Private Client Investment Managers and Stockbrokers
22 City Road
Finsbury Square
London EC1Y 2AJ
Tel: 020 7448 7100
See also www.apcims.co.uk

Student Awards Agency for Scotland

Gyleview House
3 Redheughs Rigg
Edinburgh EH12 9HH
Tel: 0845 111 1711
www.student-support-saas.gov.uk

Student Finance England

PO Box 210
Darlington DL1 9HJ
Tel: 0845 300 50 90
www.direct.gov.uk/en

Student Finance Northern Ireland

Tel: 0845 600 0662
www.studentfinanceni.co.uk

Student Finance Wales

Tel: 0845 602 8845
www.studentfinancewales.co.uk

Student Loans Company

100 Bothwell Street
Glasgow G2 7JD
Tel: 0870 240 6298
www.slc.co.uk

Tax Adjudicator

The Adjudicator's Office
8th Floor
Euston Tower
286 Euston Road
London NW1 3US
Tel: 0300 057 1111 or 020 7667 1832
www.adjudicatorsoffice.gov.uk

TaxAid

Room 304
Linton House
164-180 Union Street
London SE1 0LH
Tel: 0845 120 3779
www.taxaid.org.uk

TaxHelp for Older People

Helpline: 0845 601 3321
www.litrg.org.uk/about/activities/
index.cfm

Tax Office

See HM Revenue and Customs

Tax Tribunal

Tribunals Service (Tax)
2nd Floor
54 Hagley Road
Birmingham B16 8PE
Tel: 0845 223 8080
www.tribunals.gov.uk/tax

Trading standards offices

See *Phone Book* under name for your
local authority.
www.tradingstandards.gov.uk

Transact at Toynbee Hall

(The national forum for financial
inclusion)
Toynbee Hall
28 Commercial Street
London E1 6LS
Tel: 020 7392 2961
www.transact.org.uk

UK Border Agency

Public enquiries: 0870 606 7766
Sponsorship and employer's
helpline: 0300 123 4699
www.ukba.homeoffice.gov.uk

Which? (formerly Consumers' Association)

Castlemead
Gascoyne Way
Hertford SG14 1LH
Te: 01992 822800
www.which.co.uk

Appendix 3

Adult Financial Capability Framework mapping

There is now a second edition of the *Adult Financial Capability Framework* which has been used for this mapping. The skills, knowledge and understanding identified are the main areas. This is not exhaustive and users may feel that this *Handbook* covers other aspects.

Component	Developing level	Chapter/Section
Different types of money/ payments (a)	Understand that cash isn't the only way to pay for goods and services and recognises the alternatives.	3.1
	Understand different forms of payment including cheques, cheque guarantee cards and debit cards.	3.2 3.3
	Understand and compare different forms of payment including standing orders and direct debit arrangements.	3.3
Income generation (b)	Understand there are different forms of benefit, how they are paid and how to access them.	5.1, 7.1, 9.2, 9.4
	Begin to understand the retirement provision.	6.1
Income disposal (c)	Understand why money, such as tax or pension contributions, is deducted from earnings.	8.1-4
	Begin to understand local and national taxation and spending.	8.1
Gathering financial information and record keeping (d)	Understand keeping money in an account – eg, bank, post office, building society, credit union.	3.2-4
	Able to check for accuracy bank statements, utility and other bills.	1.6, 3.3, 5.3

Component	Developing level	Chapter/Section
Financial planning – saving, spending, budgeting (e)	Understand the need to consider saving and the potential benefits.	4.1
	Understand the variety of ways and places to save.	4.3-4
	Begin to be able to plan and think ahead.	1.4-5, 4.1
Risk and return (f)	Begin to understand the principles of probability and insurance.	7.1
	Understand money is made from money by saving and interest paid on borrowing.	4.1-2, 5.2
	Begin to understand that interest rates vary over time.	4.4, 5.2
Personal choices and the financial implications (g)	Begin to make decisions on the basis of short- or medium-term needs.	1.4-5
Consumer rights, responsibilities and sources of advice (h)	Understand we have responsibilities as well as rights.	5.8, 7.5, 8.4, 8.6, 9.6, 10.4
Implications of finance (i)	Know about the roles of financial organisations.	1.1, 10.1

Component	Extending level	Chapter/Section
Different types of money/payments (a)	Understand the implications of different forms of credit and debit including credit cards, store cards and catalogue shopping.	5.2-4
	Increased understanding of implications of credit and debit including overdrafts and different loan agreements and ways to compare interest rates.	5.2-7
Income generation (b)	Understand the need for money in retirement – pension – and how this could be paid for.	6.1-2, 6.11
	Begin to understand how companies and other organisations are financed, including shares.	4.5
	Understand how deductions such as tax, national insurance and pension contributions are made.	6.1-2, 8.1-4
Income disposal (c)	Understanding of the range of personal expenditure and how it may be managed.	3.1
	Understand local and national taxation and spending and a basic understanding of how and why government is financed.	8.1-4

Component	Extending level	Chapter/ Section
Gathering financial information and record keeping (d)	Understanding of personal finance statements including bank statements, credit card statements, utility and other bills.	1.6 3.3 (partial)
	Able to reconcile a bank statement to allow for items not yet presented.	3.3
	Understand credit card statements and other loan/credit financing documents.	5.3
	Able to gather, compare and contrast information on financial services to inform a decision.	1.3-5, 3.1, 4.1, 5.1-2, 6.1, 7.1, 8.1
Financial planning – saving, spending, budgeting (e)	Understand ways in which to plan, monitor and control personal income and expenditure.	1.4, 3.1, 8.1, 8.2
	Fully understand the difference between short-, medium- and long-term financial commitments and how the planning and decision making for these differ.	1.5, 5.2
	Able to obtain information and analyse it to decide on an appropriate service, taking care to evaluate and monitor the situation on an ongoing basis.	3.2, 4.2, 5.2, 7.2-4, 8.1-2
	Begin to understand local government finances (council tax) and the national budget.	8.1 (partial)
Risk and return (f)	Understand the principles of probability and insurance in complex situations, identifying potential risks and how to protect against them.	5.2, 6.6, 7.1-4
	Understand that both saving and borrowing are offered on differing terms and interest rates vary over time.	4.1-2, 5.2
	Understand that some loans and purchase agreements are secured while others are unsecured.	5.2, 5.6-7
	Understand the difference in risk and return between saving and investment products.	4.2, 4.6-7
	Understand the need to monitor and evaluate financial services to assess performance and relevance over time.	1.6

Component	Extending level	Chapter/ Section
Personal choices and the financial implications (g)	Understand the difference between short-, medium- and long-term needs and make appropriate decisions.	1.5
	Understand the differences between manageable, planned debt and unmanageable, unplanned debt.	5.8 (partial)
	Able to assess best buy in a variety of financial circumstances.	1.5, 3.2, 4.4-5, 5.2, 6.5, 7.2-4
	Knowledge and understanding of a range of generic financial products in the short-, medium- and long-term. Ability to identify personal requirements, obtain information/advice, analyse and decide.	1.4-5, 3.2, 4.2, 4.4-5, 5.3-7, 6.3-7, 7.2-4
	Ability to make informed choices based on personal financial information gathering on resources available, outgoings (both needs and wants) and what is left, if any.	1.4-5
	Ability to put a personal financial value on differing needs/wants and to prioritise these within the constraints of limited resources.	1.4-5
	Ability to undertake ongoing monitoring and evaluation of needs/wants/services based on changing life circumstances.	1.3-6, 6.9
	Ability to evaluate the choice of a particular product on lifestyle, etc.	1.5
	Ability to assess the financial implications of personal life choices in terms of education, life long learning opportunities.	5.7, 4.3 (partial)
	Ability to make informed choices when experiencing a drop in income or other changes to financial circumstances.	5.1-2, 7.4 (partial), 9.1
Consumer rights, responsibilities and sources of advice (h)	Know about the different sources of generic financial advice, including financial advisers and Citizens Advice.	2.2
	Know about the different sources of advice and the difference between generic and personal advice.	2.1-4, 8.5
	Be able to assess and compare different sources of financial advice and information.	2.1-4

Component	Extending level	Chapter/ Section
	Understand there are different rights and responsibilities in relation to different financial products.	3.8, 4.6, 5.8-9, 6.10, 7.6, 10.2-4
	Understand how to identify if it is appropriate to comment or complain and be able to access the procedures.	3.8, 4.6, 5.8-9, 6.10, 7.6, 10.2-4
Implications of finance (i)	Understand there is an ethical, social dimension to financial decisions.	1.5
	Understand how to plan and manage debt.	5.1, 5.8
	Understand what to do if difficulties arise in repaying debt.	5.8
	Understanding the role of regulation and consumer protection in financial institutions.	3.8, 4.6, 5.8-9, 6.10, 7.6, 10.1-4
	Understanding of the wider implications of personal finance decisions – eg, the pros and cons of ethical investment.	1.4-5, 4.4 (partial), 4.5 (partial)
	Develop an understanding of how local and national decisions may affect personal finances.	4.1, 6.2, 8.4, 9.1, 10.1
	Develop an understanding that local, national and global finances can impact on one's own life – eg, setting of interest rates.	4.1, 5.6, 10.1

	a Different types of money/ payments	b Income generation	c Income disposal	d Gathering financial information and record keeping	e Financial planning – saving, spending, budgeting	f Risk and return	g Personal choices and the financial implications	h Consumer rights, responsibilities and sources of advice	i Implications of finance
D Developing level	2. 3.1 3. 3.2-3 4. 3.3	2. 5.1 7.1 9.2 9.4 3. 6.1	2. 8.1-4 3. 8.1	1. 3.2-4 4.1.6 3.3 5.3	1. 4.1 2. 4.3-4 3. 1.4-5 4.1	1. 7.1 3. 4.1-2 5.2 4. 4.4 5.2	1. 1.4-5	3. 5.8 7.5 8.4 8.6 9.6 10.4	1. 1.1, 10.1
E Extending level	1. 5.2-4 3. 5.2-7	1. 6.1-2 6.11 2. 4.5 3. 6.1-2 8.1-4	1. 3.1 2. 8.1-4	1. 1.6 3.3 2. 3.3 3. 5.3 4. 1.3-5 3.1 4.1 5.1-2 6.1 7.1 8.1	1. 1.4 3.1 8.1 8.2 2. 1.5 5.2 3. 3.2 4.2 5.2 7.2-4 8.1-2 4. 8.1	1. 5.2 6.6 7.1-4 2. 4.1-2 5.2 3. 5.2 5.6-7 4. 4.2 4.6-7 5. 1.6	1. 1.5 2. 5.8 3. 1.5 3.2 4.4-5 5.2 6.5 7.2-4 4. 1.4-5 3.2 4.2 4.4-5 5.3-7 6.3-7 7.2-4 6. 1.4-5 7. 1.4-5 8. 1.3-6 6.9 9. 1.5 10. 5.7 4.3 11. 5.1-2 7.4 9.1	1. 2.2 2. 2.1-4 8.5 3. 2.1-4 3.8 4. 4.6 5.8-9 6.10 7.6 10.2-4 5. 3.8 4.6 5.8-9 6.10 7.6 10.2-4	1. 1.5 2. 5.1 5.8 3. 5.8 3.8 4. 4.6 5.8-9 6.10 7.6 10.1-4 5. 1.4-5 4.4 4.5 6. 4.1 6.2 8.4 9.1 10.1 7. 4.1 5.6 10.1

Chapter	Section	Adult Financial Capability Framework *reference*
1. Financial planning	1	D(i)1 E(d)4
	3	D(e)3 E(d)4 E(g)8
	4	D(e)3 D(g)1 (E(d)4 E(e)1 E(g)4, 6, 7, 8 E(i)5
	5	D(e)3 D(g)1 E(d)4 E(e)2 E(g)1, 3, 4, 6, 7, 8, 9 E(i)1, 5
	6	D(d)4 E(d)1 E(e)3 E(f)5 E(g)8
2. Getting advice	1	E(d)4 E(e)1, 3 E(h)2, 3
	2	E(e)3 E(h)1, 2, 3
	3	E(h)2, 3
	4	E(h)2, 3
3. Everyday money	1	D(a)2 E(c)1 E(d)4 E(e)1
	2	D(a)3 D(d)1 E(e)3 E(g)2, 3
	3	D(a)3, 4 D(d) 1, 4 E(d)1, 2
	4	D(d)1
	8	E(h)4, 5 E(i)4
4. Saving	1	D(e)1, 3 D(f)3 E(d)4 E(f)2, 4 E(i)6, 7
	2	D(f)3 E(e)3 E(f)2, 4 E(g)4
	3	D(e)2 E(d)2 E(g)3, 10
	4	D(e)2 D(f)4 E(f)4 E(g)3, 4 E(i)5
	5	E(b)2 E(f)4 E(g)3, 4 E(i)5
	6	E(f)4 E(h)4, 5 E(i)4

Chapter	Section	Adult Financial Capability Framework *reference*
	7	E(f)4
5. Borrowing	1	D(b)2 E(d)4 E(g)11 E(i)2
	2	D(f)3, 4 E(a)1, 3 E(d)3, 4 E(e)2, 3 E(f) 1, 2 3 E(g)3, 4, 11
	3	D(d)4 E(a)1, 3 E(d)3 E(g)4
	4	E(a)1, 3 E(g)4
	5	E(a)3 E(g)4
	6	E(a)3 E(f)3 E(g)4 E(i)7
	7	E(a)3 E(f)3 E(g)4, 10
	8	D(h)3 E(g)2 E(h)4, 5 E(i) 2, 3, 4
	9	E(h)4, 5 E(i)4
6. Pensions	1	D(b)3 E(b)1, 3 E(d)4
	2	E(b)1, 3 E(i)6
	3	E(g)4
	4	E(g)4
	5	E(g)3, 4
	6	E(f)1 E(g)4
	7	E(g)4
	9	E(g)8
	10	E(h)4, 5 E(i)4
		E(b)1
7. Insurance	1	D(b)2 D(f)1 E(d)4 E(f)1
	2	E(e)3 E(f)1 E(g)3, 4
	3	E(e)3 E(f)1 E(g)3, 4

Chapter	Section	Adult Financial Capability Framework *reference*
	4	E(e)3 E(f)1 E(g)3, 4, 11
	5	D(h)3
	6	E(h)4, 5 E(i)4
8. Tax and national insurance	1	D(c)2, 3 E(b)3 E(c)2 E(d)4 E(e)1, 3, 4
	2	D(c)2 E(b)3 E(c)2 E(e)1, 3
	3	D(c)2 E(b)3 E(c)2
	4	D(c)2 D(h)3 E(b)3 E(c)2 E(i)6
	5	E(h)2
	6	D(h)3
9. Benefits and tax credits	1	D(b)2 E(g)11 E(i)6
	2	D(b)2
	3	D(b)2
	4	D(b)2
	5	D(b)2
	6	D(h)3
	7	D(h)3
10. Protecting consumers	1	D(i)1 E(b)2 E(i)4, 6, 7
	2	E(h)4, 5 E(i)4
	3	E(h)4, 5 E(i)4
	4	D(h)3 E(h)4, 5 E(i)4

Index

How to use this Index

Entries against the bold headings direct you to the general information on the subject, or where the subject is covered most fully. Sub-entries are listed alphabetically and direct you to specific aspects of the subject.

Debt Advice Handbook

8th edition

The **Debt Advice Handbook** contains all the essential information needed by advisers dealing with debt problems, and explains the key stages and issues in money advice in England and Wales.

It has guidance on interviewing clients; dealing with emergencies; establishing liability for debts; income maximisation; prioritising debts; preparing financial statements and negotiating with creditors. There are sections covering business and student debts, and court action by creditors to recover debts and repossess property/goods. Further sections deal with enforcement in magistrates' courts, bailiffs, and insolvency.

As well as outlining the debt advice process, it helps advisers choose the most effective strategies and deal with unacceptable debt collection practices.

Every edition is revised and updated to cover recent changes to legislation, caselaw, court procedures and practice. The book is fully indexed and cross-referenced to other relevant publications and articles as well as to caselaw, legislation and the rules of court.

> *This book continues to provide welcome support for advisers and consumers. CPAG are to be congratulated on meeting this need.*
> **Institute of Money Advisers**

> *The* Debt Advice Handbook *has proved itself over the years as a comprehensive, reliable and easily accessible source of information.*
> **The Adviser (Citizens Advice)**

Price £20.00   December 2008   ISBN: 978-1-906076-21-4

Published by Child Poverty Action Group, 94 White Lion St, London N1 9PF
Tel: 020 7837 7979
Email: bookorders@cpag.org.uk
Website: www.cpag.org.uk/publications

Welfare Benefits and Tax Credits Handbook

2009/2010

The **Welfare Benefits and Tax Credits Handbook** is the definitive comprehensive guide for claimants and their advisers. It explains:

- who can claim benefits and tax credits
- disability and incapacity benefits, and the work capability assessment for employment and support allowance
- how housing benefit and council tax benefit are calculated
- jobseeker's allowance and benefit sanctions
- how to claim from the social fund
- which benefits can be claimed if you are unemployed, a parent or carer, a student, retired or widowed, pregnant, entering the UK, or sick or disabled
- challenging decisions, backdating, overpayments, income and capital, and national insurance contributions.

It is fully indexed and cross-referenced to law and regulations.

> *The best value in publishing ... All legal aid firms must have this book.*
> **Solicitors Journal**
> *The one thing that can be relied on in this ever changing world of welfare is CPAG's indispensable handbook... the adviser's bible.*
> **The Adviser (Citizens Advice)**

Price £37.00   April 2009   ISBN: 978-1-906076-35-1

Published by Child Poverty Action Group, 94 White Lion St, London N1 9PF
Tel: 020 7837 7979
Email: bookorders@cpag.org.uk
Website: www.cpag.org.uk/publications

Council Tax Handbook

8th edition

The **Council Tax Handbook** is the definitive practical guide to all aspects of the council tax in England, Scotland and Wales. This eighth edition includes all changes to law and practice, including recent caselaw and Local Government Ombudsman decisions. It includes the reforms to the council tax appeals system achieved by the introduction of the Valuation Tribunal England in October 2009, as well as detailing changes regarding benefits, collection and enforcement practice. The **Handbook** explains:

- which homes are eligible and which are exempt from council tax
- how homes are valued for council tax purposes
- discounts available, for example for people who live alone
- ways in which a bill may be reduced, for example for people with disabilities and those on a low income
- the position of students
- the powers of local authorities
- tax collection, appeals, enforcement and bailiffs' powers.

It includes practical examples and is fully cross-referenced to law and regulations.

> *A comprehensive guide to all aspects of the council tax ... easy to follow and use.* **Citizens Advice**

Price £17.00   November 2009   ISBN: 978-1-906076-33-7

Published by Child Poverty Action Group, 94 White Lion St, London N1 9PF
Tel: 020 7837 7979
Email: bookorders@cpag.org.uk
Website: www.cpag.org.uk/publications

Training at CPAG

CPAG courses provide comprehensive rights training for advisers and detailed coverage of up-to-the minute legislative changes. Our tutors are expert in their areas of work and draw on the extensive training experience of CPAG's own welfare rights specialists. Courses include:

- An introduction to welfare rights
- Benefit take-up campaigns
- AA/DLA – revisions, supersessions and appeals
- Immigration law and social security
- Tax credit overpayments
- Employment and support allowance.

For full course information and online booking please see our website (details below). Our courses can also be tailored to meet the needs of specific groups, including those not normally concerned with welfare rights. To assess your training needs, we are happy to discuss your requirements for 'in-house' training to meet the internal needs of your organisation.

CPAG's London-based courses are Law Society and Bar Council accredited and carry continuing education points. They are also approved by The Institute of Legal Executives and the UK College of Family Mediators. Courses in Scotland have Law Society Scotland accreditation.

Contacts for further information:

London   Judy Allen, Training Co-ordinator,
tel: 020 7812 5228   email: jallen@cpag.org.uk
website: www.cpag.org.uk/training

Scotland   Pauline Chalmers, Training Administrator
Tel: 0141 552 3420   email: pchalmers@cpagscotland.org.uk
website: www.cpag.org.uk/scotland/training

Money advice training at CPAG

CPAG money advice courses are an essential tool for all those dealing with clients who have debt and other related issues. They make you aware of all the options available to your clients and help you make an appropriate referral where necessary. Courses include:

- Dealing with debt
- Voluntary bankruptcy – what it means for clients
- Outline of bankruptcy procedure and responding to proceedings
- Students and debt
- Students and debt – tactics for experienced advisers

For full course information and online booking please see our website (details below). Our courses can also be tailored to meet the needs of specific groups, including those not normally concerned with welfare rights. To assess your training needs, we are happy to discuss your requirements for 'in-house' training to meet the internal needs of your organisation.

CPAG's London-based courses are Law Society and Bar Council accredited and carry continuing education points. They are also approved by The Institute of Legal Executives and the UK College of Family Mediators. Courses in Scotland have Law Society Scotland accreditation.

Contacts for further information:

London   Judy Allen, Training Co-ordinator,
tel: 020 7812 5228   email: jallen@cpag.org.uk
website: www.cpag.org.uk/training

Scotland   Pauline Chalmers, Training Administrator
Tel: 0141 552 3420   email: pchalmers@cpagscotland.org.uk
website: www.cpag.org.uk/scotland/training